HORNETS
NEVER
LIE

HORNETS NEVER LIE

and other tales from Charlotte's first NBA season

Tucker Mitchell

DOWN HOME

Down Home Press

Asheboro, N.C.

First Printing, October, 1989

ISBN 0-9624255-0-8

Printed in the United States of America

Cover design by Harry Blair
Book design by Elizabeth House

Down Home Press
P.O. Box 4126
Asheboro, N.C. 27204

For Woo, Hassie, Mom and everyone else
who showed me the wonder of books.

"Earl said that about me? Well, I guess it's true, because Hornets Never Lie."

– Charles Barkley

Contents

Birth of a Notion

"I told the guys, 'Men, bow your heads and pray they shut up. It's our only chance.'"
—Wes Unseld, coach of the Washington Bullets

In years to come, someone may claim that they saw the Charlotte Hornets' first game, first victory, or some other first of note. But unless they saw the Hornets lose to Washington that night in November they didn't really see it begin.

They did not witness the inexplicable and unexpected bonding of team and fan that was welded tight by 20 searing minutes that night. They did not see the term "Hornet Mania" defined, for the first time, by living, breathing flesh. Which is not to say that they never saw it, because once started, it happened again and again. Though not with quite the same furor.

But for the Hornets and their crazy fans that was the night it was born, November 26, 1988.

It did not start out so, or even figure to be. Until it happened. The Hornets had played surprisingly well in the first month of their first season, but they were still winners in just two of their first 11 games. And as they arrived in Charlotte at mid-morning on that November day, the numbers didn't promise to get much better. They were tired, worn from a three-night trip to Boston and Philadelphia, and perhaps just a bit melancholy. Most had missed Thanksgiving with their families because of the schedule, celebrating instead at a buffet in a Philly hotel.

For that reason and others, the Saturday night game would be a test of will. It was Charlotte's fourth game in five days, played after an afternoon of rest at home. And forward Kurt Rambis, an important player on this team, would not, in all probability, be able to play. He had sprained an ankle several days before and had missed the game in Philadelphia the previous night. What's more, the opponent was the Washington Bullets, a nondescript, NBA mediocrity that brought fire to few eyes. Even expansion teams had trouble stirring interest in the Bullets.

Hornets Never Lie

About all the Hornets had to boost them was a surprising report that the game, their fifth of the season at the Charlotte Coliseum, was going to be a sellout. "A sellout for the Bullets?" trainer Terry Kofler asked incredulously on the flight home. "C'mon."

But it was true. These Charlotte fans had not yet had their fill. By the time the starting lineups were announced just after 7:30 p.m. — with Earl Cureton starting for Rambis — the place was indeed full.

Charlotte started well, especially for a tired team. The Hornets ran the court with determination, beating the Bullets back for easy baskets. They made nine of their first 15 shots and led 22-18 with a little over seven minutes gone. But Washington's fine second team, which would pester the Hornets and many other opponents all season, wrested control from Charlotte in the second period. The Bullet reserves ran harder than their starters and rookie Ledell Eackles lit up Rex Chapman, his rookie counterpart, for 10 points in the first four minutes of the quarter.

The Washington lead climbed as high as 12 before Charlotte's first team returned to lead a late rally. Cureton's layup with eight seconds left, off a skillful pass from Tyrone Bogues, made the score 56-54 at the half.

The Hornets felt good then and even better when Kelly Tripucka hit a jumper that tied it on Charlotte's first possession of the third quarter. But then the game began to unravel for the Hornets.

Washington scored 17 points in the next four minutes, 42 in the third period. All-Star guard Jeff Malone did his work almost at will, scoring 18 in the third period, which, not coincidentally, was about what Charlotte trailed by at period's end. The Hornets needed an unlikely three-point play from Tom Tolbert in the last 15 seconds just to cut Washington's lead to 98-77 entering the fourth quarter.

Faced with this situation, fans in most NBA cities would have done one of two things: leave or maintain a grim, sadistic vigil. Just how bad would the home team get beat?

As Washington's Darrell Walker said later, "Anywhere else in the NBA they'd have all left to beat the traffic. No, I take that back. In New York and Philadelphia they would have stayed to boo."

This was not "anywhere else in the NBA," though, and for whatever reason, the fans, all 23,000 or so, stayed. And not to boo. When the teams returned to the court for the start of the fourth quarter, the Hornets were met with a rising roar of anticipation. Maybe, this being their first year and all, the fans were too naive to know this one was over. Or maybe, because they didn't know that, it wasn't.

Nothing happened for a few minutes. Washington maintained its lead, even boosted it a little. With 10:30 left to play, the Bullets led 102-79.

But then, like the cheers that had greeted them just moments before, a Hornets' rally began growing, swelling, suddenly bursting across the Coliseum floor. Charlotte, led by Tim Kempton, couldn't miss. And the Bullets, lost in the mounting sea of decibels, could barely hang onto the ball, much less throw it in the basket.

Bogues flipped in an improbable reverse layup. Robert Reid intercepted a pass and found Chapman for an easy breakaway. Reid took a charge, then Kempton gathered in a Reid miss and laid it in.

Kempton followed by tipping a ball from Bullet Terry Catledge's hand, then dashed to the other end of the court and tossed in a rolling hook shot that cut the lead to 11 and drove the fans to another, madder, level.

Trying to bring the ball upcourt after Kempton's shot, Washington's Walker fumbled a pass at midcourt. Though unguarded, except by the 23,000 voices screaming in unison, he shuffled his feet trying to recover. Traveling. But it was several seconds before anyone knew. The crowd was too loud to hear referee Bennett Salvatore's whistle.

When Salvatore finally managed to stop the game and make his call, Wes Unseld, the Washington coach, walked to midcourt and shouted at Salvatore: "Timeout! Timeout!"

Unseld tried to calm his frazzled club, but the deafening roar continued. It was hard to talk, much less explain a complex piece of basketball strategy.

"I have never heard anything like that in my life," Unseld said later. "I tried to tell them some stuff. But finally I just gave up. I told the guys, `Men bow your heads and pray they shut up. It's our only chance.'"

Asked about Unseld's message, Walker said, "Yeah, he said something about praying. I couldn't hear it all."

Kempton, his 245-pound frame fairly dancing by this point, made sure the timeout didn't slow the Hornets' rampage. On the next possession he rebounded two straight misses by teammates. The first he gathered and threw back outside. The second he laid into the basket.

Another roar. And then Malone, trying to communicate with Walker through the din while maintaining his dribble, lost track of his man, Chapman. Realizing too late that he'd left the ball exposed, Malone lashed out at the advancing Chapman with his free arm. Offensive foul.

Charlotte let that opportunity pass without further eroding the Washington lead, and a few seconds later, Malone scored the Bullets' first points in nearly five minutes, hitting a baseline jumper to make the score 104-93 with 6:50 to play.

The noise dropped just a bit and the rally threatened to wane, but Kempton lowered his head and drove down the lane past a bewildered Dave Fietl for two points. And the magic continued on defense. Reid, playing suffocatingly close on Bullets' ace Bernard King, tipped a pass into Kempton's hands. The big redhead grabbed it and started his bulky frame on a headlong flight to the basket. Some Bullets, predictably, caught up, but Kempton, a Magic Johnson this night, cruised right through them for his fifth straight basket. It was 104-97.

With the din rising higher still, Washington crumbled. Malone, hounded by Bogues at midcourt, dribbled the ball off his right foot, out of bounds. It was the Bullets' third turnover in the backcourt in 90 seconds.

Unseld tried another timeout, but again to no avail. Bogues turned it over on Charlotte's next possession, getting stuck in lane traffic and throwing a bad pass. But the Bullets couldn't get a clear pass. King, surrounded by Hornets, tried to hit Malone, who was behind him near the Charlotte baseline. Malone slipped and King's pass sailed out of bounds. Hornets' ball.

Chapman blew around Malone and flipped in a finger roll shot from the baseline to make the score 104-99 with 5:37 left, and it was now very much a game. John Williams missed for Washington; Reid rebounded, and Bogues was off on the break. He hit Tolbert cutting to the basket. Washington's Catledge prevented the score with a foul, but Tolbert made one of two free throws for 104-100 with more than five minutes left to play.

Suddenly, Washington regained its composure. Williams, a 6-9, 235-pound monster of a man, drove through a Hornet trap for a layup. Chapman missed a long jumper and King scored on the break. Another Chapman miss and Washington got another fast-break basket, a jumper from Catledge. Six straight by Washington and a 10-point lead with 4:06 left. Surely that was the game.

But no. Neither the crowd nor the Hornets had come this far to give up now. After a timeout, Reid scored on a drive and Kempton made a free throw to cut the lead to seven.

Washington got back-to-back baskets from King and Malone for 114-103, and Kempton, who had 11 points and four rebounds in the quarter, fouled out. Prospects looked bleak, but the Hornets were still not done.

With Kempton gone, it was time for Tolbert, a seldom-used rookie of little promise, to go crazy. He flipped in a reverse scoop shot, then snared an offensive rebound and put it back in for 114-107 with 1:50 left.

Washington needed a basket to clinch the win, and, to no one's surprise, went to Malone. But, to the surprise of many, Tolbert rose from the lane to block his shot. The Hornets recovered the ball, and Chapman hit one of his famous, leaning jumpers from the right wing to make it 114-109.

The crowd — incredibly still intact, except for a traitor or two who had left for the parking lot — roared its approval. It roared again when Tyrone the Pest stripped the ball from Malone as the Washington star drove past the free throw line. Chapman, guarding Malone, picked up the loose ball and headed downcourt. Cut off, he fired a pass back to Bogues, who cut to the basket. The massive Williams was in his path, biggest man on the court against the littlest in all of professional basketball. Not the most desirable matchup for the Hornets, but it seemed to work out when Bogues plowed into the leaping Williams and was knocked to the court, surely fouled.

The wild cheers of the Hornets fans turned quickly to boos when referee Ken Mauer called Bogues for an offensive foul. With Bogues yapping at his heels, Mauer flung his forearm out from his body, the signal that he was calling Bogues for pushing Williams off with his free arm.

Bogues snorted at the call later. "Now how in the world is a guy my size going to push off a 250-pound guy like John Williams?"

The answer seems obvious, but replays of the potentially pivotal play are inconclusive. There was minimal contact. It appears Bogues fell so hard from the force of having his shot blocked. Probably, no foul was committed and Charlotte should have gotten the ball out of bounds.

Instead, amidst a chorus of boos that was not as loud as the cheers before, Washington took over. A lob into the 6-5 Walker, guarded by Bogues, resulted in a missed layup, but the man who had come over to help defeat that play, Tolbert, had left Catledge free under the basket. Catledge grabbed the miss and was fouled trying to put it back in.

Catledge is not a strong free throw shooter, but he made these, and finally, that was enough. Reid followed with a three-pointer for Charlotte, but Williams and Malone hit four straight free throws as Washington won 120-113.

The fan-driven comeback, Charlotte's victory in defeat, was a shot heard throughout the NBA. Harry Weltman, the general manager of the crowdless New Jersey Nets, watched a cable broadcast of the game off the Bullets' network. When the Hornet fans sent up their cheer to start the fourth quarter, Weltman found himself snickering.

"But then," he recalled later, "they kept screaming and the Hornets kept coming back. I watched the rest with my mouth open. I tell you, they're something. They won't let that team quit."

Teams coming into Charlotte were stunned for a few more games, but soon word got around, spread in large part by the Washington tale. Down 21 and still screaming. Now that's something to see.

"Yes," said Reid, minutes after the comeback that failed but didn't, "those people out there were really something tonight. I think we may have started something here."

Indeed, they had.

Letting George Do It

I'm just God's little idiot"

— George Shinn

Every great journey, it is said, begins with a single step. But nobody says that first step has to be in the right direction.

It was like that with Charlotte's stunning acquisition of an NBA franchise. The leader of the journey, the ever-bubbling George Shinn, stalked off hard and fast right from the start, just as he does every time he puts some of his hard-earned dollars on the line. But his direction wasn't true.

It wasn't exactly false, though. Shinn did set out after a big-league franchise for his adopted hometown. But his initial heading bore roughly the same connection to basketball that a railroad would have to a man who set out to buy an airline. Same field, but no, not the same.

What Shinn wanted was a Major League baseball team. Baseball was his first love. He had been a good enough player growing up to harbor some big-league fantasies, and like a couple thousand other mill workers' sons in Kannapolis, N.C. back then, Shinn grew up a fan. He loved the game, specifically the Carl Furillo-Roy Campanella-Jackie Robinson Dodgers.

The Dodgers were not for sale when Shinn felt the call to own. Nor at any other time, for that matter. But maybe he could build his own Dodgers somewhere else. Take a new team, an expansion team, and teach it to bleed, not Dodger Blue, but whatever (team's name) whatever (team's color). Maybe.

Then another problem appeared way back then in 1984, the year in which the feisty little millionaire got his first, serious hankerings for big-league sport. Major League expansion, he learned, was years away. Not until the 1990s at least. And Charlotte, or anyone else just getting interested, would have to take a number and stand in a very long line.

The line didn't bother Shinn. As the NBA would eventually learn, he was not particularly interested in, certainly not intimidated by, the size or strength of the obstacles in his path. This pint-sized positive thinker figured he'd clear them all and end up in front anyway.

But that wait. That was something else. George Shinn, say those who've worked with him, would rather write out a big check than wait for one of his projects to go through.

So on to plan B. Was there a team he could buy and bring to Charlotte right now? Was there a way to get in right away?

Shinn, with guidance from Max Muhleman, owner of a Charlotte public relations and marketing company, began exploring the possibility. There was a chance. The Chicago White Sox were changing hands, and some minority partners were being sought.

But that idea fell through almost before it took shape, and Shinn adopted his current long-term strategy for obtaining Major League baseball.

That involves establishing himself in the minors, just like a ballplayer, so when the call comes down from the "bigs" Shinn will be ready. He owns a class A team in Gastonia and a AA in Charlotte. When, and not if, as he puts it, he obtains a AAA team or AAA membership for Charlotte, he'll have a farm system in place. How can Major League baseball resist?

But that's for the future. This was then, back when the ownership bug had bitten and nothing but the top would do.

Halted on the diamond, Shinn turned next to football, specifically to that dinosaur known as the United States Football League.

Hindsight doesn't award Shinn much credit for this choice. The USFL, which played in the spring rather than the fall, was on shaky ground almost from the minute it was on the ground at all. The original idea — a league that didn't compete with the established National Football League for either time or talent — died quickly. Deep-pocketed owners like Donald Trump, who wasn't quite so famous as he is now, quickly blew the league's salary cap to kingdom come, and not long after it had started, the USFL's only hope was an anti-trust action against the NFL.

If the USFL won a big judgment, its tottering franchises would, at worst, suddenly approach solvency, and at best join the NFL in a merger.

The USFL didn't win, of course, but there was no way Shinn could have known that then. At the time it had much to recommend it to Shinn, the most important item being that it indeed was open to expansion. In fact, all you had to do was flash a little dough and ask. The USFL was easy.

Shinn asked. Expansion was a possibility. Buying an existing team, which is both quicker and simpler, was considered, too.

In the fall of 1984, Shinn talked with league officials about purchasing the troubled Los Angeles Express, a team saddled with a huge payroll and little interest. He would have left that team in LA and owned from afar, using it as a foot in the door to pro sports in general. That deal fell through, but Shinn kept sniffing around. Talks with the Chicago Blitz, a less-troubled franchise, ensued. Nothing happened there either. Later, the USFL called Shinn to talk about buying the very successful (by USFL standards) Birmingham franchise when its owner ran into some tough financial times. But that, too, was a dead end.

Having been offered a division's worth of teams in various non-sales, Shinn returned to the expansion avenue. To see how pro football might go in the Carolinas, Shinn blew a half million dollars or so and staged a couple of USFL exhibition games in Charlotte early in 1985. They did well — a combined crowd of 33,000 attended the two games at Memorial Stadium — and that encouraged Shinn, who earned some needed recognition as a can-do player in the sports game in the process.

It did not earn him a franchise, however. Not long after the games the USFL fell apart. A federal judge ruled in the league's favor in its suit against the NFL but awarded it a token settlement in the low one figures. The USFL became a piece of sports trivia.

That trivia had, however, played its role in Charlotte's still-to-be-born quest for an NBA team. Shinn and Muhleman had gained experience in franchise chasing, and the desire for pro sports in the city had been raised.

With two sports out of the way, and hockey out of the question, Shinn finally turned to basketball. If that sounds like a strange way of getting there, well, it is. But that's just the way it happened. Charlotte's road to the NBA included a couple of wrong turns before Shinn and company stumbled onto the right exit.

Recalling the search in the heady days after it had come to fruition, Muhleman said, "We didn't plan on the NBA from the beginning. In fact, it was about as far from our plans as it could be. But once we came to the conclusion that Charlotte could support a major-league team it made sense."

• • • • •

George Shinn, one-time winner of the Horatio Alger Award for up-from-nothing achievement, can appreciate what the NBA did to position itself for expansion in 1988.

Hornets Never Lie

At the start of the 1980s the league was tottering. It was poorly perceived and received by a public that linked it with drug use and lazy, overpaid prima donnas. Revenues were down. The franchises in Cleveland, Utah, Indianapolis and Kansas City were all struggling, on the verge of failures that could mean an unsettling move at best, an unpalatable disappearance at worst. The impression was that the league's smaller markets couldn't compete with those in the big cities. Some wondered if the NBA, which added eight teams between 1967 and 1971, hadn't grown too fast for its own good.

The growth, which had lined existing owners' pockets — hence, the chief motivation for it — had turned the league into a fully bi-coastal organization. That was good in many ways. There were lots of paying customers out West, for instance. But it also produced a dramatic increase in an already numbing travel schedule for the participants. And with no decrease in the length of the schedule, which has been at least 80 games since 1961, consistency of effort suffered. Long-standing rivalries were weakened, too. For instance, the Celtics and Lakers, league powers for most of two decades, met nine or 10 times a year in the early 60s before expansion started. Today they play twice, once on each home court.

Combined with the social changes brought on by the civil rights movement and counter-culture radicalism, the NBA earned its rep for lackluster, do-what's-needed play. Like many reputations, it was only partly deserved, but truth mattered less than perceptions at the box office. Attendance declined steadily in the 1970s.

Worse still, relations with TV, a major concern of any sports league, were down. CBS, which had wrested the contract away from ABC in the early 1970s with the help of some rather devious machinations by the NBA owners, was dissatisfied with its product. It was paying relatively large bucks to televise something that not many people wanted to see, and the NBA got in the way of other sports programming. As a result, the league got its money but little else from its TV deal. Certainly not much exposure. Regular-season telecasts, invariably featuring Boston, LA or Philadelphia in some combination, were held to a minimum on Sunday afternoons and the playoffs were shown at 11:30 p.m. EST up until the finals. Roller Derby got better time slots.

Although it had established a niche in the sports world, the NBA was, in a word, a mess.

Enter, at this point, one David J. Stern, a savvy-yet-cheerful lawyer who was a surprise choice to succeed the taciturn Lawrence O'Brien as NBA commissioner. Although other forces, such as the economic upturn of the Reagan years and the timely arrival of several megastars, undoubtedly helped, Stern is credited with reversing the NBA's fortunes. In half a decade the NBA went from a weathered old war horse heading for the glue factory to a sleek stallion, streaking towards the winner's circle in the Great American Sports Derby. By the time Shinn started pitching Charlotte as a new site, the NBA's ledger was as bright as any, with only a handful of teams failing to break even. And it was a major player in the sports TV game once again.

Stern changed the course of the league with a three-point program aimed at fiscal improvement and image enhancement.

Most significant was the implementation of the salary cap, a complex document (in its current version, it numbers over 200 pages) designed to hold down and equalize league payrolls while cutting the players in for a fair share of the income. NBA players as a group receive 53 percent of the league's gross receipts. A formula that projects league income sets a spending standard for the payroll of every team. By the 1988-89 season, it had climbed to more than $7 million each for the 23 established teams.

That's a lot of money, but it's not what it could have been had the talent market been wide open to the highest bidder. And the payrolls were roughly even. The NBA's bigger cities (New York, LA, Chicago, etc.) will always own inherent money-making advantages, especially when it comes to TV, simply because of sheer numbers. But they can no longer use those numbers to overwhelm their smaller brethren on the court.

The salary cap has prevented labor problems, too. Football and baseball have both had strikes this decade. The NBA, where financial information is shared by the owners with the players, has not. The late Larry Fleisher, former head of the NBA player's union, said before he died, "I still think an open market would be better, but we've got the highest salaries and a league that's in good shape. The cap isn't the worst thing that's happened to us."

Most general managers and owners around the league would agree, even while regularly cussing the cap. It is not unlike the tax forms churned out by the Internal Revenue Service in its ability to confound and confuse. But, like form 1040, once you battle through it, you find it does the job.

Al Bianchi, general manager of the New York Knicks, says of the cap, "It's a pain in the ass, but we'd have a mess today without it."

Stern, again with the help of Fleisher and the player's union, also implemented a tough drug policy that helped reduce the problem and, more importantly, the perception of the problem in the league. Drug abusers in the league can come forward on their own for counseling and will receive help up to three times. Players who are caught using drugs before they admit to the problem are suspended for several years. Most recently, the NBA began testing all drafted rookies entering the league.

In conjunction with those programs, Stern advocated a more upbeat public relations campaign, exemplified by those "NBA is FANtastic!" commercials. He wanted to stress the point that the league, populated by stars like Larry Bird, Magic Johnson and Michael Jordan, is fun and exciting. It was not a lie, and Stern tried to make sure no one missed hearing about it. Media types were coddled. NBA officials and players are probably the most accessible in all of pro sports and not by accident. League rules dictate it.

All of this combined to make the NBA, if not a hot property, then certainly a warming one, when George Shinn began his franchise chase in the fall of 1985.

With no contacts, Shinn set about meeting people and winning friends like the Norman Vincent Pealer that he is. He spent several months traveling the country, talking with NBA folks about the league and about the possibility of putting a team in his adopted hometown of Charlotte. His receptions varied. One that stood out later for its hospitality was accorded by the general manager of the Los Angeles Clippers, one Carl Scheer.

By January of 1986, Shinn was sure enough of his chances to go public with his latest dream. He called a press conference to announce his intention to obtain an NBA team for Charlotte.

The plan included three basic components: rallying support at home, clearing the financial path, and lobbying the NBA and its franchise owners.

Shinn had worries on all three counts, but the first proved to be no problem. Charlotte, a burgeoning city in the growing Southeast, was, for many reasons, ready to enter the big time. Outsiders who had moved to the area from large metropolitan areas craved a major-league diversion. Natives equated obtaining a team with bringing another big business to town, only on a grander scale. It was a point of civic pride. The NBA would give Charlotte a way to distinguish itself from the muddle of medium-sized cities in the region.

The grass roots support was, in all likelihood, already there, but just in case, Shinn found a valuable ally in the local media. TV, radio, and especially the *Charlotte Observer* gave voluminous coverage to Shinn and his pursuit. Once the formal attack began, the *Observer* covered Shinn's every moment, printed regular season-ticket counts, and also supported him editorially.

The paper's shill factor, obviously, can be debated. Was the interest there before the coverage? Or did the coverage inspire the interest? It's the old chicken-and-egg question with which all newspapers are familiar. Whichever, the *Observer* certainly didn't mind helping hatch the plot.

Recalling his organization's involvement after the franchise had been obtained, *Observer* editor Rich Oppel said, "I felt pretty good about standing tall in the papers. We confined the advocacy, for the most part, to editorials and sports columns. Anyone is naive who doesn't think that a newspaper uses its influence in the selection of stories. This is one case where we chose to turn the spotlight on brightly."

Public opinion, and pressure, helped Shinn turn the corner on a key item — the team's lease at the new Charlotte Coliseum. Members of the Coliseum Convention Center Authority, fearful of seeing their new building begin life as a financial turkey, resisted for more than two months Shinn's requests for a substantial price break. Finally, in late May, Mayor Harvey Gantt, head of the city council which appoints Authority members but has no say in their actions, interceded. He publicly endorsed Shinn's proposals and privately lobbied for their passage.

Bombarded by Gantt and editorials in the *Observer*, the Authority gave in. Shinn received a remarkable price break, a $1 per game rental fee for the first five years. The as yet unborn team was in the new building. The Coliseum's standard fee had already been set at $3,000. After five years, an option in the agreement would allow for more substantial rental fees which would rise each year, based on the team's gross receipts.

In return, Shinn and team were cut out of all the side income at the Coliseum excepting novelty sales. Parking and concessions would go to the city.

Authority Chairman Marvin Brackett, who had successfully stonewalled Shinn for so long, said of giving in that it was a gamble for both sides. "If the gamble works, if the people of Charlotte and the area support the team, then we all win. If we lose, we'll lose and George will lose, too. But frankly, I don't think we'll lose."

Shinn hailed the agreement as a stumbling block overcome. "I'm relieved," he said. "This is as good as I could have hoped. I think it gives us a real advantage on some of the other cities. It's a tremendous lease."

NBA managers actually rank it as a good lease. Not the best in the league, but hardly the worst either. The almost non-existent rental fees in the early years were balanced by the lack of involvement in parking or concessions, and by the potentially stiff rental dollars to be paid down the road. But it was a very favorable lease for an expansion team, one that would help defuse worries in the league about early financial failure.

So, with the lease tucked into his pocket, Shinn made formal application to the NBA for a new franchise. At the same time, he also pursued some existing franchises — Utah, among others, was more or less on the market at that time — with the idea of buying one and moving it to Charlotte. That idea appealed to Shinn. He could bring a better team in and bring it in faster. He might get it cheaper, too; although at the time he didn't know what price the NBA might ask.

Shinn knew that expansion was a surer thing. All he had to do was persuade 23 very independent owners that he and his city were prepared to join them. The only problem was that he wasn't the only millionaire around looking for an NBA team. Six other cities had expressed interest in expansion, too — Minneapolis; Miami; Orlando; St. Louis; Toronto; and Orange County, California, a massive bedroom community for LA. And it was, as yet, still a mystery how many teams the NBA would invite in, or even if they'd invite any. Although expansion fever was running high in the league, no vote on the matter was scheduled until October of 1986.

So while they waited for their quests to take on real meaning, the would-be NBA cities waged, in public at least, a highly superficial war for supremacy. The primary battlefield was the box office, or rather the box office to be. The prospective franchises went to work selling season tickets for teams that wouldn't play a game for almost three years, if then. It was not an easy sell, but few were any better suited to the task than George Shinn, a cock-eyed optimist and salesman from way back. Already a regular on the civic club banquet circuit, Shinn just added a pitch for civic pride — in the form of NBA season tickets — to his message of the power of positivism and Christianity.

That did the job. Shinn began his campaign in mid-July, selling Mayor Gantt the first two tickets. He helped form an advisory group of civic and business leaders in September that pitched the tickets to area businesses, who could do the most for the cause because they could afford to buy in mass. Just three months after the campaign began, just as the ownership group went to Phoenix for the NBA meetings, more than 8,400 season tickets had already been sold. Sales eventually topped 12,000 before Charlotte landed a team.

That allowed Charlotte to at least keep pace with the opposition, and by Shinn's somewhat biased reckoning, he was ahead. "We may not have the biggest number," Shinn said at one point during the ticket derby, "but we have the most realistic number."

He had a point. While the other franchises-to-be rang up a sale anytime somebody wrote or called saying they would buy a ticket, Shinn only counted those who had sent in deposits ranging from $50 to $250. And while the others paid interest on the deposited money and offered a money-back anytime refund offer, those who signed up for Charlotte tickets were in for the duration. There'd be no interest — Shinn was already on the way to spending a million of his hard-earned dollars traveling to lobby for the team — and there would be no refunds unless Shinn failed to land the team.

At the same time he was getting the ticket campaign rolling, Shinn was also putting together his ownership group. Although his dream and eventual plan was to own the team himself, Shinn knew that he needed help. His personal worth, estimated at $50 million, was impressive, but it was not in the same financial league with the mega-rollers who own pro basketball teams. To land a franchise, he'd need some well-heeled partners who could bolster the balance sheet Shinn turned in with his application.

Shinn quickly added two players to his ownership team. One was his friend and sometimes business partner, Rick Hendricks, the Charlotte auto-dealing giant and NASCAR team owner. The other was Felix Sabates, like Shinn a rags-to-riches success story who had started at the bottom of the company, Top Sales, Inc., he now owned.

Hendricks was an obvious pick. Since meeting Shinn several years before — when Shinn threatened to sue him over a malfunctioning auto he purchased at one of Hendricks' dealerships. The two men had become fast friends. They co-owned a couple of truck dealerships in the area. And Hendricks already had some experience in throwing his money after prima donna athletes. Hendricks MotorSports had a three-team stable on the Winston Cup circuit and fielded teams in several other racing organizations as well.

Sabates, who led a Charlotte foray into professional soccer a few years before, was a natural choice even though he was not, at the time, close to Shinn. A garrulous Cuban, he was itching to be a part of the Charlotte sports scene. Besides the soccer venture, he was a major backer of UNC Charlotte basketball. And even before meeting Hendricks, he was casting an eye towards NASCAR.

Those two men enhanced Shinn's ownership package, lending it financial support and a pair of strong, impressive personalities. But Shinn still lacked the sort of financial clout he needed to sway owners who might not grant a franchise to a group they thought couldn't weather the potential financial storm associated with an expansion club. In hopes of finding the partner he needed, Shinn and Muhleman compiled a list of the 50 or so best-endowed citizens of the area and had contacted each. Some return feelers were received, but

Shinn had nothing in concrete when he and Muhleman flew to Phoenix in late October to meet with the NBA owners.

Shinn was to be allowed 30 minutes to make his case. He had two important messages to get across. One, that Charlotte was a great area, ripe for an NBA team. And two, that his was a group which, if given the opportunity, could make a franchise work there.

It was hoped that the second point would come across naturally. Shinn was a gifted speaker, and Hendricks and Sabates were engaging, if not as polished. Persuading the owners that Charlotte was big enough was more of a worry. While it was obvious to anyone who lived there that it was a booming city in the middle of a heavily populated region, there were heavy demographic numbers to fight.

Population surveys showed Charlotte had the smallest metro area (less than 650,000) of any of the expansion competitors. There were nine cities not competing for an NBA franchise that had larger city populations, 12 that had bigger metro areas, as defined by the census takers. Worse yet, Charlotte was a comparatively tiny TV market, ranking just 32nd nationally. San Antonio, which was already in the league, was worse — 42nd. But no other existing team was lower. To combat these figures, Muhleman and Shinn compiled their own figures.

• • • • •

Cities of the world know they have arrived when newspaper stories carrying their dateline are otherwise unidentified. That is, when something happens in London, the story's dateline does not further identify it as London, England. It may disappoint the Charlotte Chamber of Commerce to hear it, but not everyone knows where Charlotte is, not even when the "N.C." is included in a dateline. This was true even after the arrival of the Hornets — witness the moderately famous drug runner who mistakenly went to Charlotte instead of Charleston, S.C. to make a drug buy early in 1989. Sure, he was a foreigner, but you can bet he'd have found the right Los Angeles if that had been his destination.

Charlotte's identity remains a problem, at least until the city can wedge a couple hundred thousand more cars into neighboring Pineville, and it was even more so back in 1986 when George Shinn was trying to persuade the NBA owners that Charlotte could support a professional basketball franchise. Unless you'd been there, unless you lived there, unless you'd driven the I-85 corridor on Friday afternoon, you just didn't know how crowded the place was. And the simple numbers, which said Charlotte was a city of 350,000 or so in a state of five or six million, didn't give an accurate picture. The NBA was looking for bigger game. Why, LA has suburbs that are bigger than Charlotte. That was the prevalent perception, echoed rather vividly by a Phoenix sports columnist, who wrote while the meetings were going on, "The only franchise Charlotte will get is one with golden arches."

The demographic truth, as Muhleman's number crunchers depicted it, was somewhat different from that alleged reality, however. John Connaughton, an economist at the University of North Carolina at Charlotte, who studied the situation for Shinn, compiled a battery of statistics that showed Charlotte to be one of the most under-utilized sports markets in the country.

Charlotte was a bigger, better market, with more willing-to-spend young basketball fans than just about anywhere. The per capita income was high for a region where the cost of living was below the national average. Nearly a third of all households had an income of $35,000 or more. New businesses were flocking to the area, which was fast becoming a hub of the so-called Sun Belt's continuing growth. Charlotte's population grew by almost 10 percent from 1984 to 1986. It was already a national banking center, with $40 billion in assets, the eighth-largest total in the country.

Connaughton's study, and eventually, the Muhleman-prepared presentation, also sought to inflate Charlotte's population by redefining the metro area concept. The key point was the size of the region around Charlotte. As Shinn and other Charlotte drum beaters pointed out over and over again, 5.5 million people lived within 100 miles of Charlotte. That was 700,000 more than lived within the same distance of Atlanta, nearly 2 million more than lived that close to franchise rival Miami. And Charlotte, because of its size and position, was the hub of that area. Raleigh and a few other places might argue the point, but Raleigh wasn't bidding on an NBA team.

The effect of all this was hard to measure. Maybe it opened some eyes, and maybe not. Atlanta Hawks' president Stan Kasten, who was on the NBA committee that selected the expansion cities, said, "I don't think it was a big shock. We all were familiar with the place. We are not a bunch of guys living in cocoons you know."

Perhaps not, but just in case someone had forgotten, Shinn made sure they knew. He ripped through the presentation, bombarding the owners with the facts and his own dynamic speaking abilities. He received rave reviews and lavish praise afterwards, an occurrence that left the Charlotte party sky high as it left Phoenix to return home. They even stopped over to celebrate at one of Sabates' favorite Las Vegas hangouts on the way back.

Hornets Never Lie

Besides the favorable response to the presentation, there was another reason why Shinn left Phoenix feeling good. While he'd been rehearsing for his presentation at his Phoenix hotel room, he'd received a call from Cy Bahakel, a Charlotte communications magnate and one of the prospective investors Shinn had contacted. Bahakel, who owned Charlotte's independent TV station WCCB, wanted to join the ownership group. Bahakel owned radio, TV and cable companies from Charlotte to Denver, and his assets were more than twice what Shinn could claim.

Bahakel's interest may have swung the deal for Charlotte with the NBA owners, according to Norm Sonju, general manager of the Dallas team, who advised Shinn throughout his franchise quest. "Cy added a lot of ... prestige," Sonju said.

Color prestige green in this case.

Just after the franchise was awarded, Shinn conceded Bahakel an important position in team history. "Cy was absolutely critical," Shinn said. "He made an extraordinary impression on the league. He has broadcasting experience and the advantage that he's extremely wealthy."

When the two men split two years later over Shinn's bid to take over the entire team, Shinn changed his tune a bit. After Bahakel claimed Shinn never would have landed the team without him, Shinn replied, "That's bull. We had people lining up to be partners. He just wanted in for the TV rights. He came on first, so he got in. But if it hadn't been him, it would have been someone else."

Whatever the case, Bahakel was in, and in a big way, as Shinn led the final assault.

The months after the Phoenix meeting were filled with more ticket-pushing activities and tying up loose ends. Bahakel formally joined the Charlotte ownership group in November. Members of the NBA expansion committee visited in February. The lease agreement was given final approval in March.

In between, Shinn continued his private lobbying efforts and presided over a pick-the-name contest that was sponsored by the *Observer* and a local TV station. "Spirit" won, giving the Charlotte team a name it could use — at least for a while.

Finally, on the day after April Fool's Day in 1987, Shinn and everyone else learned that their quest had not been in vain. The NBA expansion committee recommended that Charlotte and Minneapolis, along with either Orlando or Miami, be admitted to the league. Commissioner Stern phoned Shinn first to tell him the good news, a sign Shinn took to mean that Charlotte was the first choice. Kasten and others say that's not necessarily so, but it hardly mattered.

Positive thinking had won again as underdog Shinn took underdog Charlotte into the NBA.

Said Shinn, "I guess we did a little better than some people thought. I guess this is better than the golden arches."

• • • • •

In the aftermath of the franchising victory, signs began popping up around Charlotte featuring a basketball and the words, "Thanks George." The exposure of the franchise hunt had made Shinn a celebrity, but he was also a hero, a guy who had done what others said couldn't be done.

It was a remarkable feat, but no more remarkable than many George Shinn had accomplished in his up-by-the-bootstraps life.

The youngest-ever winner of the Horatio Alger Award has a tale that sounds as much like an Alger story as anything Alger ever cooked up.

Neither Ragged Dick nor Tattered Tom, two of Alger's downtrodden heroes, had anything on Junkyard George, the poor little waif from Kannapolis, N.C. His life has produced one believe-it-or-not anecdote after another:

• Shinn graduated last in his class but went on to own a chain of business schools that span 13 states.

• He battled a speech impediment in school but went on to become a polished public speaker who commanded four-figure fees.

• He grew up wearing hand-me-down clothes but now heads a business conglomerate where employees, at Shinn's command, must wear suits and crisp, white shirts.

• As a boy, Shinn watched in tears as his father's possessions were auctioned off to satisfy creditors. In 1988, he joined in the million-dollar bidding for the physical assets of the bankrupt PTL Club.

They just go on and on. In the space of 10 years, Shinn went from a despairing, would-be businessman who didn't even have enough money to file for bankruptcy, to the head of a sprawling conglomerate, George Shinn and Associates, Inc., whose interests run from tractor trailers to Christian tracts.

Shinn likes to say the foundation of his success was laid in the sad, early years of his life, right after his father died and the family was left in dire straits. Shinn's father tried to build an empire of his own. He owned a gas station, and in 1951, the year before he died, he mortgaged all he had to build a small subdivision in Kannapolis. When a sudden heart attack felled him the next year, he was deep in debt. Everything but the family house had to be sold to satisfy his many creditors.

Shinn later said, "I'll never forget the crushing humiliation of those auctions, watching other people make bids on what had been my father's life work."

But even if that memory was forever etched into his brain, it was a long time before it ever drove him very far. Shinn was a poor student in high school with admittedly lousy study habits and a bent towards the mischievous — or even beyond. He says he walked a tightrope with the law in some of his wilder episodes growing up.

All this conspired to help him achieve his now famous feat of finishing 224th in a class of 224. And Shinn barely managed that. He had to go to summer school after his senior year to make up two courses he had failed.

Shinn jokes, "I like to say that the first graduation I attended was one where I was speaking. Well, that's not a lie. It's true." And just one more fantastic turnaround from Shinn's repertoire of personal reversal.

Shinn's career in the work force began where it did for many Kannapolis youth at that time — at Cannon Mills. He carried rolls of cloth from place to place for two years before developing back problems that forced him to look for something else.

He applied for a sales position but was turned down after taking an aptitude test that, in a yet another of those Shinnsian twists, said he'd never be a good salesman. Shinn, who not only lectures about sales but has even written a textbook on the subject, loves to tell that one, too.

After her son was turned down for the sales job, Shinn's mother suggested he get more schooling. He attended Evans Business College in Concord, N.C., one of those we'll-take-anybody-for-a-fee places, and that is where he really got his start. Shinn got a part-time job at the school to help pay his way. It was a little a bit of everything — stacking books, sweeping up — your basic odd-job/janitorial duties. That wasn't getting him anywhere fast until one Saturday morning, while he was sweeping up, fate pointed two potential secretarial students his way. Shinn answered their knock on the school door, gave them a tour, then found applications and collected their fees.

On Monday, the two students returned with four of their friends, asking for the "Mr. Shinn" who had sold them on the school two days before. They would deal with no one else. But that was a problem for school officials, because they knew of no one by that name who worked there. Finally, someone remembered that George the janitor's last name was Shinn. He was hauled out of class to sign up the new students.

That incident, and some others, helped Shinn grow close to David Ratchford, the man who owned the school. In 1964, Ratchford made Shinn his chief recruiter, giving him $10 per student signed. In 1966, Shinn was made manager of the school, and in 1968 he became co-owner. It was the kind of deal from which legends are made. Shinn, 26 years old and still living with his mom, paid nothing for his interest in the college, but agreed to share costs, and profits, if there were any, with Ratchford.

In the next four years, Shinn traded various assets with Ratchford and another owner and wound up with control of four similar schools in Durham, Raleigh, Fayetteville and Greensboro. In some ways that was shrewd business. Shinn had become an education tycoon for next to nothing. On the other hand it was dumb. The schools were not profitable. In fact, despite paying employees late and scrimping on supplies, by 1972 Shinn faced 12 lawsuits and tax claims demanding $67,000 from his business schools.

Shinn was sinking so fast that he couldn't even see how big the hole was. He paid a consulting firm $500 to tell him just how bad the situation was. It was bad, they said, and they recommended that Shinn file for bankruptcy.

"But," says Shinn, "that really wasn't an option, either. After paying them I didn't have the $400 I needed to file the bankruptcy papers.

"So," Shinn says, heading towards what he feels is the triumphant conclusion of his darkest story, "one of the consultants told me I just didn't have a prayer. But that wasn't right. A prayer was all I did have."

Shinn, a devout Christian, credits his personal conversion with turning his life around. While driving to work one on one of those dark days, wondering just what he was going to do, Shinn pulled over to the side of the road and began to cry. In his despair he prayed, asking God to help him run his business. Shinn says that in the next few moments he experienced a calm, the likes of which he had never experienced before. When he got home that night he slept well for the first time in weeks.

And, his life did turn around, almost immediately.

In the next few months Shinn dropped 40 pounds from his sagging frame, stopped smoking, cut back on his drinking, and quit his damaging habit of using a vessel-constricting nasal spray. The physical improvements carried over to his personality as well. A once crabby boss who blamed employees for all the school's problems was transformed into a positive dynamo who encouraged others and even pitched in with the manual labor. The depressing atmosphere at Shinn's schools was lifted and soon their fortunes were reversed. The colleges, now known as the Rutledge chain, went from 200 students and a $33,000 loss in 1972 to 3,700 students and a $620,000 profit in 1975.

Shinn sees his story, and often uses it, as an illustration of the power of prayer and hard work. Those are the attributes, along with the self-confidence that Shinn says will come from them, which Shinn advocates as the most important to success. His "Ten Rules for Success" include such maxims as: "Be Honest. Live with enthusiasm. Don't worry about your problems. Assume your full share of responsibility in the world. Pray consistently and confidently."

Shinn believes that. He says that "I believe motivation will, in most cases, overcome pure, raw ability." Because of his past successes, he is confident that he can work and pray his way through and to almost anything. And he thinks everyone else, with his help, can, too. Shinn's confidence is infectious and productive, but employees often find his constant prodding annoying.

"He is a dreamer," says Max Muhleman, the consultant who worked with Shinn in landing the Hornets. "He teaches that. And his approach to problems can be kind of intense."

Ironically, Shinn must admit at least a footnote of fortune when chronicling his own success. His transformation, all the prayer and hard work, might have gone for naught if not for a coincidence of bureaucracy and history that suddenly made Rutledge Colleges a hot property.

In late 1972, the North Carolina Board of Education made a policy change that allowed veterans full educational benefits, even if they attended as little as 12 hours of college per week. That was down from 25 hours and fit the profile of the part-time Rutledge student considerably better. Coupled with the influx of Vietnam veterans starting to pour in, Shinn found himself with an attractive product and a wealthy relative — Uncle Sam — to foot the bill. Rutledge enrolled more than 5,000 Vietnam vets between 1973 and 1978. The Vietnam era version of the GI Bill turned Shinn's business around, giving him the capital to pay for a dreamer's expansion.

Shinn admits as much. "Yes," he says, "as hard as I struggled, those were the keys. I'm just God's little idiot."

God's little idiot turned out to be pretty shrewd when he got some money and got out on his own. The colleges, boosted by new types of government loans, continued to churn out the cash, and Shinn poured it into other investments, ranging from oil and a printing house, to restaurants and a Kannapolis bakery that Shinn remembered from his childhood. He also collected consulting fees from colleges seeking to duplicate the Rutledge success, royalties from assorted motivational and business text books, and fees for speaking to corporations at motivational seminars.

Perhaps the biggest boost came from auto and truck dealerships he bought into with Hendricks, another up-from-nothing guy who is now listed by some publications as the country's third-largest auto dealer. The bottom line is that by 1986, when he filed a personal worth statement, Shinn listed his assets at $50 million. Because of the Hornets and other deals concluded since, it's fair to say that figure hasn't gone down, even though he decided in 1989 to divest himself of the Rutledge building block, which, by then, had lost some of its luster anyway. State and Federal reports on the institutions cited some of them for general shabbiness and an alarmingly high default rate on student loans.

Slowed by his 1988 stroke, Shinn switched gears as he approached his 50th birthday. Sports and related development will be his cause in the years ahead. He will, in the near future, be sole owner of the Hornets, and he hopes to be at least a co-owner of a local Major League baseball franchise.

Muhleman says Shinn is no different from most sports owners.

"They all have something burning in them that makes them want to do this," he said. "I don't think George is any different. He's been a big fan. He has the means now and it's something he wants to do."

Others in the Charlotte business community suspect Shinn was just been trying to feed his ego. He was the city's most visible citizen in the late 1980s, having wrested the limelight from the town's traditional leaders. For a long-time have-not, an outsider, nothing might be more satisfying.

Shinn, a proud man who is not openly boastful, is sensitive about the ego charge. As a professing Christian, he also values humility.

"I'm not doing anything crazy, and I'm not trying to support my ego," he said. "I think that my ego is very much under check. I do have one, of course. I'm human. I like to be loved, respected and admired, just like everyone else. It's just that business is what I do. You keep making deals."

Shinn also likes helping others. Before he became a sports figure, he was best known as a philanthropist. He set up the George Shinn Foundation to raise funds for theological schools and students. He headed Charlotte's drive to build a center for the homeless. Someday he even plans to turn his own home into an orphanage of sorts. The 25-room, 10,000-square foot house holds dormitory-like facilities into which Shinn and his wife Carolyn one day plan to put foster children they have adopted.

In his 1981 book, *The Miracle of Motivation*, Shinn explains his philosophy of giving. "Some see (success) as money, power, fame. But it's also the concept of 'reaching down,' of being able to help your fellow man. Material things you can buy and sell, but things like hope and courage and faith and knowledge are gifts you give your fellow man to pull him up."

Shinn sees his charitable contributions as one way of fulfilling that view of success. The success itself is another. The more Shinn does, the bigger he becomes, the bigger testament he makes to the power of the things in which he believes. The bigger he becomes, the bigger becomes the pulpit he is always eager to fill.

Shinn, who returned to the public speaking circuit four months after his stroke, says, "I've been delivering the same message for 15 years. The only difference now is that the messenger is a little better known, so the people listen a little closer."

Perhaps nothing embodies Shinn's vision of success as well as his basketball team. By bringing in a relatively wholesome entity that touched a community, a state really, without regard to lines of race or class, Shinn experienced his ultimate fantasy. He touched millions while personally making it big.

While buying the Hornet tickets and souvenirs that lined Shinn's pockets, fans could share the glory of a hard-working team, the rise of a region built by entrepreneurs like Shinn, and old time, Bible Belt religion. At Shinn's direction, Charlotte home games were preceded by the NBA's only regular invocation.

The pre-game prayer was the source of mirth in the NBA and amongst the Hornets themselves. Before one road game late in the year, assistant coach Ed Badger walked over to two writers just before the national anthem was played and said, "Okay, which one of you guys has the invocation today?" But if Shinn heard any of the cracks or laughter, he probably didn't mind. God's little idiot knew the joke really wasn't on him.

Dressing Up the Front Office

"Dick was the only one with a suit and a white shirt. He looked good. I liked that."

—George Shinn

Having done the impossible – his words for it – and obtained an NBA team for Charlotte, George Shinn now needed to figure out how to run it. The answer, of course, was to find someone else to do it.

Shinn claims his managerial style is to "get people who are smarter than I am to do the job and then get out of their way." Reality always seems different, particularly to those whose way Shinn has allegedly gotten out of, and in the case of the Hornets, Shinn was less inclined to sit back than normal. Feeling that he had given the people of Charlotte his word that *he* would make sure the team was run right, Shinn committed himself early to an active ownership. He said he'd spend 75 percent of his time on Hornets' business, a figure he later amended to 50 percent. No, he said, he did not want to be a meddling George Steinbrenner calling the papers every day to lambaste his team, charging into the locker room for an off-the-cuff firing.

"But," said Shinn somewhat ominously, "I do like the way he keeps on top of things. I'd like to be like that."

Having established that he would be very involved with the team, in spite of his lack of basketball expertise, Shinn set about determining who else would be.

One choice was obvious. Max Muhleman, the marketing whiz who had guided Shinn down the twisting path to the NBA, would have to be a part. Except for the lack of a financial commitment, he was as deeply involved in Charlotte's NBA effort as Shinn was. Shinn and Muhleman talked about Muhleman leaving his successful marketing agency to become a full-time Hornet employee. That did not appeal to Muhleman, however, who wanted to continue his work outside of the Hornets. So when Shinn announced his basic management team in late June of 1987, Muhleman fell into a slot somewhere between employee and advisor. The job title was about as nebulous as you could get — executive consultant — but there was little doubt at that time that the 50-year-old Muhleman would have a big role. He was part of a troika at the top that also included Shinn and Carl Scheer, the team's general manager.

Locating a general manager wasn't quite as simple as finding an executive consultant. There wasn't one right in town. But the choice of Scheer was just about as obvious. Sheer, who had broad experience as a basketball executive, had more roots in the area than some Carolina pines.

Scheer's wife is from Valdese, N.C., a town on the edge of the mountains only 80 miles northwest of Charlotte. He got his start in professional basketball representing a college player (Bob Kauffman) from Greensboro's Guilford College. And for four years, from 1970-1974, Scheer was president and general manager of North Carolina's "other" professional basketball team, the Carolina Cougars of the old American Basketball Association.

There were other factors on Scheer's side, too. When Shinn was calling and meeting NBA people during his franchise quest, one of the warmest receptions came from Scheer, then the general manager of the LA Clippers. That's not surprising. Scheer was at least familiar with North Carolina, and he is, by any measure, a polite and friendly man. But that's all there was to it, at least from Scheer's side. Scheer says that back in 1985 he had no illusions about Shinn's ability to acquire an NBA team for Charlotte.

"I was courteous to George when he called, I think," Scheer said later. "But I never believed that George Shinn or anyone had the capability of convincing the NBA that Charlotte was major league. When I left to go to Denver in 1974, I dreamed that someday North Carolina would have an NBA franchise. But I truly believed that dream would never be fulfilled. I didn't think any human could bring major league basketball to this state in my lifetime."

But Shinn remembered the courtesy, and as Scheer's other connections and ties became apparent, he was a natural choice. This was more than geographic cronyism, though. On top of everything else, Scheer was also the most experienced basketball executive on the market when Shinn started looking. When Charlotte won a franchise, Scheer was serving in the less-than-scintillating post of commissioner of the Continental Basketball Association. But for 16 years before that, he had been the head of one professional basketball franchise or another.

Scheer's record as a general manager was good if not spectacular. A former All-State point guard from Springfield, Mass., where basketball was born, he never displayed any great skill at judging basketball talent. But he was sharp at marketing and managing his product. Among his more impressive feats was turning Denver from a morose, ABA franchise into an NBA attendance leader. The Rockets averaged 4,100 spectators a game the year before Scheer arrived. With a new name, the Nuggets, and a new team, the figure climbed to 6,712 per game the next year. It almost doubled in the 1975-76 season. And in 1976-77, Denver's first year in the NBA, they led the league with an average attendance of 17,150.

Scheer gets at least part of the credit for that reversal and some plaudits for a rare collection of skills, all of which were acquired on the job. Of course, that's the way it usually is in sports. There are a few sports management schools these days, but they don't really prepare anyone for the myriad tasks involved in running a pro franchise. Everyone in the business takes what background they have and builds from there.

In Scheer's case, the background was law. After graduating from the University of Miami law school, he moved from Florida to Greensboro, N. C., where his wife, Marsha, had many family ties. Scheer's basketball education was less formal and not as advanced. He was a good high school guard in Massachusetts and later an avid fan. His interest in the game grew in Greensboro, where he practiced law for six years. He formed a close association with the burgeoning program at Guilford College, a small Quaker school then just beginning its climb as an NAIA power. Scheer hung around the program, providing booster-like support, even doing radio play-by-play of Guilford games for a time. Unexpectedly, he stumbled upon a new career.

Bob Kauffman, a 6-8 center who was the Quakers' first star, was an NBA prospect and needed legal representation in his coming contract talks. Scheer had the legal skills and was already a trusted figure in Quakerland. It was an obvious match. Scheer negotiated Kauffman's contract with Seattle and made a number of contacts in professional basketball. Certainly the most important was with then-NBA commissioner Walter Kennedy and his staff. Impressed by the young lawyer who handled the Kauffman deal, Kennedy hired him as his administrative assistant the next year.

Scheer served in that post for most of two seasons. It was a hectic time. The league office was grossly understaffed, and with the competition with the ABA underway, there were great demands on employees. Plus, New York, site of the league's offices, was only slightly less difficult to navigate then. Scheer, who moved his family to suburban Connecticut, remembers the long commutes: hopping off a train onto a subway, then walking for blocks to his office. It took two hours some days, and with a 10-hour day usually spliced between rides, there wasn't much room for anything else. Still, Scheer remembers, it was an exciting time, a time to meet people and, as it turned out, to build the foundations for a new career.

Ironically, the ABA, which Scheer had been fighting in New York, provided him with his biggest break. He took the job of president with the expansion Buffalo Braves of the NBA early in 1970, but quit a few months later when a slightly more powerful position was offered to him with the ABA franchise based in his old stomping grounds, Greensboro. Although it cost him some of his friendships in the NBA — Scheer says he's still not sure if Kennedy, now dead, ever forgave him — the job was too good to pass up. He could work in a part of the country that he liked, and day-to-day control of the franchise would be in his hands. Jim Gardner, the North Carolina businessman who was elected lieutenant governor in 1988, had bought the struggling Houston franchise and moved it to Greensboro in 1969. But his own business empire was in trouble, so one year later he dumped everything on Scheer and turned his attention to other matters. Scheer rarely saw him that first year, and one year later Gardner sold out to Ted Munchak, an Atlanta carpet magnate. Munchak was more involved, but he retained Scheer as the general manager of the regional franchise known as the Carolina Cougars. The team played games in Raleigh and Charlotte as well as Greensboro.

Scheer's experience at the time was just about nil. Essentially, it was just what he had heard and seen during his two years with the NBA. But that was just about par for the course in the ABA, so he learned along with everyone else. Scheer, generally mellow now, was impetuous and volatile back then. During games he darted from place to place in the arena, pounding tables and cursing as the events of the evening transpired. Cougar staff members recall the extraordinary nervousness that sometimes overwhelmed him when the team was on the road. Unable to bear the strain of listening to the broadcast of the game, Scheer would phone staff members to find out what was going on. A few minutes later, he'd call back. Finally, he'd stay on the line and have them do a play-by-play of the play-by-play of the closing minutes.

He was a wheeler-dealer, too. The Cougars made several big trades in Scheer's four years at the helm and signed free agents right and left. Some of that was Scheer's youth and inexperience, and some of it was just the times. With the additional avenue of a raid on the other league available, there were more moves to make. And largely because of that, Scheer built the Cougars into a winner before the team left town in 1974.

There were several key maneuvers. The signings of NBA stars Billy Cunningham and Joe Caldwell gave the team a superb talent base, and giving Larry Brown and Doug Moe their first coaching jobs assured the team of sound direction. With Brown at the helm in 1973, his first season as a head coach, the Cougars won 57 games, increased attendance by 40 percent, and actually made money. They slumped to 47 wins the next season, but for a franchise that had never done better than break even before those years it was a credible run.

The Brown-Scheer tandem continued to win after Munchak pulled the carpet out from under the Cougars. With the franchise collapsing, eventually to move to St. Louis, they sought work elsewhere. Denver snapped them up as a team in June of 1974 and they went there and built another winner. In the ABA's last two years, Denver won 125 games, though, notably, not the title. In the first two seasons after the merger, Denver won 98 games and back-to-back division titles. The acquisition of David Thompson was a key. Scheer traded for his draft rights, giving up almost nothing — aging guard Mack Calvin and forward Jan van Breda Kollf — to the impoverished, soon-to-be-defunct Virginia franchise, which knew it didn't have the bucks to sign the ex-N.C. State star. Then Scheer went out and signed Thompson, out-bidding Atlanta of the NBA in the process.

Two other robberies that showed Scheer's aggressiveness and acumen added the pieces to go around Thompson, who Scheer still considers the best to ever play the game. In one deal, Scheer landed center Dan Issel, giving up journeyman pivot Dave Robisch to Baltimore of the ABA, another bankrupt franchise that, as it turned out, would never play a game. In another, he swapped draft picks with the Cougars and obtained the rights to North Carolina's Bobby Jones. He signed him, too.

Those players were the staples of several excellent Denver teams, but they weren't enough to get the Nuggets —a name Scheer came up with to replace the old ABA moniker, Rockets —over the hump in the NBA. The first of two back-to-back division winners lost in the first round of the 1977 playoffs. A year later the Nuggets gritted out a semifinal series win over Milwaukee in seven games but fell to Seattle in six games in the Western Conference finals.

That convinced Scheer that the Nuggets needed more ammunition. So in the summer of 1978, he started dealing. In separate transactions, he acquired Charlie Scott and George McGinnis, two high-profile scorers, while jettisoning Jones, guard Ralph Simpson, and Darnell Hillman, the legendary ABA skywalker. Jones and Simpson went to Philadelphia for McGinnis in August, 1978, a trade that still causes Scheer occasional pangs of guilt. Jones was the epitome of an unselfish player, a great defender and a decent rebounder who seldom took a bad shot. McGinnis was ... more or less, the opposite of that.

"That just didn't work," Scheer said. "I remember the first day of practice after we got him (McGinnis); the team was training up at the Air Force Academy. Larry called me after the first workout and said, 'We've got to get rid of this S.O.B.' I felt terrible."

Scheer recouped some of his loss in the McGinnis deal 18 months later. In the middle of the 1980 season, he traded bad George to Indiana for a young forward named Alex English and a first-round pick in the next draft. English became, indeed remains, the cornerstone of a still relatively successful Denver franchise.

But the McGinnis deal may have helped break up the old gang in more ways than one. Brown, the brilliant coach, left in March, 1979, to take the coaching job at UCLA. Donnie Walsh, an assistant who is now general manager of the Indiana Pacers, took over. Denver did well the rest of that season but collapsed in 1979-80, losing 52 games. Scheer made more changes, adding another scorer in Kiki Vandeweghe. The 1980-81 team missed the playoffs, too, but in mid-season Scheer was able re-hire Moe, this time as head coach. That established a level of proficiency that is still in force in Denver. The Nuggets are never bad, but never good enough to make much of a title run either. Moe, who completed his ninth season in Denver in 1989, says of that niche, "You'd love to win the title, but hey, making the playoffs all the time ain't exactly the pits."

The circumstance says little about the abilities of the coaches and managers involved since it is exactly what the NBA system of talent replenishment would predict. A team within hailing distance, either way, of mediocrity would expect to stay roughly the same. A poor team, but not a bad one, would receive draft picks that weren't quite good enough to turn it around. A good team, but not a great one, would pick in a position good enough to insure a continued infusion of talent, but not good enough to bring the talent that would get it over the hump.

Only great fortune or some remarkable drafting would change the scenario. Scheer has been no luckier than the next man, and he's never been accused of making great draft picks either.

In fact, Scheer owns a rather dismal record in that department. He doesn't have to shoulder all the blame since he has been more willing than most general managers to share such decision making with his staff. Scheer is strong-willed and opinionated. Beneath his calm and courtly exterior, is the resolve and temper to carry on an argument. But he also came to understand fairly early in his career that picking the live wires from the duds is not his strong point.

"There are a lot of things in this job I can do well," Scheer says, "but the bottom line is when I had the right kind of people around me and the right kind of leadership, we had outstanding success. And when I got away from that formula I made mistakes. It's as simple as that."

Scheer's picks with Carolina are hard to score. With successive number-one picks, he drafted Ted "Hound Dog" McLain, Bill Bunting and Tom Riker. Although "Hound Dog," a guard who couldn't shoot, was the only one so named, all three classified as basketball canines. But when the ABA was in competition with the NBA, players were often drafted because they were signable. Scheer expended a first-round pick on Pete Maravich one year but couldn't get him signed.

In Denver, where the picture was clearer, Scheer's record was abysmal. He presided over nine drafts. Three of the players picked in the first round — Rod Griffin, Kenneth Green and James "Fly" Williams — didn't make the team. Among the rest, center Marvin "The Eraser" Webster, forward Tommy LaGarde and guard Mike Evans, who was picked after Griffin in 1978, were the best. The rest stuck for a while but didn't pan out.

Denver's draft position can be blamed for some of that. The Nuggets picked higher than 16th just twice after Denver joined the NBA. But Scheer wasted the Nuggets' best position, selecting the inimitable James Ray, a power(less) forward from Jacksonville with the fifth pick overall in 1980. It was not a strong draft, but Mike Gminski, Kiki Vandeweghe, Mike Woodson and Andrew Toney all serviceable NBA players — were available when the Nuggets nabbed Ray.

In his one draft in Los Angeles, Scheer used the third pick to take Benoit Benjamin. Scheer was one of 12 general managers who passed on current superstar Karl Malone, but all in all, that wasn't a bad pick. Benjamin is a decent center who still has a chance to be a star.

Scheer got to LA in 1984 after the management changed in Denver. Red McCombs, the Houston auto dealer who purchased the San Antonio franchise in 1988, bought Denver in 1984 and started cleaning house. He offered Scheer a lesser post, outside the basketball operations field. Scheer resigned instead and was hired by the Clippers soon after.

That quagmire of a franchise, which has played in three cities while making the playoffs just three times in 18 years, dragged Scheer down. But he made a mark there. He drafted Benjamin and made a six-player trade (Terry Cummings, Craig Hodges and Ricky Pierce for Marques Johnson, Harvey Catchings and Junior Bridgeman) that assured Milwaukee a contender's role in the playoffs through the 1990s. He fired Jim Lynam as coach.

Attendance improved marginally as the Clippers hit, relatively speaking, a high spot. They won 31 and 32 games under Scheer. That wasn't very good, but the three teams before him didn't do as well, and the two that followed didn't win that many combined. As ego friction increased, Scheer was forced out in the spring of 1986. Newspaper stories in March that year, leaked by others in the ever-amicable Clipper front office, said Scheer had been caught misappropriating more than $10,000 in team funds and had been forced to pay it back. The Clippers rallied to Scheer's defense, saying there was only a procedural misunderstanding. "We do not question his integrity and never have," President Alan Rothenberg said at the time. Nonetheless, Scheer resigned a few months later. The innuendo and bickering were more than he could stand.

Scheer calls the LA experience a "colossal mistake."

"The less said about that the better," he said. "It was wrong, number one, for me to go there, and number two, for me to let my ego get in the way to where I thought I could do what no one had done before. It was just a big mistake."

While waiting for another NBA job to materialize, Scheer took an interim job as commissioner of the Continental Basketball Association. He is credited with some modest improvements to that entity, but no one figured he was there for life and, as it turned out, he wasn't. After some heavy lobbying by Scheer and his many acquaintances around the league, Shinn bowed to the obvious in June, 1987, and hired him as Charlotte's vice president for basketball operations, and later, its general manager.

Shinn, who had wanted Scheer for the front office even before he got a team, said he really had no other options. "Everybody I talked to in the NBA gave him a tremendous recommendation," Shinn said. "I was so impressed that, outside of my relatives, I didn't interview anyone else."

Scheer, pleased to be back in the NBA after his CBA exile, said the day he was hired, "This is the best job in the NBA."

With Scheer on board, the franchise spent the next few months taking care of some nagging little details, such as the team's name and colors, and selling more tickets.

After some consultation and with help from a name-the-team

contest in 1987, Shinn tentatively called his team the "Spirit." But it had not proven to be a popular moniker. Judging by reaction to call-in shows and the jokes that cropped up ("The Spirits don't have a ghost of chance"), Shinn decided to hold a second name-the-team contest not long after winning the franchise. "Whatever makes the fans happy," Shinn said, "that's what we want to do."

In what could be called spirited voting, Hornets edged out Knights 2,916 to 2,467. Spirit finished a distant fourth with 776 votes, relegated to that position by nostalgia buffs who gave nearly 1,500 votes to the old ABA nickname, Cougars.

Hornets, team officials were quick to point out, was very fitting. Charlotte had already had a pro baseball team with that nickname, and, during the American Revolution, Mecklenburg County had been noted by the British as a "nest of hornets with revolutionary fever." Even more importantly, considerably more in all likelihood, "Hornets" offered marketable logo and mascot possibilities not readily available with the indescribable Spirit. With Spirit, Charlotte would have received an impressionistic logo and a generic NBA mascot along the lines of Duncan the Dragon, a seven-foot tall blob of lime-green shag carpet who doesn't fire up the crowds at New Jersey's home games. At best, or maybe it would have been worst, Charlotte would have had something that resembled Casper the Friendly Ghost.

As it turned out, the team came up with a silly, but entertaining symbol: a purple and teal wasp with a moderately menacing stare. And the mascot, his suit developed later by Jim Henson of Muppets fame, turned into one of the great rages of the raging season.

"Hugo," whose name was "Harvey" until just minutes before his debut, captured the fancy of kids and adults. Hugo dolls, with suction cups on their feet, could be seen affixed to car windows throughout the area. In Mecklenburg County, they undoubtedly outnumbered the similarly endowed Garfield dolls that started the window-sticking fad. And Hugo became, in the end, the most popular Hornet of all. Coach Dick Harter marveled late in the season at the phenomenon. He'd been at a Hornets appearance with Hugo and had found himself all but alone while a throng of bug-eyed fans surrounded a man in a wasp costume.

"It was like I wasn't even there," Harter said. There was no jealously in his voice. Harter doesn't want to be a major celebrity. He was only marveling at who, in this crazy town in this crazy year, got to be one.

With the team name and mascot out of the way, and ticket purchases at an acceptable level — 14,000 plus by September of

1987 — the team returned to personnel considerations.

Scheer installed a basketball scouting staff in early October, headed by 44-year-old Gene Littles, who, like Scheer, had plenty of Carolina ties.

Littles, a Washington, D.C., native, played his college ball at High Point College in the North Carolina city famous for its furniture making. He was a three-time, small-college All-American and a scoring machine. He averaged 23.3 points a game for his college career, which is still a school record. He might have done better if he hadn't spent most of his freshman season with his shooting wrist in a cast.

But that injury just served to endear Littles to High Point fans. As the first black to attend the school, he became a cult figure during his four years there. A 6-1 guard who averaged nine rebounds a game in his senior year, he was a one-man army of a basketball player, as revered for his playmaking and defense as anything. Bill Miller, a coach at rival Elon College during Littles' High Point days, says, "There are only two players in the league who can turn a game around single-handedly. Littles is one of them." The other was Western Carolina's Henry Logan. Their twice-a-year matchups were televised throughout the state back when not that many games were on TV.

Littles' path toward a basketball career was a peculiar one. After finishing at D.C.'s McKinley High one year ahead of NBA great Dave Bing, Littles went to work. He spent five years in the Government Printing Office and kept his basketball skills sharp playing AAU ball in the D.C. area. He realized that business opportunities were limited without a college degree, so when High Point College scout Mort Littman approached him, Littles, then 23, was interested. As it turned out, he was the perfect choice to break the color barrier at High Point and in the Carolinas Conference. His age, experience and low-key persona allowed him to survive the not-so-incidental contact and the cherry bombs and ice hurled his way at some of the league's less-progressive stops.

By the time he left in 1969, Littles had a degree, a pile of basketball records, a night in his honor, and a wife. A pro contract soon followed. The Cougars, trying, foolishly as it turned out, to cash in on local sentiment at the gate, signed Littles. Littles' pro career was preordained to be a short one. He was a 27-year-old rookie and passed very quickly into what the pros consider the twilight stage of his playing life. For that reason, and because Littles was never a flashy player, the Cougars kept trying to replace him. Scheer drafted guards year after year, but year after year Littles retained his position, which was usually third guard in a three or four-man rotation. "It was always the same," Littles said. "Every year they'd bring in some super new guard to replace me, and by the end of the season every year I'd be playing again."

Littles hung on until the Cougars were sold and moved to St. Louis. A general housecleaning there, supervised by Harry Weltman, thrust Littles into limbo, but the Kentucky Colonels, the ABA's best team at the time, picked him up. With Littles playing a conspicuous reserve role, the Colonels won the league title that year.

Littles started his coaching career in North Carolina, too. The year after his season with the Colonels, he went West to to start a clothing business. But a year after that he returned to North Carolina to join Bobby Cremins at Appalachian State University in Boone as an assistant coach. He spent two years there, then cashed in on his celebrity in the Piedmont Triad area by winning the head coaching job at N.C. Agricultural and Technical University in Greensboro in 1977. Littles did the job there. Picking up the pieces left by the disastrous reign of Warren Reynolds, Littles fashioned a 40-15 record in two years. Not only was Littles comfortable at A&T, he had friends and admirers in the area, and, in a remarkable stroke of luck, had even been able to buy his old High Point house back when he returned. But the money was not great and advancement was certain to be slow. The pros offered better opportunities, even though it would mean a vagabond lifestyle away from the state that he and his wife Rita called home.

In 1979, Littles jumped at a chance to join Tom Nissalke's staff. He coached with Nissalke for five years in Utah and later in Cleveland. When Nissalke was fired from the Cavs in 1984, Littles managed to retain a position on George Karl's staff. When Karl was fired in late 1986, Littles even became interim head coach for 15 games.

Such stints are usually meaningless, and Littles' was no different, though perhaps it could have been. When he took over, the Cavs were actually leading Chicago for the last spot in the Eastern Conference playoffs. But the Cavs faced a brutal closing schedule with many games on the road or against league powers or both. And, with characters like World Free and Mel Turpin on hand, it was hardly a stable mixture.

Littles got the team off to a good start. They split their first six under him, including back-to-back wins at New Jersey and Atlanta. With eight to play, Cleveland led the Bulls by two-and-a-half games, and the thought began to creep into Littles' head that he just might coach his way into a job. Make the playoffs. Show up well against Boston in the first round. How could he be denied?

The dream quickly died, however, as the schedule took its predicted toll. Cleveland lost seven straight, including four on the road. A season-ending victory over Chicago left them out of the playoffs by a single game.

Littles was left hanging in the wind for a few months. He helped the Cavs prepare for what turned out to be the pivotal draft that turned the ailing franchise around. But he wouldn't be around to see the comeback. A new general manager, Wayne Embry, was hired in June. Lenny Wilkens was chosen as the new coach three weeks later.

The ending left Littles bitter. He hadn't won a championship, but he had thought he should have found a better fate for the coaching job he did. "I just felt I really got used by management in Cleveland," he told Joe Menzer, an Ohio reporter, several years later. "I felt used not so much because I felt I had saved the team, because I didn't. The team was already destroyed. But I felt like I kind of helped stabilize the attitude fans had towards our team. I mean, we weren't winning. We weren't going anywhere, and still 8,000 fans showed up for our last game. I think the fans felt we were a good team but shorthanded, that our guys believed they could win and that they would play hard every night.

"When the season was over ... I lost all faith in management. They always talked about loyalty toward management, but I felt like management had no loyalty to me."

Littles was actually offered the chance to stay. The Gund family, which owns the Cavs, told him there would be a position for him before Embry was ever hired. But Littles knew better than to believe that. "All that meant was that the new GM can come in and say, 'Hey, I don't want this guy around.'"

So he left the Cavs and went looking for another job. Littles, with many friends around the league by this point, had no trouble finding work. He signed on as an assistant with Chicago, where he taught Michael Jordan how to play defense and do other things. "I taught him everything he knows," Littles once joked. "All that hanging in the air stuff, that's me."

Littles was getting ready for his second year in Chicago when Scheer called with an offer. It was not the first time Scheer had offered him a job. When Littles had finished the last year of what turned out to be his last pro contract, he and Scheer talked about Littles coming to Denver to play. They agreed to some terms but not all. Littles felt so sure about the deal he even began investigating the housing situation in the Rockies. Then Scheer called again. He'd like Littles to come, but for a new, lower figure.

"I told him I thought we had a deal already," Littles recalled. "Carl said, 'I don't remember that.' And so we didn't. General managers can have very selective memories."

Time heals old wounds, however. Twelve years later, Littles was glad to hear from Scheer again. And glad to take a step toward management. Although reasonably secure financially because of his wife's business talents and some successful dabbling of his own in the clothing business, Littles knew how mercurial coaching could be. As with his playing career, the chance to diversify and display new skills could only help him extend his career. He joined the Hornets in early October in his first job as a full-time scout and judge of basketball-playing men.

Hiring Littles and a part-time staff of scouts gave Charlotte the nucleus it needed. Scheer also brought in some business personnel to handle tickets and hired a public relations director. The major moves, except for hiring a coach, which really wouldn't be needed until the spring before the first draft anyway, had been made.

And then suddenly, in late December of 1987, one of the moves was unmade.

Muhleman organized a press conference, not unlike many he had organized for Shinn in his various team hunts, at which Spartanburg, S.C. businessman Jerry Richardson announced his campaign to bring an NFL team to Charlotte. As usual with a Muhleman production, it was slick. Richardson and his sons explained their financing possibilities, their concept of a privately owned stadium and the chances for expansion in the future. Despite rivalry from another football story in the area — Mack Brown's impending arrival as new coach at the University of North Carolina — the NFL bid got good play in the various media of two states. As far as Muhleman and his associates could tell, everything had gone smoothly.

But as they would soon learn, some important feathers had been ruffled — Shinn's. The NBA owner, as Muhleman and everyone else knew, had once wanted to be a Major League baseball and NFL team owner as well. What they didn't know or understand was that Shinn still wanted all those things. He was already at work preparing his own NFL campaign when his marketing man, Muhleman suddenly launched someone else's. Shinn considered this to be treason, or something very much like it. And very quickly the Hornets' top leadership dropped from three to two.

Muhleman was shocked. "I thought the NBA team had satisfied him," he said some time later. "I really had no idea."

Muhleman's first tip-off was Richardson's report on a meeting with Shinn the day before the public announcement. The family had paid a call on the city's newest celebrity, more out of courtesy and respect than anything else, to inform him of their plans and to thank him for providing the inspiration. Jerry Richardson said he'd never have believed it possible if Shinn hadn't done it in basketball first.

Mark Richardson, Jerry's son, detected some subtle coolness in Shinn's reaction to the news. "He pledged to buy 10 season tickets if we got a team," Mark Richardson said, "but he didn't sound too excited about it."

Muhleman's ouster — because of a contract, he was retained for awhile as an under-utilized consultant — put more power in Scheer's hands, especially in the area of marketing. That wasn't a bad turn of events. The three-headed leader, which Shinn had set up, was, by his own admission, a little strange. With Scheer in charge of day-to-day operations and ideas, the Hornets took a bit more normal course, and marketing was Shinn's cup of tea. Muhleman would have been, in some ways, superfluous. Perhaps, in his position as consultant, the prescient Muhleman would have noticed this and gracefully faded from the scene. As it was, his fade was more like a drop through a trap door. But it was still reasonably graceful. No public name calling, and, a few months later, not much ill will on either side.

In spite of that swell, the Hornets sailed into their debut year on relatively smooth waters. Shinn continued to push tickets. Littles and company beat the big-league bushes, and Scheer carried out various duties, among the most important, looking for a coach.

• • • • •

Ever wonder how the day after, and sometimes the day before, a coach is fired, newspapers will already have a list of his probable successors in print?

Do sports writers have ESP? Do they have ESPN, as a semi-famous football coach once suggested? Do the people doing the hiring call them up and tell them? Is it just a guess?

To be honest, it's a little bit of all of that, except perhaps ESPN.

Some information flows in, some guesses are made, and like police investigating a burglary, the usual suspects can be rounded up — you know, the guys who are up for every job: Larry Brown, Mack Brown, Billy Martin, Don Zimmer. Every case is pretty much like the one before.

And every one is different, too. The connections — the who-knows-who that so often tells the hiring tale in sports as well as other businesses — are never the same. Check the records; check the backgrounds of the hirers. Make the connections, and you will usually be headed in the right direction.

In the case of the Charlotte Hornets, the obvious connection was right on the money. Larry "the Nomad" Brown had worked for Carl Scheer for seven years. He had family in Charlotte. He played basketball at North Carolina. He coached the last pro team in the state, the Carolina Cougars of 1973-74. And he'd been at his current job, Kansas, for five years, which was, by Larry Brown time, something bordering on an eternity. He was overdue for a switch.

So the rumors and the speculation started before George Shinn had a team or a general manager with ties to Brown, long before Brown's services would be needed. And then when Shinn got the team and Scheer got the job in the spring of 1987, the rumors did not die. With reason. Brown, the perennial sad sack with a penchant for turning any team into a winner, was the first guy Scheer thought of, too. When the Hornets' coach hunt began in earnest in the winter of 1987-88, it began with Larry Brown.

Shinn, who had no personal relationship with Brown, downplayed his candidacy. He agreed Brown seemed to fit, but Shinn was pursuing his own agenda at the time, prematurely talking to candidates in what the cynics might suggest was just a series of cheap, publicity stunts.

Shinn talked with Lefty Driesell, the old Davidson and Maryland coach, in the winter of 1986-87, before he got a team, and brought in John MacLeod, the deposed Phoenix coach, in May of 1987, just after the Charlotte franchise was awarded.

Neither was a serious candidate. Driesell, outrageous and out of work, would make no one's list of potential NBA coaches. He'd never been there and the skills that made him successful in college, such as his slick recruiting style, don't necessarily translate to the pros. Driesell withdrew his name from consideration in late March.

MacLeod, who had spent 14 years with the Suns, certainly had the credentials. But the timing was off. He was too-hot a property to wait on Charlotte, unless the Hornets were willing to pay him to wait. They were not, and less than a month after he stopped by Charlotte to talk with Shinn, he had been hired by the Dallas Mavericks.

No matter. Three days before that, Shinn had hired Scheer as the Hornets' general manager, a move that locked Brown in as a certain candidate. Not a certain coach, mind you, just a candidate. But for months that was enough, and even though Scheer denied it then, for a long time that was all. Larry Brown was the man.

And why not? In 15 seasons in pro and college basketball, Brown, then 47, had compiled an astonishing record of success. He was almost 300 games over .500 and never had a losing season. Brown's ability to bob and weave and never take a coaching punch had something to do with that. He hadn't jumped onto many sinking ships. But he had jumped on to a few that weren't exactly leading the race and he had pulled them into contention. It was indisputable that Brown possessed a certain coaching magic. If in no other way, you could tell because of the way so many of his peers sneered at his reputation. Larry the Genius.

Maybe he wasn't a genius. Maybe no coach is. But there was no doubt he could coach. More than that, he owned so many of the ingredients that an expansion team would need — a renowned ability to teach the game, motivational intensity, some experience at handling young players — that he was a perfect choice. The only real question was, could the Hornets get him to take the job? Brown, one of the bright lights of the college ranks, was raking in the dough at Kansas. Charlotte would have to match that and hope Brown would agree to sign aboard a certain loser.

"There are a lot of things I love about Larry Brown," Scheer said without a lot of hope in February, 1988. "I'm sure he'd make us a great coach. But there are just so many things that would have to be ironed out before that could ever come to pass. I don't know if they could be worked out. And then there's the question of whether he'd want to come. I just don't know."

Because of the uncertainty of bagging such big game, Scheer began compiling a backup list. He made overtures to a few former and current pro coaches — Matt Goukas, Dick Motta, Jim Lynam — and talked to friends about other possibilities in college and among the ranks of NBA assistants. But he hoped he wouldn't have to go to that list.

Brown was obviously aware of the Hornets' desires. Perhaps he and Scheer even talked that winter. But, tired of constantly denying rumors about his imminent departure, Brown offered no public comment about the Hornet speculation. And Scheer said, as the NCAA Tournament began in March, that his original goal of naming a coach by May 1 probably would have to be scrapped.

The pursuit of Brown picked up during the tournament. In a phenomenal coincidence, Scheer and owner Shinn traveled to Lincoln, Neb., of all places, to scout college players in the Midwest Regional. Brown and Kansas were among those on display there. The Jayhawks, rallying late after a modest season marred by injuries and other woes, beat the death watch over the coach by winning two games and advancing. Then they won two more and suddenly found themselves in the Final Four in Kansas City. What might have happened had they checked out on time is unclear. With only his regular reputation in tow, with no special emotion coursing through his veins, Brown might have been more susceptible to a Hornets' offer.

As it turned out, as everyone knows, Kansas went on to win the National Championship. A few days later, Brown's seemingly tortured conscience led him, at a bleary-eyed public press conference, to turn down an offer to return to UCLA. Privately, he also told Charlotte no, although the formality of that offer is a matter of debate.

Brown, who eventually moved to San Antonio to coach the Spurs, said, "I considered other places, like Charlotte. I have family there. One of my best friends is Carl Scheer. And I was going, basically, to get what I wanted there. That wasn't a problem. They just didn't have David Robinson (a promising center who will start playing for the Spurs in the near future). I think it could have been done, but we didn't get any further than that."

Shinn still contends the job was offered to only one man, but there's little doubt Brown could have had it. Ten days after the Final Four, at a college All-Star game in Orlando, Fla., Scheer said that the Hornets had not locked in on Brown. "But," Scheer said, "it had progressed far enough, and enough people thought that's where we were going, that it kept some people away. It's fair to say that our talks with Larry limited us."

So in mid-April, the Hornets were, as Scheer put it, "starting over."

"Larry's out. We can't get to Jimmy Rodgers (a Boston assistant who would soon take over for K.C. Jones) and Motta isn't interested," Scheer said. "We're back to re-evaluating candidates. We're talking to people, getting recommendations, things like that. We've even talked with a few (NBA) assistants lately."

Scheer uttered that last phrase with some distaste. Looking to maximize the marketing possibilities, as well as land a more proven coach, he had hoped to find someone with NBA head coaching experience.

While in Orlando in April, he met briefly with Stan Albeck, the current coach at Bradley, previously the coach of the Chicago Bulls, San Antonio Spurs, Denver Rockets, Cleveland Cavaliers, and New Jersey Nets. He not only had NBA experience, he had coached a whole division himself.

A classic journeyman, Albeck was not happy to be called a candidate for Charlotte or any other job. He was a little tired of having his name bandied about every time a coaching job popped up.

"Every time a job is open my name comes up," Albeck said. "I kind of feel like Larry Brown."

Hornets Never Lie

The Albeck-Scheer meeting didn't produce much interest on either side. But it did mark the beginning of the Hornets' coaching cattle call, a six-week long parade of candidates in and out of the city. The list eventually ran to 10 names — 11 if you count personnel director Gene Littles, whose name popped up briefly when the other avenues seemed to be drying up. The Eternity 10 were Albeck; Goukas; Lynam; NBA assistants Ed Badger, Allan Bristow and Dick Harter; CBA coaches Bill Musselman and Tom Nissalke; Gary Williams of Ohio State; and Bob Hill, former coach of the New York Knicks who had been working for Charlotte as a scout.

The connections were as varied as Scheer's career. He had already hired — and fired — Lynam once, in LA. He and Badger had the same lawyer/agent. So did Nissalke, who like Musselman, was an old CBA acquaintance, among other things.

Bristow, at age 36 the youngest candidate, coached under Doug Moe, who had been Brown's assistant during Scheer's glory years in Denver. Scheer had known Goukas, a former NBA player of some note, for a long time, too, and he was being pushed by Norm Sonju, the Dallas general manager who had Shinn's ear since the days of the expansion contest.

The only players in the game without a major contact were Harter and Williams. They had to get by on coaching credentials.

As it turned out, they were two of the more serious candidates in Hornet eyes, though Williams quickly quit his candidacy when news of his interview leaked out.

Scheer also gave Lynam a long, lusting look, but he was taken out of play in mid-May when the 76ers re-signed him. Lynam had taken over from Goukas in mid-season, and while he hadn't done that well, he had done well enough to earn another shot.

The interviewees rolled in and out of Charlotte. The interviews dragged on and on. Badger, interviewed the first week of May, said, "They're not in any hurry. They've gone this far. What's the big rush?"

Apparently there wasn't any. Was the timing unimportant? Wouldn't the Hornets pay for Scheer to go out to lunch if he didn't take a potential coach with him?

Scheer chuckled at the length of the process as it was winding down.

"We probably have set a record for most people interviewed, one job," Scheer said. "But I just think this is so important. Some guys may think NBA coaches come and go. I don't."

"I will say this," Scheer said. "As thorough as we've been, I won't have trouble sleeping at nights once we hire someone."

If he had any problems, he could've just counted interviewed coaches passing through his office until he drifted off to sleep.

Eventually, in late May with yet another self-imposed deadline (June 1 this time) bearing down, Scheer and Shinn whittled their list down to two men: Goukas and Harter. Then down to one. They would offer the job to Harter, a 57-year-old, ex-Marine with a reputation for toughness during 18 years as a college coach. Harter had spent the last five seasons as an NBA assistant, first to Chuck Daly in Detroit, then, for the past two years, to Dr. Jack Ramsey in Indianapolis.

Harter was well-known as a head-coach-to-be in the NBA. He'd nearly landed the New Jersey job the spring before and had a shot at the Pacer post eventually filled by Ramsey. In his Indiana agreement was what might be called an expectancy clause. It was "expected" that Harter would get a call some time from another team needing a head coach, and the Pacers agreed not to get in the way when it happened.

Harter didn't possess a household coaching name, but to those on the inside, it seemed just a matter of time before he got a shot somewhere. Scheer, an NBA insider, was moved by that. He also got plenty of recommendations. All of Harter's ex-NBA bosses boosted him to Scheer, including Pacer general manager Donnie Walsh, yet another member of Scheer's old Denver gang.

What persuaded Shinn, other than Scheer's recommendation, is hard to say for sure, but at least in part it was Harter's tailor.

Among Shinn's personal quirks is his insistence on proper dress for employees. For him, that is defined by coat and pants of matching material, i.e. a suit, set off by a crisp white dress shirt. No deviations please. Not a light blue shirt, not a white shirt with stripes, certainly not a blazer with different color pants.

Explains Shinn, "I just think it's neat. It looks better. It adds something and it says something. I think it's important."

The dress code is not exactly mandatory; that is, it's not written down somewhere. But then again, it's not exactly voluntary either. The exact measure of the policy is hard to gauge because Shinn employees seldom choose to challenge it.

Coincidentally, perhaps, Harter didn't either. In the parade of possible coaches he was the only guy who met Shinn's measure. "They all looked nice, but not the same," Shinn recalled. "Some had suits but wore colored shirts. And some had white shirts but wore sports coats. Dick was the only one with a suit and a white shirt. He looked good. I like that.

"I don't know if he knew that before he came or not. It doesn't matter. If he was sharp enough to call and ask, 'Hey, how does this guy like to dress?' that's fine. That's pretty sharp, too."

Harter, who joked about the dress code throughout his first season, laughed at the suggestion. "I wouldn't have considered wearing anything else," he said. "Hey, you forget. I'm an old Ivy Leaguer (Penn). That's how we dress, too."

Well, sometimes they do. Mari Harter, his wife, enjoys telling the story of how the ejection of Ramsey one night in Indianapolis placed her husband, attired in a putrid mixture of greens, blues and oranges, in the head coach's seat. A fan sitting near her, his attention now focused on the previously obscure assistant, wondered aloud, "I hope that guy can coach. He sure can't dress."

Good thing George Shinn wasn't in Indy that night.

Negotiations with Harter went on for about a week. Shinn's policy of not giving his employees multiple-year contracts stood in the way for some time. He wanted to guarantee Harter's extended employment with a handshake. There's nothing wrong with that, of course. More deals ought to be done that way. But Harter, cynical from years of contract conflict in the college ranks, wasn't about to agree. He didn't have much leverage, but if the Hornets wanted him they'd have to do better than a year with a firm grip.

Finally, they did. Sort of. Harter got a two-year contract, which paid him an average of $200,000 per season, and Shinn's public assurance that, "If he still feels like coaching at age 77, he'll be here. He's our man." He also received a year's supply of white shirts. Nah, not really.

Harter wasn't thrilled with the deal, but he had achieved his goal of becoming a head coach in the NBA. And he was confident he would do well enough to keep the job. "I figured it would come sooner or later," he said. "This may be a little later than I would have have liked but it's fine. And the contract doesn't bother me. I've always believed that if you do the job you'll be rewarded for it."

• • • • •

Harter may have believed that, but he hadn't always seen it come true. He did a remarkable coaching/program-building job at the three colleges he served, but twice had to leave just as the lynch mob was being formed.

Part of that is just the nature of coaching. Welcomes wear thin everywhere. It's impossible to continue the escalation of success every year. Eventually, every coach and team must come to some reckoning: Yes, he's the best we can do; or No, maybe he's not.

But part was Harter himself. Intense even for his profession, he did not, during his college years, allow a lot of compromise or invoke many mixed feelings. Folks either loved Dick Harter's hard-hitting brand of basketball or they hated it.

The love was essentially based on success. Harter's teams won. In 18 college seasons, he had just four losers and overall won 98 more games than he lost. He coached the finest teams in Penn's long and gilded basketball history. He did as well as any Penn State basketball coach ever has, and at Oregon. ... Well, at Oregon he was a legend.

The funny thing is, Harter's Oregon teams weren't that different from the Penn teams that preceded them or the Penn State teams that followed, but they were very different from what anyone had seen in the Pac 8 up until then.

Bruce Coldren, a reserve for Harter at Oregon, remembers that "Everyone out here thought the things we did were a wonder. But then we'd go back East for a tournament and everyone played the same way. Coach Harter brought the eastern style here. It was like a revolution."

The Pac 8 was dominated at that time by John Wooden's UCLA teams, clubs which relied on speed and finesse. Harter brought in a physical, no-holds barred brand of ball predicated on defensive intensity. Harter's boys got in your face and stayed there. They growled if you didn't like it.

There was bound to be a clash and there was. For six years, Harter exchanged salvos with Wooden who, before playing Oregon, liked to say stuff like, "Oh, we've got to play the wrestlers again."

Harter's teams won enough falls to make the match more or less even. Oregon beat UCLA three times during Harter's tenure, once ending a 98-game Bruin win streak in Pauley Pavilion. The league ceased to be a one-team affair, although neither Harter nor anyone else could fully break UCLA's grip until after Wooden was gone.

During those halcyon days, when Harter built Oregon into a legitimate Pac 8 threat, the 10,000-seat campus gym known as McWhorter Court was sold out for 79 straight games. And somewhere in his third season, a Eugene sports writer nicknamed Harter's team the "Kamikaze Kids," a tribute to the head-first, hell-bent fury with which its members played.

Harter didn't like that. He thought it sounded too negative. He even took the writer out for a little talk, to try to straighten him out. But it was too late. The name had caught on. Students started wearing leather jackets and aviator caps to Duck games.

Harter gave up and gave in, even encouraging the rowdiness in an effort to make Mac Court, as it was called, an even tougher place for visitors to play. He was, forever, the Kommander of the Kamikaze Kids.

It was a fitting description, for Harter asked his players to sacrifice a lot. He drove them through punishing practices to make the games seem easier. He emphasized contact and physical play. He taught them to be tough.

Among other tasks, Harter's players had to practice diving on the floor for loose balls, practice taking charges, practice running into each other. They performed what are called grass drills in football — while running in place, they'd dive and bounce their chests against the floor every time a coach's whistle sounded, then bounce back up and continue marking time.

They did defensive drills while holding bricks painted in the school colors, climbed ropes, and ran, literally, until they could run no more.

One Oregon behemoth, Gary Nelson, saved his teammates from unnecessary toil by throwing up nearly every practice. Someone had to, the player's surmised, before the running would ever end. Another Duck avoided that agony one afternoon by simply running away. Instead of stopping a sprint at the prescribed line, he just kept going, right out of the gym. Harter sent a manager after him, but all he got was a glimpse of the player's behind, on a bicycle, as it turned a corner leaving the gym.

Harter muses now, "He must have had that planned. No way he could have gotten on that bicycle that fast if he wasn't expecting to do it."

Harter's college charges remember the brutal practices before anything else.

Mike Drummond, a tiny point guard at Oregon, said, "Practice dominated my life. That's all I thought about. It's all any of us thought about. It was that bad."

Added Coldren, "I was reading the Bobby Knight book, *Season on the Brink*, not long ago, the one everyone was so shocked by. I got about halfway into it and I said to myself, 'What's the big deal?' There was nothing in there any worse than what we had to do."

Hearing the old war stories — such as the time he had his Penn players put their hands on a hot radiator when they fouled up a rebound drill — make Harter smile now. He is somewhat embarrassed and chagrined by some of the things he once did, but then, as Harter noted, aren't we all?

"There are a lot of things I might change now if I went back and did it again," Harter said. "Practice would be shorter and more fun for one thing. But I still don't see anything wrong with being tough on the basketball court."

Harter has relished that commodity all his life. Not a gifted athlete, he worked his way into a contributing role for the Penn varsity through hustle and fearless play. To his dismay, his college coach, Howie Dallmar, did not put a premium on his attributes.

"Howie was an ex-NBA guy, a laid-back Californian who coached laid back," Harter said. "He treated you like a gentleman. That was great, but the thing is, he was nice all the time, no matter what you did. It didn't matter if you dove into the eighth row for a loose ball, or if you just stood there and watched it go out of bounds. He'd still be nice to you.

"That killed me. I was sort of a hustling, not-too-good player who wanted to play more. I'd do anything. I mean, I went a whole training season without a Coke to make myself better. I cared that much. But it didn't matter to Howie. He played the best players no matter what they did. I decided right then that when I was coach, the guys that tried the hardest would get to play."

Few tried any harder than Harter, who swallowed defeat as if it were a football and celebrated big victories with uncommon glee. For instance, after trouncing Villanova one night in the Far West Classic, a beating that avenged a five-year-old personal humiliation suffered by Harter at Penn, Harter says he stopped his car while driving home and laughed for 20 minutes. "It meant that much to me," he said.

Nothing speaks to Harter's intensity and competitive spirit like the Chancellor's Cup incident, though.

The Chancellor's Cup was a 50-year-old basketball competition between Oregon and Oregon State, decided by a best-of-three series each year. With Harter whipping up emotions in all of Oregon's opponents, in particular in arch-rivals like OSU, the series began to overheat in the mid-1970s. And the chance of riots and fan violence led the leaders of both schools to decide to cancel the cup competition.

But the series was already scheduled in the year the decision was made. And as fate would have it, Oregon State was the winner. With the Beavers holding a commanding lead in the rubber game, an OSU cheerleader hoisted the Chancellor's Cup trophy above his head and began a victory jog around the court. All went well until he passed the Oregon bench. There, a leg whipped out in front of him, causing him to go sprawling head first down the sideline. The cup flew from his hands and clattered to the floor, acquiring a big dent in the process.

Stu Jackson, one of the stars of that Oregon team, recalled, "That sucker went flying. And he landed hard, too. Coach really laid him out."

Although Jackson seems sure what happened, there is debate as to just whose foot caused the tumble. At least one Oregon player,

Mark Barwig, still claims he did it. But his teammates figure he's just covering for a coach they sometimes hated and sometimes loved.

"I think most of us probably like him now," Mike Drummond, now a bond salesman in Seattle, said of Harter. "But if you'd asked me three or four years ago, I might have told you something different.

"When I finished at Oregon, I, quite frankly, didn't like Coach Harter at all. He had made me sick of basketball. I didn't even pick a ball up for about five years. But, I see it differently now. He helped me. In my business, you win or lose every day and you've got to be ready every day, got to be tough. Coach Harter taught me how to do that."

Some find it hard to believe that a coach who tripped cheerleaders and measured his players by the length of their floorburns could survive, indeed, would even attempt to survive in the pros. There's some sense to that. NBA players are more disciplined than they're often given credit for, but pro basketball is nothing like college, where a coach can expect and receive almost total control. And Harter was the ultimate controller.

His college players dressed well and wore their hair in a near copy of Harter's semi-Marine crewcut. They hit opposing players on defense and made the prescribed number of passes on offense, or they had a seat. They went to class. They followed the rules.

Harter was an extremist in this sense, and for that reason, one of the least likely college coaches to be a candidate for NBA duty. He even owned a long-held prejudice against the pro game, dating back to the early years of his career when pro coaches were looked down on by many college coaches. As Harter himself says, in deliberate understatement, "I think you could say I had more of a change to make than most coaches."

Harter made the change, though. He become a pro basketball convert. But it wasn't a sudden revelation. He was no basketball Saul struck down on a court near Damascus. No, Harter's conversion was forced upon him, a hard reality of life in a hard profession.

He left Oregon, with some bitterness, in 1978 to try to build a program at Penn State. Clashes with football coach Joe Paterno, the school's unofficial saint, and an administration that quickly found itself wishing for a more gentle soul in the men's basketball office, put Harter in a contract bind five years into his stay. He asked for an extension on the one year he had left and was denied. To him, that was handwriting on the wall. He went looking for a new job, away from (Un)Happy Valley.

Not a pro job, just a basketball job of any kind. But there wasn't much out there for a man of his skills and position. He was overqualified. In semi-desperation, he decided to give the pros a try. There was an opening for an assistant in Detroit where Chuck Daly, who had followed Harter at Penn, was now the head man, and Jack McCloskey, the guy who had preceded Harter there, was the general manager. It was as natural an entry into the pro game as Harter was going to find. He took the job.

Basketball people wondered about it. Kelly Tripucka, a Piston at the time, said, "Dick's reputation preceded him. We'd all heard the stories. We wondered, 'Now what in the world are they doing bringing in this guy?'"

As it turned out, Harter, then 52, was more malleable than anyone could have imagined. Taking his cue from Daly, a master of the NBA's player-coach psychology, Harter learned the essential personnel differences in the pros. And the old defensive doctor fell in love with the faster, stronger, and yes, tougher NBA game.

Because he still has many ties, many friends in the college ranks, he's reluctant to praise his present world for fear of trashing his former. But there's little doubt he has become an NBA coach.

"I know this for sure," Harter said. "Any college coach who spent just one year in the NBA would be so far ahead of the game it wouldn't be funny. I know if I went back I'd be 30 percent better than I was before.

"It's just so different. The whole player-coach relationship is different. The season is different. You have to come back faster from the losses. The game is different, too, although that was probably the easiest part. It's still basketball."

And Dick Harter will always be a part of that.

"Yeah," Harter said, "when they finally get rid of me here, I'll probably go coach in some CYO (Catholic Youth Organization) league somewhere."

Not long after hiring Harter, Scheer completed the basketball staff. Personnel director Littles received the added title of assistant coach, and Ed Badger, one of the other interviewees, became assistant coach and director of basketball administration. It was an odd pairing in some ways. Though Badger and Harter knew each other, the assistants were more Scheer's friends than Harter's. And, in a kooky twist, both assistants had more head coaching experience in the NBA than Harter did.

Badger, in fact, was an old hand. He'd coached two pretty good teams in Chicago (combined record: 84-80) and had been an assistant and scout with Cleveland and Boston. A long-time junior college and college (Cincinnati) coach, he had ties throughout the basketball world. In terms of experience, he was a good addition to the Hornets' staff. And with roles and power as yet undefined, that was about the only way to judge it.

"The staff is as good as I'd hoped it would be," Scheer gushed after hiring Badger. "We've got some great coaches."

Now all they needed were a few great players.

Meat on the Hoop

"The fact of the matter is ... most of them won't be around two years from now."

– Carl Scheer

Dick Motta, the coach who led the Dallas Mavericks from the hapless days of expansion to the relative happiness of respectability, noted once, with an unfortunate degree of accuracy, that there are only three kinds of players available to new teams coming into the NBA.

"What you have," said the always blunt Motta, "are bad players, bad people or bad contracts."

Actually, there is a fourth kind. As Motta later observed, sometimes you get a combination of the three. The good news for expansion teams is that there aren't too many of those guys around.

Starting an NBA team has never been a bargain. It cost George Shinn and his partners $32 million plus change just to get in -- and all that got them was a place on the schedule plus a half-dozen tickets to the All-Star game.

It certainly didn't buy any slack or sympathy from the existing teams. No reason to think it would, of course. If your team had lost 60 or so games out of 82 the year before, would you go out of your way to give some new guy a break, a chance to beat you?

The answer from the existing NBA ports was a resounding no. Not surprising. After all, one of the chief benefits of owning an existing franchise is that you don't have to go through the pain of starting a new one. Even so, what the league offered the new teams in the way of building blocks bordered on the embarrassing.

Oh, there were plenty of avenues to pursue, and some even looked promising at first glance. But no matter the route, there was always a catch, an unseen toll booth or traffic jam up ahead. It was sort of like driving in New Jersey.

For instance:

A new contract between the players and the league opened the door to expanded free agency the summer before the Hornets and the

Miami Heat were to begin playing, but the league imposed a limit on salaries the new teams could pay their first season, effectively eliminating them from the bidding for the big stars available.

The league proposed relatively equitable rules for an expansion draft but didn't change them when new circumstances imposed by the new league-player contract greatly reduced the talent pool offered to the expansionists.

The NBA graciously offered the new teams a first-round pick in the college draft, but wouldn't let them get into the lottery for the top pick. They wound up with choices eight and nine.

The college choices were tolerable. The eighth and ninth picks in recent years have generally yielded serviceable NBA players as well as an occasional star. Recent treasures from those draft positions include All-Stars or near All-Stars like Tom Chambers, Jack Sikma, Robert Parish, Ron Harper, Charles Oakley, Dale Ellis, Otis Thorpe and Cliff Levingston. Those spots also produced Brad Sellars, Lancaster Gordon and Larry Demic, three NBA players of dubious value, but who's counting?

The elimination of the free-agent windfall was a bit more disappointing, but since it hadn't been expected at the outset it wasn't that great a loss.

When George Shinn landed the franchise, back in the spring of 1987, free agents were still just a theory in the NBA. The old contract between the owners and players contained the concept, but the practice was much different. Because the team that held the rights to a player could re-sign him by matching any written offer to that player, and because the team that signed a free agent had to pay with a draft pick, free agents were limited to a small group.

If a player were too good, his old team wouldn't let him go, no matter the price. If he were too bad, a new team wouldn't pay the price – a draft pick – for signing him. The line between was extraordinarily thin.

But the new player-owners' agreement, hammered out by Commissioner David Stern and Larry Fleisher, then the counsel for the NBA Player's Association, put free agency on baseball terms. That switch, in fact, was the linchpin of the agreement that kept the league from a strike.

Under the new rules, adopted in a contract agreed to in the spring of 1988, players with seven or more years of service who had completed two contracts were available – no strings attached to the highest bidder. The length of service clause will be even shorter in years to come.

Ramifications of the change were immediately apparent to the

Hornets. As highlights of the new contract were spit out of the telex in the Hornets' office that spring day, personnel director Gene Littles whistled and said, "That changes a few things."

The Hornets had been looking at a long, long building process, aided only by draft picks and, eventually, by the deals they might be able to make once they got enough currency (i.e. useful players) to make them. Now, they might just go sign up some instant help. And they might do it the first year.

But at this point, the friendly, neighborhood NBA owners stepped in and shrank the expansion teams' salary caps. There'd be no fast rises for these teams.

It eventually became obvious that the Hornets would do most of their early building via the expansion draft, plus the one or two draft picks who made the team.

Therein lay some hope. The prescribed system for the draft allowed each existing team to protect eight players on its roster from being drafted. The expansionists would then draft players on a set day, alternating picks and selecting one from each team. No team lost more than one player and each expansion franchise would wind up with about a dozen NBA vets of one description or another.

While it was obvious that some NBA teams didn't have five, much less eight or, more to the point, nine players worth having, it was just as certain that there were many teams that did. Even teams that didn't play eight men on a regular basis had players who could blossom usefully. The expansionists could and did point to the stories of Dale Ellis, a Dallas scrub who became an All-Star with Seattle, or Frank Brickowski, a non-entity with Seattle and the Lakers who suddenly transformed into a serviceable NBA center in San Antonio. Brickowski's scoring average quadrupled, from four to 16 points a game, in one season.

As he peered into the murky, personnel future ahead in the spring of 1988, Carl Scheer, the Hornets' general manager, said about 20 times, "If there's another Dale Ellis out there we want to find him."

To keep track of the burgeoning Ellises and Brickowskis, Scheer and Littles both constructed situation boards in their temporary offices in the basement of team partner Cy Bahakel's TV studio.

Scheer displayed the players on each team in alphabetical order. Littles arranged and re-arranged his rosters constantly according to whom he thought was in the protected eight and whom he thought was out.

It was a tricky business even then when it really didn't count. Littles, an NBA assistant in three different cities, could figure out the talent rankings pretty quickly, but factors like age, health, potential and a player's contract all had to be weighed, too. A team might expose an aging veteran, secure that an expansion team wouldn't grab him. Or it might place a not-so-useful player with one of the NBA's many inexplicably large contracts on its available list. Would an expansion team blow its limited cash reserves on such a guy?

Ironically, one of the examples often cited of the latter was Kelly Tripucka, a million-dollar-a-year guy whose career was at a dead end and whose value in the league was close to nil.

"What I'm doing," Littles conceded, "is just one big guess."

Even so, a number of the guesses wound up previewing Charlotte's first-year roster. They didn't all come the Hornets' way by the expansion draft, but Tripucka, Dell Curry, Kurt Rambis and Tyrone Bogues all did wind up on the team.

Scheer viewed the rosters on the stark, cinderblock walls with a wider view, tempered by history.

"The fact of the matter is," he said one morning in February, 1988, "that whoever's out there, whoever we take, most of them won't be around two years from now. That's just the way it is."

This assertion was almost self-proven. Expansion teams must get better, and to get better they must, obviously, change players. But previous expansion teams had proven this true as well.

The most recent example, Dallas, the only team entering the league in 1980, plucked 22 players off existing rosters. Two years later, Jim Spanarkel was the only expansion Maverick who remained.

That sweeping change was somewhat distorted by the fact that Dallas was able to convert some of its original retreads into the future draft picks that helped the team "arrive" somewhat faster than anticipated. That was due to the presence of one Ted Stepien, an unpredictable man who owned and ran (into the ground, some might say) the Cleveland Cavaliers in the late 1970s and early 1980s. With legendary foresight, Stepien swapped three first-round draft picks in future years for stalwarts Mike Braatz, Richard Washington and Jerome Whitehead, three mediocrities who showed up on the Mavericks' original roster.

Perhaps without much real hope, Scheer talked about making similar maneuvers with the herd of dispersed players he was able to bring in. Because Whitehead and Washington were big men, Scheer eyed the 7-footers on his board who might be available and engaged in what proved to be ironic musing. The Hornets just might, Scheer suggested, take some extra big men as trade bait.

As it turned out, much of the winter's speculation evaporated in the spring, when the new bargaining agreement set a large number of players free. In a strange, and for the expansion teams, painful twist, the same free-agent bonanza in which they effectively could not participate also impaired their chances in the expansion draft.

After a bit of study, the teams realized that a side effect of the new contract was an increase in the number of players who would effectively be protected in the dispersal draft. For that reckoning, "free agents," as they were known, didn't matter. A team could expose an unsigned player to the expansion teams, secure in the knowledge that if the expansion team drafted him it would have no more call on him than anyone else. It would be a non-pick, as it were, and it would not be made.

The real beauty of this unforeseen loophole, though, was that the free agents could be used to cover other players. By not protecting a free agent, a team in effect got to protect a ninth player – the eight on their protected list plus the free agent. If they had two free agents, then they could protect 10. It soon became apparent that some teams might not have to expose more than a player or two.

Timing opened this loophole. The expansion draft was set for late June. July 1 was the date when free agents became fair game for all 25 teams. Players a team wanted to re-sign would likely be signed by the time of the draft. Those it didn't would still be around, though, to act as shields for players a club wanted to save from expansion.

Hornets Coach Dick Harter, in one of his many moments of frustration to come, characterized the free-agent loophole in the dispersal draft as "the biggest screw job of all the screw jobs the league gave the Heat and Hornets coming into the NBA."

He may have been right, although the league disputes the notion that the Hornets got conned.

Gary Bettman, the NBA's ultra-smooth attorney, said in 1989, "Anybody that says something wasn't fair about that doesn't know what they're talking about. We knew about the free agents before the draft. It was just obvious that there wasn't going to be much of a problem. There just weren't that many out there.

"If there had been a problem, we would have changed the rules before the draft, just like we did this year."

In 1989, when more free agents were on the market, the NBA created a new rule that gave the second wave of expansionists an escape from the free-agent snag. The teams who drafted in the summer of 1989, Orlando and Minnesota, didn't have to take a player from every team, provided a team had only one player and he made more than $600,000 a year.

That was a good idea, but that rule only kept a new team from being saddled with an unwanted financial burden. It did nothing to aid it in the procurement of serviceable talent hidden by the new free agency. And that was what Harter was talking about.

As it was, the Hornets got to the business of locating players long before Harter arrived.

Littles and a part-time staff of scouts spent the entire 1987-88 season surveying the basketball landscape. They looked at the NBA, the minor-league Continental Basketball Association, as well as the colleges. It was an exhausting process, although it did earn Littles a lot of frequent-flyer points.

But it was also frustrating in the sense that Littles was, for a long time, a personnel director with no personnel. All he had was a paper team stuck to the side of his office wall.

When he finally got his hands on a few players, at the team's inaugural free-agent camp in late May, Littles breathed a sigh of contentment.

"It's nice that we're starting to get some bodies involved instead of just names," he said as camp opened.

Twenty players participated in the camp, held at the old Charlotte Coliseum. Five eventually played in the NBA in the 1988-89 season. One, ex-Davidson star Anthony "Ace" Tanner, later won a slam-dunk contest staged as a halftime show at a Hornets' game.

None of the players ever appeared in a game in a Hornets' uniform, though. At the time, Littles thought Ennis Whatley, a point guard with 237 games of NBA experience, was a good bet. But subsequent draft choices made Whatley feel he'd be the odd man out in Charlotte so he didn't come. Late in the season he was signed by Boston.

The camp was basically a bust for finding players. Even for expansion teams most such camps are. If you find one player you've done well. But it was a start, and at this point the Hornets couldn't ask for much more.

Early June, after the coaching staff was put in place, was spent discussing strategy for the two coming drafts.

The first hard decision was made June 13, when Scheer flew to New York, watched NBA commissioner David Stern flip a special coin, replete with a Hornet logo on one side and a Heat logo on the other, to determine draft order for the expansion teams.

Both Scheer and Lew Schaffel, Miami's general manager, looked a little pale as the coin floated in the air. One of them was about to make his first act of player procurement for his new team, and neither wanted to blow it. Both had refused to specify their preference publicly – first pick in the expansion draft or eighth pick in the college draft – prior to the flip, underlying the surprising tension that followed this should-have-been minor event. Both realized the safe way out: have the other guy make the choice for you.

The coin came down "Hornet" so Scheer lost. Or won. Depending on how you look at it. He made his choice: the Hornets would take eighth in the college draft. Schaffel immediately claimed he was going for the expansion draft pick anyway. Big surprise.

"I don't see the draft in maybe the same light Carl does," Schaffel said. "I see it to be much broader than that. The expansion draft has more possibilities to it because it's not just the player that you take, it's the possibility of what that player means to 22 other teams – or 23 other teams."

Schaffel was making a veiled reference to some soon-to-be-revealed deals between established teams and the expansionists in which draft picks were ceded to the new teams in agreement for not picking certain exposed players. In effect, teams would pay a price, a draft pick, to be able to protect a ninth player.

Scheer was aware of these possibilities. Established teams had been talking to him, too. But he didn't see those deals as being as lucrative. A preliminary examination of the college field by Littles and his associates had drawn the conclusion that a break of some significance came between the anticipated eighth player taken and the ninth. So the Hornets thought the eighth pick more valuable than the ninth by a power that mere ordinality would not indicate.

This marked the beginning of the philosophical debate – if such a term can apply to something as comparatively trivial as basketball – between the two new franchises. It provoked thought in both cities throughout the year to come.

• • • • •

The expansion draft, the NBA's first since Dallas had sorted through everyone's roster back in 1980, was held on June 23. In Charlotte and Miami, braintrusts of the two teams gathered in heavily guarded – well, heavily guarded for a sports draft – hotel rooms where their only link to the outside world was a telephone. The NBA provided security agents for each site, apparently to insure secrecy. At stake was the identity of the players who had been left unprotected in the draft.

That might not seem like much of a secret, but to some NBA executives it was considered quite a problem. The theory was that a player exposed might be embarrassed/depressed/angered (choose one or more) that his team had given up on him and that if he were not the player chosen from that team, he would be hard to handle in the season ahead.

It was and is a somewhat spurious argument. Players so bad as to be exposed but not taken would not, in all likelihood, figure prominently in most teams' plans anyway. Furthermore, because the NBA is a gossipy, insider organization, it was extremely unlikely that anyone on the list could be unaware of his or her plight.

As best as can be discovered, this was true. All the Hornets and Heat drafted said they knew their plight before the fact. Most knew who all the uncovered players on their old teams were.

Generally speaking, almost everyone knew. Bit by bit, the list of available players began appearing in newspapers around the country, and for most teams anyone with even a passing knowledge of the NBA could whittle the possibilities down to a half-dozen names or so.

There were a few surprises. The Lakers, wanting to hold on to a couple of seldom-used younger players (Mike Smrek for instance) exposed all-time great Kareem Abdul-Jabbar, and Boston exposed veteran Dennis Johnson. Both those clubs later made deals to prevent those players from being taken.

Utah put ex-All-Stars Tripucka and Darrell Griffith on the exposed list, a stratagem that sounds crazy but really was not. Tripucka, for reasons not clearly defined, was in Coach Frank Layden's doghouse and wasn't playing or ever going to play, and Griffith was coming back from knee surgery.

Detroit, the league's deepest team, probably faced the toughest call. After coming just a couple of points short of the NBA Championship, the Pistons weren't inclined to let go of any of their key components, but they were an honest-to-goodness nine-deep team. Someone had to go. After some debate, they exposed guard Vinnie Johnson, figuring, correctly as it turned out, that the expanders would not waste a pick on so volatile a player with so big a salary.

Those players, along with some well-known "names" like Norm Nixon and Otis Birdsong, offered spice to the draft lists which otherwise were about as expected: i.e. disappointing. As it turned out, not many NBA teams were very deep in proven talent.

George Irvine, the personnel director of the Indiana Pacers, surveyed the prospects not long before the draft and tersely described the possibilities:

"About the best you can get will be some players who just haven't gotten their chance yet," Irvine said. "So many players blossom when they finally get some time. Maybe these teams will find some."

Irvine didn't have to make any picks, though. The guys that did were less optimistic.

Stu Inman, Miami's director of player personnel, said on draft eve, "There's not a whole lot out there."

Dredging up a consumer metaphor that Charlotte's upwardly mobile middle class could understand, the Hornets' Scheer said, "You don't find a Mercedes in a used car lot. I think the list is very sobering."

In their pre-draft meetings the Hornets discussed the possibilities, however meager, on every team. Not surprisingly, some differences of opinion arose.

Harter, with his short contract weighing rather heavily, lobbied for a more liberal sprinkling of experience and talent. Owner Shinn worried about the cost of such players. The others in the braintrust, Scheer, Littles and Badger, had their favorites, too.

In the end, the most important course of action to come from these meetings was the courting of Utah with regard to Tripucka. Although the Hornets could have picked him straight up, the idea of carrying his massive salary (nearly $1 million) was more than Shinn could bear. Negotiations were opened with the Jazz, who desperately wanted to unload him, to work a deal where Utah paid part of Tripucka's contract.

The two sides finally agreed that the Hornets would trade one of their last three picks in the expansion draft to Utah in exchange for Tripucka. The Jazz would pick up about half of Tripucka's salary.

Scheer was also on the line listening to other deals. The Lakers, Mavericks, SuperSonics and Celtics all eventually made deals to protect extra players. Some were open-ended, meaning that either Charlotte or Miami could activate them. Some were not. A few teams called to line up trades for players the Hornets might be able to take in the draft.

But aside from the Tripucka deal, which also hinged on Miami not picking him, nothing could be worked out. Miami's ownership of the first pick in the expansion draft put the Heat in the driver's seat when it came to dealing at this point. The Hornets might say they would pick a certain player if he was available, but the Heat could, for at least one pick, guarantee it.

As it turned out, the Heat did just that. In exchange for a first-round pick in the college draft five days later, the Heat opened the expansion draft by picking one Arvid Kramer off of Dallas' roster.

It is not necessarily a slight on Kramer's playing abilities to report that his selection drew laughter from all three parties (the Heat, the Hornets and the NBA) connected on the draft-day conference call.

Kramer, a 6-9 forward who left tiny Augustana College in 1979, actually played eight games in the NBA. But the last one was in 1980.

Hornets Never Lie

He was acquired by Dallas in the 1980 expansion draft, making him one of just a handful of players to be honored with two such selections. He never showed in Dallas, although as events eight years later revealed, the Mavs did cling tenaciously to his rights. Kramer chose instead to play basketball in Europe. It was thought when the Heat drafted him that he was still there. Nobody, including the Heat, researched the matter closely, however, so the question asked of Miami after the pick – "Where is Arvid Kramer?" – remains one of the NBA's enduring mysteries.

An ironic twist: The man who brought Kramer into the league, and hence into the expansion draft eight years later, was Carl Scheer, who signed Kramer as a free agent for Denver at the end of the 1979-80 season. What goes around, comes around, they say, even if they don't know where it is.

Miami's first pick was not such a surprise. The Hornets had expected the Heat to make some sort of deal with the first pick. All it really did was take off the board Bill Wennington of Dallas, perhaps the most promising big man available.

Charlotte followed by quickly snapping up Dell Curry from Cleveland, a young guard with a fine shooting touch who many rated as the most valuable, in all senses of the word, player offered in the draft. As Littles noted, "He is the kind of guy you could think of scoring 20 a night on down the road."

Miami countered with a choice arranged in another deal, taking the Lakers up on their offer of a second-round pick in the future (1991 or 1992) in exchange for not taking Abdul-Jabbar. To boot, the Heat also got to pick another Laker, in this case Billy Thompson, a young forward who eventually turned out to be a pretty good choice.

Charlotte used its second pick to take Dave Hoppen, the next best center prospect. Miami came back with yet another deal, selecting Fred Roberts from Boston, instead of the unprotected Dennis Johnson, and getting a 1988 second-round pick for doing it. A few minutes later, they traded Roberts to Milwaukee for yet another second-round pick, this one in 1989.

Charlotte next chose Tyrone Bogues, the 12th player taken in the 1987 college draft. Like Curry, the 5-3 Bogues had trade potential. Denver, whose fast tempo would seem to suit Bogues' game, had already called both expansion teams about him and had made at least a tentative offer of a first-round draft pick in exchange. But because they'd had a 54-victory season, the Nuggets' pick was 23rd overall. At the time, the Hornets were able to turn their backs on that.

The point is arguable. The jury was, at least in some quarters, still out on Bogues. Indeed, in some ways it always will be. And with throngs of teal-clad fans storming the coliseum only a pipe dream at this point, the acquisition of an attraction like Bogues carried some non-basketball value. The smallest player in NBA history retains an innate appeal that would give any box office a boost.

The picking continued with Miami taking Atlanta's Scott Hastings, San Antonio's Jon Sunvold and then making two more deals for second-round picks. Charlotte took Mike Brown, a beefy power forward who was languishing on Chicago's bench, Portland guard Michael Holton, and Utah vet Rickey Green.

Green, the 10th choice overall, seemed to seal the Tripucka deal for the Hornets. Miami couldn't take him now, and all that remained was for Charlotte to pick up three dogs at the end of the draft to exchange for their first star.

In due time, that's just what the Hornets did. With their seventh and eighth picks they took two forwards, Michael Brooks and Bernard Thompson, whom they figured had outside chances to make the team. With their last three, they chose Detroit's Ralph Lewis, Indiana's Clinton Wheeler, and the Knicks' Sedric Toney, three guards on the border between CBA stardom and the 11th and 12th spots on an NBA bench.

Good guys that they were, the Hornets did the Jazz an extra favor by drafting three guys who wouldn't cost them any money. Lewis, Wheeler and Toney were all free agents, meaning that while Utah would technically obtain the rights to one of them, they were under no obligation to pay.

It looked like a good deal for Charlotte when Utah suddenly tore up the contract, telling the Hornets that the NBA probably wouldn't approve a trade of a Tripucka for, in effect, nothing. At once, the Hornets' biggest expansion draft plans were up in the air. The NBA ruling was uncertain, but so were Utah's true intentions. Did they have a deal cooking with Miami, too?

The Hornets went back to the Jazz with a new proposition. Was there another player they'd consider? The Utah braintrust, led by coach Frank Layden, perused the list. They had hoped the Hornets would choose Sunvold, a point guard who could back up John Stockton. But Miami had taken him. Various names were discussed. Finally, the two sides settled upon Brown, a useful player but one who seemed a bit superfluous in Utah, which already had a roster full of big men.

It was not a disastrous loss for the Hornets, but it definitely had more impact than the loss of Sedric Toney. The muscles that the 250-pound Brown could have offered were missed sorely at times in the days ahead.

Hornets Never Lie

Even so, the Hornets left the draft claiming victory.

Owner Shinn crowed at a post-draft press conference. "Our guys did great. We got three of our top five and got two we'd have taken if we had the first two picks. I'm ecstatic. How much better can you do?"

Miami thought it did well, too. Schaffel pointed to the extra draft picks, six in all, and said, "That makes a very loud statement. We're committed to building with young players."

Scheer bristled at the notion that his team had missed the boat. "Miami stocked up," he said. "But in our view the kind of players available there (in the second round of the draft) aren't as good as the ones we drafted today.

"You can talk about building for the future through the draft, but we didn't exactly pick a bunch of over-the-hill guys. We only got one guy over 30 (Rickey Green), and most are very young."

Charlotte's acquisitions were backcourt heavy. Of the players retained, only Hoppen and Brooks could qualify as inside players. But the staff thought that was relatively unimportant. Trades could balance the roster later. On this day, just picking up as much talent as possible was the key item.

And the key to that was Tripucka. Harter, who had coached Tripucka in Detroit and had hired his college coach, Digger Phelps, as an assistant when Harter was at Penn, pushed the deal. He knew the 29-year-old Tripucka was a tough, offensive player who could score in the NBA, something expansion teams had traditionally struggled to do.

"You take the kind of guys we'll probably get, put them in positions, and it's tough to figure out how we'll score 80 (points) a night, much less 100," Harter said. "Throw in a 20-point a night guy and you at least have a chance."

Tripucka, the son of ex-pro quarterback Frank Tripucka, had proved he could score. In his first five years in the league he had averaged 21.5 points a game and twice was selected to play in the All-Star game. But in 1986, as the Pistons were starting their climb to their current position atop the NBA, Tripucka was traded to Utah for Adrian Dantley.

The swap didn't have much effect on Dantley, other than to earn him some extra playoff money. But it was murder on Tripucka, who went from starter to seldom-used reserve. His scoring average fell by half his first season, then to just 7.5 points a game the year before he came to Charlotte.

Harter saw that as a plus as much as a minus, though. "I think Kelly's got something to prove," Harter said. "He'll be inspired when he gets here."

Tripucka agreed with that. "It feels like I've been in a barrel for two years," he said after arriving in Charlotte. "It's time for me to play ball again."

• • • • •

Though they'd been scouting, studying and otherwise preparing for the college draft for months, the Hornets found themselves scrambling to get ready in the four days between it and the expansion draft. The reason? Their expansion acquisitions were so lopsided towards backcourt players that suddenly the idea of picking to fill a need threatened to overwhelm the long-held theory of simply taking the best player available when their turn came around. Specifically, they began to wonder if they didn't have to take a big man to go with the respectable stable of perimeter players –Tripucka, Curry, Bogues, Holton and Green – already on hand.

Just minutes after the expansion draft was completed, Harter urged this course, beginning a refrain he was to sound all season.

"You've got to have big people to compete in this league," he said. "We've got to take a look at that with our first pick."

On the same day, Scheer seemed to agree.

"We know now," he said, "that we're pretty well fixed at two and three (numerical terms for the off guard and small forward positions), and we know we don't have to draft a point guard at pick 34 (Charlotte's second-round pick). But what we don't have, obviously, is a bona fide center or any real size to speak of.

"That," Scheer concluded triumphantly, "is what the eighth pick can do for you. If we had taken nine,it might be a problem. But I just don't see any way we don't get big guy ... unless something really crazy happens."

The NBA draft is a curious event, overblown in a sense, yet its importance really can't be emphasized too much. Teams spend hours and many dollars evaluating hundreds of players only to make a couple of picks that any fan armed with a timely basketball magazine usually could have made. These days there aren't many upsets in the draft. Then again, a team that consistently makes the right pick will consistently find itself at the top of the league, and vice versa.

The college draft is the simplest, surest way any team has of acquiring new players. No one wants to screw it up, so each team spends lots of time preparing its own evaluations.

These days, those evaluations extend well beyond the jump shot. Nearly every team flies in prospects for personal interviews before the draft. Most spend some time calling coaches of rival college teams as well as the player's own. And lately, some teams have even taken to hiring private investigators to probe players' backgrounds. Does he use drugs? Associate with those who do? Is he a stable guy, or a menace to society? With big money and a franchise's future on the line, inquiring teams want to know.

Charlotte was no different than anyone else in this respect. They flew in a dozen or so prospects for interviews, dug up background information on each, then began balancing their findings against their basketball opinion of each. Finally they managed to identify a group of eight players – Danny Manning, Charles Smith of Pitt, 7-3 Rik Smits, Syracuse center Rony Seikaly, Temple shot-blocker Tim Perry, and guards Mitch Richmond, Hersey Hawkins and Rex Chapman – whom they considered the cream of the draft. That was the easy part. Next, the Hornets had to figure out what everyone else was going to do. Though scouting takes up considerably more time, intra-league intelligence is the crux of all the pre-draft planning in the league. Other teams' actions affect all but what one team can do on draft day. So everyone wants to know what everyone else is thinking, but that is not easy to find out. For months before the draft, truth is just a theory in the NBA. The good news is, everyone also knows that.

Donnie Walsh, general manager of the Indiana Pacers, says, "The best advice I've heard about the month before the draft is 'don't talk to anyone in person.' That way you don't have to lie to their face."

Agreed Littles, a few weeks before his first draft with the Hornets, "They're all lying. What you have to find out is who's lying the best."

As usual, trade rumors and assorted pre-draft bull clouded the picture before Charlotte's first draft. Everyone had a deal in the fire. That was part of the game. But few, if any, would come to fruition. The Hornets, for instance, were offered, among other things, Wayman Tisdale, then with the Pacers, in exchange for their first-round pick. Maybe it wouldn't have been a bad move. Though somewhat disappointing as a pro, Tisdale was a former number-two draft choice and no one the Hornets could land with the eighth pick figured to be a great deal better. But they would be younger and they would be untainted by the blood of any other NBA team. That offer shriveled almost before it hit the table. And so did most of the other deals formulated that year. It was, despite the two new teams, business as usual.

The one given in the 1988 draft was that the LA Clippers, who owned the first pick, would take Danny Manning. Negotiations had already begun. His jersey had already been made and retired. Well, it should have been retired. Few clippers have been any more famous. At any rate, the top spot was a lock. The Hornets didn't need to worry about drafting Danny Manning.

Further investigation led them to believe they could scratch Smits and Smith off their list. The Hornet braintrust figured both those big men would be gone long before Charlotte picked. That left left Seikaly, Perry and the three guards.

A few days before the draft, the Hornets were still thinking there was a chance that either Seikaly or Perry might float their way. Philadelphia, which was sure to draft a guard with the third pick in the draft, liked Chapman, and there were at least two other teams, Phoenix and Golden State, that could use a player at that position, too.

But on Monday afternoon, less than 24 hours before the Tuesday draft, Scheer said new data – specifically word that Phoenix would pick Perry if he were available – indicated the Hornets would probably wind up with one of the guards, probably Chapman.

"That's the way it looks right now," Scheer said. "I could even see all the big men being gone and the three guards going six, seven and eight. The way I rate the guards, Chapman is third. If that's the case, then that's who we will take. I think it would be a serious mistake to pass on him."

In the scenario Scheer saw building, indeed that he hoped was building, the Chapman pick would be a virtual automatic. The other players rated highly by the Hornets would be gone, and the alternatives would be picking taller but inferior players like 7-1 Wil Perdue of Vanderbilt or 6-9 Harvey Grant of Oklahoma.

"That's why we think it would be a bad idea to pass on him (Chapman)," Scheer said. "Obviously we're concerned about our lack of size right now, but to take someone else, a Perdue or someone, just because they're a few inches taller, seems to be a very bad idea. Not to knock those guys, but they're just not as good."

Having created a world in which the Hornets would "have to" pick Chapman, Scheer must have been a little disappointed when reality failed to match. The first three picks went as anticipated, but New Jersey, a long-time wild card in NBA proceedings, snapped up the talented-but-mecurical Chris Morris of Auburn with the fourth pick in the draft. That assured the Hornets of having at least two of their chosen eight to pick from when it was their turn and left them, suddenly, with a choice. Golden State and the Clippers, who also picked sixth this year, grabbed guards Richmond and Hawkins. When Phoenix, as expected, took Perry the Hornets were left with an unexpected choice between Seikaly and Chapman.

Hornets Never Lie

Had the expansion draft come after the college draft this would not have been a big problem. A case could be made for either player. As it was, the Hornets had a roster of sorts in place, and it was just crying out for a 6-11 guy who, local fans were likely to remember, had wasted J. R. Reid in the NCAA tournament a few months before. This additional factor created a public relations problem for the Hornets' managers over the first big decision they would make. How could they justify taking another guard?

To their credit, they didn't let that sway their thinking. After turning down owner Shinn's last-minute appeal for a big man – a mirror of many fans' simplistic thinking on the subject – the Hornets went ahead and picked their man, Rex, the Wonder Boy. Then they set to the task of defending the choice.

Scheer was feisty as he announced the pick at the Charlotte Convention center where an estimated 6,000 fans had gathered for a draft party. Forgetting that the day before he had said Chapman was the third-best guard in the draft, Scheer marveled, after the fact, that Chapman was still available.

"You know," Scheer said, "you hear 'Seikaly-Chapman, Seikaly-Chapman,' but it wasn't that hard for us to pass the other guy up. Chapman was the best guy available. Easily."

Added Littles, the personnel man, "If you've talked to anyone you know that everybody thinks Chapman is a better player. It's just not in question."

The defense of Rex Chapman also included a fair amount of Seikaly bashing.

Littles compared the Syracuse star to Jose Vargas, which is not a compliment. Scheer noted that "six other teams passed on him." Of course, six others passed on Chapman, too.

Harter got to the crux of the matter. "We think Rex might be an All-Star," Harter said. "We certainly didn't think that about the other guy (Seikaly)."

Most of the talent assessors around the league agreed. When Chapman first announced he was leaving school early, there was a lot of interest. The sharper scouts had already been scouting him, figuring he'd leave after his junior year anyway. As Littles said, "It was obvious that here was a pro."

Chapman's surprising physical package (36-inch vertical leap), combined with his inbred "star" mentality, created a very interesting commodity. In the kind of rash overstatements that follow any young stud, he had been compared to both Oscar Robertson and Jerry West.

In truth, neither comparison fit very well. Chapman plays a

different style from either of these Hall of Famers. But the idea that he might one day reach a similar level was not so far-fetched.

Ed Badger, Charlotte's director of basketball administration, said, "There were only three guys in the draft who excited us, and Chapman was one of them. There just aren't many like him."

It was obvious early that the Hornets would have no shot at the other two, Manning and the giant, Smits. But there was enough uncertainty about Chapman, his age for one thing, that the Hornets could see long before the day actually came that they'd have a shot at Rex. He quickly became a target.

And in many ways he was the perfect match for the fledgling team: a rising southern basketball star in a rising southern city. The two could mature together.

Everyone except Chapman conceded that he was two or three years away from realizing, much less reaching, his potential. But the Hornets, barring a momentous player acquisition, were further than that from undertaking any serious competition. They could afford to wait while Chapman developed. An established team could not.

Philadelphia scout Bob Weinhauer, whose team chose Hawkins over Chapman because it thought Hawkins could help sooner, said, "Charlotte is really a good place for Rex. They can let him play, let him make mistakes, and not worry about it because their games won't mean anything for awhile. I mean, he can fire all those shots in Charlotte and not worry about shooting them out of the playoffs. I think he'll get better, faster there than anywhere."

Of course, there was the possibility he'd be a bust. Just 20 years old, Chapman's future vistas were broad, but that didn't mean they all looked out on the land of milk and honey.

Marty Blake, the superscout who supplies player ratings for every NBA team, pooh-poohed the idea of Chapman being the next star.

"If I had $100 for every 'next Jerry West,' " Blake said, "Whoo! I'd have retired long ago. I think he'd be doing real well just to be the next Danny Ainge."

That might seem like a bit of a letdown if Jerry West is the target, but in truth Ainge wouldn't be a terrible eighth pick (he was actually taken 31st). Taking Danny Ainge with the chance he might become something very much better is not a bad expenditure of draft day capital.

Still, at the moment of conception, the Hornets' first baby was not greeted with open arms. Dell Curry, the first expansion pick and a player who thought he had first dibs on Chapman's position, didn't take it very well. He left the draft party not long after the pick was announced. "I can't understand what they're thinking," a disappointed Curry said.

He wasn't the only one in the convention center crowd to feel a little let down when Chapman was chosen. When the pick was announced there was a lot of murmuring and more than a couple of boos. A few fans even chanted "Sei-Klee, Sei-Klee."

That reaction frustrated even the even-tempered Littles who said, "I can't understand that. Do they expect us to put a team together in one day?"

To placate the mob, the Hornets rushed a hastily prepared Chapman highlight film onto the big screen TVs around the convention center. It contained about three clips of Rex in action for Kentucky.

One of those stood out. As his future fans watched, Chapman streaked downcourt on the break, essentially jumped over a defender, then fired off a 25-foot shot as he came down.

Unfortunately for Chapman, he was less than 15 feet away.

That didn't seem like much of a way to sell a debatable draft pick, but at least it started preparing the crowd for the future.

With its other two picks, the Hornets made a stab at their size deficit. It was sort of a horizontal stab.

Charlotte landed Tom Tolbert with its second pick and dug up Auburn's Jeff Moore with its third. Tolbert was a 6-8, 245-pounder who played center for Arizona's Final Four team. Moore, of Auburn, was talented but not heavily motivated. He was, however, motivated to be heavy. Moore appeared to measure 6-7 just about anyway you turned the tape.

Not long after the draft, an NBA scout said of Moore, "Well, they won't be able to play him when there's a full moon."

"Why not?" the scout was asked.

"Because he'd just howl all night. He's a fucking dog."

Even if Moore and/or Tolbert panned out, the Hornets had still finished two drafts with only one certifiable inside player – the inimitable Hoppen. And in his finest NBA game he'd scored all of 17 points. That meant that as the team headed towards its first season, it bore a striking resemblance to a doughnut: it was sweet on the outside, but there was nothing in the middle.

After the college draft was finished, Harter joked about the army of jumpshooters he had been given.

"We ought to be pretty good at H-O-R-S-E," Harter said.

In case you've never played, that's a basketball game in which size, and all its advantages, has absolutely no role. All you've got to do is shoot.

Meat on the Hoop

After a few days off for much-needed post-draft vacations, Scheer and company went to work finding a few good (big) men to fill out the lopsided roster. Naturally the first move of the summer was to trade for another guard.

Okay, to be honest, he could play forward, too, but for a team that had perimeter shooters stacked up like jets over Atlanta, landing Robert Reid three weeks after the college draft was a bit of a shock. In 10 seasons with the Houston Rockets, Bobby Joe Reid, as he was sometimes known, had played the point, off guard and small forward. He had been, at various times, productive at all three, and now he was coming to Charlotte to ... do what?

Well, basically to try out. The Hornets picked up the aging guard (33) in a fire sale. Houston was turning over its talented but seemingly incompatible roster and Reid had to go. The Rockets already had a contract with free-agent Mike Woodson waiting in the wings and they needed both Reid's position and his salary to make him fit. So they offered him up as trade bait: anything, anything at all, for Robert Reid, so long as it's not too expensive. The Rockets would even surrender a second-round pick.

It seemed a minor deal at the time, but Scheer thought it was just too good to pass up. He could get a draft pick (in 1990 as it turned out) and a potentially helpful player in exchange for a player (Bernard Thompson) the Hornets weren't sure could make their team. Best of all, it wouldn't cost him a thing but plane fare for Reid to Charlotte. Due to some quirky circumstances, Reid held a contract that did not guarantee him his salary of about $400,000 per year. If he stuck with the team that owned his rights, be it Houston or Charlotte, past the NBA guarantee date in late December, he'd get the full amount. But up until that point he could be cut at will, like some raw rookie.

Scheer marveled at that.

"I was amazed when I saw it," Scheer said of Reid's contract. "It's really an unusual contract for a player that old. It's surprising, but I'll tell you this – we'd never have made the deal without it."

Reid signed the unusual pact because his previous contract was signed at a time of personal turmoil. He was in the midst of a not-too-friendly separation with his old agent, Houston-based (but not bred – you should hear his answering machine) Lance J. Luchnick, and he was coming off surgery to remove a Baker cyst from inside his left knee. It was not major surgery, but some muscle work was involved, and Reid was not young by NBA standards. The Rockets wondered a bit and wanted to hedge on his contract.

Reid, at times an overly optimistic man, felt secure enough in Houston to agree. He had strong ties to the community and thought his ties to the team, to the Rockets' finest moments (he was a starter on both Houston teams that reached the NBA finals in the 1980s) gave him all the security he needed. So he signed. The contract offered a proviso by which the money would be guaranteed if Reid played 1,000 minutes – a relative pittance for a regular – prior to the All-Star break. He also had, so Reid said, general manager Ray Patterson's handshake on the deal. No matter what the paper said, the team would take care of Reid.

Reid felt pretty good about all of this until the season started. He didn't get a lot of playing time, and soon it was obvious that he wasn't going to make his 1,000 minutes. He didn't, though as far as he was concerned, the knee was fine. The All-Star break passed and Reid was still stuck with a free agent's contract. Then in the second half of the year, with Houston struggling for playoff position, Reid started playing more. And more. He got his 1,000 minutes the second half of the year when it didn't count, and naturally he smelled a rat. "Well," Reid said, "what would you think?"

His relationship with the Rockets was still good after that season. Patterson had again assured that his contract would be worked out. But Reid was not completely surprised when the trade came. Hurt – he was traded with a second-round pick for *Bernard Thompson* – but not surprised. He had seen it coming. So he would go to Charlotte and see if a Houston handshake was any good there.

• • • • •

As he was scooping up Reid, Scheer also began negotiations with two free agents who could help the Hornets' practically non-existent inside game. One was journeyman Earl Cureton, a veteran of eight NBA seasons, who was signed two days after the Reid deal was completed. The other was the better-known Kurt Rambis, a starter on several of the Lakers' championship teams.

They were essentially the same player – seasoned rebounder/defender types with limited offensive skills and astonishingly similar career statistics. In eight seasons, Cureton had averaged 5.3 points and 4.6 rebounds a game. Rambis' numbers were 5.3 and 5.9 in seven years. Cureton's best year was slightly better 8.6 points, 6.3 rebounds a game vs. 7.5 points and 6.8 rebounds for Rambis. Both were a little small for their position (Cureton 6-9, Rambis 6-8). Both had been third-round picks.

On the surface, they seemed to offer just about the same things, but their negotiations were very different.

Signing Cureton, who had played for Harter in Detroit, was a relatively quick and painless experience. He was anxious to leave the dreadful LA Clippers, wasn't pursued by a lot of teams, and was wanted by Charlotte. The two sides came to terms (roughly half a million dollars for two years), and Cureton became a Hornet.

The addition was lauded, though not in glowing terms, at the time. Cureton was a role player whose strengths were rebounding and defense. He ran well for a man his size, which afforded him some offensive opportunities in transition. But in general, he was not a scoring threat due mostly to an extraordinarily heavy shot which could ricochet off a rim or backboard with startling force. Harter said, "Earl has great enthusiasm, plays hard and knows the game. He's not a great scorer. He can play some center. I think he's a pretty good addition."

Said Scheer, "I think he goes a long way towards stabilizing our team."

The generally mellow Cureton looked at the signing as a chance to play a little more and to further extend a career that had already run a surprising distance. He did not get to play as much as he thought he should have his last season in LA, a victim of the Clippers' alleged youth movement.

"That was the first year in which I really felt like I didn't get the minutes I should have," Cureton said. "But I understand. I'm just glad this came along. I knew what Dick would demand and I was comfortable with that. I'm looking to be in the top seven or eight and to contribute, just like always."

Rambis was a different story. Though comparable to Cureton statistically, he was better paid, better known and, thought some observers, a better player, too. This was just a suspicion, though. Evidence was hard to come by.

Even as a starter, Rambis never averaged as much as 24 minutes – half a game – in his best year. His career average was 18 minutes a game. The idea was that as productive as he'd been in those minutes, in a very limited role on a superstar-filled team, he could be even more on a team where he would be much of the show and would get a better chunk of the minutes. Said one NBA scout, "If he was a regular he might get 15 points and 10 rebounds a night. He could be that good."

The Lakers retained some interest in re-signing him, but as usual they were faced with salary cap problems caused by the massive contracts of Magic Johnson and Kareem Abdul-Jabbar. At a half-million plus, Rambis did not seem to be the best use of their dollars. Others, including the Hornets and Knicks, had a different view. Rambis had some useful skills and was a good team player, a label he had solidified the previous spring by not grousing over his dwindling role in the Lakers' most recent title run. Rambis played just 180 minutes in the 1988 playoffs and wasn't used at all in five games, but he didn't complain.

Later, when he had become a Hornet, he said, "I could have made life miserable for Pat Riley last spring, but what would have been the point?"

As Rambis coolly reckoned, there was none. That was a fairly typical response for the man with the horn-rimmed glasses and the long, stringy hair. Although he cultivates, and in fact deserves, his reputation for laid-back California zaniness, Rambis can be quite thoughtful and pragmatic.

He demonstrated this again while choosing his professional options in the summer of 1988. Along with wife Linda, a smart woman with a nice career of her own in tennis promotions, Rambis weighed the various offers. His objective was to provide for his family (two children) in the best possible way, live in a nice place and play, actually play, more basketball than he had in the past. Like a high school recruit, Rambis even made trips to the sites of the teams seeking his services.

Eventually he decided that Charlotte was the only place where all three criteria would be met. The money was just as good some other places, but playing time was a worry. Other locales didn't offer acceptable living conditions. Rambis, on his first visit to North Carolina, was impressed by the trees and yards of Charlotte's endless neighborhoods.

Some haggling over contract length and term followed. The Hornets at first suspected Rambis was using his offer from Charlotte – four years at 2.4 million – as a lever in negotiations with the Lakers. But he turned out to be a more faithful bargainer than that. On July 27 he finally agreed to terms very close to the original $600,000 a year offer.

Scheer said on that day, "He (Rambis) just wanted a few more dollars, that's all. We got it worked out."

Praise for the former Santa Clara star was on a slightly higher plane than that issued to mark Cureton's arrival.

Scheer said, "He's not a great player, although we do think in our situation, with a little more time and a less star-studded cast, his production could pick up. But he's one more piece. He'll help."

Harter praised Rambis' famous work ethic, "No one's ever questioned that," Harter said.

Amongst the two successful signings, the Hornets also flailed about in a sea of aborted ventures to put more size on the roster.

One of the more interesting was a mid-summer's dalliance with Artis Gilmore, a massive center who at age 38 was obviously a bit past his prime. Gilmore, who knew Scheer and Littles from the days when all three were in the ABA, came down from Chicago for lunch and a meeting one afternoon while the Rambis negotiations were in full swing.

Before the meeting, Scheer said, "I really don't have any secret feeling that he can still play or help us in any way. But it's worth talking about I suppose."

Gilmore, who had just finished a contract that paid him more than $800,000 his last year, was anxious to continue his NBA career. He got the Hornets to agree to further talks. There even was the suggestion of a no-risk tryout in September. Sad to say or maybe not, depending on your point of view – nothing ever came of that.

Scheer chased after some other big ghosts that summer. One that would prove to be a recurring haunt was the Indiana Pacers' Stuart Gray, powerfully built 7-footer who was a free agent, though not an unrestricted one. Once upon a time Gray had been ranked as the second-best high school center in the land, just behind Ralph Sampson. But he progressed slowly in college (UCLA), and at the end of his first pro contract had shown himself to be little more than a very large person with a willingness to initiate contact.

Having left college a year early, he was young, however. That meant he had a chance to improve. He was also a favorite of Harter, who had developed an uncommon bond with the hard-nosed center during their two years together in Indiana. Harter also knew that Gray was available. The Pacers, for whatever else they didn't have, had plenty of big men. Following the selection of Smits in the college draft, Gray became just one of five Pacers taller than 6-11. And he wasn't number one in that group.

At Harter's urging, Scheer called his old friend Donnie Walsh in Indiana. Walsh was the general manager there, but he had been Scheer's choice to replace Larry Brown as coach in Denver one year. And just as in any business, friendship figured heavily in NBA deal-making.

The Hornets didn't have a lot to offer, but Scheer and Walsh managed to work out a deal. Charlotte could get Gray by sending Michael Holton back to Portland, which in turn would send Indiana a draft pick. The maneuver collapsed because of an NBA rule that prohibited a team retaining for at least a year, a player it lost in the expansion draft for at least one year. But Scheer thought he and Walsh still had an agreement to work something out.

For that reason he was a little stunned to read, in mid-July, a quote from Walsh in an Indianapolis newspaper that said the Gray deal was dead. "There is no deal for Gray," Walsh said.

Said Scheer, "I'm surprised. I really thought we had something."

As it turned out, Scheer was to think that again, about the very same player, several times before the season was done.

• • • • •

The Hornets continued their talent roundup in July and August with that NBA tradition, the summer camp. Ah, summer camp. S'mores and songs around the campfire. Arts and crafts. Hiking. Boating. Morning announcements. What a blast.

That is summer camp when you're a kid, but once you grow into a professional basketball player the images conjured up become quite different. Sweat. Basketball drills. Sweat. Basketball drills. Scrimmage. Dinner at Shoney's. Get cut. Move on to some other city. What a drag.

But that is just the way the summers go for the army of would-be and former stars, groping for a grip, just a fingerhold, on the NBA's mountain of money. From late June until mid-August they try their luck – and most say that is just what it is, luck – at a seemingly endless series of NBA cattle calls.

Ralph Lewis, one of the Hornets' expansion picks, knows those tiresome ropes. Before he made the Pistons in 1987, he visited five other NBA camps.

"All you can do is work hard and hope it works out for you somewhere," Lewis said. "But once you're in, you're way ahead of the game. That's what everybody's trying for."

The Hornets' first camp, conducted the first week of August at the old Charlotte Coliseum, would be different from most. Both as a public relations ploy and in a desperate effort to dredge up some more talent, the Hornets invited almost twice the summer camp norm: Thirty-six players are expected, including representatives from every nook and cranny of the non-NBA professional basketball world.

The biggest part are CBA players, many of whom have been up to the bigs for the proverbial "cup of coffee." Some, like Duke's Billy King and Colorado's Scott Wilke, were fair college prospects just passed over in the college draft. There are well-known players like Louis Orr, who played eight years in the NBA, and utter unknowns like John Spencer, who averaged eight points a game in college at Howard University, and little Ralph Miller of South Carolina State who mailed the Hornets films of himself to earn a tryout. Littles, a former "little guy" from a small school, liked what he saw or at least felt enough compassion to extend a tryout.

Although it is technically called a rookie camp, the only Hornet draft pick in attendance was the rotund Moore who showed up in Charlotte in early July weighing so much that the Hornets were embarrassed to release the figure. Rumor was it was over 300. Moore himself admitted to 275.

The team's other draft choices, Chapman and Tolbert, didn't show as part of the standard contract mating dance.

Adding some pathos to the melodrama are the older players who come to give it one last try, or perhaps next-to-one-last try. They include Sam Foggin, a big forward who had played overseas (Australia, Brazil and England) for nine years, Mike Clark, who played for Harter at Oregon, Reggie Gaines, a former Winston-Salem State star, and 7-footer Brett Vroman, who at age 32 was the camp's old man.

All the older guys know their chances are limited by their age. No NBA team, and especially not an expansion team, is going to stock up with a bunch of old guys. But they also have experience on their side. This is not their first tryout camp, and through the years, they have developed a feel for what the coaches are seeking.

Gaines, a shameless gunner in his college days, said nine years of camping taught him an important rule: don't shoot.

As he watched some of his "campatriots" scrimmage the first day of camp, he said, "A lot of these boys here are shooting their way right out of here. You see that a lot. They want to impress, but it's the fastest way out of these things. The coaches don't come to these camps looking for a guy who can score 25 or 30 points a night. They're looking for people who will rebound, pass and play that defense. You know, those things most guys don't like to do.

"So," Gaines said, "that's what I try to do – please the coaches.

"Who else matters? And if you never take a shot, then they'll never know you can't make one."

Tim Kempton, a young, beefy center who spent the past year playing in Naples, Italy, had already discovered the truth in Gaines' message. Smart and worldly, this son of a New York police officer (his mom) knew the Hornets, or any other NBA team, went to summer camps looking for steak rather than sizzle.

"This is not a glory job," Kempton said on day two of the workouts. "You stand in there and fill up the middle on defense, play tough in the post, grab some rebounds, set picks for the scorers and get the ball to the point guard. Not everyone would want to do that, but I can see a career in it."

As it turned out, the Hornets could, too. But when camp opened no one was particularly optimistic about finding a player. Littles, whose duty it was to find players to fill the beds at the Holiday Inn across the street from the coliseum, suggested, hopefully, that as many as a half dozen players at the summer camp might be invited back to the preseason camp in October. But he also said, "This is a real collection."

Harter, looking over his roster, struck a similar note. "It's a bunch of guys," he said. Which means? "Which means," Harter said, "the odds (of finding a player) aren't very good. But you never know. And our situation, I'd rather have a bunch, too many, than not enough. Maybe someone will turn up."

The first day of camp brings some disappointment. Enis Whatley, the point guard who was the star of the Hornets' May camp, doesn't show. Littles had heard he might sign with Milwaukee. As it turns out, he just went to the Bucks' mini-camp. Russell Cross, an agile big man who was the number-six pick in the 1983 NBA draft, is absent, too. Nobody has a clue as to what has happened to him, nor do they especially care. Cross was terrible in the NBA the first time around, and it's easy to cross him of the list.

Harter and his staff began cutting players the second day. But the coach is wary of making any bold pronouncements.

Does he really like Ranzino Smith, the one-dimensional, ex-Carolina guard who keeps surviving cuts? Harter shrugs.

What about the veteran Orr?

"He's been around," Harter said.

The big guys have shown some good things haven't they?

"Well," Harter said, "they are trying hard. That's good I guess."

Smith's staying power, which looks suspiciously like an attempt to sell a few more tickets for the free-agent games to be held at the end of the camp week, is a surprise. So is Howard Spencer, who makes it to the games' roster despite owning one of the worst shooting touches, among those who are really trying, on the planet. He is aggressive, however, which explains a lot. He is also realistic.

As he makes it down to the last 15 or so players, Spencer is asked if likes his chances any better than before. "Yes," he says, I'd say they're down now to about a million-to-one."

Others who showed well in the twice-a-day pony show are forward Gary Plummer and forward-center Mike Gibson, a former Washington Bullet. Kempton is also impressive, in his own way.

Outside observers like Ray Hall, a big guard from Canisius. He can shoot, dunk it in a crowd and makes a lot of flashy plays. But, remembering Gaines' warning, it is no surprise that the coaches have no interest in him.

Center Vroman, the biggest guy in camp, clanked about in the scrimmages like one of those Russian guys in the 1972 Olympics, which causes Littles to remark, "He's been in Europe so long he plays like a European."

The Hornets cut him the day before the exhibition games against three other teams' free agents are to begin, but he wouldn't go away. He showed up the next morning at practice and begged his way back on to the team even though on his knees Vroman was less than five feet tall.

"Some people from Europe are coming to the game tonight to see me," Vroman said. "The Hornets didn't owe me anything, but when I explained my situation, they agreed to let me come back."

Said Harter, "We wanted to do the right thing. When I talked to his agent I'd said he'd get in for some games."

Vroman got in for one, a 98-87 victory over a motley group of free agents with the Atlanta Hawks. The first-ever triumph for players wearing anything like a Charlotte Hornets uniform prompted a banner headline on the front page of the next day's *Charlotte Observer* sports section that read, "Bring on the Lakers."

More than 4,000 fans paid to see the utterly trivial proceedings which elicited some surprise from old NBA hands who were present, and foreshadowed the coming boom. Robert Reid, visiting his new employers, marveled, "If they get 4,000 for some guys who may not even make the team, what will they do when the real 12 gets here?"

Good question, Robert.

The Hornets' roster for all the exhibition games was bolstered by the addition of several "real" players who dropped by. Michael Holton played one game. Dave Hoppen played all three.

The Hornets won three games in Charlotte, then went to Miami for three more and lost them all. Ed Badger, leading the team with Littles while Harter watched from a safe distance, managed to draw a technical foul in one of the games in Miami. As it turned out, that was one of the more memorable accomplishments of the exercise which many NBA teams think is a waste.

During camp, though not necessarily because of what he did at it, the Hornets signed Lewis to a guaranteed contract for the coming season. A few weeks later they came to terms with Kempton, also giving him guaranteed money for the coming season, as well as a small, partial guarantee for the year after that.

The two signings gave the Hornets 10 players with guaranteed money for the coming year, and that didn't count Chapman, Tolbert or Reid and his funky contract. The lack of flexibility inherent in this situation would dog the Hornets later, but at the time Scheer thought it was the thing to do. Kempton and Lewis, he said, intrigued the staff enough to warrant a further look, but neither player was willing to come to fall camp without a guarantee. So the Hornets gave them what they wanted.

Everyone else left the camp without that commodity, including the pathetic Vroman, who, after being cut a second time, showed up the next morning begging for a job with one of the other teams in town for the three-day tournament.

There weren't any takers.

A Puzzle with too Many Pieces

"Guaranteed is the most important word in the league"
– Michael Holton

There is a certain, unavoidable exhilaration to pre-season camp in the NBA, even amongst veterans who know its drudgery and boredom all too well. One of the league's great appeals to players, as Rex Chapman gleefully observed late in his first season, is that you play games more than you practice. But in camp the cycle is reversed. For a long time you play no games at all, except scrimmages, and even after exhibition season starts, practice still consumes more time than play. Yet, when it first starts, it is exciting.

And in the case of the Charlotte Hornets, it was more exciting than normal simply because it was different. Most of the Hornets had been to pre-season camps before, though only one had been to an expansion team's first camp.

He was Marty Byrnes, a 32-year-old forward with modest skill and a baleful outlook. In another October, seven years before, he had been amongst the teeming masses at Dallas' first camp. Now, on what was certainly his last basketball leg, he was in Charlotte.

The odds of him making the team were poor. He was here as yet another favor to Cincinati lawyer Ron Grinker, the man who was Byrnes' agent. Grinker, who represented perhaps a tenth of the NBA's active players, though few great ones, was well connected throughout the league. That was especially true in Charlotte where three-fourths of the basketball staff – everyone but Harter – called him either "my friend," or "my lawyer," or both. Harter felt mildly uncomfortable over being in the midst of so many Grinkos when he first arrived in Charlotte. Early in the season, he joked, "They've got me surrounded. Grinker's got the last one the other day. He signed up Irene." That referred to Irene Lavelle, the multi-talented basketball secretary, who in fact remained unsigned throughout the season.

Hornets Never Lie

Grinker wasn't so sure Byrnes could still play in the NBA, but Byrnes wanted to try. With expansion looming, he and Grinker had agreed upon a plan the year before. Byrnes would play in the CBA, which he did, and either catch the eye of an NBA team or prove to himself that he could no longer do it.

But the results were, to Byrnes at least, inconclusive. In 31 games for the hapless Charleston, W.Va., Gunners, Byrnes averaged 8.7 points and 3.9 rebounds a game.

"I managed not to succeed at either one," said Byrnes, as the Hornets' camp began. "So here I am."

Byrnes wanted very much to play again. The motivation was hard to describe, though. It was not so much the money, although that would be nice. Neither was it the feeling of never having had a shot. As Byrnes himself admitted, he had been fortunate to play as long as he had. "There aren't many guys around like me," he said. "It's very hard to think of a player my age getting back into the NBA."

It was just that basketball was so much fun. And he had done it all his life. Since high school and before. On through Syracuse, where he was an All-American. Then into his stop-and-go pro career in six NBA cities and a half dozen more around the world.

Now, with his career headed for its last showdown, Byrnes thought back to a prophecy made when he was leaving college. In a national magazine article rating prospective draft picks that year, Pat Williams, general manager of the Philadelphia 76ers at the time, said of Byrnes, "He'll be a good journeyman forward."

Byrnes sneered then. "I thought, 'Ah, what does he know.' But you know, he was right. I have fulfilled his words."

In fact, he had become a personification of the term. By his own count, Byrnes' basketball sojourn had taken him to 14 cities in 10 years. Dallas and Phoenix, where he played most and best, were his favorites, he thought, but it was hard to tell. The street names, the neighborhoods, the interstates – they all ran together after awhile.

"I don't know what to tell people when they ask where I'm from," Byrnes said. "I think I'm registered to vote in about 18 states. It's kind of nice, though. I meet someone, start talking, and when they tell me where they're from I can say, 'Oh yeah. I lived there once.'"

Byrnes laughed and seemed to mean it. His jokes were not graveyard humor, even though the hole has already been dug for his career. He enjoyed, and is proud of, the fight he put up. And as the Hornets' camp began, he was ready to go one more round. If he was knocked out, as expected, would he finally give up?

"Yeah, I guess so," Byrnes said. "My family is tired of following me around the world just so I can play basketball. Still I would like to play some more. Damn. It's just so hard to quit."

Oddly enough, Byrnes was not alone in the futility of quest. Among the 19 players who opened camp, half a dozen had virtually no chance to make the team in spite of the coaching staff's promise of an open mind. This surprising development – the perception is that an expansion team's first camp would be a wide-open cattle call – was the byproduct of Scheer's contract handiwork over the summer. In addition to the six guaranteed contracts the Hornets' assumed in the expansion draft, Scheer had secured five more over the summer.

He had signed Kurt Rambis and Earl Cureton in mid-July, then added Ralph Lewis, an expansion draftee whose contract did not contain a guarantee, at the first of August. After the free-agent camp, Kempton was signed up, and just before Labor Day, the Hornets finally came to terms with second-round pick Tom Tolbert, guaranteeing his first year's pay, too. That gave Charlotte 11 guaranteed pacts with first-rounder Chapman still unsigned and Robert Reid and his non-guaranteed salary still on hold. It was a mess that defied NBA logic, especially for an expansion team. The last two newcomers in the league, Dallas and New Orleans, had both gone through more than 20 players in their first season. But Charlotte's high percentage of guaranteed contracts prevented the installation of a revolving door.

Michael Holton, the astute guard drafted from Portland, shook his head at the opening roster. It just didn't make sense.

"Guaranteed," Holton said, "is the most important word in the league. It decides everything. But we've got so many (guaranteed) contracts here. It's odd. It makes things very interesting, though."

Dick Harter, the Hornets' coach, wasn't worried about the situation yet, although he wondered how willing the frugal Shinn would be to dump guaranteed contracts. Time would tell.

As for Scheer, he didn't like having his hands tied, or being thought of as a soft touch, but he thought there was no choice. The Hornets were committed to the expansion contracts they picked up, and signing Cureton and Rambis was a must. Guaranteeing money for Lewis, Kempton and Tolbert was a bit iffier. The Hornets might have held their ground and gotten away with it. Then again they might not. Would the NBA waiver wire or the CBA have given them as good players had they let Kempton or Lewis go unsigned? It was a hard call, because no one yet knew just how good they were. Tolbert was a rookie. Kempton had one NBA season as a backup center, and Lewis had been the 12th man on a very good team, so he had seldom played.

"There was no way we'd even get to take a look without the

guarantees," Scheer said. "I don't like it, but that's business in this league right now. You've just got to make those kinds of investments. You have to expect that somewhere along the way you may have to pay someone for not playing."

The system of guarantees, which as Holton said, did mean so much in the NBA, didn't quash all competition at Charlotte's first camp, though. Another roster quirk, the overabundance of guards, made some of the guarantees look shakier than others. Charlotte opened camp with five guards of varied NBA experience under contract with the as-yet-unsigned Chapman still to come. The 6-8 Reid could play guard, too. Compared to most NBA rosters, it was a real glut. Few teams in the league carried even as many as five pure guards, and four was the norm.

Harter hoped the situation might turn into a positive. "I think it could be the great thing about this camp," he said. "There are going to be some pretty good – I don't want to call them battles – but situations here. That can be pretty good. Of course, it's not exactly Kevin McHale fighting Robert Parish (two All-Star 7-footers who play for Boston) to decide who's going to be the center. But for a first-year team it's not bad. Better than you might expect."

The obvious competition caused some tension. Lewis, whose grip on an NBA job was more tenuous than the rest, said he sensed it as soon as he arrived. "The competition began the minute you stepped off the airplane," he said. "It's kind of sticky. I don't think you'll make many friends like this."

Not all the guards shared his feelings, though Holton was, as usual, wary. And Reid, worried by his contract situation, was ready for anything. Any fool could count the numbers, he said, and come to the same conclusion that he had: "That without a doubt, management is still on the phone (making a deal). Something's got to happen."

Thirty-four-year-old Rickey Green, the veteran obtained from Utah, was less concerned. He owned a major edge in experience on the assembled guard corps, and it was obvious he'd get the first shot at the point guard spot. The Hornets had all but told him that. Likewise, little Tyrone Bogues wasn't concerned either. He knew that he still had to prove, indeed would always have to prove, that he could play in the league. But one year after Washington made him the 12th pick in the draft and offered him a contract commensurate with that position, he knew he would be a bitter pill to swallow as a cut. He still had three years left.

Asked about the crowded guard situation, Bogues said, "Hey man, my money is guaranteed."

But so, it was pointed out, was the money of every other guard in camp, excepting Reid, who also played forward. Bogues grinned a I-know-more-than-you-grin and rolled his eyes. "Yeah, but there are different years involved. There are guarantees and there are *guarantees*. Know what I mean? I'm not sweating it man. I'm just going to play."

As uncertain as anyone was Dell Curry. Though he was the team's first pick in the expansion draft, though he had proven capabilities as a shooter in the NBA, he just wasn't sure. In the first two years of his career he had been stuck in untenable situations on two different teams. Utah, the team that drafted him, never gave him a chance to play. The Jazz were on the rise, and off guard, Curry's position, was filled with veterans. Darrell Griffith and Bob Hansen were ahead of him. So was Green, who was slowly being eased out of his position by a young point man named John Stockton. Frank Layden, the Utah coach, found a backcourt of Stockton and Green was sometimes effective. But minutes for playing Curry were hard to find.

Much to Curry's relief, he was traded to Cleveland at the start of training camp in 1987. He still faced some playing time problems. The Cavs had Ron Harper, a more versatile player taken seven picks ahead of Curry in the 1986 draft. But it was only one man. At worst he'd be a backup. And Cleveland really wanted him. In fact, the Cavs had debated between Curry and Harper when making their selection in 1986.

In the end, Harper's speed won out over Curry's incredibly deft shooting touch. That, plus Harper was a homestate boy from Dayton and had played in college at Miami of Ohio. That was a consideration for the Cavs, who struggled at the gate. Ron Harper might sell a few tickets that Dell Curry might not.

It had turned out to be a good pick. Harper had blossomed quickly and was likened to a poor man's Michael Jordan, an explosive player of great physical skill. But Curry still had his appeal, and when the Cavs found they could obtain him for almost nothing – in exchange for overweight centers Mel Turpin and Darryl Dawkins – they did it. For most of the year, it seemed like a good move for Curry. His minutes per game doubled to a respectable 19 a night, and he managed to average more than 10 points per game. On opening night, he came off the bench to score 20 points, and when Harper went down with an ankle injury in December, Curry stepped in and averaged 18 a game in his absence. All season, Curry provided instant firepower off the bench. He was a big contributor for a young team rising toward the top.

Then the playoffs arrived, the time of year when players really love to play, and Curry was suddenly forgotten. Coach Lenny Wilkens, who had thrown up his hands at Curry's defensive failings all year, barely used him in a five-game set against Michael Jordan and the Chicago Bulls. Instead, he went with Craig Ehlo, an obscure college player, a one-time third-round pick who had battled his way through the CBA to the NBA, as Harper's chief backup. Ehlo was not as deadly a shooter as Curry, but he played better defense. In the Chicago series, Ehlo averaged 22 minutes a game. Curry played just 17 minutes in the entire series, and sat out three whole games. After that, Cleveland didn't seem as good an idea to Curry. And, Curry didn't seem as good an idea to Cleveland. The Cavs still liked some of the things he could do, but faced with a choice of protecting him or Ehlo in the coming expansion draft, they chose to keep Ehlo.

Although he was disappointed to leave a team that figured to be a contender in the years ahead, expansion was fine with Curry. He figured to finally get his chance to play. Charlotte, not far from his home in western Virginia, was okay, too. At least for two or three days. Then the Hornets drafted Chapman. Curry was stunned. The nightmares of his first two years in the league, the ones he thought he had finally left behind, were coming back to haunt him. Chapman was an off guard, too, and there was little doubt that he, as the franchise's first, first-round pick, had the edge for playing time. "I just don't understand what they're doing," Curry said the day Chapman was drafted.

Over the summer he'd had time to reflect, time to hear the Hornets' side of the story. They thought there was room for both players at the position, possibly even as a high-scoring backcourt tandem. Chapman, they said, could play the point. Curry thought about it. By the time camp started he was ready to concede the possibility.

"I guess we could play together," he said. "I really haven't seen Rex play that much. Just a few times on TV. So maybe he can. Management thinks he can. Of course it's their right, their duty, to say things like that. Time will tell what they really think."

Time was on Curry's side as camp began. He was there and Chapman was not. As per modern NBA custom, contract negotiations with the agents representing Charlotte's top pick were rolling along at a leisurely pace. The two sides had met several times over the summer and had finally begun talking money in September. But when Scheer flew to Washington, D.C., on October 4 to meet with David Falk, Chapman's chief representative, the deal wasn't done.

Said Scheer then, "We're at the point where we could finish fairly quickly. But, we've been at that point for awhile. It's just a matter of who's going to move and when."

The reason for the Chapman contract agony, which is typical for the NBA, is not readily apparent. The league has no salary scale, but a general idea of every player's worth is known almost from the moment he is drafted. It's based on what players in the same draft position or playing the same basketball position received the year before. Add a little cost-of-living boost – NBA salaries don't go down – and you have something better than an approximation of what the player will make. There's not much deviation from this. Almost without exception the negotiators on both sides are seasoned. They know the market, and mistakes will not be made. They know a contract will be signed.

Ron Grinker, Scheer's friend and one of the NBA's more active agents, says of the process, "When was the last time somebody went back into the draft (which, technically at least, is an option for every player drafted)? It never happens. You hear a few guys say Europe, but that doesn't happen much either. Most deals are going to be done."

But not until the last minute. Or beyond. The two sides wait for the market to develop. What one draft pick is paid depends somewhat on what another, just above or below him, gets. They wait for time to apply the only available pressure. Eventually, summer will end and camp will start. The team wants its picks in camp. And the agents know their players will do better if they're there. When camp starts, everyone gets serious.

Until then, they burn up travel dollars and blow smoke each other's way. Donnie Walsh, general manager of the Indiana Pacers, says, "I always like to hear what the agent is going to say. I don't know why, though. I never listen."

Likewise, at one of their meetings at the Charlotte airport, Scheer says he interrupted a Falk monologue on the merits of Rex Chapman to tell him it wasn't working. "I said, 'David, we can go through this dialogue. You can impress your client with how much you're working, and we can have these public cries of outrage, or we can just sit down for an hour here and do it.' "

Falk, an old friend of Scheer's, laughed and continued to press his case. Incredibly, in that three-and-a-half hour meeting, salary figures weren't mentioned once. Spencer Stolpen, George Shinn's legal counsel, attended the meeting with Scheer and left shaking his head.

Figures were on the table when the negotiations intensified on October 5, the first day of camp. But two lengthy sessions produced no breakthrough. The two sides were stalled, about $100,000 apart, when Falk broke off talks to fly to the West Coast and finish up a few contracts there. As chief basketball negotiator for ProServ Inc., one of the giants of the sports representation business, Falk was a busy man in early October. Chapman would have to wait a few more days.

In the meantime, the Hornets began practice, having graciously been given three extra days to work by the NBA through the player's association. The enthusiasm of Harter and the veteran players, most notably Kurt Rambis and the well-conditioned Robert Reid, dominated the early days.

Rambis, more or less a caricature to North Carolina fans from his playoff days with LA, showed himself to be a flesh-and-blood leader early in the drills. Though not vocal in the standard sense – he doesn't shout at teammates very often – he is assertive, hustling both physically and mentally. Often in the early practices, as Harter and his staff were installing the Hornets' basic offenses and defenses, Rambis would pipe up with a question about how it was to be done in certain situations, or a suggestion about how it might be done better. They weren't ignored, and a leadership role was quickly, subtly established.

The garrulous Reid provided a less-serious counterbalance, dashing through drills with uncalled for flair and ribbing teammates who failed at various tasks or in scrimmages. It was easy for Reid to be in such a mood. A summer of hard work had left him in superb condition, the best in the last four years, he thought, and he opened camp playing well. None of the other shooters was on yet, and only Bogues and Green, the speedy point guards, appeared to be running as fast.

Of course, this was not by accident. Reid had been rebuffed over the summer when he had asked the Hornets to renegotiate his contract. He wanted to have it guaranteed, a change he says the Rockets had agreed to orally. Additionally, he thought the Hornets should increase the amount. His Houston contract included numerous incentives based on winning 50 games, a division title, etc. Reid could add more than $50,000 to his contract with that in Houston, but with the expansion Hornets the numbers were meaningless. Joked Reid, "I'm sure the Hornets wouldn't mind guaranteeing the incentives."

Perhaps, but Scheer was adamant about not guaranteeing the rest. He wouldn't have acquired Reid if his roughly $450,000-a-year salary had been guaranteed, and that hadn't changed. "Robert's a veteran and all," Scheer said, "but our thinking hasn't changed. We still want to take a look and see what he can do."

There actually wasn't much question about what Reid could do. In 10 NBA seasons, including a couple of title runs, he had proven himself a player of great versatility and character. He could handle the tough, big guards in the league defensively, could pass and rebound better than most at his position, and was, on occasion, a deadly scorer, though with the Rockets that had seldom been his role. He was also superb in the clubhouse, a veteran trouper who maintained the tricky balance of good relations with teammates and those outside the team (management, fans, press) as well as anyone in the league.

So really, there was no doubt about what he *had* done. It was all about what Reid *could* do. At least superficially, the point of his Houston contract was management's worry about Reid's health. In the summer of 1987 he'd had a Baker cyst, a knot of muscle, removed from behind his knee. That surgery, coupled with Reid's age, made Houston want to hedge its bet. And Reid, foolishly he admitted later, had agreed to the non-guaranteed contract. Now, a crazy summer later, he was stuck. Only one way to guarantee his money now. On the court.

Led by Reid's spirited example and spurred by uncertainty, the backcourt competition was heated even from the opening bell, as Ralph Lewis had predicted. The first scrimmage featured a lot of rugged contact among the guards.

That was more notable because of the lack of contact up front. Harter had expected a tough duel between Rambis and Earl Cureton at power forward, and had hoped something would develop at center. But nothing of note materialized. Rambis and Cureton, befitting their journeyman stations and their reputations for good citizenship, hustled and paid attention. Mike Gibson and Brian Rowsom, two free agents trying to make the team, played hard but remained decorous, too. No fights broke out.

At center, it was even worse. Tim Kempton, the free-agent signed out of the summer camp, knocked some people around, but Dave Hoppen, the expansion pick, played a timid, finesse game. And free agents Jerome Henderson and Marty Nessley were practically docile.

Henderson, a career CBA man who had played for Harter once in a summer league, was not a powerful player anyway. There wasn't much muscle or meat of any kind stretched across his 6-11 frame, a shortcoming compounded in the early drills by his apparent disinterest. Henderson loafed through sprints and almost never asserted himself. Nessley, a huge man two inches over seven feet and at least 270 pounds, was different. He tried, as befit someone coming out of Mike Krzyzewski's Spartan program at Duke, but he shied away from the kind of teeth-rattling collisions that might have earned him a long look from a team so low on sheer bulk.

That is a highly valued commodity in the NBA, regardless of the accompanying skills, and the possession of such mass had allowed Nessley to play a year in the NBA. Despite a college career in which he achieved near-mascot status because of his inept play, Nessley had hung on for most of the 1987-88 season with the LA Clippers, filling the number-three center role that Kempton had manned the year before. After being waived in March, he was picked up by Sacramento, which carried him the rest of the year. The Kings let him go one day after the end of the regular season.

Oddly enough, Nessley's NBA experience had left him somewhat complacent. He sought out the Hornets because they seemed a good match for his skills, such as they were. "They don't have much bulk or anyone who can block shots," Nessley said. "I've got bulk, and I can block shots." Ergo, he was just what the Hornets needed. He told his training camp teammates as much. Having seen Nessley play, they were somewhat doubtful. Whether Nessley himself believed this is hard to say. Certainly he was somewhat less confident when, five days after practice started, the Hornets made him the first cut in team history.

The team suffered a more significant loss several days before Nessley departed, when Curry broke a delicate bone in his left wrist. The injury was flukish. In a halfcourt drill, Curry jumped to make a pass, was knocked off balance by a moving defender, and fell. He tried to brace his fall with his left hand, but something gave as he did. The injury was iced and Curry left the morning practice feeling okay. The swelling wasn't too bad. He didn't think it was serious. But it was. X-rays revealed a crack in the navicular, a tiny, fragile bone in the wrist. A similar injury had wrecked Bob Horner's baseball career and had led Atlanta fans and management to think of him as a malingerer because it took him so long to return. In truth, it was just a slow-healing injury. Curry would be out for eight to 10 weeks at best. "I can't believe this has happened," said Curry of the worst break in his slow-developing career.

The injury caused the first shuffling of personnel. Harter had begun camp with a "coincidental" lineup of Curry, Green, Tripucka, Hoppen and Rambis working together in team drills. Ralph Lewis, the ex-Piston benchwarmer, now moved into the lineup in Curry's place. The injury also caused some shuffling in the Chapman negotiations. ProServ, which heard about the X-ray results almost before the Hornets did (Bogues, another ProServ client, relayed the results), figured this improved Chapman's position. He was now the number-one off guard in their eyes. The Hornets differed. "They think it (Curry's injury) is a factor," Scheer said. "I do not. We're not going to make a long-term business decision based on one, 12-week injury."

Charlotte took a breather from its first week of practice for an intrasquad scrimmage at Duke University. It was a ragged affair, as such games tend to be. A lot of the shorter players played well. Most of the taller ones did not. That was to be a standard refrain during the season, but this game really didn't say much about the team. The real exhibition season began the following weekend as part of a Friday night doubleheader in New York.

Before that game, Chapman signed. Falk returned from the West Coast, having signed three players over the weekend, and talks resumed on Monday afternoon. The discussions went on for four hours before a break for dinner. That night, beginning around 9:30, the talks resumed at owner George Shinn's home.

That was Shinn's first direct involvement, and both sides credited him with breaking the deadlock. Although he had a vested interest, Shinn acted almost like an arbitrator and managed to cut through some of the smoke and get right to the fire. That was something Scheer and Falk were, at this point, unable to do. "George allowed us to escape with our egos intact," Scheer said.

Shinn also suggested the unique strategy of putting the meat itself onto the table. Chapman and his father, Wayne, who were in town because of the increased gravity of the negotiations, were summoned to the Shinn mansion around 10:30. They stayed for about two hours. Shinn met privately with Chapman for part of that time, a face-to-face that Shinn says led him to up the ante once again. That, in turn, gave Falk some room to maneuver without losing face, and that led to a contract.

"We weren't that far apart, less than 10 percent, really," said the ever-smooth Falk. "But that last 10 is always the hardest. George met with Rex, which we thought was good because it allowed the positives (in Chapman) other than basketball to come out. I think when George saw some more of the intangibles, he felt justified to go up. And when we saw that flexibility, we decided maybe we could come down."

After meeting with Shinn, Rex hung around a while longer, as more details were hammered out. It was an enlightening experience. "They kept right on talking like I wasn't even there," he said.

The Chapmans went home a little after midnight. The rest stayed until about 2:30. Incredibly, they resumed talking at the Hornets' offices again about 11 a.m., accompanied by an army of mini-cams and sports anchormen who filled up the tiny lobby. The talks finally broke up around 6:30 that evening, and at 7:15 p.m. Scheer announced, appropriately enough in the lobby of a bank building, that an agreement had been reached. Chapman, who had just turned 21, would receive more than $650,000 a year for the next four years. He was the 19th highest-paid guard in the NBA.

Chapman went to his first practice the Wednesday before Charlotte's exhibition opener in New York and immediately demonstrated his good and bad sides. He was dazzling as a shooter. But in the practice-ending scrimmage, he fumbled away a pass on a possession that could have given his team a victory, then got beat for the game winner at the other end. Not because of any that, Harter decided that he'd probably hold Chapman out of the exhibition opener. "Maybe if we needed a three (point shot) to tie it at the end or something, some special situation like that, I might put him in," Harter said. "But I doubt it. It's just not fair, after only two practices."

Chapman's first-day practice was the last for three other would-be Hornets. While the media swarm surrounded Chapman after his first workout, Harter quietly spoke to Byrnes, Gibson and Kenny Fields, telling them thanks, but no thanks. It was no great surprise. Byrnes and Fields were older players, without guaranteed money, trying to break in at a position that was heavily stocked. Gibson, a 6-10 player from Spartanburg, S.C., had a better chance because of his size. He had played a year with Washington when it had the "Bruise Brothers" – Rick Mahorn and Jeff Ruland – and had some experience. But he was older than Rowsom, his chief competition, and no longer as big. Once, because he thought playing for the beefy Bullets demanded it, he had pumped himself up to nearly 250 pounds, well above his collegiate playing weight. But after several bloated years in Washington, the CBA and Europe, he realized he couldn't play like that. He'd lost most of the acquired mass through a self-imposed diet of bologna sandwiches and water.

Now, back to his old weight of 210 pounds, he could run again. He was fast for someone 6-10. But, as the Hornets' coaches noted, he was not much else. He couldn't shoot well enough to be small forward and he couldn't bang inside well enough to play there. And he was 28. So, goodbye.

Charlotte took 15 players, including Chapman, to New York for its first game, plus a planeload of fans. Harter was going to play as any normal team would. He planned to start by platooning two five-man units, then he would add the other guys as the game progressed. No one would play a lot. But it was obvious that this wasn't just another game. The Hornets entered the exhibition season an unknown, even to themselves.

"If this were a normal team, the first exhibition game, the whole exhibition season, would be no big deal," said Reid. "You'd just go out and play your minutes and not worry about it. But this is not a normal team. We're all kind of wondering what it's going to be like."

Even in the meaningless opener, Harter hoped the team would begin to lay a foundation for the season ahead. He hoped the team would hustle. He hoped it wouldn't quit. "We've got to learn to scrap and scrape all the time," he said. "We might as well begin now."

It did not go very well. The New Jersey Nets, hardly an NBA power, jumped on Charlotte early. Tripucka had trouble defending against Roy Hinson and Walter Berry, New Jersey's tall small forwards, and the team's defense was not, as yet, coordinated enough to offer much help. Rambis turned an ankle early in the game and never returned, and that helped an already larger Nets' team maul the Hornets on the boards. Then at halftime, with his team down by eight, Harter walked into the locker room and found most of his players naked, or nearly so, from the waist down. This was not standard procedure and he wondered what was happening. Were they so discouraged by the first half that they were quitting and going home?

No, the problem, as it turned out, was more serious than that. No one had remembered to wash the players' brand-new athletic supporters before the game, and the combination of sweat and chemically treated nylon had created some major itches in some areas of major importance. The players busily sought whatever relief they could find – powder, vaseline – while Harter talked.

The Hornets' uniforms in general were a problem on this night. The unorthodox togs, designed by North Carolina sportswear designer Alexander Julian, were either ugly or innovative, depending upon the point of view. They had pin-stripped jerseys with pleated pants and shooting jackets with wide, alternating stripes of purple and teal. The shooting jackets were tapered, which was fine, except the tapering made them fit tighter and restricted arm motion, something many players find essential to shooting. The pleated pants sounded like a neat idea, but the execution was faulty. The unusual material made the uniforms hotter than other NBA suits, and in the larger sizes, the pants legs flared outward and upward to an alarming degree. The Hornets' bigger players, especially Kempton, looked as if they were mincing about in tennis skirts.

The problem was corrected by having each suit altered after the first two exhibition games, and by mid-season no one was talking about Charlotte's funny uniforms any more. But at the start, the Hornets' uniforms made a real impression.

Charlotte's first game was not without its redeeming qualities.

Hornets Never Lie

Tripucka displayed his scoring skills, piling up 23 points in not many minutes. Kempton grabbed eight rebounds. Holton and Reid were effective on the second team. But all in all, the 21-point defeat (118-97) was not particularly heartening. Perhaps the most dejected was Lewis, who had gotten to start. Midway through the rather ugly game, he had taken a hit on his left thigh and had to miss the rest of the rout. Worse still, hours after the injury, his thigh still throbbed. It could be serious, and one thing a guard on this team didn't need to be was hurt.

Two nights later, Charlotte played its second exhibition game in Columbia, S.C., part of Scheer's regional showcase plan, and a funny thing happened. The Hornets beat the Knicks 126-113. It was exhilarating for the Hornets, depressing for the Knicks. New York starter Charles Oakley said, after becoming an unwanted part of Hornet history, "You don't want to lose to no expansion team when you're playing for fun, when it's an exhibition game, or any other time."

The mitigating circumstances were numerous. Pat Ewing, New York's shot-blocking star, sat out the game with a sore knee, and the Knicks' vaunted press was not exactly in mid-season form. The Hornets, led by Tyrone Bogues, tore through it for piles of easy baskets. Kempton, who started at center, was a major beneficiary. He sprinted downcourt for easy baskets against the press and finished with 20 points.

But Charlotte played well, too. They passed the ball well, rebounded effectively despite the absence of both Cureton, who pulled a hamstring in the first quarter, and Rambis, who didn't dress, and shot 55 percent from the floor. Reid, who had 18 points, said, "We were pretty good out there tonight. I'd think even the Knicks would admit that."

Rowsom, filling in for Cureton, scored 11 points and had seven rebounds, a performance that opened the door to his making the opening night roster. Chapman, in his first game, hit his first three shots and scored 13 points in 13 minutes. He felt pretty good about that.

But Harter was less impressed. "Shooters are shooters," he said. "I think you could wake Rex up at 4 a.m. and he'd make his first two." Later in the year, later in the exhibition season, Harter may have been tempted to try that theory out. Then, making two straight would have represented a great improvement.

But for now it was not a problem. Nothing was. The victory over the Knicks lifted Hornet spirits to such a height that at practice the next day Harter even talked with some enthusiasm about the team's situation at center. But not that much enthusiasm. Hoppen was still too timid, Kempton still too small. Henderson wasn't any help. Harter cut him at the end of the week, just before two exhibition games against Chicago that pointed up Charlotte's problems in the middle.

The Bulls of Michael Jordan are not an overwhelming team in terms of size, but on back-to-back nights they were more than Charlotte could handle. In game one, played in Jordan's old college haunts in Chapel Hill, the Hornets' big men couldn't shoot. The centers and power forwards were a combined eight for 42. Kempton, a starter again, was especially noteworthy. He missed three layups, including one he fired off the glass and to the other side of the court without hitting the rim. He failed to score. Rambis, back in action, was three for 11 from the floor and moderately angry in the locker room. "There's no excuse for missing those easy shots," he said. "We're doing the right things and then missing inside, and it got away from us."

Despite the interior follies, Charlotte hung in the game until seven-footer Brad Sellars scored 16 points in less than four minutes in the third quarter to help the Bulls pull away. The final was 115-99. Tyrone Bogues deserved credit for keeping the game so close for so long and for making sure it never got any worse than it did. For the second straight game he scored 15 points and had eight assists. "Thank goodness for his creativity," said Harter. "We don't have many options in the halfcourt offense, and if he didn't give us some things, sometimes we might lose by 50."

For Bogues those were sweet words, although he knew they were essentially meaningless. Coaches, as he saw it, could appreciate what he sometimes did without actually appreciating him. He might hold a team in a game, or lead it to victory, but he would still be the little guy who was a liability most of the time in their eyes. That didn't seem fair, but Bogues realized that was the game he was in. Nothing he could do but play as hard as he could, the way he always did. "That's just the way I am," he said. "Pickup game or NBA playoffs, up 100 or down 100, I'm not going to let up. At my size, you just can't."

The next night, after a four-hour bus ride to Richmond, Va., Charlotte was even worse in the middle, and neither Bogues nor anyone else was able to hold the line. The Bulls raced to a 29-11 lead after the first quarter and were ahead 60-42 at the half. Poor shooting hurt the Hornets, but it was their inability to stop anyone inside that sealed the verdict. Bill Cartwright, the center Chicago had acquired a few months earlier from the Knicks, scored 12 in the first quarter and drew three fouls from Hoppen. In the second quarter, rookie Wil

Perdue scored eight and Jack Haley, a 6-10 free agent, powered his way past several Charlotte defenders for 10 points.

The latter performance was still on Harter's mind at practice a few days later. While working on defense, he told the team, "We'll double team when we have to, guys, but I really think we ought to be able to handle Jack Haley one-on-one. Okay?"

Roster positions were just about established by this point, as indeed they had been when camp began. Larry Spriggs, a muscular 6-7 forward who had earned championship rings with the Lakers, was still around, but was destined to go. Spriggs had played well most of the preseason, but not that well. And, it was getting to be an old refrain for the free agents trying to make the team, he wasn't a young player anymore. He was 29, and the skills that had once allowed him to press Jamaal Wilkes for playing time in LA were greatly diminished. Rambis, his former teammate, noted that in particular Spriggs could not or did not jump as he once did. When he arrived in the NBA, out of tiny Howard University, he was a great leaper, a dunker extraordinaire. With the Hornets, his dunks, even in practice, were few and far between. He was considerably more ponderous.

Spriggs thought he had a chance, though. He could help Charlotte at two positions (both forwards), and he'd been in the big-time before. That haunted him a little bit because, he felt, it really wasn't his fault that he wasn't there anymore. After a good season in LA in 1985-86, he had set about negotiating a new contract. Because he played well for two straight years, he and his agent, Fred Slaughter, thought he had some leverage. When the Lakers wouldn't budge on their offer, Slaughter recommended that his client stay out of training camp. Spriggs did and the Lakers, apparently not too distraught at his absence, didn't call again. Neither did anybody else, so Spriggs wound up playing the next two seasons in Spain. Now he was back, but two prime years had been cut out of his NBA career, and he wasn't good enough to make it in the league unless he was in his prime or very near it. Still, Spriggs thought there was a chance. The league had expanded. Twenty-four more players had to make a team this year.

After Spriggs, the roster figuring was a little more complicated. Tolbert, the rookie forward, hadn't done much, but his contract was guaranteed for a year, and the jury, Scheer at least, was still out on him. The team needed to lose a guard, but that battle was relatively even. Lewis, who hadn't practiced since the exhibition game in New York, was behind everyone else. But it wouldn't be fair, and perhaps not prudent, to cut him without seeing more. Reid was a possibility, but only for economic reasons. If they cut him, the Hornets didn't have to pay. The same was true of Rowsom, but Harter, who had coached him the year before in Indiana, liked him a lot. And not without reason. Alone among Charlotte's big men, he seemed to possess untapped potential. He was a hope for the future, and he probably would stay.

Harter had gone to some length to get him, too, coaxing him away from Dallas' camp, which he had already agreed to attend. That move didn't please the Mavericks, and it almost didn't happen. With Rowsom on the fence just as camp was to open, the task of confirming his appearance in Charlotte somehow fell to Bill Branch, an administrative assistant who helped Littles. As Harter walked into his office after the team's first practice, he overheard Branch leaving a message for Rowsom with Rowsom's roommate. Knowing how uncertain that was, Harter leaped into action. He made sure Branch contacted Rowsom in person that day. Had he walked into the office a few minutes later, he would never have known, and Rowsom might well have been a Maverick.

With Rowsom likely to stick, a guard was still the most likely man out, but who? The uncertainty heightened team tensions heading into the last weekend of exhibition games.

Charlotte had three straight games on this weekend. The Hornets opened with Dallas in Charlotte, then played Cleveland in back-to-back games in Winston-Salem and Fayetteville. It was a tough slate. Dallas had reached the Western Conference finals the year before, and Cleveland, unbeaten in the exhibition season, was a projected contender in the East. With the regular season just a week away, Harter's player rotation would be the first tangible signal as to where they stood. One who would not find out was forward Earl Cureton. The hamstring pull he had aggravated early in the exhibition win against the Knicks was slow to heal. Indeed, it seemed to have regressed. He wouldn't play any the last weekend of exhibition season and might not be ready for beginning of real play.

That was a disappointment to Harter and the Hornets who had hoped Cureton would be a major boost to their inside game. A journeyman, he had shown himself a capable rebounder and defender during eight previous seasons in the league, but he hadn't been even a shell of his former self at Charlotte's preseason camp. "He certainly hasn't been the Earl Cureton of old," said Harter just before the Dallas game. "I really thought he'd help us, but his preseason has been a real downer."

Even without Cureton, Charlotte beat the Mavericks. Bogues played well again (10 assists). Holton continued his solid preseason play, and the centers just went crazy. Hoppen and Kempton combined to make 12 of 14 from the floor and score 35 points. Hoppen, finishing fast breaks and scoring in the lane, had 19 points himself. "It's always a challenge for me to play well," Hoppen said. "But I can play. I deserve to play here."

Like the victory over the Knicks, the 104-93 triumph against Dallas carried an asterisk or two. John MacLeod, the Mavericks' coach, played it less like a regular-season game than Harter did. Star forward Mark Aguirre burned Charlotte for 18 points in the last seven and a half minutes of the third quarter, but he played only a minute of the fourth. And Rolando Blackman, another starter, didn't play at all in the final period.

"You could say that made the difference," Blackman said. "But you could say a lot of things. The bottom line is, the team they had on the floor in the fourth quarter beat the team we had."

Similarly, the Hornets and their fans weren't inclined to quibble over details, such as whether they could ever have stopped Aguirre if he had stayed in the game. It was, as all Hornet victories would be this season, one to savor. A crowd of just under 14,000 – there wouldn't be that many empty seats for a Hornets game in the coliseum the rest of the year combined – whooped it up in the closing minutes. After the game, owner Shinn roamed the halls, telling everyone he saw, "How 'bout them Bugs?"

Cleveland sucked up some of that euphoria the next two nights. The young and talented Cavaliers whipped Charlotte soundly, pulling away in the third quarter both nights. Holton and Kempton continued to play well for Charlotte, but rookie Chapman looked severely overmatched against Cleveland's Ron Harper, a third-year player with All-Star possibilities. Harper's ability to beat Chapman at will in the third period just about decided the Winston-Salem game by itself. And in the two games, Chapman was a miserable 5 for 25 from the floor. That made him 12 for 47 (28 percent) since his successful (six for 11) spree in his pro debut against the Knicks. Observed Harter, "He is not shooting very well."

Worse news than Chapman's slump was an ankle injury suffered by Rambis in the game played at Fayetteville. Fighting for a loose ball late in the third period, Rambis jumped, then stumbled as he came down and re-injured the ankle he hurt two weeks before in New York. Harter was depressed. As Rambis hobbled out of the ramshackle Cumberland County Auditorium, he did not look like a man who'd be able to play basketball four days later. That was bad news. Rambis was a leader – he was elected co-captain along with Reid – and with Cureton out, he was Charlotte's only guaranteed inside force.

But much to Harter's surprise, when the team practiced Tuesday in Charlotte, less than 12 hours after the injury, Rambis participated in part of the drills. "I'm unbreakable," Rambis said.

"He's amazing," said Harter. "I think if we had a playoff game tonight, he'd play, which is hard to believe after last night. He's one tough guy." Harter beamed at that. Tough guys are hard to find.

On the same day, a Tuesday, the team cleaned up its roster for the big franchise debut on Friday. An unhappy Spriggs was cut "I didn't get much of a chance," he said – and Lewis was placed on the injured list. Lewis' thigh bruise had turned out to be a more serious injury than first thought. But, it was also convenient. With Lewis injured, the Hornets could at least postpone a contract-eating decision. And who knows? While they waited someone else might get hurt.

The exhibition season had not shown Harter many things he didn't know before it started. Tripucka had demonstrated that his two-year exile in Utah hadn't affected him much. Harter, who had pressed for the deal that had made Kelly a Hornet, was relieved by that. Rickey Green, the other ex-Jazz on the roster, had looked, to Harter at least, a little worn. Though Green had retained the starting role throughout camp, the point guard job was essentially up in the air.

Center was just as bad as Harter had thought it would be. Kempton had a few encouraging moments, but he was too small to play the pivot in the NBA, and he was inconsistent. Hoppen had played one good game, but was probably a little worse than what Harter had hoped. Cureton was a mystery, but Rambis was as good or better than advertised. Chapman looked like a boy playing with men, which was true and expected. Curry's injury had been a blow, but Reid's condition and play had softened that.

A major, but not-unexpected plus, seemed to be the team's chemistry. The Hornets had shied away from problems, in part because of Shinn's community-service decrees, but also because they were smart enough not to get bad players who were bad people, too. Losing a bunch of games would be pain enough. But how many would they lose – or win? The exhibition season had not really answered that, and heading into the opener the team's fortunes were a mystery.

Harter had a number in his head, he said, between 10 and 20 wins. "I know what my number is. I just hope I'm not right."

Littles just wanted to win 10. "That way at least we won't be the worst team ever," he said. Philadelphia in 1972-73 won just nine games.

Hornets Never Lie

Tripucka said, "I have no idea what will happen. I think we could win between 10 and 40 games, but I'm not predicting either one. If I say 40, then everyone will think I'm crazy. If I say 10 or 12 then we might start believing that, and that's all we would win. So I'm not predicting anything. You'll just have to wait and see."

The wait wasn't long. And what was seen early made many folks wonder if the predictions that had been made weren't very wrong.

Take the Hornets and Points

"Losing this game, to that team, would have been like losing four in a row."

– Akeem Olajuwon after Houston came from behind to beat the Hornets.

Dick Harter began his first season as an NBA coach at age 57, but he was not old. Not even close.

For one thing, he had a wife, his second, who was in in her early 30s and could pass for a college cheerleader, which she once was, and who made Harter something of a legend amongst his colleagues. When Harter first came to the NBA, in Detroit under Chuck Daly, a writer covering the Pistons kept noticing him in the company of this very pretty, very young, blonde. Could it be his wife? He finally asked Daly for confirmation. "Yep, it's his wife," Daly said, "which is why Dick Harter will always be my hero."

Slowed perhaps by young love, Harter's personal clock ticked away at roughly half speed. No matter what everyone else's calendar might say, Harter knew retirement and all that old stuff wasn't just around the corner. As far as he was concerned, it wasn't even on the same block.

In this, his 57th year, Harter still worried about his tan and his waistline, and could still carouse well enough to keep up, though not, his friends say, quite as well as he once did. He was very young back then. Now he's just sort of young, middle aged perhaps, but no more. Thoughts to the contrary just don't enter his head.

In a casual conversation once during the Hornets' first season, a reporter tried to kid Harter by telling him that he'd understand a particular feeling when he got old. Harter nodded in agreement, missing the insinuation entirely. "Yeah," he said, "you're probably right."

Of course, Harter couldn't afford to think differently. Beginning a new career when others his age were thinking of ways to end theirs, he had no choice but to imagine he had many, many years left. Or to put it another way, only someone who thought that way would have done what Dick Harter did. And now, with Charlotte, he had the chance to prove he was right.

Ironically, though not altogether accidentally, Harter's first team was filled with players at similar stages in their careers. The Tripucka and Reid trades, the signing of free agents Cureton and Rambis, the acquisition of Rickey Green in the expansion draft, all of these moves had served to age the Hornets' first roster. On opening night, the Hornets averaged 26-and-a-half years old. That was slightly above the NBA median, and a source of some ridicule around the league. Even before the season began, Harter quickly tired of answering the question, "What's a new team doing with all these old guys?"

"What are they talking about?" Harter said one day. "What old guys?"

Indeed, most of them weren't even in their 30s yet. But athletic ages are different, sort of like dog years. You have to multiply them by something. The Hornets' veterans, if not on their last legs, were at least on their next-to-last legs. They were older guys whose stars had once risen but were now in descent. Expansion and the Hornets represented a chance to stay in the NBA sky a little longer – and to show those who had cast them out that maybe they were just a little wrong. They could prove that letting them go, whether by not protecting them in the expansion draft or simply letting them become free agents, was a mistake. Getting a payback was a recurring theme in this season. I told you so, a common refrain.

Said Houston castoff Robert Reid just before the season began, "I think there are a lot of us here who have something to prove."

The proving began amid pomp and ceremony that included two governors, a symphony orchestra and several thousand dollars worth of rented tuxedos. It was the night of November 4, 1988, when the Charlotte Hornets finally played their first, real NBA game. It was George Shinn Day in Charlotte, and much of the hoopla before the opener was devoted to honoring the man who brought Charlotte its franchise. Fans watched a video, which touched on the highlight's of Shinn's life and his exertions in bringing the team to town. They heard various dignitaries make various speeches. They saw Mark Stegall, who had bought the first season ticket, make an honorary first toss at the center jump circle. It went on and on, so long, in fact that the visiting Cleveland Cavaliers returned to the locker room, lest they stiffen up while listening to the various proclamations. As befitted the night's unspoken theme, the Cavs stayed too long and missed their introductions. When public-address announcer John

Edwards said, "And now, for the visiting Cleveland Cavaliers ...", there were no Cavaliers in sight.

All of this was distracting, but it could be excused. This was a night to remember, and months later many of the players still recalled it as their fondest memory of the first season. Reminiscing in April, Earl Cureton said, "You just don't get to be part of the first something very often. It was a big night. No matter what happened."

Ah, yes. What happened. While it was a night to remember in many respects, it was a night the Hornets would like to forget on the court. The Cavaliers, who had roughed them up in two exhibition games, savaged the fledgling Hornets as they leaped from their nest. The final score was 133-93, and it was over before the amazing Hugo appeared out of a cloud of smoke at halftime. A devastating second quarter, in which Cleveland ripped the Hornets 40-16, decided the issue. A rash of Charlotte turnovers, produced in part by Cleveland's aggressive defense, fueled the Cavs' depressingly quick breakaway. The Hornets went from a few ahead to 24 down so fast, in fact, that owner George Shinn missed the carnage. He left the building after the first quarter, the score was tied at 26-26, to have photos made and meet dignitaries. When he returned a few minutes later, it was 64-40 Cleveland. Shinn dashed over to Carl Scheer to get an explanation. "He told me about the Cleveland run," Shinn said. "And I told myself right then, `George, you've gotta realize you have a bunch of young kids on your basketball team. Just brace yourself.'"

The Cavs subs padded the margin at a slower pace in the second half. The Hornets, numbed by the quickness of their demise, were powerless to stop the onslaught. When it was finally over, they stumbled into their locker room bearing a look that resembled shell shock.

Coach Dick Harter said, in classic understatement, "This wasn't a very enjoyable way to start the season. I can't think of anything good to say."

Groping for a bright spot, veteran Rickey Green observed, "I guess the best thing I can say is it's not likely to get much worse than this."

Green was right. The Hornets would not lose by a wider margin all season.

The effect of all of this on the sellout crowd of 23,300 was strange, to say the least. Curiosity and the excitement of something new was more important, on this night, than any partisan feelings of disgust. They had not yet learned to boo or to rag Dave Hoppen, so no matter what happened, they cheered. They cheered after the first quarter, and rightly so, and they cheered at the half, when public-address announcer John Edwards may have said, "Ladies and gentleman, how about the first quarter!" The exhortation is a modest, first-night legend. Several observers on hand say that's what they heard, but Edwards, a cautious man not given to offending management, says he didn't. Well, it would have been a good line.

There is no dispute as to what happened at the end of the game. As the Hornets limped off the court – literally at least in the case of point guard Green who pulled a hamstring in the first quarter – the crowd, about two thirds of which had stuck out the rout, rose to their feet and delivered a standing ovation. For what was hard to decipher. A job well done? A nice try? Just for being there?

"I suppose," said co-captain Kurt Rambis, "they think we're going to get better."

• • • • •

One of the nice things about the relentless NBA schedule is that there isn't time to brood about depressing turns of event. Less than 12 hours after getting mashed by Cleveland, Charlotte was winging to Detroit for its first road game of the year. Much to Harter's relief, the outcome, even though it was another loss, was within the bounds of competitiveness. The Pistons won the first game ever played in their new building, The Palace at Auburn Hills, 94-85. Charlotte did not have a great chance to win even though Detroit was, in the words of sixth man Dennis Rodman, "in a very nonchalant mode for this one." Having pulled to within 50-46 early in the third quarter, the Hornets watched helplessly as the Eastern Conference champs tightened their famous defense. With Pistons hounding them every step of the way, the Hornets missed 13 of their next 14 shots and fell behind 60-48, then 71-54. A late Charlotte rally made it look better in the record book, and the team flew home in a better mood than in which it had left.

Though the Cleveland debacle was somewhat hard to take, Charlotte was essentially on track after two games. The Hornets did not figure to beat the Cavs or the Pistons, two of the league's strongest teams, in their first year. Just where the victories would come was hard to predict. Since the Hornets probably would not be favored, except when they played co-expansionist Miami, the best chances figured to come at home against teams from the NBA's lower echelon. No team fit that description better than the LA Clippers, Charlotte's opponent for an election night game on November 8. At the start of the 1988-89 season, this ill-managed, unfortunate franchise had not had a winning season in 10 years, hadn't been to the playoffs in 15. And in the last two seasons, they had become almost synonymous with NBA futility, winning only 29 games over the two years.

For that reason, it had not boded well for the Hornets when they opened training camp with four ex-Clippers on the roster. But Harter had the good sense to cut two, Marty Nessley and Kenny Fields. The remaining ex-Clips, Tim Kempton and Earl Cureton, had played together on the famous 1986-87 team that won just 12 games. "Not a fun year," Kempton recalled as the Clippers' game drew near. "You lost a lot, and nobody got along very well."

The current Clippers were reckoned to be a cut or two above that. The upside of having terrible records is that you get better draft picks. With the help of some trades, the Clippers had corralled six first-round draft picks in the past two years. Only five would come to Charlotte. Danny Manning, the number-one pick in the 1988 draft, had yet to sign a contract and was not with the team. But Charles Smith, picked third overall was there along with Gary Grant, another rookie. Ken Norman, Joe Wolf and Reggie Williams, rookies in 1987, were available, as was Benoit Benjamin, the erratic, but hugely talented center Carl Scheer had drafted for the team in 1985. It was, as veteran coach Gene Shue noted, the kind of team you'd love to coach for about five years. It was also, as he prophetically noted, the kind of team he probably wouldn't get to coach for five years.

It was also, for the time being, not very good. The players were so new and their talents were not that complementary. There were too many potential stars on the team, not enough role players. The Hornets did not exactly chalk this one up as an automatic "W," but because of the Clippers' odd mix and their inexperience, they figured at least to have a shot. So November 8 loomed as a big day in Hornet history. Perhaps the day they would win their first game.

It turned out to be an even bigger day than imagined. The Hornets did indeed gain the first, regular-season victory, but before that happened, the team and town were stunned by the news that owner Shinn had suffered a stroke. It happened sometime after lunch, while Shinn was talking to a group of area radio executives. He began rambling towards the end of his speech and seemed disoriented to observers but continued his schedule, attending a meeting at his offices in downtown Charlotte. Shinn complained that he didn't feel well after the meeting and went to his office to rest. A few hours later, around 3 p.m., he hadn't gotten any better, so Spencer Stolpen, the legal counsel for Shinn and Associates, drove him to Charlotte's Presbyterian Hospital. Shinn walked into the Emergency Room but was soon hospitalized. Dr. Craig Van Der Veer examined Shinn and discovered the stroke, which he termed mild. It was caused when a blood vessel burst in Shinn's brain, just above the right eye. For a stroke victim, the news was good. There was no paralysis and no medication needed. Shinn's life was not in immediate danger, but he would need months to recover. The illness put a cloud of uncertainty over the game, though, and indeed, the season itself. Would Shinn be incapacitated? And if so, for how long? Who would run the show in his absence?

Perhaps already pondering these questions, Carl Scheer was tense prior to the game with the Clippers. It was a dark time. But his mood was brightened somewhat as people continued to file into the coliseum. With the modest on-court start to the season combining with the low appeal of the Clippers and the lure of watching the election results at home on TV, Scheer was expecting the worst. The season-ticket sales, now over the 15,000 mark, guaranteed a decent financial gate. But Scheer figured there would be a lot of no-shows and doubted that the true crowd would even match the season-ticket numbers. Yet they kept coming, almost 19,000 in all. It would be the smallest home crowd of the season, but ironically it was the comparatively puny turnout that first led Scheer to contemplate the box-office bonanza that eventually appeared. Thinking about the spectator landslide later, Scheer said, "That game on election night was the first time I thought we might have something special here. It was supposed to be a wash, and 18,000-some showed up."

Those lucky fans saw the Hornets' historic first victory, a triumph that was a tribute to teamwork and a lack thereof. Led by the veteran triumvirate of Rambis, Robert Reid and Kelly Tripucka, the Hornets led almost all the way against the fractious, unfocused opponent. Rambis collected 14 rebounds, the first of many big board nights for him, and Reid grabbed nine as the Hornets beat what should have been a pretty good rebounding team 55-48 on the boards. Tripucka scored 24 points, serving as the linchpin for a Charlotte attack that rolled up 117 points.

Two improbable baskets by rookie Rex Chapman at the end of the third quarter – an off-balance 20 footer followed by a high-arcing shot from the right baseline – gave the Hornets an 11-point lead entering the last 12 minutes. LA somehow managed to rally within six with less than three minutes to play, but Charlotte's veterans, inserted by Harter for just this effect, kept their heads and put this one away. Reid, in his 11th pro season, made one especially clever play. With the score 105-99, he grabbed a rebound away from LA's Grant Gondrezick, and then, noticing that Gondrezick was off balance, leaned against him so that the Clipper player had to fall on him.

Gondrezick tottered briefly, trying not to hit Reid, but finally couldn't avoid him. He was called for a foul, sending Reid to the line and saving the Hornets the trouble of having to run a successful play to score more points. Reid scored seven of his 18 points in the last two minutes.

The game left Harter and his team in a good mood. They had played well together. "Probably the best thing," Harter said, "was that we had so many guys contribute." And of course they had won.

"It's a good feeling," said Reid, "just to get that monkey off our backs before it starts getting heavy."

The good feeling continued on a weekend road trip. In Washington on Friday, Reid led the Hornets to a quick start that produced a 22-11 lead in the first quarter. Washington, another team on Charlotte's list of probable victories, recovered and went ahead at the half. But it was still tight entering the fourth quarter. Washington's shooters, most notably Bernard King and rookie Ledell Eackles, warmed and the Hornets struggled to keep up. A steal and two free throws by Tyrone Bogues, who extracted a measure of revenge this night against his former teammates, pulled Charlotte to within three with 2:19 left. After a Washington miss, the Hornets had a chance to pull within one. But Reid missed a wide-open 15-footer with 1:43 to play. "That's the kind I'm paid to make," he said. And at the other end, Bullet rookie Harvey Grant swished one from 18 feet out, more or less the limit of his range. Washington held on for the victory.

The next night, in Atlanta, Charlotte's chance wasn't as good. The Hawks' arsenal of All-Stars past and present was more than the Hornets could hope to handle on all but the most extraordinary nights. But, as had been the case in Detroit, Charlotte didn't draw Atlanta's best effort, and the Hornets managed to stay in the game. Holton, who had taken over as the starting point since Green went down, played his best game of the year, hitting seven of 10 from the field for 17 points. Hoppen, a one-time Hawks' draft pick, did a little damage inside, and Brian Rowsom battled his way to 14 points and seven rebounds. Down by 14 after one quarter, the Hornets pulled to within six after three quarters and cut the lead to 96-93 90 seconds into the fourth quarter when Tripucka hit a three-pointer from the corner. If that gave the Hornets a glimmer of hope the Hawks quickly blacked it out. Like a formula racer dueling a pickup, they shifted into another gear and sped away to a 132-111 victory.

Chapman, who'd been at the front of the third-quarter rally, said, "I guess Atlanta played okay, but it looked like if we ever got ahead or close there was another level for them to go to. Not much to do about that."

Harter, whose college teams sometimes didn't surrender 132 points in a month, was not particularly thrilled about the Hawks' fourth-quarter getaway. Atlanta shot 64 percent in the decisive period and scored 40 points. "I'm sick of not being able to stop people already," Harter said. "Offensively, we're getting pretty close to what we can do, but defensively we're just not doing it."

Accepting such problems and the defeats they brought was not easy for Harter. He vacillated all season between a realistic evaluation of his personnel, which frustrated him, and his long-held belief that effort and toughness could carry the day, which frustrated him even more. Could the Hornets really stop a team like the Hawks when it mattered? Would the thick-legged Tripucka, who once gave up 50 points to Atlanta's Dominique Wilkins in a playoff game, suddenly rise up and throw the Human Highlight Film's shots back in his face? No, of course not. But what if they played as hard as they could, as smart as they could? On a particular night that might be good enough. They might win. So, even when it didn't seem likely, you had to try. Or, in Harter's case, you had to get someone else to try. "Not being able to do it is 90 percent of the problem," Harter said. "It's the other 10 percent I've got to worry about."

• • • • •

Five games into the season, Charlotte's long-standing roster problems still hadn't changed. There were still too many guards, even with Dell Curry out until Christmas. There were still too many players. Ralph Lewis, who had opened the season, more or less legitimately, on the injured list, was ready to play. And having served the mandatory five-game minimum on the IL, he was eligible. But activating Lewis meant someone else would have to go. And although Green and Cureton were both still hobbled by their hamstring pulls, neither was volunteering to go off active duty.

This was a fairly common NBA personnel dilemma, but it seemed to perplex the Hornets' braintrust. There were two players on the team without guaranteed contracts – Reid and Rowsom – who could be cut without financial loss. But Harter was against dropping either. The veteran Reid had been invaluable thus far, and Rowsom appeared as though he could become that way. Another option was to cut someone with a guaranteed contract. Tom Tolbert, the carefree rookie, seemed a likely choice. He hadn't shown much in the exhibition season or the opening days of the regular season – the coaches were sure he was a wash – and didn't seem inclined to push himself to greater heights. His money was guaranteed, he had a fast car and, most significantly, the company of a striking young woman who had accompanied him east from Arizona. It was like he had uncorked a genie who had granted him three wishes, one of which was not to be a great player, and now he was living them out. In any event, he was the least useful Hornet, especially when his girlfriend was taken out of the calculations. Scheer, who for unclear reasons was Tolbert's biggest booster in the front office, more or less agreed. "I think he may be able to play in this league, but maybe he never gets a chance," Scheer said.

He would get the chance for a little longer, however. For whatever reason – Shinn's absence, the paralysis of management by committee, the as-yet-undefined power structure of the front office – the Hornets couldn't pull the trigger. So they waited. The day before the sixth game of the season, Harter said, "We may just shuffle them around (on the injured list) for awhile."

That meant Lewis had to watch games while wearing a suit (though not necessarily with a white shirt) for a little while longer. That did not suit him very well. "I'm very frustrated. It's not easy to watch the others play," Lewis said before game six. "I'm ready to go now, but I don't know if I'll get the chance."

Harter, who liked Lewis' defensive skills and the fact that he was from a Big Five school (LaSalle), was non-committal about his interest in Lewis. "To be honest, we really haven't seen him that much. I have my opinions, but I'm really not sure," he said.

So, as New Jersey – another possible Hornet victim – came to town, Ralph Lewis wondered about his basketball career.

He did not have to wonder for long. Midway through the second quarter of the New Jersey game, Rowsom landed funny on his left foot and broke a bone in it. So much for cutting someone or eating a contract. Providence had made procrastination pay off.

Sort of. At least a decision didn't have to be made now.

It was hardly a cause of celebration, though. Lewis, another guard, would replace Rowsom, an inside player whom Harter characterized the night he was injured as, "Our MVP so far." It was an overstatement, but not a huge one.

"What am I going to do now?" Harter moaned. "Earl's hamstrings are killing him. Rambis can't get in shape where he can run more than five minutes at a time. We didn't have enough big guys as it was. Now we've got three or four big guys and a bunch of guards. That's not very good."

Worse still, the big guys on hand weren't all that big. Joe Barry Carroll, a well-traveled center who had come to rest with the woeful Nets, had just driven home that point. Carroll, a seven-footer with good offensive skills when he chose to display them, had looked like Abdul-Jabbar in his prime in the second half. Against a variety of smaller defenders he had made 10 of 13 from the field in the last 24 minutes and scored 21 points. That had helped New Jersey erase a six-point halftime deficit and pull away to a 106-99 victory. "Not much you can do when he gets on a roll," said Tim Kempton, one of the rolled-on Hornets.

Harter seethed at the idea that Carroll was unstopable. Everyone else could stop him. The Hornets needed to be tougher and the point guards, Tyrone Bogues in particular, taller. As much a problem as the centers' defense against Carroll was the inability of the guards, most notably the 5-3 Bogues, to harass the Net guards who were making the passes in to Carroll. With Bogues unlikely to grow much in the next few days, Harter went on the road to Texas in a bad mood.

The Hornets' two-game swing would take them first to Dallas, which in the NBA veterans' travel manual was a pretty good place to be. The city was clean and safe, with many fine restaurants, and, most importantly, seemed to have more than its share of beautiful women. Noted Kelly Tripucka, "You can walk through the Dallas airport, any hour of the day, and be amazed."

The sights were not confined to the airport, however. Just before the national anthem was sung this night at Reunion Arena, the ever-vigilant Ed Badger spotted a comely blonde in high heels and a light-green, almost teal, miniskirt walking down the aisle behind press row and the bench area. A nudge to the ribs of coaches Harter and Littles resulted in the Hornet staff conducting a neat about face as the music started.

The rest of the evening was less appealing, although for a half the Hornets did turn a few heads. They played Dallas, then thought to be a Western Conference contender, even for the first 24 minutes. Kempton, on the way to a 5-for-5 night that would boost his field-goal percentage to a league-leading 72 percent, led the charge. But in the third quarter the Hornets collapsed. They hit just 19 percent from the floor, and Dallas, taking advantage of the misses, ran to a 34-12 advantage in the quarter, easily enough to decide the outcome.

Harter was livid and had plenty of spleen to pass around. The whole team had quit on him. Rambis still wasn't in shape. Reid had hobbled about in the third quarter like an old man. And none of his shooters were shooting. "When you're paid to make shots you should make them," Harter said. "I don't know. I guess it's hard to keep playing so far above yourself. I know it is, but that's what we've got to do. That's all there is to it."

A man who took both winning and losing hard, Harter seemed

very near the bottom on this night. He knew his team was undermanned, but if it played well there was a chance. If the effort was there –and the toughness – he would figure something out. Kempton's surprising shooting touch in the early season, and the possibility of trading for another soft-shooting big man such as Portland's Richard Anderson, had led him to muse about creating a new position. "Maybe we'll invent the point center," Harter said whimsically before the Dallas game. "You know, sort of like Don Nelson's point forward. Get you some big guys who can shoot it from 15, 17 feet out, and build an offense around that. It could be pretty tough to defend."

In San Antonio the next day, an off day, Harter was in better spirits despite being in his least-favorite NBA city. Perhaps it was the opposition.

The Spurs, flying in from a road game at Denver, were off to as poor a start as Charlotte. Larry Brown, who had signed on as the coach for a salary three times greater than Harter's, was in misery. Sometimes that seems to be his perpetual state – he is one of the world's great pessimists – but this time he had reason. He couldn't get David Robinson, the center the team had drafted the spring before, out of the Navy. Mysterious headaches, which made him nauseous, dogged Brown, and his past was a constant haunt. Because of him, Kansas, where he'd coached the year before, was about to go on NCAA probation. Worst of all, the players he inherited in San Antonio either weren't very good players or weren't very good people. Or both. A few were injured. A few were sulking.

Charlotte, which would be a little more rested, looked to have a chance. San Antonio was not big inside and hence, couldn't wear Charlotte down as some teams did. And this was a cause game for Robert Reid, an air force brat who was raised in the city. Growing up, he'd sold concessions at Spurs' games when they were an ABA team. He went to college in San Antonio, too, at tiny St. Mary's. "The greatest gym in the free world," Reid said. "Had this funky floor with springs in it or something. Made everyone look like they could sky. The scouts came down here to see old Robert Reid and thought he was the next Dr. J." Reid smiled at the thought. His game had changed since then. He was older and smarter. But not, he conceded, as good a jumper. "My game used to be running and jumping. I liked that dunk. 'Here I come. Whoomph!'" Reid said. "Now I usually just lay it in. It's still two points." Not as much fun, though. He could use his old floor.

Charlotte's hopes dipped a bit on game day. Rambis, the starting power forward, came down with a stomach virus. Or maybe it was food poisoning. Whatever, team members were treated to a strategy session in Harter's hotel suite which featured the sounds of Rambis' discomfort emanating from the bathroom. "It was distracting," Tripucka said.

It was enough to knock Rambis out of the game. But it was not enough to kill Charlotte's chances. The Spurs were as bad as advertised, lackluster and unfocused. They let Hoppen dominate the boards for a brief-but-spectacular spell in the first half, let Tripucka roam about as he pleased, and found themselves down by nine at the half. Though the Hornets played fairly well, it was clearly not an impressive performance by the hometown boys and their big-time coach. They left the court to boos from a small-but-boisterous crowd in delightfully dingy HemisFair Arena. Even the public-address announcer, the most partisan partisan in most NBA cities, wasn't happy.

Narrating a halftime contest in which fans shot free throws in hopes of a winning a Thanksgiving turkey, he said, "They're shooting for turkeys out there. Or maybe it's the turkeys shooting. ... Or, maybe it's the Spurs who are the real turkeys."

The turkeys rallied late in the third quarter. Alvin Robertson, an All-Star guard earlier in his career, led the charge. Charlotte's Tim Kempton aided the cause when he fumbled the ball away on back-to-back possessions late in the period. San Antonio trailed by just four entering the fourth quarter.

Led by Tripucka and Earl Cureton, who played well while picking up most of Rambis' lost minutes, Charlotte clung to its lead. San Antonio pulled to within three at 100-97, but a steal by Tyrone Bogues that resulted in a Tripucka layup made it 105-99 with 1:43 left. That lead looked reasonably safe, but two Spur baskets, sandwiched around a Robert Reid miss, made it 105-103 with less than a minute to go.

For the first time all year, Charlotte faced crunch time, but there wasn't much debate about what to do. Harter pushed Tripucka's button, just as he knew he would all along.

"When we were talking about getting Kelly back in June I told George and Carl that there would be so many times we'd put it in his hands at the end of the game," Harter said. "There aren't many guys in the league like that, who you can just give it to them and say, `do something,' but he's one of them."

Tripucka wasn't prompt on this night, but eventually he delivered. Harter called his number, isolating him against Robertson on three straight possessions in the last 55 seconds. It was classic NBA stuff. One of the league's great one-on-one scorers against one of its finest defenders. Robertson, three inches shorter and 30 pounds lighter than Tripucka, had been named to the league's all-defensive team three straight years. Tripucka, a master at the art of personal offense, had averaged 20 or more points a game in four of his seven previous seasons in the league.

In this duel, Robertson won two out of three. The first time down, he cut off Tripucka's dribble, bumped him without drawing a foul, and watched with satisfaction as Tripucka threw up an air ball. That allowed San Antonio to tie the game, but here came Tripucka again. Once more, Robertson was in his way. The fake was a little better this time, and Tripucka escaped around Robertson's right side. Just as he cleared his man, though, a whistle blew. Tripucka, the ref said, was traveling. Spurs' ball again.

San Antonio worked patiently, and eventually found Greg Anderson, a 6-10 second-year player, free for a layup. But as Anderson went up to score, Cureton came flying across the lane and blocked the ball, missing both a foul and a goal-tending call by just a few inches. It was a remarkable play that saved the day for Charlotte.

At the other end, Harter went to Tripucka again, same play, and this time when the whistle blew as Tripucka backed in, it was a foul on Robertson, his sixth. It sent Tripucka to the line with three seconds left. An 85-percent free-throw shooter for his career – "It's stupid for anyone to hit less than 75 percent," Tripucka once said – Tripucka swished both tries, capping off a 13-point quarter and a 31-point game. San Antonio's desperate shot at the buzzer missed, and Charlotte had another first for the scrapbook: first win on the road.

Not surprisingly, Robertson and Tripucka had different versions of the closing plays. Brandishing a rivulet of blood on his right bicep, Tripucka said, "He fouled me before. Just look at this blood. He clawed me, he gave me a head butt. It was like karate.

"Of course," Tripucka said, "you don't expect those calls on the road. I guess one out of three wasn't bad. At least they gave us that one."

In the San Antonio locker room, Robertson rolled his eyes at Tripucka's assertions. "Aw, that (blood) is probably from my elbow. I got cut and it probably rubbed off on him. We were pretty close together out there.

"I'm just disappointed the ref (veteran Dick Bavetta in this case) made that call. Usually they let the players decide it."

Of course, Tripucka thought he had decided it by having the courage to take it to the hoop, draw the big foul, and sink the big shots. That was his style, his way of winning, and he loved it. "Those situations when the game is on the line," Tripucka said, "those situations are what the game is all about for me. I love that."

Hornets Never Lie

A member of a great sports family – his dad, a pro quarterback, threw the first touchdown pass in American Football League history – Peter Kelly Tripucka was accustomed to excelling, accustomed to carrying the load on the field of competition. He had done it all his life and in a lot of sports. Basketball eventually became his specialty. He was tall, almost 6-7, and despite a large frame that could and did support a lot of weight, reasonably quick. Because of his background, he was also very tough and competitive. Because of some good coaching at various points in his career, he was sound fundamentally.

That was enough to make him a college star at Notre Dame, and enough, despite some obvious physical shortcomings, to make him the 12th pick in the 1981 draft. He went to Detroit, along with Isiah Thomas who was picked second that same year, and helped turn that franchise around.

Tripucka was a starter from the day he arrived in Detroit. He averaged 21.6 points a game his rookie season, and was on his way to a monster year in 1982-83 (26.5 points per game) when injuries to his back and other areas slowed him down. He played just 58 games that year and earned the first bit of his reputation as a somewhat fragile player.

There was truth in that. Tripucka hated to play at less than full speed. It limited what he could do, reduced his production. And it was just damned inconvenient. The treatments took time and were sometimes as bad as the problem.

For instance, playing in Detroit one year, Tripucka's back knotted in spasms. To keep him going, trainer Mike Abdenour fitted him with an electric gizmo that sent tiny shocks into the muscles, keeping them more relaxed. It worked for awhile, but the system was designed to eliminate pain in resting patients, not in moving, sweating ball players. As the game wore on, the sweat caused the pads on Tripucka's back to slip. Suddenly the electrodes were in direct contact with his skin.

"It was like getting stuck with a million pins at the same time," Tripucka recalled. "I screamed and called time. Mike comes running out and reaches in to pull the wires off but he forgot to turn the box off so he's out there getting shocked, too. We were both jumping around. It looked pretty strange I'm sure."

Tripucka survived that, but he continued to get hurt, to miss games on a fairly regular basis. Not many, but always some. It seemed perplexing at the time, but it really wasn't all that hard to figure. Simply put, Tripucka's style of play was self destructive. Tripucka had to score to play. He did nothing else well enough to justify staying on the court. And to score he had to do something more than just shoot jump shots. Although he was very good at that, it was too hard to get open that much, too uncertain. He needed a faster, surer, more efficient way to score, and like all great point producers, he quickly came to understand that that way was to stand 15 feet away, straight on, and shoot set shots with nobody guarding you.

Tripucka lived by and for the free throw. He averaged nearly seven attempts a game during his Detroit years, enough for a good shooter like him to add considerably to his scoring average. But getting to the line meant giving up various body parts to the ravages of opponents who were at least as big and strong as he. That was not a great deal of fun, but there was no other way. So his game became a mixture of jump shots and wonderfully creative, yet sadly destructive drives to the basket. Tripucka would rumble into the lane, looking for the foul while waiting to invent the shot that would assure him of two free shots, and which might just go in. That skill, or perhaps it was will, made Tripucka a great scorer, but it also took its toll. Constantly battered and beaten, he would suddenly give out. A muscle or other body part would rebel, and Tripucka would be gone for a week.

"I'm afraid," Tripucka said later in the year when an old back injury flared up, "that I'll end up like Sidney Moncrief (a former star player in Milwaukee). He kept taking it in there until there was nothing left of his body. But that's the way I've got to play."

It was his injury woes, along with his defensive shortcomings, that ended Tripucka's career with Detroit. One year after signing him to a five-year, $5 million contract, the Pistons sent him to Utah, more or less even up for Adrian Dantley, another ex-Notre Dame star who played the same position and did roughly the same things as Tripucka.

It was a weird deal, one of those that makes outsiders scratch their heads. But, as usual in the NBA, there was more to it than met the untrained eye. In Utah, coach Frank Layden, the franchise's omnipotent director, had been feuding with the fragile-egoed Dantley for several years. He had finally determined that there was no solution but to trade away his problem. He found a taker in Detroit, which, after improving with the Tripucka-Thomas nucleus, had stalled with back-to-back 46-win seasons. General Manager Jack McCloskey had come to the conclusion that changes had to be made if the team was going to advance any further.

The main problem was defense. The run-and-gun Pistons ranked in the top 10 in scoring every year Tripucka was there, and in 1983 played in the highest-scoring game in NBA history, a 186-184 win over Denver. But they gave up nearly as many points, and few gave up any more than Tripucka, who was ill-equipped physically to stop most of his counterparts. Deficits in speed and size and jumping ability that could be hidden on offense were there for all to see at the defensive end. The Pistons' braintrust had seen. Most vivid in their memory was a 50-point explosion by Atlanta's Dominique Wilkins in a 1986 playoff series won by the Hawks three games to one.

Tripucka had been helpless against that onslaught, McCloskey remembered. Coach Chuck Daly also remembered the many nights, 58 in five years, when Tripucka couldn't answer the bell because of some niggling injury. Oddly enough, Dantley had actually missed more – an average of 14 absences per season – but this trade was less about logic than about feelings and perceptions. The Pistons perceived Tripucka as a fragile player with a major liability even when he was healthy. Even though he was a good guy and a remarkable scorer, they had reconciled themselves that he must go. He wasn't the answer, and he wasn't, in their eyes, worth the money extorted from the Pistons when Cleveland had made free-agent Tripucka an absurd offer in the summer of 1985. Ironically, Gene Littles, Charlotte's personnel director and assistant coach, was a member of the Cleveland staff that prepared the offer. "We tried to think of something so high there was no way they'd match," Littles recalled later, when his new team was footing the bill. "We said, `Let's try $900,000.' And Detroit came in and gave him that plus a little more. We couldn't believe it."

Tripucka was not happy to be leaving Detroit. He had an identity there, enough notoriety to be lucrative, and a comfortable life. Utah meant change, entrance into a strange new world, for in the NBA there is no city more different for players to live in than Salt Lake City. But Tripucka did not think it would be that bad for his career. As a team, Utah was roughly on par with Detroit, and he figured to inherit Dantley's substantial role. "A.D." had led the Jazz in scoring seven straight years, and the season before the trade he had averaged 36 minutes a game, plenty of time by any standards.

"It did not look like a bad playing situation," Tripucka said.

What he didn't know was that he would also inherit Dantley's feud with Layden. Well, that's the way Tripucka sees it at least. His playing time and production shrank dramatically in Utah, and the only thing Tripucka could figure was that they just didn't like him.

"They would never explain it to me," Tripucka said. "That burned me up. I'd ask and they'd say, `What's the problem? You're still getting paid aren't you?' I couldn't believe that attitude. I was (getting paid), and I should have been. But there's more to it than that. They treated me poorly and took some of the best years of my career. They made me feel like I was living in a barrel. They really injured me.

"And the worst thing is that I think they knew it was going to be that way when they made the trade. It was a trade to get rid of Dantley. From day one, they were in a fog, as far as I'm concerned, about me."

Layden, the rotund comic who coached the Jazz while Tripucka was there, says that's not quite the way it happened. Utah thought Tripucka would pick up much of Dantley's slack – he did play a lot when he first arrived. But the team began to develop along other lines. Two young forwards, Karl Malone and Thurl Bailey, emerged as major stars the same year Tripucka joined the Jazz. They needed minutes and Tripucka was the natural playing time reservoir from which they should drink. Layden experimented some with Tripucka at guard, a position his size, but not his speed, dictated he should play. But there was a crowd there, too. The oft-injured Darrell Griffith required some time, and young Bobby Hansen was developing as well. Griffith was a better athlete than Tripucka, Hansen a better defender. He was squeezed out again.

"What happened," Layden said, "is that there was just no place for him. That was tough on him, and it was tough on us. Maybe we shouldn't have made the deal, but overall it has worked out for us."

Tripucka voiced his displeasure at the situation midway through his first season in Utah, and that sealed his fate. The team would try to trade him, and even though it lacked depth and scoring punch, it would not try to meld Tripucka into the essential mix. A seemingly ideal sixth man was left to languish on the bench.

Whether he would have filled such a role is a matter of debate. During his first year with the Hornets, Tripucka talked excitedly about the future when he could come off the bench and light a spark. But in Utah, teammates sensed an unwillingness to be a mere spark after having once been the main fire.

Mark Eaton, the massive center who was Tripucka's best friend in Mormon country, said, "There were a lot of factors, but really I think it was just that Kelly couldn't stand not being in the spotlight. He thrives on that."

Tripucka may indeed revel in filling the role of BMOT (Big Man on Team), but it's often hard to tell. He is proud of what he's done and can do on the court, but sends out mixed signals about his feelings towards celebrity. He is bright and talkative in public, a natural speaker who can be quite engaging before a large audience or a small group. But around his teammates he is quiet and introverted, seldom engaging in locker room banter, or banter of any type. On the road he holes up in his hotel room – no calls received – and is seldom seen until time to go to the game. After home games, partly as a response to the needs of his off-battered body, Tripucka is almost always the last player to leave the coliseum. He usually missed the post-game interplay while treating some injury.

Is this a way of setting himself apart as the star he once was and still wants to be? Or is he embarrassed by the points he scores and the money he makes? Money may be the root of all evil, but in the NBA, shots taken has been known to nurture a little bad blood as well. Tripucka, as the highest-paid, highest-scoring player on the team, was in an unenviable position in regard to relations with his teammates. And he was well aware of that. When injuries and illness wore him down the second half of the season with Charlotte, he fretted over his teammates' possible reaction.

"I just feel guilty about sitting around home," he told Harter one night in February after he'd missed several games and practices.

"Ah, that's bullshit," Harter said. "Listen, you don't have to worry about it. I don't care what anybody says. You do what you have to do to get well. We need you."

"Yeah, well, thanks Coach," Tripucka said, "but I still feel guilty. I shouldn't miss things."

If any of this really did bother Tripucka's teammates during Charlotte's first season, they didn't let it show. Tripucka was liked, or at least not disliked. Most of his teammates, especially those who had been around him before at other league stops, wrote off his idiosyncrasies with, "That's just Kelly."

"This whole team gets along," Robert Reid said late in the year. "Even Kelly, in his own quiet way, works well with everyone. He communicates enough to get that done."

What Tripucka communicated most was joy. Of all the players born again in Charlotte, none was a happier baby than Kelly Tripucka. "I'd forgotten just how precious it is to be on the floor, how much fun that is," Tripucka said.

The thrill danced through every facet of Tripucka's life. He built a house in south Charlotte, mingled with the locals, and a month before the season started, conceived his first child with his wife Janis. It was not a coincidence, Tripucka thought, that that happened after he got to Charlotte. "No, no way," he said shortly after the event had been medically confirmed. "That never would have happened in Utah."

Tripucka's heroics in San Antonio signaled to everyone, but most importantly to Tripucka himself, that his two-year exile, as he called it, in Utah had not hurt his game. If anything, the added maturity seemed to have improved it. He was still a scorer, but he was more of a team player than before, just more of a player, period.

Harter, who'd coached Tripucka for three years in Detroit, said, "He's diving for loose balls, doing things nobody thought they'd ever see him do. I know I didn't."

Tripucka thought growing up made the difference. "I'm more patient, smarter, just more mature," he said. "I think I understand the game better, and I think I can beat you more ways than I used to. I much more well-rounded than I once was."

• • • • •

The San Antonio game touched off a Tripucka rampage that propelled Charlotte through the first six weeks of the season, the crucial time when the fledgling franchise was feeling its way, trying to build confidence and gain respect. Following an 11-point night against his ex-teammates from Detroit, Tripucka went on a month-long tear in which he averaged 28.4 points a game and shot better than 52 percent from the floor. At the peak of that run, in early December, Tripucka experienced a shooter's nirvana when almost everything went in. He made seven straight three-pointers and 39 of 40 from the free-throw line.

This offensive explosion offered a much-needed focal point to Charlotte's offense, and indeed to the team itself. Opposing teams had to start reading their scouting reports. They couldn't just let Tripucka run wild. If they did, he'd score enough by himself to keep the game close. This realization led to what Tripucka saw as the ultimate compliment: the double team. He almost beamed the first time he saw a team running an extra defender his way.

"You earn respect in this league," Tripucka said during his early December streak. "I guess the double-team is the best way there is of knowing when you've earned some as a scorer. It does feel good, although when I'm out there playing I don't really think about whether somebody likes me or if I'm all the way back."

Tripucka's brilliance ignited, or at least coincided with, Chapman's first good streak of the season. Shooting a miserable 29 percent from the field after the San Antonio game, Chapman suddenly exploded on Thanksgiving's Eve in Boston, making 10 of 16 from the floor, including his first three-pointer and his first dunk. "It felt good to shoot well for a change," Chapman said afterward.

It helped Charlotte's offense, too, lending support to Tripucka and to Reid, who was starting to come on as well. The Celtics, without

Larry Bird or a great deal of cohesion, were stunned by Charlotte's onslaught. The Hornets led by nine with 3:45 left in the first half, and by four at the break.

Boston pushed ahead in the third quarter and led by seven when star forward Kevin McHale was injured with 5:46 to play. Charlotte immediately rallied, cutting the lead to two with less than a minute left. But in the closing seconds, Reggie Lewis, a rising Celtic star, hit a tough jumper and forced a miss from Reid. All the Hornets had was a near miss.

They repeated that performance two nights later in Philadelphia. The Sixers, off to a quick start for the year, jumped on the Hornets early, building a nine-point lead in the first quarter, leading them to think they'd done a night's work. But Charlotte rallied behind Tripucka and Reid, who combined for 60 points on this night. The Hornets took a six-point lead into the fourth quarter and were up eight with five minutes to play despite yet another absence by Rambis, out this time with one of his recurring foot injuries.

But the Hornets couldn't hold on. Philly's Cliff Robinson, a good offensive player with a long history of physical problems, burned Reid for three baskets and an assist in the last two and a half minutes, and the Hornets' offense, brilliant for the most of the night, disintegrated. Tyrone Bogues made two turnovers. Kempton threw an uncontested pass out of bounds, and because of Rambis' injury and Cureton's foul trouble – he picked up his sixth personal with eight minutes left – rookie Tom Tolbert wound up on the court in the crucial, closing minutes. Not only on the court, but, in fact, taking one of the crucial shots. Down two with just over a minute to play, Tolbert saw an opening in the lane. He went up, maybe was bumped by the Sixers' Ron Anderson, and missed. There was no call. Robinson scored again for Philadelphia, and that was that.

Tolbert, happy to finally get some playing time, was philosophic about the turn of events. "I thought there was a foul," he said, "but that's immaterial. They're not going to give a rookie like me that call. Of course, knowing that, maybe I shouldn't have taken that shot. I don't know. I don't get many chances."

Harter wasn't happy with the shot or with having to play Tolbert in that situation. But with Rowsom and Rambis out and his roster filled with guards, he didn't have much choice. "Well, who else was I going to put in there?" he asked.

He was depressed. His worst dreams were coming true. The team was playing well, but it still couldn't win. "There's no asterisk in the record book that says, 'Good, you played hard.' It's just another 'L.' That's all people will see."

Another heartbreaker followed. Down 24 late in the third quarter to Washington, the Hornets rallied behind Kempton and a raucous Charlotte Coliseum crowd and pulled to within four with more than three minutes to play.

It was a miraculous, inspiring rally, the high point of the season in many ways. While watching it, a light went off in the head of Tom Sorensen, a dry-witted columnist for the *Charlotte Observer*, who was battling a tight deadline that night. With the clock ticking away, Sorensen's light made it into print, and Kempton became "Dr. K." It was a clever piece of basketball parody. Julius Erving, the graceful stylist who in the 1970s had almost personally revolutionized the way basketball was played, was known as "Dr. J," or sometimes, "the fabulous Dr. J." Kempton, gawkish, with red hair and a hefty body that did not seem to move quite as fast as he wanted it to, was almost the antithesis. To label him with an appellation similar to Erving's was funny stuff.

The humor was not lost on Tom Tolbert and Kurt Rambis, two of Kempton's not entirely serious teammates. When Kempton arrived at practice the day after what became known as the "Dr. K game," he found the letters D-O-C written on the heel of his basketball shoes in black magic marker. "Hi, Doc," teammates greeted him.

Kempton made a show of downplaying the nickname and trying to nip it, as Barney Fife might have said, in the bud. But it was too rich to die. Assistant coach Ed Badger, who liked to stick the needle in as much as anyone, quickly took to calling Kempton "Dr. K." Explaining a play, he would dryly, matter-of-factly, say, "Now on this one, Dave, you and Dr. K have got to set this pick higher. Got it Doc?" That assured it would catch on, even though Harter continued to call Kempton "Timmy," making him sound like the star of the old "Lassie" show on TV, which probably was worse. It was "Doc this," and "Doc that," with great grins for a few days. Then it just became "Hey Doc," as a matter of course.

For the record, Kempton continued to struggle mildly against the tidal wave of sentiment, but his actions told different feelings. He grinned when the nickname was spoken and eventually consented to be photographed dressed in surgical scrub clothes for a picture to go with a follow-up column by Sorensen. Though he never admitted it, this must have been fun for Kempton. For no matter how good-natured he is, seldom does an ex-free agent on the fringe of the NBA become one of his team's most popular players. But it happened this crazy season in Charlotte. He became, of all things, a celebrity, a star.

When that star finally, inevitably perhaps, began to fall, his fans couldn't understand. Why wasn't Dr. K playing, they wondered as the season went on. Why, asked a caller on Carl Scheer's weekly radio show one night, was coach Harter saying all those nasty things about Dr. K? "He seems like a such a nice young man," the caller said.

The caller was right. Kempton was a nice young man. But his M.D. was a fake, just a newspaper hoax, and his early season magic just an illusion. After two amazing months the Doctor stopped operating, his practice drying up, some teammates theorized, when he really started to believe he could heal. "He read all that 'Dr. K' shit, and it went to his head," said one teammate as the season drew to a close with Kempton barely contributing.

Perhaps. But for a few games, and certainly for a few minutes that night against the Bullets, Kempton had as much right to a doctorate as any Hornet. The rebounds, the running hooks, the drives through the lane – Dr. K pulled them off as well as any basketball scholar ever had. The magic was not quite enough, though. The Bullets pulled it out, running the losing streak to four games and extending Charlotte's near-miss depression. But good times were just around the corner.

• • • • •

They appeared first wearing the black-and-orange, non-designer uniforms of the Miami Heat, Charlotte's expansion brethren. The Heat came in three days after the Washington loss, providing an almost certain opportunity to win. The Heat, which had gone with younger players than had Charlotte, was paying a terrible price early in the season. They had yet to win a game and hadn't come close very often.

Hornet spirits were dampened a bit when Tripucka pulled a hamstring in practice the day before the game. It was an odd injury, suffered while running rather easily up the court, and was typical of the little aches that seemed to dog him throughout his career. He tested the leg when he got to the coliseum that night, but it was still too tight, too sore. He couldn't go.

The Hornets won anyway, rather easily, in fact, 99-84. Chapman picked up Tripucka's scoring slack, pumping in a career-high 22 points, and the Hornets' defense managed to blunt Miami's anemic offense down the stretch. It was a big win because of the teams' obvious rivalry. But it was expected, or at least as expected as any win Charlotte would have that season.

Victory the next time out, two nights later at home against Philadelphia, was not. The Hornets delivered anyway in one of the classic games of their first season.

Take the Hornets and Points

It began with a searing start that helped Charlotte roll to a 23-point lead early in the second half, and ended with a frantic finish in which Charles Barkley's game-tying basket at the buzzer was waved off by referee Lee Jones. The veteran official called Barkley for charging into all of Rex Chapman and Tim Kempton, and into parts of several other Hornets.

The 260-pound Barkley, a man for whom the term colorful was invented, was furious. He had to be restrained while he shouted at Jones, lest he be called for his second technical foul. In the Philly locker room he blasted Jones, saying, "No way you let guys go at it like that for 48 minutes, then make that call. No way. It's just not good officiating sense. But then that man ain't got no sense."

On the face of it, it was a curious call by NBA standards. Though not under orders to do so, at least not under publicly acknowledged orders, the league's officials do try to let the game be decided by timed plays rather than at the foul line. And, as any aficionado of the college game knows, they do let more contact go by without tooting their whistles.

Did any of those traditions apply to the call against Barkley? Barkley took an inbounds pass near midcourt with about four seconds left and drove, under full steam, into the lane from the right side. There wasn't much doubt about what he intended to do. The only question was, "Would the Hornets let him get away with it?" They didn't. Chapman stepped over. So did Kempton. The force of the blow was such that Kempton was knocked sprawling onto the floor and Chapman went flying into the basket support.

"Not many people take a charge from Charles Barkley and live to tell about it," Chapman said after the game. "It was quite a blow. But you've got to stand in there and take that if you're going to win."

Chapman may have been motivated by assistant coach Ed Badger's pre-game offer of $50 to any group of Hornets on the court who singularly or collectively took a charge from Barkley. Technically, offering such a bonus is a violation of NBA rules, but the league passed on that one. It got all the fine money it needed from that game from Barkley, courtesy of his tirade against referee Jones.

The victory, Charlotte's second straight and fourth overall, was especially sweet after the many close misses in recent weeks. The team had blown its lead, but had held on and made the big plays at the end. "When you do that, it really pays off," said Tripucka.

Besides the defensive courage of Chapman and Kempton, there were two clutch jumpers from the rookie guard, a steal by Kempton, and Tripucka's winning layup with six seconds to play. That was an odd play, too, in that Tripucka was all alone for an easy one off an inbounds play under the Sixers' basket. Two Philadelphia players failed to switch as Tripucka slid off a Chapman pick and got the ball in a shocking position – wide open under the basket. He couldn't believe his good fortune, so he pump faked once, twice, then a third time before he finally went up and deposited the lay in.

"I just couldn't believe there wasn't anybody there," Tripucka said. "I'm sure I looked like a fool, but I knew somebody had to be right on top of me."

Charlotte followed those successes with a credible performance in Houston on Robert Reid's homecoming night. Of all the many get-back nights the Hornets played in their first year, this was probably the sweetest. Reid, a 10-year veteran of the team and a former goodwill ambassador for the sprawling oil town, was incensed at the way he had been treated by the Rockets and the pittance for which he had been let go, namely Bernard Thompson.

On the eve of his return to the banks of the Buffalo Bayou, Reid was still hot. "I mean, I can understand being traded and all. This is a business," Reid said. "But *Bernard Thompson*? No offense to Bernard, he's a great guy and all. But really. When I heard, I thought, 'They've got to be kidding.'"

They were not. The Houston management saw Reid as an aging player with a potentially troublesome knee to whom they were, at least ethically, wed to the tune of some $500,000 a year for three more seasons. They wanted younger blood for their on-the-brink team, a better player for that money, so they dumped him. And now, just five months later, he was back, a key cog, if not a star, for an expansion team – and with a good memory. "They did not treat me right," Reid said on the eve of his big game. And he dreamed of revenge. "I'd like about 45 points, 15 rebounds and 12 assists, and about three blocks, too," he said, half joking. That would be nice. In reality, he just hoped he could show the fans that management had been wrong.

He did that. In a magnificent, under-the-gun performance, Reid made 12 of his last 16 shots, scored 24 points and grabbed seven rebounds. That, plus a 30-point night from Tripucka and better-than-normal play from the centers helped the Hornets gain a 66-49 lead in the third quarter. Houston came back behind all-star Akeem Olajuwon and guard Mike Woodson, the free agent signed to replace Reid. They led a steady, Rocket parade to the free throw line that paved the way to victory. Houston shot 47 free throws and scored 16 of its last 18 points from the line. Charlotte got to the line just 19 times and shot just two free throws in the last four minutes.

"All I can remember in the fourth quarter is standing there, watching them line up for a free throw," said Tripucka. "That's a pretty good play."

Despite the free-throw onslaught, Charlotte still had a chance to win in the last five seconds, if they could make a three-pointer. But Tripucka and Michael Holton botched an inbounds play, and the last-gasp hope expired.

The Rockets, an alleged contender in the Western Conference, were relieved. "Losing this game, to that team, would have been like losing four in a row," said Olajuwon.

Respect was hard to come by. The prevailing opinion in the league was, "Expansion team, they must be terrible." The truth was they weren't much more terrible than a lot of teams in the league, and they had the advantage of low expectations. Many of the teams just above them in terms of talent were burdened by the souring of spirit and morale that comes from knowing you could have been, should have been better. As David Stern, the NBA commissioner once said, when asked if the league was being fair to the expansion teams, "Hey, we've got some established teams that still look like expansion teams. It's not the rules that decide who's good and who's not."

One such expansion look-a-like was the New Jersey Nets, a bumbling organization left over from the ABA merger that seemed, at times, almost without hope. They played their home games in the Brendan Byrne Arena, a fairly nice basketball building located on a depressing piece of swampy landfill in northern New Jersey known as the Meadowlands Sports Complex. There was nothing there except a football stadium (home of the Jets and Giants), a race track, the arena, some hotels and a very, very large parking lot. Though located right beside an interstate that led to New York City and Newark, it was hard to get to because of a twisting maze of exit ramps and access roads that confused even veteran cab drivers. And it always smelled of some long-forgotten, long-hidden hazardous waste accident, a suspicion confirmed by the story that the horses that raced at the local track no longer stayed there. Having munched some Meadowlands' grass, they got sick, so now they were trucked in each night for the races.

All this, combined with the fact that it wasn't really *anywhere* and that the Nets were at best, a mediocre team, kept the fans away in droves. The team actually had four straight winning years in the 1980s, but had changed coaches seven times since 1981. In the 1986-87 and 1987-88 seasons, the Nets had won just 43 games combined. Interest in the "Exit 16W Nets," as some in the league referred to the team, was not high. Corporate sales kept the Nets' reported attendance at respectable levels, but on many nights the crowds were so sparse that every epithet hurled from the stands echoed about the arena. And some were always hurled. After all the uninspiring years, the Nets "fans" had turned a bit cynical. No, more than a bit. They made fun of their own mascot, shouted sexual vulgarities at their own cheerleaders, the scantily clad "Jersey Girls," and ragged the poor players on both teams.

As luck would have it, the Nets turned up on the Charlotte schedule, for a doubleheader no less, just as the Hornets were reaching the first peak of their feeble powers right after the Houston game in early December. The teams played in Charlotte Friday, then moved on to New Jersey Saturday. Although those who just followed the scores in the paper might have thought otherwise, the mood around the Hornets was that the impending doubleheader was almost an even match. New Jersey, searching, as always, for that elusive chemistry, had made some major moves just before the season started, acquiring Carroll, the center who had ravaged Charlotte early in the year, point guard Lester Conner and off guard Mike McGee.

The results had been promising at first. McGee, a noted gunner, had scored a lot. Carroll, a noted underachiever, had played all right, and the Nets' two quality players, Buck Williams and Roy Hinson, had been good. But things had quickly started to go wrong. The many misfits on the team – Carroll, McGee, Walter Berry – had started living up to their reputations. New Jersey came into the two-game set with Charlotte riding a five-game losing streak and pulling its collective hair out. Willis Reed, the ex-Knick star who coached the team, said, "I've asked the guys what's wrong, pleaded, begged, but I don't know. This is a mess."

Charlotte took advantage of the mess to win the opener 96-95. Chapman, playing well again, led a second-quarter assault by the Hornets' second team. He poured in 16 points in the quarter and got support from fellow second-teamers Kempton and Bogues as Charlotte piled up a 32-14 advantage in the period. New Jersey had come back. Carroll, who possessed an astounding magic all season against the Hornets, went crazy again, scoring 12 in the last 10 minutes of the game. Clutch offense by Tripucka and a couple of pressure free throws by Bogues held New Jersey off and raised Charlotte's record to a more than respectable 5-11.

The Hornets nearly made it two in a row the next night. New Jersey, playing with a bit more enthusiasm on their home court, pounded the smaller Hornets on the boards. The final rebound total was an amazing 60-35. But Charlotte hung on, and when Chapman and Tripucka combined for three three-pointers in the last three minutes, the Hornets were able to erase a nine-point lead and forge a tie at the end of regulation. The overtime started well enough, too, but then Carroll, the Hornets' recurring nightmare, did his thing again. Working against Earl Cureton, four inches shorter and 20 pounds lighter, Carroll scored five straight points to open the overtime. Then, when the Hornets tried double-teaming him, he flipped a nice pass to Hinson for a dunk that put the Nets up by four. Charlotte couldn't recover and another opportunity was lost.

Immediately afterwards, Harter was upset with assorted calls down the stretch and once again depressed by a near miss. But after he'd had a day or two to ponder the outcome, his feelings changed. "To be out rebounded like that and still go into overtime," he said. "If we had won that one, it would have been one of the all-time great victories. You'd have had to put it in the hall of fame."

As the Rockets had been a week before, the lowly Nets were relieved to have dodged the expansion bullet at home. In their case, it seemed especially important. "It was embarrassing enough at their place the night before," said Buck Williams. "If we'd have lost this one, the lid might have come off our pot. It almost did last night anyway. You can't lose to a team like this."

But five teams already had, and some more were destined to suffer the same fate. Even though opposing players still felt embarrassed about losing to the Hornets, coaches and others in the league were beginning to notice the new team. They were not an automatic "W." They had some weapons, and they could hurt you.

Full realization of this never occurred, however. Some opponents, even some already burned, were taken in right down to the last week of the season. But as scouting reports and game film began to make their way through the league, some began to learn that the Hornets were indeed serious business.

• • • • •

The first layer of Charlotte's early season magic may have worn off just before Christmas when Milwaukee took two solid blows from the Hornets, yet still won back-to-back games. The games were remarkably similar. Both teams shot well in both games, and both nights Charlotte carried a lead into the fourth quarter only to see the Bucks blow them away in the last 12 minutes. In Milwaukee, the Bucks won the fourth period 37-26. In Charlotte one night later, it was 31-18.

There are a lot of ways to explain that: Milwaukee is just a far superior team; Milwaukee's big guards, among other things, gave the

Hornets too many match-up problems; the Hornets were under strength, with Rex Chapman out with a back injury and Tyrone Bogues hobbled by an ankle injury. There's some truth in all of that, but Del Harris, Milwaukee's white-haired, straight-talking coach, figured as big a reason as any was that the Bucks simply weren't as surprised as some other teams had been.

"Early in the year I think you could tell your players, 'Hey, this is a good team. You know these players. They can play,' but they just wouldn't believe you," Harris said after the second Milwaukee win. "Now you can bring out some statistics, pop on a tape of Philadelphia getting beat and get their attention. I think our players believed us now."

That made sense to the Hornets who saw the oppositions' fury rising almost every game.

Earl Cureton, who was nearly recovered from his preseason hamstring problems by the time of the two Milwaukee games, said, "Teams know we're not a cakewalk now. I think they used to think that no matter what they did it was still a 'W.' But no more."

"Yes," agreed Kelly Tripucka, "teams are learning that if they take the night off against us they'll be fighting for their lives in the fourth quarter. We're starting to take some pretty good shots now because of that. And I guess we'd better get used to it."

For Dick Harter, this downside to gaining recognition and respect for a job well done brought on more frustration and some bitterness. He'd handled his task, perhaps as well as anybody could have expected, and what was his reward? He'd probably get beaten even worse, he thought, the rest of the way.

"People are starting to figure us out," Harter said, nearly sneering, after the second Milwaukee loss. "There's no magic to it. You push on Kelly a little bit, and if no one else is hitting, we don't look very good. And if you give it to one of our big guys, they're not always going to go up and jam it down, you know?"

That was the first of many cries for help Harter would issue in Charlotte's first season. He was doing what he was supposed to do, turning a bunch of cast-offs (and that's exactly what they were, for as Harter was always pointing out, the Hornets owned only one player who wasn't dumped, in one way or another, by another NBA team) into a credible team. The not-so-old, old coach had done the job in every way. The Hornets' offensive and defensive schemes, given the physical limitations of the players, were superb. Charlotte ran, as it is said in league parlance, "good stuff," complex stuff, and ran it well. Indiana's Reggie Miller noted in February that "Charlotte runs the motion offense (a standard NBA set) as well as anyone except

Detroit." Atlanta's Jon Koncak, after getting lost in the Hornets' set offense one night, said, "It's amazing. They run counters (a counter is a play devised to counter what an opponent might do against the original play) for the counters of their counters. You never know what's coming next."

Beyond the Xs and Os, the league marveled at Harter's motivational skills. He had coaxed a lot of long nights out of a lot of old legs, had coddled a very young rookie through some very tough times, and had made 6-9 centers and 5-3 point guards play very much taller than that. And he had made them do it night after night after night. That was the thing. The team with no real hope played as if it had everything on the line every time out.

For the first two months of the season, 27 games, Charlotte shocked with the consistency of its effort. The Hornets won eight of those games and had a chance in six more. They were blown out just once, in the ill-fated opener, hanging on, coming back time again when it would have been considerably easier and seemingly more practical, just to cave in. But they did not. Twenty-seven games. A great effort in all but two or three. It was a real accomplishment, a wonder, said general manager Scheer.

Few wondered more than those who are inclined to bet on professional basketball games, for the hustling Hornets covered the spread in 19 straight games after the opener. Such records are not kept, at least not for public inspection, but it may have been the greatest such streak of all time.

Harter made note of the spreads, not out of any interest in gambling but as further supporting evidence that he was indeed bucking some serious odds. Pondering his team's mounting string of book-making successes one day in December, Harter's face lit up.

"You know," he said, "somebody betting on us could have made a lot of money."

But would the Hornets be a good bet for the rest of the year? Harter wondered about that.

Dancing in the Aisles

"What are these people doing here?"
– Kurt Rambis

There are plenty of theories, but no one will ever know for sure just what happened.

George Shinn cajoled and impressed the NBA into putting a team in Charlotte, a sparkling, new coliseum was finished just in time for the first season, and then ... all hell broke loose. The people of Charlotte and its environs just went nuts for a team that lost three out of every four it played, that lost its opener by 40 points, that would, in even the rosiest of scenarios, be eliminated from the playoffs several months before they began.

Almost a million of them came to see the 41 home games. That was 23,172 a night, or 99 percent capacity at the new coliseum. It was the best in the NBA. It was the first time an expansion team had led any professional league in attendance. It was the biggest thing to hit Charlotte since ... well, maybe just the biggest thing.

Max Muhleman, the marketing man who guided Shinn in his expansion quest, thought about the significance of the phenomenon that eventually came to be known and may even have actually qualified as hysteria or mania, and said, "This is the most catalytic thing that happened to Charlotte. I thought for a minute and compared it. There's statehood, the Civil War, and the Hornets." And not, he thought, necessarily in that order.

Hyperbole to be sure, but it was not outrageous. The Hornets were just big beyond belief, dominating a city's social life and supplanting the weather as a source of small (and not so small) talk. They became so big that the bigness itself became a topic. By mid-season, when a sellout every night was assured, one of the biggest cheers was always reserved for public address announcer John Edwards' attendance update. "Ladies and gentleman, you've done it again," Edwards would say. And the crowd would burst into one of its deafening roars, drowning out the figures being announced. That's how big and how crazy it was. And it just made no sense.

No, that's not quite right. It made some sense because it was new. Novelty and curiosity still sell, and there hadn't been an NBA team here before, and there hadn't been a new coliseum in 30 or so years. But that wasn't it, not really, because the crowds got bigger, not smaller, as the season wore on. The enthusiasm increased, doubling, tripling, quadrupling, maybe growing ten-fold. Who could tell? There is no true measure of such, only the finite clicking of the turnstiles and the unending ring of the cash register. The former deviated for a month or so, then settled unerringly on 23,338, the capacity of the Charlotte Coliseum. If interest grew beyond that point, there was no way to tell, at least not at the box office. There just weren't any more tickets, or at least not enough to bother counting. Truth is, you could have gotten into most Hornet games right at game time, providing you came alone and had $50 to spare. That was the price of expensive, courtside seats that were always the last to sell out completely. As for the latter measure, well, it was just as inaccurate, if for exactly the opposite reason. Hornet paraphernalia – shirts, caps, license plates, posters, etc. – sold like the proverbial hot cakes. But it sold at so many places, through so many vendors, that there was no way to count it all.

The Hornets themselves were deliberately vague about the figures. They admitted that Belk's stores in North Carolina sold more than $1 million worth of Hornet stuff before Christmas. "And that's about all we're going to say," said general manager Carl Scheer.

Other figures drifted in. A supervisor at a coliseum novelty stand reported sales of more than $13,000 *in one night* at just his stand when Chicago and Michael Jordan visited town December 23, and estimated that novelty sales for the whole building totaled more than $50,000 that evening. NBA Properties, which licenses the logos and namesakes for all 27 NBA teams to national distributors, added further definition to the mania that swept Charlotte. By dividing the number of fans attending NBA games into the dollar value of all league-licensed merchandise sold, the NBA arrived at a figure of 40 cents per head. That is, every fan attending an NBA game buys about 40 cents worth of league novelties. When Charlotte's novelty sales were divided by the Hornets' league-leading attendance, the figure came to roughly $1.25 a head. Hornet crazies were buying three times the stuff that their average rivals did.

But just how much was sold and to whom was impossible to gauge. The NBA licenses more than 140 vendors for everything from apparel to sunglasses to automobile windowshades, and then there's the Hornets' own novelty arm, much of which is controlled by Rick Hendricks, one of the team's minority owners. Suffice to say that that first year the money poured in from all directions and the countryside soon became littered with assorted teal and purple souvenirs. Owning and wearing a Hornet shirt, hat, sweater, or whatever became something of a patriotic duty in Charlotte and, to a slightly lesser degree, in the area beyond. It showed civic and regional pride. It proved that one knew how to jump onto a bandwagon.

More than anything else, it was those two elements that produced the near hysteria over the Hornets in the fall and winter of 1988-89. For a variety of reasons, Charlotte was ready for an NBA team that year. Certainly the business and political leaders of the bustling banking center felt it was time to step up, officially, into the big leagues. And, in various ways, this idea of the entrance into the NBA serving as a coming out party for the city caught on with the echelons below. There was no mistake now. It said so in the papers every morning, all across the country. *Charlotte* at New York. Boston at *Charlotte. Charlotte* vs. LA. That said it all. Being paired against teams from those cities meant belonging with them whether those cities liked it or not.

Generally they did not, or, worse still, maybe didn't even care. For despite the trappings and the team, Charlotte certainly did not qualify in 1988 as a really big city. It belonged instead to a sub group, just outside the major, metropolitan ring of cities advancing on or just past the one million mark in population. There was already a group of similar cities in the NBA: Indianapolis, Phoenix, Portland, Sacramento, Salt Lake City, San Antonio, Seattle. Denver and Milwaukee might be included, too, although being a little older in their bigness, they did not quite fit.

A first glance, it seemed these towns would struggle to hold their own in any competition with their larger world-class brethren. And for a time it had been so. The ability of New York, LA or Chicago simply to overwhelm the opposition financially via TV rights fees had been one of the NBA's problems in the 1970s. The little guys had had no chance. But the salary cap had done much to redress the imbalance or at least prevent the huge metropolises from bringing their full, financial weight to bear. Phoenix could never demand the local TV and radio fees that New York could. There were five to six times more viewers and listeners in the Big Apple. But if the two franchises were limited by the same salary ceiling, it didn't matter. Phoenix only had to earn enough to cover the cap limit and meet its other expenses. It didn't have to match New York.

And that was quite possible, even without massive broadcast revenues, because at the gate there was almost an advantage in being small. True, NBA teams in the larger cities had more potential ticket buyers. But they had to compete with the NFL, the NHL, Major League Baseball, and who knows what else for the local sports dollar. Losing teams lost that competition, but even the winners didn't always fare so well. Fans became somewhat desensitized to the thrill when they could see it any night of the year. But the smaller cities were often one-horse towns where one went to see the NBA or one saw no pro sports at all. The novelty and the thrill remained, and, as a consequence, almost all of them did well at the gate. Some were unbelievable.

Portland, which entered the league in 1970 with a population of roughly 300,000, was the classic example of this effect. Interest was strong in the Pacific Northwest from the start, but it was not until three or four years later, when Bill Walton arrived, or rather got healthy, that what later came to be known as "Blazermania" began. It swelled quickly, as such movements often do. Little Memorial Coliseum, a 12,666-seat building, was filled every night. Season tickets had to be capped at 11,500, and the spillover from the ticketless at big games often filled the Paramount Theater, one of those old-style movie houses not carved up into a half-dozen mini screening rooms, where Trailblazer fans went to watch the games on close-circuit TV. And they'd come whether the game was blacked out or not. That way they could still be a part of a cheering throng. Everybody watched. When Portland won the championship in 1977, beating Philadelphia in the title series, the final game was seen on 96 percent of all the TVs in Oregon, an unofficial record for penetration by a single event.

It was only natural, a dozen years later, for old NBA hands to compare Charlotte with Portland. Philadelphia's Jimmy Lynam, who spent one season as an assistant coach with the Trailblazers, thought the effect just the same after his second trip to Charlotte in January. "It's a bunch of crazy people screaming for their team," Lynam said. "It's just like the old Portland crowds, only the place is twice as big."

While that may have been true, the Hornets' grip on the local populace was probably more similar to what was going on in Sacramento, the most successful of the submetropolises when Charlotte joined the league. California's capital city became an NBA town in 1985 when some local businessmen bought the stumbling Kansas City franchise and moved it west. They had no building ready, but played to packed houses for three straight years in a glorified warehouse known as the ARCO Arena. And they did it despite the Kings playing like paupers every year they were in Sacramento. In their first four seasons there, they were 106 games under .500. No matter. The fans still lined up to see them, and Oakland and San Francisco, two major-league ports, were just a two-hour drive away.

This should have been encouraging news for the Hornets, the bulk of whose fans were at least four hours away from the nearest big-league action. But management entered the first season worried nonetheless. The potential advantages notwithstanding, Charlotte was still a very small market. And the Charlotte Coliseum was a very big building, the biggest in the NBA now that the Pistons were moving out of the Silverdome. General Manager Carl Scheer looked at co-expansionist Miami and its comparatively cozy, 15,000-seat building with a degree of envy in the days before the season began. With a building that size, a team could hope to build some demand for tickets. There would be a genuine fear of sellouts. But in an arena that held more than 23,000? No, not there. Once the newness wore off, Scheer and everyone else figured, the Hornets would be doing well if they could just keep the echos muffled.

And they were not, as a glance at the NBA map seemed to show, without competition for the local basketball-ticket dollar either. The city and the region were right in the middle of that mythical highway known as Tobacco Road. It was the right of way through the Atlantic Coast Conference, one of the most fervent hotbeds of college basketball in the nation. Fans in North Carolina held allegiances to four in-state schools in the league the University of North Carolina, N.C. State, Duke and Wake Forest. The UNC following, as rabid as any with the possible exception of Kentucky, would have been enough of a challenge. But the other three, combined with the other members of the famous, eight-team league, soaked up all the stragglers. The Hornets weren't exactly entering a vacuum of allegiance. That was worrisome indeed. Would long-time UNC or N.C. State fans want to become Hornet fans, too? And if so, how big a fan would they become? Would they go twice a year or 20 times?

It never dawned on Scheer that they could actually win away some of those fans. Though in obvious competition with the local college teams, the Hornets entered their first season bearing an olive branch. They hoped it wouldn't be defoliated. "We're not in competition with the ACC," Scheer said hopefully. "There is room for both."

In fact, in Charlotte there was room for more. While the city was in the midst of ACC country, it was not actually in an ACC city. Winston-Salem, home of Wake Forest, which was the weakest of the ACC's North Carolina entries in terms of fan attachment, was about a 90-minute drive away. The Raleigh-Durham area, where Duke, N.C. State and North Carolina were situated, was a 140-mile drive on agonizingly slow roads. Clemson, another league member, was not quite three hours away to the southwest in South Carolina. Charlotte, the biggest city in the Carolinas, had no ACC team to call its own. It was an anomaly that had led to a joke amongst some North Carolina sports writers. Why not, they suggested, only partially facetiously, move Duke to Charlotte? The Blue Devils constantly complained about their position as the poor athletic sister in the Research Triangle. Charlotte was a mass of people with no team to root for.

The fictitious move was never made, never even contemplated, of course. What happened was the Hornets came instead. They became the local team that Charlotte never had. And the timing turned out to be exquisite.

"There was," said Scheer, with the benefit of hindsight, "a great yearning here for a team. It was remarkable really, the way this community wanted something like this."

It was also a complete surprise. Scheer, a veteran marketing strategist who gets a lot of credit for reversing Denver's attendance fortunes in the late 1970s, thought he had Charlotte's audience and its probable attendance figures pegged. With more than 14,000 season tickets sold by the start of the season, he figured the Hornets could average around 18,000 a game their first year. With some luck on the court and some aggressive marketing late in the year, when sales were bound to lag, they might do a little better. But not much.

"I really thought 18,000 would be a very good season," Scheer said, "even with that (season ticket) base because I thought that we had done a good job of tapping and penetrating what I thought was our main core of real fans. I knew there'd be others who'd come to a game or two just to see, but I thought that would be it. We hadn't had much of chance to get into the areas around. I just didn't see where the other fans would come from."

As it turned out, they poured out of the woodwork from day one and never stopped coming. The opener was a sellout, as expected, but the next home game, an election night tilt with the boring LA Clippers, drew 19,015. Scheer was preoccupied that night with the team's first victory and Shinn's stroke, but a few days later he blinked a few times at the figures. Nineteen thousand for the Clippers on Tuesday? On election night? What was going on here?

As in that other Wonderland, things in Charlotte got curiouser and curiouser. The nameless New Jersey Nets drew almost 22,000 the next Tuesday. Washington, another box office dreg, sold out a Saturday night game not long after that. How strange. All Scheer's marketing experience, all his advice, told him that the team would do best by selling not the Hornets, but the opposition, the stars of the NBA. The first year, that's who they'd come to see. But here they were buying tickets for the Nets, Bullets and even the Indiana Pacers. Was the desire to see Vern Fleming and Herb Williams play really that great? Then the answer dawned in some brains. The fans were gobbling up tickets to see teams they thought the Hornets could beat. Now that's a sophisticated fan.

"Some people say that," Scheer said in early December. "I'm not so sure. But I don't know. This whole thing doesn't make any sense."

It was not a complete mystery. The team was doing well enough to inspire true loyalty. They won half of their first 14 games at home, pulling upset after upset to the roar of crowds who could claim at least a little responsibility for the unexpected events which transpired. As Kelly Tripucka noted, "Our fans make up their own little universe, one where we don't lose."

Considering the option offered by reality, that was a better place to be. It was exciting, and with a 50-50 chance of success, the games were fun to attend. A peppy-but-sophisticated atmosphere, orchestrated by Scheer's staff, helped. The franchise went the extra mile to please its fans. The Hornets hired a local disc jockey to help them select music that matched their fans' tastes. They priced nearly a third of their tickets under $13 and toned down the commercialism that so often runs rampant in NBA arenas.

All that pleased Shinn who had said when he landed the team, "We may not be able to guarantee them a great team on the floor right away, but we'll do everything we can off the court to make the games as enjoyable as possible."

The raucous, party-time crowds at those early games indicated the strategy was working. All those bankers whooping it up in the aisle weren't faking it to impress their clients. They were having a good time. But as the first month of the season passed, some worry remained. The newness had not yet worn off. The ACC season was just starting. What would happen?

The Phamous Philadelphia game helped answer the question. A crowd of almost 22,000 watched the Hornets' blistering start, saw the Sixers come back, and erupted in noise when veteran official Lee Jones, perhaps the unsung hero of Charlotte's success, waved off Charles Barkley's would-have-tied-it basket at the buzzer. Many more heard the thriller on radio. Thousands were talking about it the next morning. The phones at the Hornets' offices were ringing the next morning when the first staffer – Scheer – came in. The callers wanted to buy season tickets.

Sales of all tickets jumped in response to the Tuesday night thriller. The Hornets sold out the next game, New Jersey on a Friday, pulled in 22,000 for the uninspiring Indiana Pacers, sold out a game against Dallas, and on December 21 pulled in 23,010 for the Milwaukee Bucks.

In franchise attendance history, the Milwaukee game that Wednesday night was a landmark. Officially, and in this case real life wasn't much different, there wasn't an empty seat in the house the rest of the year. Want to find a real Hornet fan? Don't find one who saw all their victories, or their most exciting games. Find one who saw the five games, or any one, that weren't sold out.

It was all madness after that. Not only were the crowds filling up the place, they were loud. And loyal. They booed Michael Jordan, the national basketball icon who played at UNC and whose parents lived in Charlotte, and a few complained that the Hornets were supporting "the enemy" when they gave out Jordan posters that night. They cheered Kelly Tripucka and Tim Kempton, two products of Notre Dame, a school that inspires a good deal of natural animosity. They dressed up like Kurt Rambis, the Laker hatchet some undoubtedly used to hate. That stuff didn't matter anymore, though. It was them against us, the Hornets. And it was amazing

Rambis, who had seen one of the best teams in basketball, the LA Lakers of the 1980s, not sell out the much-smaller Forum for five straight years, was dumbfounded. "I come out and look every night and I wonder to myself, 'What are these people doing here?'"

The Hornets' fans quickly gained notoriety around the league. When the Lakers arrived in town in March, the stories about Charlotte's fans had already become legend. Josh Rosenfeld, LA's public relations director, asked the day before the game, "Is all that stuff about the crowds true?"

Assured that it was, he said, "Good. All the guys are really anxious to see it. They were hoping it wasn't just a joke."

Aside from gawking, there was the more practical point of not letting the crowd influence the game. The Hornets' fans made it into scouting reports before some of the players did. Don't let the crowd get into the game, coaches told their teams. After a month or so, the word got around, and visitors in Charlotte developed hair-trigger mentalities toward timeouts. Any sign of a Hornet rally and there it came. A stop in the action, and, hopefully, a reduction in the noise upon which the Charlotte players, for a time, seemed to feed.

"From start to finish it's the loudest crowd in the NBA," said Milwaukee coach Del Harris. "You just want to do anything you can to stop them. But you can't. You get the feeling this must really be important to these people."

Boston's Jimmy Rodgers said, "I had about decided anytime they scored two baskets in a row I was going to call timeout. You just can't afford to get these people excited."

Rick Pitino, the New York Knicks' coach then, apparently gave the matter a lot of thought as Charlotte beat his team on its first trip south to the accompaniment of a roaring throng. When he returned a few weeks later, he was full of theories. Pitino went against conventional wisdom and said timeouts should be avoided like the plague. "The crowd gets even louder during the timeouts," he said. "If you use one you just get 'em going."

But if one could stop the action without officially asking for it, well, the lull might be beneficial. Pitino gave it a try that night when he used a dead ball to run out the novel ploy of complaining to the referees about the din. "They can't play music while the game is going on, can they?" he asked during the second quarter of New York's March visit to Charlotte. It was an ironic request, coming as it did from a coach in whose home arena organ-directed clapping is a way of life. But it caused a pause in the game – it was better than a timeout really – because the refs, understandably, weren't absolutely sure on the section of the rules that pertains to music. Finally they ruled, as Charlotte coach Dick Harter had argued, that Pitino was nuts. Of course you could play music during an NBA game.

Pitino tried to talk his way out of it afterwards. "I didn't know," he said. "But I had to do something. I don't know if it's the music or what, but the noise in this place can just kill you."

Ah, the noise. Are acoustics better in the Charlotte Coliseum or the Mormon Tabernacle? It's a question for sound engineers, but surely the Tabernacle doesn't get as loud. With the Hornets on the run, building a lead or chopping one down, it was deafening in the coliseum. Officials' whistles went unheeded and visiting TV and radio crews, their sound equipment tuned to mortal settings, couldn't hear each other talk over the air. The noise was so great you thought it shook the rafters, except there weren't any. You hoped it didn't shake the scoreboard too much. A lesser power – an electric winch – had already brought it down once, the summer before.

But roars like that could happen any time. What was really special were those magic moments when the Hornets surged early in the fourth quarter and the opposition had to call time, and then *the song* came; the power and public emotion of the instant brought chills and goose bumps. It was that good when Otis Day's "Shout!" burst from the coliseum sound system while 23,338 sang and danced along.

It stayed pure and good like that almost the whole season. League veterans laughed at the blind partisanship and the politeness of the fans. But slowly they did begin to learn. By December, Olympian Jeff Grayer of Milwaukee was treated to a shout of, "Hey, Grayer. Where's your bronze medal?" Forget that USA stuff. We're for the Hornets.

Opponents began to get rougher treatment, but it was a long time before the Hornets were booed or heckled, collectively or solo. They were heroes. Muggsy, Kelly, Rambis, Rex had signs in their honor nearly every game. There were even some loyalists with season-tickets in a corner of the lower arena who faithfully brought Earl Cureton banners to every game. "Nice people," said Cureton, who stopped by to chat one night.

Eventually that feeling changed a bit, too. Fans began to sigh at appearances by Dave Hoppen and groan when Rex took yet another bad shot. By the home finale, they were even ready to help Dick Harter coach the game. Dell Curry was playing well, but not all the time then, so a fan behind the bench held up a sign that read "Dell Curry Coach." And Curry did get a big ovation that night when he went in for Rex Chapman.

The 30-game run of sellouts that began with the overflow crowd for Michael Jordan and the Chicago Bulls (sounds like a rock group, doesn't it?) was not assured at its December 23 start. The Hornets still weren't sure. But by the turn of the year, Scheer could see the amazing run of full houses lining up. The enthusiasm over the team's strong December produced a string of unanticipated advance sell-outs in early January – Utah on a Monday, Phoenix on a Thursday – and the schedule maker had already assured Charlotte of some big gates down the road. The Lakers came to town in March. Chicago had two more trips, and the Celtics, a Division rival this year, didn't make the first of three appearances until February 1. All those games had been sold out long ago, and with something akin to a buying panic beginning to grip the public, there seemed a chance that all the gaps might just be filled.

Fans were already kicking themselves for not buying into to this hot stock when they could. A fairly substantial trade in black – or would that be teal? – market tickets ensued. They became so tough that for the really big games, like Jordan's initial visit in December, Scheer could boast of turning down governors, congressmen, even Jordan himself, when they asked for extra tickets.

The crunch, for those in the Hornet office rooting for a sellout string that would never end, would come in late March and early April, when the schedule maker was not as kind and Carolinians might think of something better to do than go indoors and watch a bad team lose another game. But by the time those games rolled around, the question was moot. The Hornets had become too big a deal and fans who had missed the early laps were grabbing any opportunity they could to jump on board. Any Hornet game would do.

Most curious perhaps was a March 12 match up with Sacramento, an obscure and not very interesting team. It had looked like a wash on the schedule when the season began. Who'd want to watch the Hornets and Kings play, much less on the same afternoon as the championship game of ACC Tournament? Though Scheer denied it, this was not a makeup call from the same schedule makers who had given Charlotte the Lakers at home two days before, the day the ACC Tournament had opened. And, as it turned out, the two crowds weren't that different in size. The 23,338 said to be hand for the Lakers may have included a few more than that, and the 23,338 who were said to have watched the Kings were certainly a few less. A casual check of the seats at the end of the first quarter revealed a few empties here and there. But not a lot.

Most of those who had tickets, came. And a few who didn't, came that day and bought one. They booed some when the Hornets wiped from the coliseum scoreboard screen the broadcast of the ACC title game – a nightmare matchup in Hornet eyes between those bitter, in-state rivals, North Carolina and Duke – and there was a Walkman or two more than normal in the crowd that afternoon. But mostly they came and watched the Hornets, cheering as much as they could a rather dismal performance, even booing a time or two for the first time all year.

The stampede through the turnstiles caught the Hornets off guard. Scheer, to his credit, never took credit for anything more than having positioned the franchise well to take advantage of the boom. "I'd like to say we had this all planned out," he said. "But the truth is we didn't."

Although the money tumbled in hand over fist, the miscalculations were costly, and figured to be more so in the future. Charlotte's lease, once viewed as a major coup by owner Shinn, looked a little less shrewd with the coliseum raking in parking and concession funds and running thousands of dollars ahead of its projections. The coliseum authority had hoped to turn a modest, $50,000 profit its first year. In the summer of 1989, thanks almost entirely to the Hornet boom, it looked to be more in the neighborhood of $3 million. By January, the Hornets would have been glad to boost the dollar-a-game rent by thousands in exchange for even a small piece of the concession pie. But a deal was a deal.

Others who failed to see the Bug Boom coming were kicking themselves, too, everyone from retailers who didn't stock Hornet items to fans who didn't buy season tickets when they were available. Local radio and TV stations who didn't win or didn't pursue a contract for Hornets' broadcast rights were thumped by their competition who did. Cy Bahakel's WCCB TV, an independent station with a fittingly small market share, made nice gains because of the viewers switching over to watch the 31 games the station offered. And WBT, already a powerful AM radio station, saw its ratings soar because of its identity as the "Voice of the Hornets." WBT gained up to 7 points on game nights, a huge increase in a world where tenths and halves of points could mean thousands of advertising dollars. That station also attributed a one to two-point rise in daylight, drive-time ratings to carryover from the NBA broadcasts. It was as an old radio trick. Dials tuned in the night before for a particular show, often weren't moved the next day.

The Hornets reacted as best they could to the unexpected hit, but there really wasn't much to do. They saved a pile of money by pulling most of their advertising after November and pored over the seating charts by the hour, looking for ways to accommodate the never-ending demand for season tickets after the season had begun. A boost in the ticket staff, from two to seven, helped, but eventually they ran out of seats before they ran out of would-be season ticket buyers. They had to quit selling at just under 16,000. So many future games were sellouts via single tickets, the team couldn't give a late-coming season-ticket buyer the same seat for every game.

Marketing director Tom Ward, who had come to Charlotte after several years beating his head against the wall in a similar post in Washington, felt a little superfluous in this real-life situation that surpassed even the rosiest of the contemplated scenarios. "It's a marketing man's dream I suppose," Ward said in December, "but the truth is I could have taken the fall off."

The spring, too, except that he was needed to help take calls from fans who wanted to buy more tickets – for next year. There were a lot of calls to take. By the summer of 1989, the Hornets had requests for more than 24,000 season tickets – slightly less than 1,000 over capacity at the coliseum. Yeah, that coliseum. The one Carl Scheer used to think was too big.

Centers of Attention

"Stuart Gray? They want Stuart Gray? I'm better than he is."
– Dave Hoppen.

The Charlotte Hornets rolled toward Christmas with a full head of steam, at least as full as an expansion team could manage. They were an unqualified box office success, and they weren't too bad on the floor either. Through 16 games, they were a very respectable 5-11, not even in last place in their designated division, the Atlantic, and well ahead of their expansion competition, the still-winless Miami Heat.

Kelly Tripucka's superb offensive play was now being augmented by Robert Reid, who went on a scoring tear and averaged nearly 19 a game during a three-week stretch, and by Rex Chapman, who had pumped his field-goal percentage into the mid-30s – a 82-percent gain since the day before Thanksgiving. The point guard tandem of Tyrone Bogues and Michael Holton, occasionally expanded to a trio with one-time starter Rickey Green, was performing well, too. In mid-December, Coach Dick Harter rated that group "a definite plus." And General Manager Carl Scheer said, "Not many teams have three point guards as good as those, do you think?" He wondered why no one was calling about a trade.

Even the center position looked okay. Earl Cureton's hamstring was finally getting better. Dave Hoppen was still meek, but Tim Kempton – Dr. K – was playing so well that it didn't seem to matter. Kempton still didn't get much respect around the league, however. After beating Charlotte December 17 in Detroit, the Piston big men ribbed each other about surrendering baskets to assorted Hornets of obscure repute.

Bill Laimbeer asked Rick Mahorn, "Hey, how'd Tolbert get his hoop? He didn't get that over you did he?"

Since Tolbert had done just that, Mahorn didn't bother to answer. Besides, he'd seen something worse happen to Laimbeer.

"Wasn't that Kempton driving around your butt for a basket?"

Mahorn asked, then snorted. "Hmmmph. Let that big ol' red-headed motherfucker score on you. Hmmph. He runs like my mother."

"Fuck you," said Laimbeer, ending the exchange.

Even if he didn't strike much fear in the hearts of the Pistons, Kempton was playing far above expectations. A former sixth-round draft choice and ex-Italian League star, he was averaging almost 10 points a game, shooting close to 70 percent from the floor, while laying some meat on opposing big men. The Hornets were happy with that. Kempton would never be a star, but it looked as if he could be a useful backup or number-three center after the team got good. And he'd been free, found in a free-agent camp of all places.

Yeah, that was a pretty good find, and this was a pretty good team. No jerks. They got along well. And they were good enough that when combined with the ever-present element of surprise, they often had a chance. "We're something like the Japanese at Pearl Harbor," said Reid one night, dipping into his unique bag of descriptive phrases. "We come out of the clouds, get the job done, and get out of there before they know what went wrong."

But some clouds were beginning to drift into this rosy picture. And no matter how one held the camera or posed the Hornets, there was no way to block out those ominous, looming clouds. All the hustle and outside shooting they could muster, all the clever plays Dick Harter could think of, couldn't change the fact that they were the league's shortest, lightest team. If the inside players scratched and clawed for all they were worth, Charlotte just might stay even in rebounding for the night with any given opponent. And that, as chief rebounder Kurt Rambis noted, was about all they could hope for. "Anything we get beyond break even," Rambis said early on, "is just gravy."

Even though they were staying in most games and managing to win a few, the Hornets were eating most of their meat dry. They were out rebounded in 11 of 13 games to start the season. A brief recovery followed that included the rather astounding feat of out rebounding the Houston Rockets, but then in one, brutal, three-game stretch in mid-December, they were pummeled on the boards 172-115. The Hornets actually managed to win one of those games over New Jersey – and went to overtime in another. But it was clearly not a good sign. Opposing teams were starting to pound away at the team's weakest link, and it seemed just a matter of time before it gave way.

The only answer was to strengthen it, and the most obvious way to do that was to add a bigger, stronger player, a course of action Harter had advocated all along. But such players don't come to expansion teams. A few possibilities were contemplated, among them Paul Mokeski, a bad-kneed seven-footer who played for Milwaukee, and Stuart Gray, the center Harter had wanted the team to obtain the summer before. Both popped up in preliminary trade talks. But nothing went further than that. To the general manager of a first-year team that was playing close and raking in the dough, the crisis did not seem all that serious. To a 57-year-old coach with a two-year contract and a smoldering desire for victory that occasionally burst into flames, it did.

As happened so often during Charlotte's first season, a temporary solution materialized while everyone was waiting for someone to do something. In late December, Rambis began peeling away his Clark Kent clothing to reveal his true identity as Super Rebounder. Beginning with back-to-back home games against Indiana and Dallas, in which he grabbed 13 and then 21 rebounds, Rambis, a slightly-built power forward and ex-Laker sub, went on a 12-week tear in which he averaged nearly 11 rebounds a game. Twelve times in that span he had 14 or more. And in the heart of the rebound run, a 12-game string in early January, Rambis averaged 13.4 bounds a game.

It was a remarkable performance, produced by nothing more than Rambis' pride and desire to play better. Coasting along in early December at a respectable eight-rebound-a-game clip, Rambis had pulled Harter aside for a frank discussion. Seven years with the Lakers had given Charlotte's co-captain an acute sense of team dynamics and psychology. The Hornets were not the Lakers, but even so, he knew his continued status as a starter and major minute taker might not sit well with teammates who watched the time being expended in a mediocre way. They might think it was in deference to Rambis' salary, his pedigree, or even his age. So Rambis told Harter to feel free to bench him, just in case the coach hadn't thought of it himself.

"I didn't want to be starting just because I'd started the season starting or something," Rambis said. "And the way I'd been playing I didn't deserve to. I thought he should think about it."

Harter really hadn't considered the idea. His options were too limited at that position to think about reducing the role of a player who was at least performing at an average level. He hadn't even gotten around to demoting Dave Hoppen, whose temerity drove him crazy, and who, by the first of December, was Charlotte's third most effective center. On the other hand, he wasn't happy with Rambis' work so far and was pleased that Rambis wasn't either. In Harter's view, the problem was essentially conditioning. Rambis, undersized and under-talented, depended upon huge amounts of desire and hustle to produce results. If he didn't go harder than everyone else, he was nothing special, his only other assets being the on-court savvy built over the years and a bit more quickness than the average inside player possessed.

With the Lakers, this had not been a problem. He had averaged less than 19 minutes a game during his career there, and even in his most active year, 1982-83, he had not played, on average, in half the game each night. On those terms, great bursts of energy and emotion were not so difficult to produce. Play seven or eight hard minutes to start the game, five or six more to start the second half and a few others here and there.

But for Charlotte it was different. Rambis had to play more. That's why the team got him, and that's why he chose to come. The problem was that it wasn't that easy. Harter was appalled early in the year at Rambis' condition. After one especially dismal performance, Harter said in one of his typical overstatements, "He can't run up and down the floor three times without needing a rest." Rambis also had showed some unsuspected fragility, missing three of the team's first 12 games with his San Antonio sickness and a recurring injury to his ankle.

Rambis would miss just one more until the very end of the season, however, becoming, in the process, a study in toughness and professionalism. For most of the season both his feet remained swollen at one point or another, and after especially brutal games, those appendages would take on a gnarled, misshapen look.

Rambis did not like to discuss the injury. It seemed an excuse, and it might give the opposition some advantage if they knew. But his condition was hard to disguise. He limped about the locker room after almost every game with bags of ice wrapped around one foot or the other and often both. He had sore ankles and sore insteps and sore arches. As trainer Terry Kofler observed one evening, "He just has bad feet."

But Rambis played through that, and played through his conditioning problem, a problem which he never really acknowledged. And suddenly he began playing like a man possessed.

The two-game burst against Indiana and Dallas was a sample, and Rambis wore the hero's laurels when his buzzer-beating follow shot beat Chicago on December 23. But the real coming out was on December 30, against the Knicks, a modestly surprising team which was, at the time, running away with the Atlantic Division race. New York came to Charlotte at the end of a four-game-in-five-day stretch, a situation that lends itself to upsets. But it was by no means a certainty. The Knicks' power players, Patrick Ewing and the newly acquired Charles Oakley, were both overmatches for the Charlotte counterparts, a fact that quickly became evident in the first half, as Ewing whipped through the attempted defenses of Hoppen, Kempton and Earl Cureton for 19 points, and Oakley grabbed 10 rebounds. That helped the Knicks, who were otherwise playing atrociously, to stay within three points, 59-56, at the break.

It also drew Harter's first technical foul of the season. Frustrated when Ewing once again got the ball too easily and had to be fouled by Chapman to be stopped, Harter screamed and stomped, demanding a push-off call on the Knicks' center. That wasn't the call he got.

At the half, the Hornets' coaches decided to try the smaller, but quicker, Rambis on Ewing. It was one of the sharpest basketball decisions of the season. Fronting the agile 7-footer, Rambis kept the ball out of his hands and helped hold him to just six second-half points. "He was a pest," Ewing said.

Rambis, who also contributed 21 points and 13 rebounds to one of Charlotte's best efforts so far, called the game his best of the season. "And maybe my best ever. That felt very good," he said.

The victory left the Hornets in high spirits. They finished the first two months of the year at 8-19, with very few blowouts and a lot of near misses. And they seemed to be playing well. A week before beating New York, two days before Christmas, a huge crowd had watched Charlotte rally from 15 down in the first quarter to beat Jordan and the Bulls.

Robert Reid and Michael Holton combined to play superb defense on Jordan, whose 18 fourth-quarter points left him with just 33, only an average night. And Tripucka had poured in 30 points, including a daring three-pointer with less than two minutes left. Then, with the game tied and 26 seconds to play, Charlotte cashed in on a crazy bounce and perhaps a missed call to win the game. With the game and 24-second shot clock ticking down, Reid escaped defender Craig Hodges to the right of the lane and went up for the shot. Jordan rushed at him and tipped the ball, which fell short of the basket. Rambis swatted it off the backboard, then gathered up the carom and laid it in just as the buzzer sounded.

There was no question about the basket, but since neither Reid's nor Rambis' shot had hit the rim, shouldn't the shot clock have expired? That's what the rules say, but the referees left the scene without blowing a whistle, wisely ignoring or missing that technicality as the coliseum erupted into a scream that lasted for almost a minute.

Harter, giddy after a victory that he said "was the best we could do," waved off questions about the missed call. "Ah, who knows what happened. The red light went off after the shot went in, and that means we won. That other stuff, who cares?"

Harter was more interested this night in talking about the shoes he slipped on after the game: a pair of teal-and-purple suede loafers sent to him and the other coaches by a Charlotte shoe store owner. "I was going to wear them the whole game," Harter said. "But I didn't have the balls to do it. Look pretty good don't they?"

Three days later, Charlotte played well again, but for the second time in a month, blew an opportunity to upset Houston. In this one, Charlotte rallied from seven down with five minutes left to tie at 95-95 with 3:24 to play. The teams managed only one basket between them the rest of the way, that coming on Akeem Olajuwon's alley oop dunk with 63 seconds left. Charlotte botched four chances after that. Tripucka lost control of the ball on a drive to the basket with 40 seconds to play, then had it stolen from him by Sleepy Floyd with nine seconds left. Tyrone Bogues stole the ball back from Floyd three seconds later, but on the ensuing inbounds play, Rambis and Kempton set up on the wrong sides of the court, fouling up the timing of the play. Tripucka's inbounds pass was intercepted, ending the Hornets' chances.

Harter liked his team's defense down the stretch in that one, but was not thrilled about the final play. "It's my responsibility to get the play drawn up right, but it is one of our normal plays. I don't think we've run it but about a thousand times this year."

Charlotte went to Cleveland after that for their second thrashing of the year by the Cavs. It was not quite as bad as the first – just 24 points at the end – but Harter didn't see much difference. Or much good. At one point in the second half, when Cleveland was pulling away for good, he screamed at one of his players then turned toward the bench and said, "I don't know what good yelling does. Every player they've got is better than every player I have."

• • • • •

Late December brought bad news for some Hornets. One was rookie Tom Tolbert, who was released in person, though not in salary, on the 29th, when Chapman returned from a seven-game stay on the injured list because of a sore back. Chapman had gone on the list, somewhat reluctantly, in mid-December when Dell Curry returned to action as the Hornets once again dodged a decision. They had a similar option when they brought Chapman back. Tyrone Bogues had sprained and then re-sprained his ankle late in the month and hobbled through the Houston and Cleveland games. He was an injured list candidate, but the Hornets decided to bite the bullet and let Tolbert go.

The decision came down to either Tolbert, Ralph Lewis or Rickey Green. With hope that someone still might want Green in a trade, Charlotte held on to him. And though Tolbert held more promise than Lewis in some eyes, Harter thought it proper to let him go first. It was a message, he thought, that players who try hard on his team get a break. Lewis was a hard worker who often accompanied Green and Curry on voluntary pre-game runs. Green, the old pro, knew after a month or so that his opportunities with the Hornets were limited. Running was his game and he had to keep his legs as ready as he could so he could make the most of whatever he got. Lewis, smart and thoughtful, realized he was a player on the border. He had to work extra hard to keep up with the other players, and of course, that never bothered a coach.

Tolbert, on the other hand, never showed much interest in doing anything extra. A nice person, but not particularly intense, he coasted for two months then coasted on out of the NBA. Three weeks later, he had signed on with a professional team that was based in the Canary Islands. It seemed a fitting destination.

A few weeks before Tolbert's departure, the Hornets also said goodbye, temporarily, to David Thompson. The ex-N.C. State star who had been an all-pro in Denver during Scheer's tenure there, had been hired by the Hornets to work as the team's director of community relations. It was a benevolent gesture, spurred by Scheer's relationship with Thompson, Thompson's regional ties, and owner Shinn's fervent belief that he should help people. After several brilliant seasons in the ABA and NBA, Thompson ran afoul of drugs. His addiction to cocaine carried him into a personal hell that ruined every part of his life and left him, in his mid-30s, living in his native Shelby without much money or hope.

The Hornets offered him a chance to recover. It was not a bad plan. Thompson's name was still legend in the Carolinas, and his testimony against the evil of drugs, carried, for obvious reasons, a great deal of weight. He joined the team and quickly began a speaking schedule that rivaled Shinn's. It seemed to be going well, but then in September Thompson was involved in a suspicious, late-night fight near his home. As fall turned toward winter, he began to miss speaking engagements and other assignments. Finally, in mid-December, he checked back into the NBA's addiction rehabilitation program near Los Angeles to fight the new problem of alcoholism.

After his departure, Scheer and others chastised themselves for contributing to the problem. The endless speeches about how he had ruined his own life had depressed Thompson and driven him to a new poison to make him forget. They had piled too much on him. When he returned, his role would be less public, they said. They wouldn't make the same mistake again.

• • • • •

On the strength of Rambis' roll and the two, late-December upsets, Charlotte charged into the new year – and immediately hit a brick wall. New Jersey, with Joe Barry Carroll wreaking havoc, won in Charlotte on January 3. A lucky three-pointer by the Nets' Lester Conner with 40 seconds to play KOed a late comeback bid in that one.

The next night the team just fell apart in Washington. Down 12 after one period, Charlotte played its worst quarter ever, one of the worst in NBA history. The Hornets didn't score for nine straight minutes, missing eight straight shots and committing six turnovers. They trailed by 29 at the half, and only Rambis' never-say-die second half kept them from major humiliation. It was pretty bad as it was. Tripucka was three for 17 from the floor. Hoppen was 0 for 7, none from very far away. The team shot 35 percent from the floor.

"I guess the best thing you can say about it is that it's over," Harter said immediately after the game. "If this were college we might practice tomorrow at 7 a.m. But it's not."

What Harter would have preferred was to wake up early the next day and find his general manager hard at work, trying to find him a center. He and Scheer were at loggerheads over the issue. In a conversation the day of the Bullets debacle, Harter had predicted that without pivot help the Hornets wouldn't win two games after the mid-February All-Star break. Scheer was, as usual, not as impressed by the direness of the team's straits. And he felt that the trade prospects were not good. He was against dealing first-round draft picks, the Hornets' most prized commodities at the moment, and was wary, too, about sending off any of the team's newly created celebrities. As he told a reporter from a newspaper in Columbia, S.C., "If I were to trade away one of these players, I think I would have a revolt on my hands."

Scheer's reluctance to move frustrated Harter, who launched a not-so-subtle media campaign to rally support for his point of view. It began with the Washington game where, ironically, the centers really weren't the problem, at least not all of it, no center ever having played poorly enough alone to cause a debacle like that. Nonetheless, Harter summed up the proceedings by saying, "Until there are some big people to help inside, there are going to be some nights like this.

David Rolfe

At left, Hornets Coach Dick Harter makes his point. Below, General Manager Carl Scheer with his game face on. At bottom, the Hornets' brain trust: (l-r) Terry Kofler, Ed Badger and Gene Littles.

David Rolfe

David Rolfe

Steve Matteson

Kelly Tripucka goes up against Boston's Robert Parish.

Steve Matteson

Rex Chapman tosses one in over Cleveland's Mike Sanders.

Steve Matteson

Tim Kempton goes up for a rebound against Hot Rod Williams and Craig Ehlo of Cleveland.

Steve Matteson

Dave Hoppen defends against Boston's Robert Parish.

Hornet fans cheer their team in different fashions. Some just get up and yell; others go dancing in the aisles.

David Rolfe

Steve Matteson

David Rolfe

WIth fans like these, it's easy to see why the Charlotte Hornets led the NBA in attendance – the first-ever expansion team to do so.

David Rolfe

The Charlotte fans caught Hornet Fever early – and kept it all season.

Steve Matteson

Steve Matteson

While Hugo the Hornet whips the crowd into a frenzy by starting wave after wave (above), Coach Dick Harter has a word with Muggsy Bogues (below).

Steve Matteson

David Rolfe

The Charlotte Hornets averaged over 23,000 fans per game, and sometimes it seemed that every one wanted an autograph. Below, Earl Cureton obliges waiting fans.

Steve Matteson

Steve Matteson

Despite his height disadvantage, Tyrone Bogues went after every loose ball – and frequently won the battle.

Steve Matteson

Rex Chapman slams one home. He skipped the NBA's annual dunk contest, but might have done quite well in it.

Steve Matteson

Michael Holton takes it to the hoop against the Celtics.

Steve Matteson

Kelly Tripucka gets two points the easy way.

Former Los Angeles Laker Kurt Rambis was a key element in the Hornets' first-season success. At right, he takes a drink from manager David Jovanozic after injuring his ankle. Below, Rambis in action against the Milwaukee Bucks.

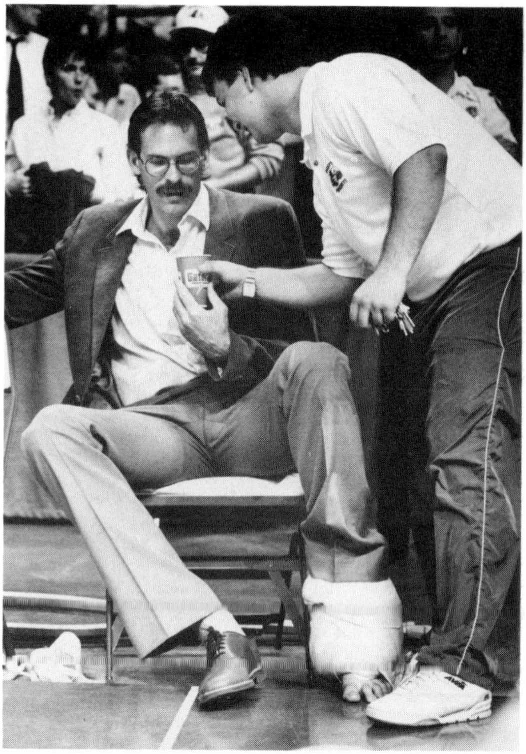

Steve Matteson

David Rolfe

When you start out with no game around the basket, it's tough."

That was said matter-of-factly. Harter then switched to sarcasm. A Washington writer asked about the play of the Bullets' Dave Feitl, a big center who, the year before, had actually played fewer minutes per game than Hoppen while both were with Golden State. Feitl had 10 points and five rebounds against the Hornets, one of his better performances, and Harter said, "Oh, the Bullets don't have any problems at center. Feitl's All-World. At least he looked that way tonight."

And a few seconds later, just in case someone had missed the point, Harter lambasted his pivots again. A radio reporter wondered what advice Harter would give to the coming expansion teams from Minnesota and Orlando. Pausing for about a millisecond, Harter said, slowly but very surely, "Find ... some ... big ... men."

Harter's venom was triggered by a sudden decline – as much as that was possible – in the play of the larger Hornets.

Earl Cureton, who replaced Hoppen as the starting center the day after Christmas, when Hoppen caught the flu, was cured of his early season injuries and was playing well. He averaged 9.6 points a game the last six games of December, and was starting to rebound well, too. But for all his wiles and skills, Cureton was too small for the task. Just a bit bigger than Rambis, he'd been asked to play center, at least briefly, at almost every stop in his eight-year, four-city career. But it was never supposed to be a full-time job, and when he was paired with Rambis, the Hornets were woefully small.

Kempton had provided the missing beef for a time. Sound fundamentally and a decided surprise to Hornet opponents, the big, red-head from Long Island had been a big plus. The team had held out some hope for him then as a potential building block, had even fielded a few trade calls. But possessing minimal NBA skills and less strength than his burly, 245-pound body would suggest, Kempton, somewhat like Rambis, was faced with the prospect of having to play very, very hard every night, or very, very poorly. Inconsistency of effort led to wild swings in effectiveness for Dr. K, as Harter understood very well.

"With Tim," Harter said one day, "it all depends on how often and how well he plays to his potential. There are guys in the league, superstars, who play near their best all the time. And there are guys who shouldn't be in the league at all on ability who do that, too. Tim could fall into the latter class." That did not mean a subsistence-level role for Kempton either, for Harter put players like Detroit's Bill Laimbeer, a personal favorite, in that same boat. "Other than shooting the ball a little, what other skill does he have?" Harter asked about Laimbeer. "But, he comes to play every single day. That can make all the difference."

• • • • •

Kempton was not at odds with Harter's plans, though at one time he had imagined something a bit better. Kempton's dad, Vince, who had played center for a Jack Ramsey-coached team at St. Joesph's that had gone to the Final Four, had passed on basketball fundamentals, as well as useful bulk, to his son. That had made Kempton a dominating prep player, a high school All-America whose good grades and disciplined background – his mother is a New York City policeman – made him a recruiting target of all the Eastern college bluebloods. Duke and Virginia wanted him. So did Notre Dame. To the surprise of no one, Kempton, a product of the intense Long Island parochial school league, chose to play for Digger Phelps and the Fighting Irish.

Kempton was part of a much heralded recruiting class, and his choice looked like a good one when he grabbed a lion's share of the playing time – more than 27 minutes a game – as a freshman. He averaged 10.6 points and 5.8 rebounds that year and shot 60 percent from the field. But, as it turned out, that was the highlight of his career. In a strange down period, even for Phelps, Notre Dame in the mid-1980s kept signing big-name players without producing big results. Kempton kept being superseded, and his production declined accordingly every year. Not even dating the coach's daughter helped. By his senior year the one-time All-America was little more than a glorified pick setter, one more player whose talents were smothered in Phelp's suffocating system.

Even so, he managed to get drafted, in the sixth round, by the LA Clippers. That troubled franchise was then at the anti-zenith of its famous failings and was willing to try anything. Kempton knocked people around and looked enthusiastic in training camp – a decided contrast to many of his teammates – and he made the team. He battled his way through the Clippers' disheartening 12-win season without distinguishing himself, but he did stick all the way. He was in the NBA, which, considering the odds, was pretty good. Only four sixth-round picks have made a team in the past 10 years. Curiously, three of them did it in 1986.

Kempton was not so fortunate the next year. Three, first-round draft picks cluttered the roster, soaking up spots previously allocated for hangers on. He was cut before the season started. His agent, the late Larry Fleisher, was able to land him a spot in the Italian pro league, in Naples, however, so his career was alive. And, in some ways, it was just what the doctor ordered. Or, in this case, needed.

Italian teams are restricted to two Americans, or foreigners, per team, so those "strangeri" must, by definition, be stars. That was not a great match for Kempton's known skills. Stars, after all, are not stars because they can set a good pick or hold position in the post. But he adapted, improving his scoring and ballhandling and becoming more aggressive.

When he came back to the states the next summer to the Hornets' camp, he was a changed player, much closer to the prep star he had once been than to the hulking bruiser of Fighting Irish non-fame. "I sort of stagnated in college, for whatever reason," Kempton said the summer before joining the Hornets for his second NBA season. "It helped when I got out, got away and just started playing again."

Kempton's progression at that point had allowed him to dream a bit. But he still had a good grasp of his situation. "I think I could contribute as a backup center or maybe even as a power forward on a team with a real big 7-footer at center," he said in December. "I could give someone a good, solid player who played all the time. I think that would be pretty good."

That seemed possible for a time, but as the year changed to 1989, Kempton began sinking into a slump that would last the rest of the season. Large opponents pushed past him, as they did the Hornets' other centers, and the surges of offensive power that had sometimes offset such shortcomings came less and less frequently. His magical shot even deserted him. From an NBA high 69.7 percent at the end of November, his field-goal percentage fell steadily. Had he missed four more shots, he wouldn't have hit 50 percent for the season.

Many factors were involved in Kempton's decline. One was that opponents began playing him with more preparation. Others included a January hand injury, and especially later on, a failure of confidence.

Like most players, Kempton believed much of the blame lay in how he was used. When Harter applied the verbal lash to his centers after a February loss to Boston, suggesting that the lack of an inside scoring threat was helping the opposition to shackle his outside shooters, Kempton bristled. "But how do they know we can't score in there?" he asked. "The ball never comes in there. Boston throws it in to everybody. They even throw it to Ramon Rivas (a Celtic rookie of unremarkable ability) for crissakes. We don't throw it in to our starters or anybody else. We just shoot the jumpers and go chase the long rebounds. Then they say they're not happy with the big men. I don't know what's going on."

Kempton wasn't happy that Harter was looking for a replacement, either. "He obviously feels we need some help," Kempton said in January, "but I don't agree. I think Dave and I can get it done."

• • • • •

David Dirk Hoppen wasn't as upset as Kempton, though he found the choice of potential subs strange. When the first Stuart Gray rumors popped up, Hoppen shook his head in disbelief and said, "Stuart Gray? They want Stuart Gray? *I'm* better than he is."

This self-administered slap in the face reflected Hoppen's understanding of reality. He knew that he was not yet a good NBA player, but he also knew that with his size and physical abilities he had a chance and would receive an opportunity. As Hoppen once noted, "I was born tall, and if I continue to progress, maybe some day I can be good and tall." He was like Kempton in that he had difficulty playing to his potential, but unlike him in that his potential was greater. Hoppen was a little taller, a full 6-11 compared to Kempton's exaggerated 6-10; he could jump better, run faster and possessed a defter shooting touch. He could be, at times, quite graceful and athletic on the court, although he also could appear to be a klutz.

The basic difference, though, was in temperament. Kempton lived up to the red-head's billing, piling up a team-high (for players) five technicals during the year and instigating the only practice fight when he squared off against Hoppen during an especially spirited scrimmage. Hoppen managed a technical but, much to Harter's dismay, spent most of the season eschewing contact and confrontation.

Harter thought a lot about how to reverse Big Dave's passivity, but could never make up his mind what was best because, for most of the season, nothing seemed to work. He would alternately cajole and castigate Hoppen in games, with an emphasis on the latter, sort of a like a one-man bad cop/good cop routine. He even thought of roughing him up a bit. One day while musing about the attributes of Stuart Gray – the rugged Indiana center whom Harter coveted because he was available and big, and because he would do almost anything a coach asked, particularly if that coach were Dick Harter – Harter offered this scenario. "Stuart is the kind of tough guy we need. If I told him, 'Run through that wall over there,' or ..." Harter's face brightened as a new idea popped into his head. "... or 'Knock Hoppen through that wall,' Stuart would do it."

Harter flashed a big grin. He was joking. Probably.

Hoppen was not unaffected by all this. He understood Harter's words, grasped the meanings of his harangues ... and generally accepted his fate as Harter's whipping boy.

On a bus ride to Madison Square Garden in February, the night of the NBA's 9 p.m. trade deadline, it was noted to Hoppen and Kempton, seated as always near each other, that if they made it to halftime they were probably safe.

"Now wouldn't that be something?" Kempton said. "You go in at halftime and they say, 'Can we please have our uniform back?'"

Hoppen sighed and said, "Yeah, but if it were me they'd probably do it at the end of the halftime ... just so coach could rag on me one more time."

It was not a pleasant experience to be so targeted, especially not by Dick Harter, whose intensity could produce, by all accounts, some classic ass-chewings. But Hoppen seemed genuinely perplexed as to what to do to avoid it. A nice man who had avoided the arrogance sometimes created by athletic adulation, Hoppen was genuinely shy. In the Hornets' locker room at the Charlotte Coliseum, his stall was on a wall by itself, the chair in which he sat almost always facing into the locker, away from his teammates, as if he didn't want to face them. He was not embarrassed necessarily, for although he undoubtedly let them down occasionally, they all had such moments that season. It was just that the idea of intense contact, of being in someone's face, seemed foreign to Hoppen, on the court or otherwise. He heard Harter's pleas for more physical play and unabated aggressiveness, but he couldn't make himself understand them.

On the same January night in Washington that Harter was doling out pivot jokes, Hoppen was still grasping.

"I'm just not sure what he means," Hoppen said while staring at the locker room floor in the Capital Centre. "The way I've been playing I don't blame coach for saying things. But I don't know that I understand what it is he wants when he keeps talking about 'play aggressive, play aggressive.' There's not a minute I'm out there when I'm not playing as hard as I can. I'm just not sure what he means."

Harter rolled his eyes at that news. "Maybe I'll have to tell him again," he said, thinking, perhaps, of Stuart Gray.

• • • • •

It's easy to imagine, though difficult to prove, that Hoppen and Kempton are simply typical products of their regions. Kempton, aggressive and outwardly confident, is a Long Islander who brags about the wonders of New York City, or "the greatest city in the world," as he calls it. He learned basketball in a tough and highly competitive high school league where the meek did not survive. Indeed, they didn't even get to play.

Hoppen was born and raised in Nebraska. He is not the farm boy his teammates sometimes made him out to be. He's from Omaha, a city about the size of Charlotte, the son of a telephone worker who gave him a reasonably comfortable life. He grew as high as an elephant's eye, as the song says, sprouting to 6-10 before he was a junior in high school, and naturally became a basketball player. That's not a big deal in Omaha, or Nebraska in general, and the competition wasn't great, although at the time it was about as good as it has ever been. Besides Hoppen, the Class A league around Omaha contained Ron Kellogg and Kerry Trotter who both went on to decent college careers. Kellogg played at Kansas. Trotter went to Marquette. They were the Big Three of the Omaha Metropolitan League, which was one of the few truly integrated prep leagues in the state.

Hoppen's team was Benson High, an old, inner city school whose athletic teams were known, honest to God, as the Bunnies. Dick Harter may find that appropriate. Local headline writers in the Hoppen era thought it marvelous ("Bunnies Hoppen Now" etc.). They got to write lots of headlines, too. For with Hoppen in the pivot and a not-too-bad supporting cast, the Bunnies just Hoppened to be the best team in Omaha for several years running. In Hoppen's junior year, they went to the Class A (Nebraska's highest classification) finals. In his senior year, Hoppen scored more but had less help, and Benson was knocked out in the semi-finals. Hoppen was good enough to make a few All-America teams and draw major recruiting attention. Notre Dame, Missouri, Creighton, Nebraska, and Kentucky called, among others. Those five made his final cut.

On his visit to UK, Hoppen was cornered in Joe B. Hall's office and given the old ultimatum treatment. "We've got one scholarship left," Hall told Hoppen. "It's between you and another guy. If you sign right now it's you."

"Well, I've got some other visits left," Hoppen remembers telling Hall.

"No, that's not the way it works, son," Hall said. "It's today or not at all."

This might surprise Dick Harter, but Hoppen says he told Hall, "Well, then I guess it's not at all."

Hoppen walked away from the Big Blue, made his other visits, and picked Nebraska. It was a major coup for Moe Iba's Cornhusker program. The school had never been able to land the best players in Nebraska or a tall guy who could play. Suddenly they had both, and

Iba made sure no one forgot. Hoppen became an instant starter, and fairly quickly, a star, in no small part due to Iba's post-oriented offense. He averaged 13.9 points a game as a freshman, 19.9 points as a sophomore, and 23.5 points and 8.6 rebounds during a sensational junior season in which he shot almost 65 percent from the floor. By then, most Nebraska basketball fans, and there were a few, could mimic Iba's constant exhortation. When the Cornhusker attack bogged down, they would sarcastically holler, "Get it in to Hoppen."

Nebraska did, and Hoppen's senior year was nearly as good as the one before. He was a certain first-rounder and a possible lottery pick in the NBA draft, when he blew out his knee in a February 1 game against Colorado. It was a terrible injury, similar to those that ended Mitch Kupchak's career and sidelined Bernard King for almost two seasons. Hoppen's surgery went well. The replacement part for the torn ligament, grafted from elsewhere in his body, was implanted with enough tension to keep the joint from wobbling, and Hoppen was able to come back. By the time he joined the Hornets he wasn't even wearing a brace.

But it still took him a year to recuperate. He spent most of it in Atlanta, under surveillance by the Hawks, who had gambled by drafting him in third round in spite of his knee. But Hoppen never played a game in Atlanta. After more than a year of rehabilitation, he was waived by the Hawks just after Christmas, 1987. He latched on with a CBA team for a few games, then Milwaukee signed him to a 10-day contract on January 12. When it was up, the Bucks offered to sign him for the season, but Golden State offered more – guaranteed pay for the rest of that season plus the next. Hoppen couldn't resist. He became a Warrior.

It was a good half season for Hoppen. When injuries felled Ralph Sampson and a few others, he got a chance to play. Hoppen started eight of the last 11 games in an ugly, 20-62 season, and averaged a respectable 10.6 points and 6.3 rebounds in that stretch. He shot 86 percent from the foul line and looked like a player who might be promising enough to keep. But new coach Don Nelson had other plans. He exposed Hoppen to the expansion teams, and Charlotte gobbled him up. Big men with any chance at all were hard to find, and there were plenty of people in the NBA who thought that maybe, one day, he'd be a player.

It looked that way early in the year. Hoppen had a few decent games. He shot the ball well. But after contracting the flu on Christmas Day and missing the Houston game, an absence that Harter thought showed little intestinal fortitude, Hoppen's production followed Kempton's down the tubes. In a brutal, five-game stretch just after he came back from his illness, Hoppen averaged 1.8 points and 2.8 rebounds a game. He was also in the midst of an amazing 30-game stretch – more than 500 minutes on the court – in which he did not block a shot. Hoppen was never a great shot blocker, but he is after all 6-11.

Part of the problem may have been residual weakness from the flu, but Hoppen was basically just playing bad basketball. "I've never had a slump like this, in which I was just terrible at everything," he said.

• • • • •

Dick Harter might have argued the point, but he didn't really have time. Instead, he replaced Hoppen in the starting lineup with Cureton and milked "Earl the Twirl" for all he was worth. And he continued to brood about centers who could be had and general managers who wouldn't make trades. The Hornets had to get bigger. If not, the pounding of an NBA season would accelerate the demise of this small team because it could take less of a whipping, and, in the second half of the year, many teams would be in assorted competitions for higher playoff spots. The Hornets wouldn't catch as many slack nights.

Scheer didn't agree, didn't want to agree, since it would mean rocking a fairly smooth-sailing boat, and he didn't like Harter's continued whining to the press. But after some huffing and puffing about the matter, he decided he owed it to his coach to give it another try. The deal wheels started turning again.

While they did, the Hornets sputtered along. After the Washington massacre, Charlotte was beaten soundly in Boston on a Friday night. The Hornets flew home to meet Washington again for their fourth game in five days, the maximum NBA schedule grind allowed, with a three-game losing streak in tow. Harter was not optimistic about his team's chances and was once again down, but after an afternoon of watching college basketball on TV, his energy levels climbed. He was almost bubbly before the game. He talked enthusiastically about the building ACC race and said, "That really rejuvenated me."

Basketball is Dick Harter's fountain of youth, and unlike many men, constant immersion in his profession did not make him sick of it. Quite the contrary. He spent a great deal of time watching basketball and football games, live and on TV. While coaching with the Pacers, he had slipped away to see, and reveled in, the famous

Indiana high school tournament. In Charlotte, he attended perhaps half a dozen UNC-Charlotte games, not as a scout, just as a fan.

If a day's rest in front of the TV had recharged Harter's batteries, it had done something less for his team's. Rickey Green and Ralph Lewis were both out with the flu, and everyone else was sagging. Fortunately for the Hornets, Washington wasn't in much better shape. The Bullets had also played the night before, and had gone into double overtime with Milwaukee in Baltimore.

Perhaps it came from being at home, or perhaps it was from the coliseum crowd, wired out of its mind as usual, but Charlotte found its legs first. Led by Tripucka, who scored 20 in the first half, the Hornets jumped in front early and stayed there almost all the way. Miraculously almost, Hoppen contributed a season-high 11 rebounds. Michael Holton played well and Rambis rallied to grab 10 rebounds in the second half. A fast-break basket by Robert Reid with 9:24 to play made it 91-75 and Washington looked tired and beat.

But, as so often happens in the NBA, the situation reversed itself very quickly. Washington rallied, the Hornets ran into a cold snap, and when Bernard King hit an off-balance 12-footer with 74 seconds to go, it was just 102-100, Charlotte.

The two tired teams, like battered heavyweights, threw a lot of futile punches down the stretch. Tripucka missed a layup, and Rambis threw an easy pass into the stands. Washington's King, after a superb move to get open on the baseline, fired a short, turnaround jumper into the side of the backboard. Washington's Ledell Eackles finally broke the double drought, hitting a free throw with 32 seconds left that made it a one-point game.

Charlotte muddled the crucial possession that followed, moving tentatively against an animated Bullet defense. The 24-second shot clock ticked down and they still weren't close to a shot. With about five seconds left, Cureton found himself holding the ball at the top of the key with his back to the basket. Not a promising position, given that Cureton isn't a great shooter when he's even closer and facing his target. But then, out of the confusion, an opportunity appeared. The youngest legs on the court, those of Rex Chapman, left a tired Washington defender behind on the right wing and flashed free, taking Chapman in front of Cureton at the top of the key. Cureton made a lateral pass to Chapman like a man getting rid of a bomb. Chapman swished a three-pointer with two seconds left on the shot clock.

Noted Cureton afterwards, "In a situation like that, the best thing I can do is give the ball to someone who can shoot. Luckily, Rex showed up just in time."

That was enough to hold off the Bullets, though just barely. Eackles, like Chapman, a rookie, answered with a three-pointer of his own with six seconds to make it 105-104. Chapman was fouled with five seconds left and nearly grew horns through his laurels when he missed both shots. But he was saved by his own bad touch. The second shot came off so hard that Washington's inside rebounders could do no more than give it a quick bat as it flew by. Teammate Holton chased it down in backcourt and hit two free throws in the final seconds to seal the victory. It was Charlotte's ninth of the season, a milestone of some importance since it tied the Hornets with the 1972-73 76ers for fewest victories in a season. One more win and Charlotte could assure itself of leaving no truly, ignominious legacy. Such an assurance was, however, a few games away.

• • • • •

In the second week of January, Charlotte entered a strangely vitriolic period. One advantage the Hornets possessed for most of their first season was that they were so new and so undermanned that the opposition didn't get much blood in their eyes when Charlotte popped up on the schedule. The Hornets contributed to this with meek play. As coach Harter complained later in the season, "We must be the only team in the league that hasn't gotten into a fight. We don't make anybody mad." That was an exaggeration, though only a slight one. But in this one, odd week, there was a lot of venom directed their way.

Actually, both confrontations were predictable. One involved the Utah Jazz, former resting place of Hornets Tripucka, Green and Curry, and was a classic familiarity-breeds-contempt situation. The other included Charles Barkley, the technical foul king and noted junk-talker, who excelled at raising dander.

The Jazz and the Hornets' confrontation really boiled down to three men: Tripucka, his ex-coach Frank Layden, and Utah star Karl Malone. Tripucka saw Layden as something bordering on evil incarnate. He was the man who had wrecked his career by trading for him and then benching him in the Mormon capital. He was almost a curse word in Tripucka's vocabulary; any mention of his name was always accompanied by one.

Now, this was not exactly a secret. Tripucka hadn't spouted off much in Utah, but he hadn't praised Layden either. Nonetheless, when Tripucka lampooned the rotund Layden in the *Charlotte Observer* the morning before the game in Charlotte, Karl Malone took great offense. Tripucka was quoted as wondering if Layden had gotten two turkeys for Christmas – so his family would have one. He'd said that one evening several weeks before while walking through the coliseum press room – probably not an ideal place to make off-hand remarks. The *Observer'* s Rick Bonnell had remembered it and used it in his story. That angered Tripucka who thought it a breach of off-the-record confidentiality. In truth, it was one of the more complimentary things he'd said about his former boss. For instance, after Layden was kissed by Morgana, the heavy-chested stripper who dashes onto playing fields to kiss various sports celebrities (including Tripucka), Tripucka wondered how the two could have gotten their lips together. "I mean, she's out to here and he's out to here," he said, demonstrating the physical problem with his hands.

Nonetheless, Tripucka was hot about the story. But the guy it really angered was Malone, who is the NBA's biggest Frank Layden fan. When Layden, who drafted Malone in the first round in 1985 after 12 other teams had passed on him, resigned as Utah's coach in December, the free-spirited Malone took to writing "Frank" on the backs of his basketball shoes. Sort of a memorial. When Tripucka desecrated the memorialee in public, "the Mailman" as Malone is known (because he delivers, get it?), was not impressed.

But Tripucka wasn't through. Though he denied it was a dig at Malone or Layden later on – "Why would I want to take on anyone that big?" he said, presumably referring to Malone – Tripucka raised a few more hackles when he appeared in the game with the word "Dick," for Dick Harter, written on the back of his shoes.

"It's just something I thought I should do," Tripucka explained innocently after the game. "Dick took a gamble bringing me here, but it saved my career. I want to thank him for it." And, wouldn't you know it, he wanted to thank him with Utah in town.

Malone thanked the Hornets with a 38-point, 19 rebound performance. He played all of the third quarter and most of the fourth in a game Utah led by 27 at the half. Malone was finally pulled with four minutes left and Utah leading by 28. The Hornets smelled a rat. "I don't understand what he was still doing in there with four minutes left," said Earl Cureton. "You don't need to do that."

Countered Malone, "We weren't trying to show anybody up. I just wanted to play."

Asked what he thought about Tripucka's shoe message, Malone said, with much the same innocence Tripucka had mustered, "Who's Dick?"

Two losses later – a narrow miss against Chicago and an ugly blowout in New York – Barkley arrived in Charlotte for a Sunday afternoon game.

Hornets Never Lie

All went smoothly in the tightly contested game – for whatever reason Charlotte, in its first season, could handle Philadelphia – until the middle of the third quarter. Then, on a routine play, Cureton was running downcourt, approaching Barkley near Charlotte's foul line. Boom. Down went Cureton. Then, boom, up went Cureton. He poked Barkley in the face, then chased him around the court for nearly a minute. It was not one of those baseball-fight type chases either, where the assailant has to be restrained, but really doesn't. Cureton wanted Barkley. But all he got was a technical foul. Barkley stayed in the game, too, and helped the Sixers overpower Charlotte in the fourth quarter.

For the normally laid-back Cureton, the minute of rage seemed a queer event. But Tripucka, Harter, and a few others who had been around him for a while said occasional outbursts were standard for Earl. They remembered, among other things, the night he chased Atlanta's Cliff Levingston up a tunnel leading to the locker room after a game in Detroit. "I do have a temper," Cureton admitted, "but it takes something big to set me off."

Barkley's forearm shot was big enough. Cureton called it a dirty play. Barkley, as usual, was flippant, but tried, in his own way, to be apologetic.

"I don't know what happened," he said. "Me and Earl were talking about PMS one minute, and then the next he's coming downcourt and I guess I had a flashback to my football days. I thought I was a linebacker, so I hit the first guy that came down the court. It was no big deal, just part of the game, I thought. I hope he understands. I hope he's still my friend."

Reporters told Cureton about Barkley's olive branch. He was not impressed. "If I knock him out, I guess we'll still be friends, too, huh?" Cureton asked. "It was cheap."

Reporters, with plenty of time to write since it was an afternoon game, now raced back to the Philly locker room to get Barkley's reaction to Cureton's reaction. Barkley listened and, uncharacteristically, thought for a moment before speaking.

"Did Earl really say that?" he asked. Assured that he did, Barkley said, "Well, it must be true, 'cause Hornets never lie."

That was good news, but it raised a question: Even if Hornets don't lie, do they get even? A scheduling coincidence put Charlotte in Philadelphia the next afternoon for a Martin Luther King Day game at the Spectrum. That offered a ready opportunity for revenge to Cureton, who had said menacingly on the afternoon before, "Barkley can die just like I can." Before the game, Cureton smiled when the subject came up. A day and an airplane flight later, he had mellowed.

"I have no special plans for today," he said. "Unless Charles has some."

Barkley had none. Indeed, he couldn't even execute his normal course of action. Despite a pre-game kiss from Morgana, who seemed to be making a tour of Hornet enemies, Barkley couldn't get loose. A chronic back problem flared into pain. He missed the third quarter and was ineffective in the fourth of what turned out to be terrific shootout.

Charlotte surprised Harter, who thought his team looked listless before the game, with a fiery start. The Hornets shot 62 percent in the first quarter and grabbed a six-point lead. Philly took control by pounding the ball inside in the third quarter, even with Barkley out, but the Hornets rallied in the fourth, and the game went down to the wire. Chapman, who was surpassing Tripucka as the team's deadliest three-point shooter, tied it with a three pointer with 15 seconds left. The Sixers couldn't get a last-second shot to go in, and the game went to overtime.

The Hornets dominated the overtime, scoring on all but one of 11 possessions in the extra period. Tripucka, who had 40, and Chapman, who had 25, did most of the damage. Tyrone Bogues, playing his finest game in Charlotte's set offense, had 14 assists. Cureton grabbed 17 rebounds.

"Every win by this team is like an NCAA Tournament win," Harter said. "They're so delicious, and so difficult. And I really didn't think this would be one we'd get. They seemed so quiet, so down on the bus coming over here. I was concerned."

Tripucka said Harter was just misreading the situation. "We weren't down," he said, "we were just asleep. I think sometimes Dick expects us to walk on the bus like the Seven Dwarfs. Hey, we're excited. We just don't show it. We're not going to sing, 'Hi-ho, Hi-ho.'"

• • • • •

Even if Harter didn't expect the team to act like the Seven Dwarves, he still sometimes thought they reminded him of them. Three straight poundings followed the euphoric afternoon in Philadelphia, and quickly returned his thoughts to the big man he didn't have. On certain nights, it didn't seem to matter. The team played around the problem, the big guys played hard enough to stay even, or the opposition wasn't equipped to exploit it. But on other nights, typically against the better teams in the league, the Hornets could just be overwhelmed. Milwaukee and Phoenix rolled over Charlotte, and on January 21, just as the team was about to embark on a five-game, nine-day road trip to the West Coast, the Hawks hammered them 137-113 in Atlanta.

That defeat was more depressing than embarrassing. Charlotte played well, even sensationally, for a time. They shot 73 percent from the floor in the first quarter, despite Tripucka's absence with his soon-to-be chronic sinus infection. Chapman drew his first start in Tripucka's place, scoring 14 in the first period. But despite the offensive fireworks, Charlotte led by just one at the quarter break, and when the jump shots stopped falling, the Hawks zoomed ahead. Atlanta rammed the ball inside and dominated the boards, out rebounding Charlotte 46-25. It was like teams from different leagues. "Maybe like junior high against high school, or maybe against a junior college," Robert Reid offered. "We couldn't touch them."

Harter just shook his head at the proceedings. As he often did during the season, he wondered where the next win was coming from. He felt he was out of options with the personnel on hand. But he also knew that the personnel might change very soon. A trade with Indiana for the omnipresent Stuart Gray was heating up. The Pacers, a huge disappointment, were preparing to shuffle their deck. Gray, a spare part on the team, was available. Maybe the Hornets would give up Dell Curry, who was in a similar situation in Charlotte.

By the time the team reached Phoenix, first stop on the western swing, the discussions had reached a serious level. The Curry-for-Gray trade, a simple, one-for-one deal, had turned into a multi-player affair that was complicated by salary cap concerns and other problems. The Hornets would now send Curry and Rickey Green, the seldom-used point guard, to Indiana for Gray and swingman John Long, yet another tough guy from Harter's assistant-coach past. The problem was the Hornets were so close to the salary cap allocated by the league that they couldn't fit both Gray and Long in at their current salaries. Gray had just signed a new three-year contract, worth about $400,000 a year. Long was in the last year of contract that paid him $500,000 annually.

The two sides looked for ways around the problem. The Hornets spoke with Long's agent. His client might be willing to take a cut if the Hornets offered a guaranteed extension. But it wasn't clear if the league would approve that as an end-run to the cap's myriad rules. If Indiana was going to take Green off Charlotte's hands, they had to dump Long. Perhaps they could waive him, and the Hornets would be able to claim him and sign him to a new figure that fit their cap. No, that wouldn't work either. The part of Long's $500,000 not paid by the Hornets would still count against Indiana's cap and that would put the Pacers over the limit.

Draft picks were thrown in, then pulled out of the discussions. Various options were considered. January 24, the day Charlotte played Phoenix, it looked as if the deal would go through. And the day after, when the team traveled to Utah, there still seemed to be a decent chance. In Indianapolis, where the Pacers were getting ready for a road trip to Washington, the equipment man packed extra jerseys, just in case Curry and Green could join the team there, and Gray gave the Indy media a farewell interview. In Salt Lake City, Curry, now alert to the possibility, took the phone off the hook in his hotel room. They'd have to tell him to his face.

But by the next day everything had collapsed. "It's dead," Scheer said.

Ironically, Curry had been a near-savior in the Phoenix game. With Tripucka out – the team's scoring leader accompanied the team West but couldn't play – Curry joined Chapman for a time in the lineup as a small forward. And with Charlotte desperately trying to stay close in the fourth quarter, he had scored 12 straight points. Curry's burst pulled Charlotte within four points, but Eddie Johnson, the Suns' sharp-shooting sixth man, made the Hornets pay for the funky lineup, going over Chapman for eight straight points that produced a 10-point lead with 3:36 left.

The Hornets sliced it to four one more time, but Kevin Johnson, Phoenix's phenomenal point guard, backed Bogues in and dropped in two tough jumpers over him in the last 40 seconds to nail down the Suns' victory. Although Charlotte had held the high-scoring Suns to their lowest home point total of the season, Harter was frustrated by the closing defense. His young players had not played tough. Bogues, whose grit he loved but whose size made him cringe, had been defenseless at the end. And worse still, Phoenix had stopped Charlotte at a crucial juncture of the fourth quarter when Mark West, a burly center who was adept at blocking shots, had swatted back two Hornet tries in a row.

"Will we please go out and get some big, tough guys so we can play?" Harter asked no one in particular outside of Charlotte's dressing room.

His wish did not come true, but two days later a fantasy did. In a rock 'em-sock 'em defensive battle, just the kind of game Harter adores, the Hornets beat Utah. Michael Holton charged into Mark Eaton, Utah's giant center, and knocked him out of the game in the third quarter, enabling Charlotte to wipe out a 13-point Utah lead. Then Rambis, the epitome of on-court grit, scooped up a loose ball in the lane and laid it in at the buzzer for an 89-88 victory.

Harter loved it. He literally bounced off the floor after the game.

"We dug in and did the job," he said triumphantly. "That's the way you have to play, and that's the way we will play in the future. You just watch."

Harter's euphoria was fueled by the emotion of the night. The match with Utah two weeks before in Charlotte weighed heavily on Hornet minds. Charlotte still thought the Jazz had deliberately run up the score. They wondered if Malone was still mad at Tripucka, and if so, how mad? Privately, some team members thought Tripucka's cold had lingered because he feared what the Mailman might deliver. The 256-pound Malone looked like a statue chipped from chocolate marble, and if he had the mind to ...

But before the game, he said he did not. "If you mean am I going to hurt him or something," Malone said, "the answer is no, I'm not. But I'm not going to invite him out to dinner or anything either. Our lockers were side by side for two years and he probably didn't say 50 words to me the whole time. We're not exactly close."

Tripucka, whose sinus infection was much worse than even he had imagined it would be, wasn't afraid. He cleared his nose as best he could and came off the bench to score 16 valuable points. The sellout crowd even gave him some applause. "I wouldn't have missed this for anything," he said.

Neither would Harter, who also had an ax to grind in Salt Lake City. The competitive pride in him had been wounded by Malone's "Dick Who?" remark in Charlotte. During his post-game radio show, when he was asked by Hornet radio man Gil McGregor about Charlotte's effective defense on Malone, who was a miserable 9 for 28 from the floor this night, Harter snapped back, "Malone? Malone? Who's that?"

Harter stomped away, leaving McGregor with some air time to kill and everyone else wondering if Harter were indeed the winning coach. He looked angry. In truth, he was about to burst with the glee that only sweet revenge can produce. Seconds later, inside the Charlotte locker room, he was grinning from ear to ear as he grabbed assistant coach Badger and said, "Hey, Eddie, this is great. Listen to this line I gave Gil ..."

• • • • •

From Utah, it was on to LA for the most celebrated of the Hornets' many "reunion" games that first year. Since the entire team, with the exception of Chapman and a few others, was grafted from other NBA rosters, almost every other stop on the road was a return to some Hornet's former playing arena. Some, like Tripucka, Bogues and

Reid, held grudges and wanted to show the employers who dumped them that they were wrong. For others, such as Michael Holton and Ralph Lewis, the feeling upon their return was warmer. They remembered the good times with their former teams and either understood or did not linger on why they were no longer there.

Kurt Rambis felt all of this, and perhaps felt it more strongly than the rest. He had not just been part of another team. He had been part of THE LAKERS, an NBA dynasty of historic proportions, made up of legendary players. He had traded practical jokes with Kareem Abdul-Jabbar, sat next to James Worthy, had helped run the clubhouse alongside Magic Johnson. He had played on four championship teams, and despite statistically meager contributions – for his Laker career he averaged five points and a little less than six rebounds a game – he had become nearly as big a star as the rest. His appearance was part of the reason. With his stringy blonde hair tucked under the NBA's only pair of prescription glasses worn on the court, Rambis looked different. He played differently, too, which is to say, not indifferently. He cared. He dove for loose balls, hustled after rebounds, and surrendered his body in bone-jarring collisions with bigger opponents. He had an unmistakable presence on the floor, and despite not being as physically gifted as other players, he added something to the Lakers' famous "showtime" mix. He was, perhaps, more important in the regular season when his non-stop hustle could lift and inspire coasting teammates who got up on their own in the playoffs. But Rambis was no post-season slouch either. He was a crucial player in the 1985 championship series against Boston, averaging better than eight rebounds a game while less than half the minutes against the Celtics' massive frontline. And he was careful never to hurt the team. He played defense with heart and intelligence and didn't take bad shots. In fact, he is the NBA's all-time leader in field goal percentage (59.2%) in the playoffs.

For all of this he was revered and adored. Early in his career, fans began dressing up in mock-Rambis attire. His second season in LA an informal fan club was formed. It was called "Rambis Youth," and its young, bespectacled members all bore some resemblance to its founding father. He could not appear publicly in the sprawling city without being recognized, although in LA that may not have been such a curse. The public there is desensitized to celebrities. A Laker in the drugstore does not cause a riot.

This happy marriage broke up when Rambis' second contract ended in 1988. He was a useful member of the team, but his role had been reduced. Instead of a spark plug, he was more like an insurance policy. If a Laker regular was hurt, Rambis could fill the gap. But when that didn't happen he didn't play very much. On the back-to-back title winners in 1987 and 1988, Rambis played very little in the championship series. He was a non-factor, but, to his credit, a quiet one. "I could have made Pat Riley's life miserable," Rambis said. "I wasn't happy. But when a team is winning, how can you complain? And besides, I don't see where that serves any purpose."

The parting was sweet. Rambis was roasted at a going-away party. A soft-drink company in LA produced a run of lemon-lime soda in commemorative Rambis cans. And as he boarded the plane for North Carolina, several strangers made a point of wishing him luck.

Going into the LA game, Rambis still did not see the point. Although he had ample ammunition for the same sort of I-told-you-so Tripucka and Reid experienced, he continued to hold his tongue. He was on a major roll coming to LA, averaging 11.9 rebounds a game over the past three weeks. And the Lakers were not, comparatively speaking, playing that well at the time. They lacked fire and weren't a great rebounding team. Perhaps, more than one Laker fan thought, Rambis would help.

Surely Rambis felt some of that. Like every professional athlete, he has pride. But, from his years in LA on a very public team that did a good job of hiding its inner self from a prying press, Rambis was guarded in what he said. He rolled his eyes when the subject of his possible contribution to the Laker team he was no longer on came up.

"You know, every year I was in Los Angeles there'd be this period of the season when they'd hit a little lull, a slump," Rambis said two days before the game. "Maybe we'd lose a couple in a row or just play .500 ball for awhile or barely beat some below-.500 teams. And everybody would start talking about why they got rid of this guy or how they should get someone else. I guess this is that time this year. I've heard that some people think they miss me, but they'll forget about that theory faster than most."

Rambis won't say that he understands LA's decision not to re-sign him from a basketball standpoint. He still thought, as he left, that he could help that team. But since the Lakers didn't agree, and since he still had to make a living, he did comprehend the move in business terms.

"You always know, or should know, that you're just a piece of meat. That's kind of a cold way of saying it, but it's true," Rambis said. "Yes, you're just a piece of meat, and when your tenderness, or usefulness, or whatever, is gone, they're going to get rid of you.

"No one has avoided it yet. Everybody has to be gotten rid of sometime. If the greatest player ever, Kareem Abdul-Jabbar, can be traded, then it can happen to anyone."

This particular piece of meat was near tears before the game, however, when a sellout crowd gave him a two-minute standing ovation after Abdul-Jabbar had presented him with the championship ring from the season before. Later, after the Lakers had shrugged off Rambis' 19-point, nine-rebound performance and steamrolled the Hornets 114-97, he joked about the evening as various Laker personnel came by to pay their respects. Of the ring ceremony, he said, "Well, it's better than if they'd sent it UPS, I suppose."

But the tears came back when Worthy stopped by – and grabbed a handful of hairs attached to Rambis' chest.

"Haven't been able to do that in a while," Worthy said.

"It still hurts," said Rambis.

• • • • •

Charlotte finished its West coast swing, and the month of January, on a Monday night in Portland. The Hornets had a late-night flight back, and, in typical getaway-game fashion, they played as if they were worried about missing it. Tripucka poured in 21 as Charlotte kept pace with the run-and-gun Trailblazers in the first half. But Portland's superior athletes dunked the Hornets into submission in the third quarter.

Clyde Drexler, the ex-Phi Slamma Jammer from Houston, took off from just inside the foul line on one, held the ball up as if it were on a tray, then turned it over and rammed it home. Minutes later, Kevin Duckworth, the team's 290-pound center, caught a lob pass in the post over Kempton, and wheeled toward the basket. Hoppen gamely tried to move over from the weakside and stop the assault, but as often happened to Big Dave during this part of the season, all did not go as planned. Duckworth fended off Hoppen's defensive effort by whacking him across the face with his left forearm. Then he went up and spiked the ball through the basket. It hit Hoppen in the face as it came out of the net and knocked him to the ground.

A stunned Hoppen sat on the floor under the basket while the ballboys chased down the basketball. The end of the Hornets' bench snickered and Rickey Green hollered, "Get up, Dave! Get up. You're embarrassing us."

The dunk quickly became a famous play in Hornet lore. While waiting to leave for the airport, voices in the back of the bus could be heard discussing it.

"Man, did you see Dave just sitting there? It was like he was sitting there saying 'Terry, come get me.'"

"On a play like that," said another, sounding suspiciously like Green, "you've got to get right up like nothing happened. Just sitting there ... unnh. That makes you look worse."

Later, at the airport, assistant coach Gene Littles was chuckling over the play with radio announcer Steve Martin when Chapman walked by. Rex stopped for a moment, picked up the topic and said, "Now *that* was funny."

Hoppen wasn't as amused. And neither was Harter, who was only too accustomed to seeing his players getting knocked down. He needed some beef, but Gray wasn't coming any time soon.

Harter was still brooding about this month-old problem during a stopover in Dallas on the way home, when a muscular arm appeared around his shoulder. It belonged to Matt Millen, a Penn State linebacker whom Harter had gotten to know during his stay at State College, Pa.. Millen was now an NFL star. On this morning he was coming back from the Pro Bowl.

"Coach," Millen said, "got your guys hitting anybody yet?"

Harter shook his head.

"Yeah, I didn't think so," Millen said. "I saw you on TV a couple of times, on cable. It didn't look like your team."

Getting on his plane a few minutes later, Harter gushed over Millen. "What a great guy. One tough SOB, too."

Too bad you can't sign him, it was suggested.

Harter shook his head, affirmatively this time. "Yeah," he said, "too bad."

By the time the plane had landed in Charlotte, he'd had another idea. "I think I'll call Chaney," Harter said, referring to the LA Clippers coach, "and see about Greg Kite."

Kite, a tall Brigham Young grad who had failed to distinguish himself in five NBA seasons, was even bigger than Matt Millen, though not quite as mean.

Education of the Boy King

"Will shoot anywhere, anytime. Run at him. He'll miss."
– The Denver Rockets' scouting report on Rex Chapman.

Legend has it that Davy Crockett killed him a b'ar when he was only three, but Rex Chapman was more precocious. At age two, he made his first steal, swiping one of those red-white-and-blue American Basketball Association balls during a timeout of a Kentucky Colonels' game and tottering downcourt towards one of the baskets at Louisville's Freedom Hall. Witnesses say he had just pulled up at the three-point line and was cocking his arm when Mom caught him from behind. Rex wasn't as fast back then.

Chapman tales are as plentiful as bluegrass now, 20 years after that opening feat. Father Wayne Chapman, a proud but slightly embarrassed Kentucky Colonel guard on that night long ago, recounts the early adventures with a good deal of pleasure. He mounted a basket to a telephone pole, about two feet off the ground, when Rex was still two and watched him dump in shot after shot. He raised the goal slowly, but steadily. By the time young Chapman was five, it was at the regulation 10 feet and he was scoring regularly. When he was seven, he could make them from 20 feet. "Of course," Wayne Chapman said, "it was just sort of a push shot."

Chapman grew and explored other sports. He was a good, Pop Warner quarterback and an All-Star little leaguer, one of those pitcher-shortstops that all the other kids envy. But he loved basketball as few his age can or do. He began playing at the rec center when he was six, and by the time he was 12, he had decided to make that his sport of record. Wayne Chapman, a coach since his playing days ended, rolled his eyes at the idea. He figured it was one of those typical, semi-adolescent decisions that would be forgotten in a week or a month, whenever the next football or baseball season started. "And I thought it was kind of dangerous, too," he said. "What if he didn't grow? You could already tell he had a lot of talent for the game, but he was still very little. If he stayed like that and stayed in basketball, I thought, it may break his heart. It seemed like a gamble to me."

But Rex did not forget and the gamble was an educated one. Wayne Chapman is a shade over 6-6 and doesn't know of any Chapman male, living or dead, under 6-2. Sure enough, after his freshman year in high school in Owensboro, Ky., Chapman spurted. He stretched from 5-8 to 6-2 in a single year. And that is where the legends really began, for now, besides skill, he had size. He had more than that, too. For reasons that are best left to theologians and genetic engineers to debate, Chapman did not, as so many youngsters do, lose his coordination when he grew. And he found that he had these springs for legs. Light and gangly, he could jump like most white people cannot, like most people cannot, as far as that goes, and this was a great wonder. Also a great aid in playing basketball. Chapman could dunk a ball long before he finished growing. He could soar and slam it through the rim, slacking the jaws of all who figured him for just another heady, white guard from Kentucky. There were hundreds of those but there was only one Rex Chapman.

Chapman's reputation as a leaper soared to a national level when, after his junior year in high school, he won the first of several dunk contests. This one was at an AAU tournament in Las Vegas, and of the 75 or so contestants, exactly two were white. As Chapman took off for the first of his rim-rattlers, John Whitmer, his high school and AAU coach, remembers the astonishment from the peer group watching. "They couldn't believe it," Whitmer said. "They'd say, `look at the way he jumps ... and he be white!'"

Chapman struck again after his senior year, winning a dunk competition in which his final slam was executed by jumping over a fellow competitor seated six feet in front of the basket in a chair. The stooge Chapman picked for this act was 7-2 Felton Spencer, who played some, but not much, at Louisville. That was an amazing feat, but by then Chapman's reputation was such that many just yawned. What? He won another dunk contest?

Just how that happened is not entirely clear. Some events do stand out in the legend-building process, but observers of the process grope to finger anything in particular.

Gene Abell, who covered Chapman's high school exploits for the *Owensboro Messenger-Inquirer* said, "I don't know what happened. He wasn't all that well known, and then by the time he went to the state tournament his junior year, everyone was buzzing. Everywhere you'd go the gyms would be full, and contrary to what most people think outside of the state, high school basketball in Kentucky does not draw that well. But they came to see Rex. Of course, people here tend to get a little crazy over basketball at times. Maybe that explains it."

Whitmer, who had thrown Chapman and two other freshman into his starting lineup when they arrived at Owensboro's Apollo High, said it was that precociousness, plus Chapman's flair for the game, that did the trick.

"First of all," Whitmer said, "I think there's his name. Rex Chapman. Kind of catchy, isn't it? And then he started playing as a freshman. He really wasn't the best of the freshmen then, but he got known that way. And then he grew. After that, he just kept doing things. He won a free-throw shooting contest at a big summer camp after his freshman year. Then he grew and started winning the dunk contests. Then he'd always be doing things in games. No one thing, but something all the time. He had such imagination and versatility and could do things with such a flair. You never knew what he was going to do next. He'd be going in for a layup and you didn't know what he was going to do with it. It drove me crazy, of course, but it sure was exciting to watch."

Whitmer's favorite example of that flair comes from a summer All-Star trip to Europe. Whitmer and another man rounded up a group of prep stars, including Chapman, and led them on a playing tour of the continent. Partisan refs and international rules dogged them all the way. In particular, the U.S. team had difficulty with traveling calls on fast breaks. They'd catch a pass and rise toward the basket without dribbling. The refs didn't think, or didn't want, that to be possible. They thought at least one dribble was necessary.

"After a while," Whitmer recalls, "they'd called it on us so much that when the whistle blew we knew what it was for. Rex knew. He'd hear it, and knowing what the call was, would go on up anyway and stick the ball between the rim and the backboard, just wedge it in there. Then he'd trot back downcourt. You'd have some 5-6 Italian ref trying to figure out how to get it out."

Chapman himself just shrugs at what he does and can do. He does not plan all that stuff. Ask him what he was thinking when he made this or that play and he'll stare at you as if you'd asked him to compute Pi to 50 places. He doesn't know the answer. He just does things on the court. They just happen. Wayne Chapman calls his son's flair a gift and defends it. "That's the way the game should be played," he says. "Everyone should do it like that. He's not showing off. That's just the way he pictures it. Ask him and he'll tell you he never thinks of it ahead of time. He couldn't. Nobody could."

It was the natural aptitude for the game that made Rex a

playground hero in Lexington, Ky., after he started his college career, and made him so enticing to NBA scouts when he decided to turn pro after two seasons at the University of Kentucky. Gene Littles, Charlotte's director of player personnel, marveled at Chapman's playground reception. "When he drives up and gets out of his car, the other players chant, 'Rex, Rex, Rex,' " Littles said. "He's the guy they want on their team. He learned the game there and has that feel you cannot teach."

Everyone who had a hand in Chapman's development agrees that constant exposure to the game and Chapman's non-stop devotion to it were the keys to his rise. But both Chapman and his father rebel somewhat at the notion that he's a product solely of that environment. That makes it sound as if he did not work, did not achieve, to reach his incredible level of proficiency. "People think it's easy for me," Chapman said once during his first pro season. "It's not."

Wayne Chapman says, "You'd have had to have been there to see. He worked hard at the game. He overcame more than anyone will ever know. But he really loved to play. People talk about burnout, but you don't burn out on something you love. Rex loves basketball."

The elder Chapman remembers his son's serious attitude about summer camps, an adventure that is often a week-long lark for players of Rex Chapman's ability. It was not for Rex. He would bring home a list of things his counselors said he needed to work on. "Then," Wayne Chapman said, "he'd go out in the backyard and work on them. He worked on them in pickup games, and if he couldn't find a game, he'd work on it by himself. Nobody's practiced more, no matter what you may think."

Chapman also fought past the failings of his body. He grew so fast in his mid-teens that his muscles and ligaments could not keep up with his bones. He suffered from Osgood-Slaughter's disease in his knees, and also a form of it in his back. Specialists told the Chapmans that playing basketball wouldn't cause any further damage, so Rex played all of his sophomore year while wearing a series of cumbersome back braces. He beat that challenge then created new ones. When the high school game became almost a bore for him his senior year, he began to experiment in games. He'd shoot turnaround jumpers, whether the situation called for it or not, and he'd wait for a quarter or more before he'd really start firing them up, working on passing and running the offense while he did.

The latter maneuver was also aimed at placating his teammates. Chapman was sensitive to the attention he received and the resentment it might cause. Some of his Apollo teammates were his best friends, members of a loosely organized neighborhood group that called itself "the fellows." They were intensely loyal to Chapman as he was to them. But others might not be, especially after reading all those Chapman headlines for years and years. Knowing this, Chapman bent over backwards not to appear to be too high on himself. He developed his low-key, low-yield interview style that has frustrated reporters throughout his career, and spent much of his time praising others.

In truth, Chapman didn't have much support during his high school years. Teammate and close friend Greg Baughn went on to play small-college ball for Chapman's dad at Kentucky Weslyan, but there was no other college talent on the team. During the Rex years, Apollo was mostly Rex. But Chapman did his best to make it sound like the 1971 Knicks anyway. When his scoring average rose to 27 points a game his junior year, making him one of the state's highest scoring players, Chapman said, "It's nice, but I wouldn't be able to average that many without my teammates. They're very unselfish."

Coach Whitmer, with Chapman's avid support, made up media rules designed to spread the glory around. Any reporter who showed up for a Chapman interview at Apollo also had to interview another player. And if he didn't use something the other player said, he might find it a little tougher to get an interview the next time he asked.

Still, there was some resentment. Abell says the *Messenger-Inquirer* got complaints about covering Chapman too much. "There were people living in Owensboro who believed that nobody coming out of Owensboro could be that good," he said. "They resented it, thought we were doing the wrong thing writing about him that much."

That resentment spilled out into the open Chapman's senior year when he was involved in a fight with a player from nearby Breckenridge County. Actually, it wasn't much of a fight. The Breckenridge player, like a gunfighter looking to make a name by taking on Billy the Kid, had grabbed and taunted Chapman the star for most of the game. Finally, as they were running downcourt, Chapman decked him with an elbow.

Dick Harter, the Hornets' coach who pushed Chapman to be aggressive when he reached the NBA, might have liked that, but it did not play well in Owensboro at the time. The *Messenger-Inquirer* was filled with letters – more than 100 – condemning Chapman. Then a wave of supporting letters rolled in. After that, another wave of condemning cards. Then it became a postal melee that the paper finally had to stop. It ran an announcement, saying that no more letters concerning the Rex Chapman fight would be printed. A few weeks later, the letters stopped coming. But Chapman's celebrity continued to grow.

A few months earlier, he had signed up to play basketball at the University of Kentucky, spurning offers from just about everywhere, but specifically from a final group that included the Wildcats, their in-state rival Louisville, plus North Carolina and Georgia Tech. He had announced his decision at an Owensboro hotel, in front of a crowd of more than 300. They whooped wildly when they found out Chapman would be a Wildcat. Chapman says such a reaction – and its likely antithesis had he done the unthinkable and become a Tar Heel or something – didn't affect his decision. He based it on comfort level – several of his friends were already headed to UK – and perhaps on Kentucky's lower-key recruiting. The other schools besieged Chapman. Coaches couldn't talk to him except during certain, NCAA-specified periods, but they made their presence known, hanging around outside classrooms or gyms where Chapman might "happen" to show up. Coach Whitmer thought one Louisville assistant coach assigned to the Chapman case had a twin brother. "He'd be at the airport waving goodbye when we left for a summer tournament," Whitmer said, "and then he'd be there to say hello when we landed." Kentucky eventually pulled out of this every-waking-moment derby. The last few weeks before the decision, UK recruiters were hardly seen at all in Owensboro, something many took as a sign that Rex had eliminated the Wildcats from consideration.

He had not, and when he picked Kentucky, the already intense interest in his career increased. Every game he played now was not only a sellout, but a lockout. And when a few Apollo games got canceled because of snow, an extra game was added in Lexington, site of the university, just to showcase the wonder kid. It was against Lexington's Henry Clay High, another state power, and was played in Memorial Coliseum, the old building that had housed UK basketball back when 12,000 seats would do. For Chapman, all those seats were full, and three Kentucky TV stations carried it live.

Chapman, as was to be his trademark, did not disappoint in the big game. He scored 37 points and, with Henry Clay leading by one with four seconds left, caught an inbound pass, turned and banked in the game winner as he was falling out of bounds. It was an amazing shot, though not the one Whitmer had planned. Figuring Henry Clay might just be expecting Chapman to get the ball, he had diagrammed a play to free a freshman named Thompson for a cut to the basket. Chapman would get him the ball. The play worked perfectly, though Chapman did have to struggle a bit to get the inbound pass. When

Chapman turned to shoot, there stood Thompson, wide open, under the basket. He was, as it turned out, in perfect position to catch Chapman's shot when it came out of the net.

Not wanting to spoil the moment, Whitmer didn't mention this for several days. "But, a couple of weeks later, I asked Rex, 'Didn't you see Thompson open there under the basket?' " Whitmer said. "Rex said, 'Sure coach.' 'Well,' I asked him, 'Then why didn't you throw him the ball?' 'Coach,' Rex said, 'I wasn't sure he would catch it.' "

The summer leading up to his first season at Kentucky, Chapman's following continued to build. When he ran onto the court for the first practice of the year, a giant banner was unfurled. It read, "The Chapman Era Begins." Before he ever played a game, "I ❤ Rex" buttons and replica jerseys, bearing Chapman's trademark number 3, were hot sellers at the many Wildcat mania gift shops. They sold out completely after his first game, which again was no disappointment. He opened by making his first shot – a three-pointer – then he made his next four in a row. A few weeks later, in the bigger-than-life Kentucky-Indiana game, Chapman matched Hoosier ace Steve Alford point for point. Each scored 26. "He was amazing," said Rob Lock, a teammate of Chapman's that year. "Every other freshman comes in scared to shoot outside of two feet because he knows it will be an air ball, and Rex opens up firing from downtown. He is not like anyone else."

Chapman is not, but he was more like them the rest of the way. He cooled after his fast start. Defenses paid him more attention. But he still averaged 16 points a game his freshman year. In his sophomore year, his average went up to 19 a game. He hurt his back again – it wasn't related to his high school growth problems, though – and missed some of that season. But he returned to score 30 in the NCAA Tournament against Villanova, 26 in the second-half during a stirring-but-failed, one-man comeback.

It was a good two years in college by most standards, but under the electron microscope at Kentucky, some flaws were detected. Chapman's shot selection was criticized. He was said to be at odds with his teammates and his coach, Eddie Sutton. Some thought he was out for himself.

Those close to Chapman admit it was not a happy time for the generally carefree young man. He could not live normally in Lexington. Well-wishers and not-so-well wishers overwhelmed him in public, and Chapman was just beginning to develop the callousness necessary to occasionally say no. The criticism did not rankle so much. At his father's suggestion, Chapman quit reading about himself. But the invasion of privacy was a pain and his celebrity seemed senseless. "It's all so silly," he said midway through his freshman year. He withdrew into a small circle of friends. And despite what the rumormongers said, several teammates were within that circle.

The attention and publicity Chapman received were astounding. Some Kentucky fans even wrote him proposing marriage, either to themselves, or to a friend or relative. But the other guys on the team understood. They had to sign autographs, too. They knew just how crazy "Big Blue" could be.

"We didn't mind," said Rob Lock. "We'd been there. I think we really felt sorry for Rex. It was bad enough for us. All that stuff about him not getting along, that was just made up, just the media. He got along, in fact he was one of the most popular guys in the (Wildcat) Lodge (where the UK basketball team is housed). He's a funny guy, a practical joker, although not many people get to see that."

Lock did one day when he brought out a video camera to make a tape to send home to his parents in California. He wanted all his teammates to say hello. It was all pretty conventional until Chapman appeared, clad only his underwear, and did a belly dance for the camera. When the Hornets were in town to play Lock's Clippers late in the year, Lock wondered about the whereabouts of the tape. "I should have saved it," he said. "It might have been worth something some day."

• • • • •

Chapman left UK after two years for reasons he still won't completely disclose. Certainly, the pending investigations of the Wildcat program by the NCAA were a factor. The desire to maintain Rex's string of precocious achievements may have been another. Both Wayne and Rex were full of confidence that Rex would play soon and well when the Hornets made him the eighth pick in the 1988 draft. "I expect to contribute and probably a lot sooner than people think," Chapman said the day after the draft.

That was a measure of Chapman's well-founded self-esteem. He had yet to fail a basketball test, and he had found himself capable of competing with the pro players, ex-Louisville and ex-Kentucky stars, who returned to the Lexington playgrounds in the summer.

But he was just 21 when he was drafted, and was just reaching the point where all his competition could run and jump as well as he could. Some disappointments followed. Chapman was unceremoniously cut from the Olympic team, dropped even before it began its summer tour. He had shot the ball abysmally at the Olympic trials in May and didn't recover enough on a European tour to catch Coach John Thompson's eye. Maybe there was nothing to catch. Thompson eventually captured the bronze medal with an odd group of players that did not include many obvious college stars. He had a certain style of play in mind, and he selected players to fit it. That rankled Wayne Chapman, who one year later said, "I'm still trying to figure out why Rex didn't make it."

The episode may have cost Rex some confidence, although after finally signing his multi-million dollar deal with the Hornets, he reported to camp in fine fettle. On his first day, he zipped in his jump shots and seemed to mesh well with his teammates. "He didn't come in like a prima donna," said Robert Reid, who would take Chapman under his wing early in the year. "He came in like somebody who wanted to belong. Nobody, no player at least, takes holding out against you. You've got to take care of business."

Chapman had done that. The contract was a good one and companies were lining up to sign him for endorsements. He was young and reasonably handsome and he was a white guy who played as few others could. Corporations with consumer goods to sell wanted to cash in on that. Before the year was over, Chapman would have contracts with Coca-Cola, Wendy's and Converse, the shoe company. Experts estimated his one-year take at well over a million dollars.

Chapman was impressive in his first game, too. In the exhibition victory over New York in Columbia, S.C., he knocked in six of 11 from the field and scored 13 points in just 11 minutes. It was a good start, but it was as good as he was going to be for a long time.

Chapman struggled throughout the rest of the preseason schedule. He couldn't understand the professional concepts of defense and his shot disappeared. He made just 12 of 51 in the last six exhibition games, a slump that carried over into the regular season. In Charlotte's first nine games, Chapman made just 40 of 134 shots, a miserable 29.9 percent. And he took it hard. After going 3 for 15 against Washington four games into the season, Chapman sat in the Charlotte locker room, chin on his hands, staring at the floor. "Cheer up Rex," said Gene Littles, the assistant coach. "There will be another night. A lot of them."

Chapman didn't acknowledge the words of solace. He just continued to stare.

A remarkable aspect of Chapman's early slump, indeed, of the slump which dogged him to a degree all season, was it's volume. Most players who are shooting poorly quit shooting for one reason or another. Either they are too embarrassed, don't want to hurt the team, or are sitting on the bench after the first few failed volleys. But Chapman, as the team's number-one pick and hope of years to come, was going to play. His effectiveness might determine the exact quantity, but the future demanded that he play. And embarrassment or fear of hurting the team did not seem to enter into his mind. "The only way to get out of a slump is to keep shooting," Chapman said a few weeks into the season. "I'm a good shooter. Not a great one, but a good one. I've always found a way to get the ball into the basket, and I will again."

Every other team Chapman had played on had needed him to score. It had become second, or perhaps first, nature for him to fire when ready. He was the guy. When he scored, his teams won. And to score, you shot. Chapman did, and in the process, managed to build, in record time, a league-wide reputation as a gunner. In Dallas, a week before Thanksgiving, fans yelled, "Shoot, shoot!" when Chapman first entered the game. And during a timeout one bleak January night in Washington, when there were so few fans in the Capital Centre that coughs and sniffles could be heard, a man stood and shouted, "Hey, Rex, did you bring a ball for the rest of the team?"

Chapman's guilt-free shooting was, at times, astonishingly brazen, but there was a certain appeal in it to pro coaches. Chapman wanted to shoot. The situation didn't matter. Pressure didn't seem to bother him, or at least he didn't shy away from situations that included it. He was a "gamer" in the parlance of the profession, a guy who wanted to win the game himself. That was good. There weren't many of those types around.

Chapman admitted to a certain enjoyment of the money-time challenges, when it was do-or-die for the outcome of the game. "That," he said, after he had in fact won one for the Hornets, sinking a clutch three-pointer to beat Washington in early January, "is what you play for. Those situations. You want to control it. I've been in them a lot. I think I've about broken even, missing or making shots, but its fun either way."

If Chapman could retain that interest in the big shot while refining the execution of it, the Hornets might really have something. And, as everyone had noted when Charlotte drafted him, an expansion team was just the place to learn. It would be a long time before it really mattered if the shots went in.

In the meantime, the Hornets strove to improve Chapman's defense and to raise his shooting percentage. The former was, as always, largely a function of desire. Although in the case of the frail Chapman, a 180-pounder at best when he came to the NBA, there was a certain physical element to it, too. Harter had trouble getting Chapman to understand just how physical he had to be. Chapman, quick and lithe, had always relied on finesse to play defense. Harter and most NBA thinkers knew great defense in the pros depended more on speed and power. As Chapman learned, one had to play the passing lanes less and the players more. Plus, the officials allowed more contact, even hard blows at times, and a player had to take advantage of it. A player who couldn't or wouldn't dish out a lick when it was needed, was easy pickings. Chapman found this the hardest lesson. Even as late as March he complained, "I just can't get used to all the holding."

Harter tried to impart the message of toughness in a number of ways. He talked about it constantly, sometimes cajoling, other times haranguing, Chapman about his defense. The kid gloves came first. On the team's first trip to Boston, Harter, who was old enough to be Rex's grandfather, took Chapman on a personal tour of the Garden. He mentioned all the great players who had been there. He told him how this was the first time he'd ever come into this NBA shrine and not seen Larry Bird, now injured, out shooting early, before anyone came. That was how Bird became great, Harter said. Rex could be like that, too, if he was willing to put in the same kind of effort. Chapman was unfazed by this. He hardly spoke a word during Harter's soliloquy and later, when asked for his impressions of the Garden, said, "It's kind of old and dirty. It looked better on TV." Which, was a true enough statement, but also sad.

When that approach failed, Harter got tougher. Chapman ranked second only to Dave Hoppen as a target for Harter venom. He screamed at Rex when he took him out of games. Once, in Cleveland, he even minced about on his tiptoes on the sidelines, trying to show Chapman that he was playing like a wimp. Chapman didn't take it well. Whereas Hoppen usually just hung his head when Harter let go, Chapman always had a reply. An excuse. "I don't need someone slapping me on the back or telling me what I did wrong all the time," Chapman said late in the year. "When I foul up I'm the first one to know it."

Occasionally, Harter used games as personal labs for Chapman. Early in the year, the Hornets were playing Detroit. It was a 10-point game starting the fourth quarter, when Vinnie Johnson, a 6-1 knot of muscle who plays guard for the Pistons, just overwhelmed Chapman, scoring eight straight points and making it a 17-point game. Harter inserted Robert Reid into the lineup, and Johnson didn't score on two trips down the court. A timeout was called.

In the Hornet huddle, Harter said, "Okay, Rex has got Vinnie ..."

Reid raised his eyebrows and in a startled tone, said, "What! I've got him. He can't score on me."

"No," said Harter, "Rex has got to learn to play that kind of guy."

Reid looked at Chapman, who sort of winced and went back out and did the best he could. Fortunately for him, Johnson soon left the game.

Through such experience, including his own problems trying to get free of an especially rugged defender, Chapman eventually got the message. Certainty of his enlightenment came in late January in Atlanta, the same night that Chapman was finally granted his wish to become a starter. In the midst of a torrid first quarter in which Chapman was personally keeping the Hornets in the game, the Hawks' Reggie Theus burned Chapman on two straight jumpers. Harter jumped up and said, "C'mon Rex, you can't let him do that."

And for a change, Rex didn't. Two possessions later, the smooth Theus glided upwards for another shot. Chapman ran at him, leaped and smashed a forearm into his chest, knocking Theus into the courtside seats at the Omni. He was called for a foul, but Theus' hot streak was over. Harter leaped off the Charlotte bench and ran several feet onto the court, applauding and screaming, "Attaway, Rex, attaway!"

Later, Harter said, "Rex really got after Theus. I like that. He keeps that up, he'll start and play all he wants."

Chapman smirked when Harter's reaction came up. "Yeah, I know he liked it," Chapman said. "I've always been conscious of what he wanted. He didn't want Theus to get hot so you should hit him. I guess I'm going to try that way for awhile. I need to experience different things. There's no one solution to playing defense or anything else."

Chapman's shooting seemed to defy any solution at times. He had a pretty shot, great range and an uncanny touch, as evidenced by his free-throw percentage, which hovered in the low 80s all year. But he did not take much care to be consistent in form or technique when he got off the line. That was a serious flaw. A physiologist once did a film study to determine the important factors in the jump shot. Studying hours of NBA footage, he charted shooter after shooter, result after result. Finally, he decided that elbow angle (90 degrees) and shoulder position (level and perpendicular) were the most crucial, and that Bailey Howell, a perennial All-Star of the 1960s, was, technically, the finest shooter ever. Howell's elbow and shoulders seldom varied.

Rex Chapman was uncharted in this study, which took place a decade or so before he joined the league. But it's safe to say he would have ranked somewhat behind Howell. He fired his shots from every conceivable angle, and some that weren't conceivable. He shot falling away, leaning in, with his legs splayed apart like the bottom of a jumping jack, and with legs drawn tightly to his body. This looked to be, and was, creative when it was on the end of a drive in the lane. When it occurred after popping off a screen on the perimeter it just looked foolish. During the first few weeks of the season, Chapman looked foolish fairly often. He looked harried and uncertain, and he rushed his shot like a man who was afraid Bill Russell was always just a step away.

Russell, in fact, was on the west coast, and Chapman's shooting was caused more by his lack of familiarity with his surroundings and his desire to succeed immediately. Even Wayne Chapman, who rarely says a discouraging word about his son, admits that Rex has trouble with his patience. "He is not always as good as he should be letting things come to him," the elder Chapman said.

The Hornets counseled Rex on the same topic. When Chapman finally did get off to a good start one night in Boston, he followed it with a pair of bad shots back-to-back. Harter called time and told the young, would-be star, "Rex, wait for it. I'd rather see you go 4 for 5 even though we need your scoring, than do another 4 for 15." Chapman followed the advice, somewhat reluctantly perhaps, and had one of his best nights of the year.

In another effort to help his shooting, the team produced a special film for Chapman. Fletcher Gregory, the assistant coach in charge of assimilating the many miles of video tape an NBA team now requires, put together a Rex Chapman lowlights film, depicting his many off-balance tries.

It's hard to say if any of that really worked. After the first nine games of the year, Chapman finally hit pay dirt with the 10-for-16 night against the Celtics. He had his first three-pointer of the year in that game, also his first dunk. It was a relief, and Chapman followed it with several decent games: 4 for 7, 8 for 19, 8 for 20, 8 for 15. But relapses were never very far away. After finally raising his field-goal percentage above 40 in late January, he went 21 straight games without hitting better than 50 percent from the floor. He broke that streak with his best game of the year, a 16-for-28 afternoon (37 points) on March 12 against Sacramento. From that point to the end of the season, Chapman shot 44.9 percent from the field, respectable if not really good. But by then, the book on him had been written. He was a force to be feared for the future, but for the moment he wouldn't beat you by himself. Not most nights. Most teams followed the advice a Denver assistant coach scrawled on the grease board in the Nuggets' locker room in Charlotte one night: "Will shoot anywhere, anytime. Run at him. He'll miss."

Chapman missed enough early that even with a late rush his field-goal percentage for the year was 41.4 percent, or just slightly above the miserable percentage his dad shot in three ABA seasons. Are stats genetic, too? Among NBA players who tried more than 400 shots – about five a game – only Joe Kleine and Nate McMillan hit a lower percentage. "And that," said Chapman at the end of the year, "is not very good."

• • • •

Chapman's switch to the starting lineup on Jan. 21 was a great relief to him. He had never come off the bench before and had found the role unsettling if not embarrassing. He whined about the problem publicly, suggesting that one reason he was shooting poorly was that he wasn't accustomed to coming off the bench. Wayne Chapman also complained. "All this going in and out of the game, coming off the bench stuff, isn't helping Rex," he said in December. "He's not used to it." He told Scheer the same thing, in an unprecedented situation for the NBA where a general manager took suggestions from a player's father. And that may have led in part to Chapman's elevation to the first string.

Harter, who had found Chapman's earlier complaints about not starting incredible, was oblique in explaining the move. "I just thought he deserved it," he said.

He did not say then that the elevation was permanent. Chapman got his start when Tripucka first developed his sinus infection. Reid moved to forward and Chapman stepped into the backcourt beside Holton. When Tripucka had missed a game earlier in the year, however, Harter had gone a different way and had kept Chapman in the sixth-man role. So this was different. And when Tripucka returned to a condition close to full health, Chapman remained a starter and Reid became the sixth man.

Chapman was playing better by this time. When a college back injury flared up in December, he had had to sit out seven games. He returned a more relaxed player, the bench having helped by giving him time to reflect and watch the game that seemed to be passing him by. Chapman was reluctant to admit this at first. Later, he acknowledged it.

"At the beginning of the season, I wasn't just shooting bad, I was bad," he said. "I was confused. Maybe it was a blessing to get hurt. You know, the first pro game I ever saw I played in. And that's a little much. This is very different. You need to step back and take a look."

His first game back from the injury, the December 30 victory over New York, was one of his most restrained and one of his best. He made six of 12 shots, scored 13 points and a season-high seven assists, three of which were as remarkable as anything he did all year. Twice on fast breaks, Chapman threaded high-speed chest passes to teammates. Then, in another transition situation, a pass intended for him sailed wide of its mark. Chapman lunged after it, and as he was going out of bounds, flipped the ball behind his back to Tripucka for a layup.

That was, most of the Hornets agreed, a rare combination. Chapman is a wondrous passer. It might be the best thing he does. But his first year in the NBA he did not do it very often. His 176 assists – less than 2.4 a game – ranked him below such noted playmakers as Tom Chambers and Ken Norman, and teammates, who knew how he could pass when he did, wondered why. Harter said, "A guy who can pass like that should have more (assists). It doesn't make sense."

In general, Chapman did not seem selfish. With his teammates he was genuine and not self-centered, but he didn't pass much in games, particularly not to set up Tripucka, his scoring rival, for a shot. Perhaps this was coincidental or subconscious. It's hard for basketball mortals to imagine that a player in an arena as fast-paced as the NBA could factor in such considerations while making the split-second decision to throw or not throw a pass. But NBA legend says it's happened before. The first blacks on some teams didn't get the ball from their white teammates, and in Michael Jordan's first All-Star game, so the story goes, Isiah Thomas and some other East teammates froze the new star out. Jordan started but got just nine shots that day. Maybe that was a coincidence, too. Nobody could ever really be sure.

The Tripucka-Chapman situation was equally cloudy. They did pass to each other, just not as much as some other Hornets thought they should. It was a nebulous thing, hard to prove. But maybe it could be cured. A subtle act was needed, and as Tripucka neared the 10,000-point milestone of his point-filled career, co-captain Reid thought of a plan. He suggested to Harter that he draw up a play in which Chapman passed to Tripucka when Tripucka went for number 10,000 at home on March 8 against the Nuggets. It would be easy to set up. Tripucka entered the game with 9,998 points. The Hornets would be going to him on their first possession anyway, trying to get the milestone early so they could get on with the game. Harter thought it was a good idea and explained it to the team before the game. "I said, 'Okay, we're going to go Rex to Kelly on the first play to get the ten thousandth. We'll do it. That's something that's gone for us all year,'" Harter said later. "I made a big deal out of it. But I think it (Harter's irony) went right over Rex's head. I don't know."

Whatever he thought, Chapman made the pass and Tripucka hit the shot that night, and nothing more was said. If there was any animosity between the two, it was hard to tell. Chapman didn't talk about Tripucka or anyone else very much in public, and Tripucka seldom talked about Chapman. Once, after a west coast game in which Chapman had made some big shots at the end, but also missed a few wild ones at inopportune times, Tripucka berated him for "not knowing that stuff by now."

"We've played 60 games," Tripucka said. "He's had time to learn."

They were not great friends, but they didn't seem to be great enemies either. By and large, Tripucka and Chapman just didn't pay much attention to each other, a circumstance that could be attributed to Tripucka's loner mentality as much as anything else.

• • • •

Chapman continued to play at a higher level into January, improving in all areas. He even won a defensive player of the week award from ESPN, although that same week Harter was still wondering about Chapman's abilities in that area. Watching warmups in Philadelphia, Harter said, "He still doesn't understand. I'll bet he gave up 30 last night by himself. But he's a rookie. You figure any rookie would give up 12 more than he should, so I guess that's about right."

Harter's rookie had at least progressed to the point that he wasn't detrimental when he became a starter. To Chapman's chagrin, however, that move was no great boon to the Hornets either. February was one of Charlotte's best months, the last really good one, but Chapman wasn't the difference. A favorable schedule left them with no long trips and two winnable games (Indiana and San Antonio) at home. They augmented that with a pair of home upsets the first half of the month. The Hornets surprised road-weary Seattle on February 3, then capsized the Hawks six days later.

Chapman helped on both occasions. He played 42 minutes against the Sonics, his longest run of the year, and made a key defensive play, as well as a blunder, down the stretch. He played a big role against the Hawks, too. Harter wasn't using many players at this point. But the real hero on both occasions was Robert Reid, the veteran about to be eclisped by Chapman's rising star. Subbing for Tripucka, who suffered a relapse of his sinus infection, Reid poured in 28 against the Sonics and delivered the game winner. With four seconds left in a tied game, he went up for a jumper from 12 feet away and drew the defense to him. That left Tim Kempton open on the baseline. Reid threw a pass to the big redhead, who laid it in for the win.

The next week, Reid came off the bench to score 28 again, including 14 in a nifty fourth-quarter comeback. With Charlotte trailing Atlanta by one with 11 seconds left, Reid flushed a 15-footer from the left side. Tripucka took a charge from the Hawks' John Battle with four seconds left to wrap that one up the day before the All-Star break.

The fourth quarter of the Atlanta game was heaven for Reid. His peculiar jump shot, in which he brought the ball back over his head and then kicked out his left foot as he fired, was on target. The Hawks couldn't stop him. They couldn't believe him. Running back downcourt after making a particularly improbable shot, Reid caught the eye of Dominique Wilkins, who was resting on the Atlanta bench. The Hawks' star shook his head and covered his eyes with his hand, then mimicked Reid taking a shot with the other. Reid laughed and shrugged.

That, more than anything, was what the game was about for Reid. Acceptance and respect from his peers meant everything. Fortunately for Reid, he had been good enough during his 10 years in the NBA to attract both. He was not a great player. He'd never been to an All-Star game, never been voted to any all-league teams. But he was a good, solid, NBA player, valued for his versatility and known for his upbeat personality. Few players seemed to have as good a time playing in the NBA as Reid.

Ironically, this had not always been so. After five seasons with the Rockets, including his brilliant play in the 1981 playoffs, Reid quit. He sat out a year. It was not a contract problem, and it was not, as it has often been portrayed, a religious conversion, although Reid did spend some of the year working with youth in a church-sponsored program in Miami. What happened was that Reid just got tired of basketball. "It got to me, and I'd had enough," he said. "So I took a year off. It was something I just needed to do. When I came back, I felt better. I felt like playing again."

A more mature Reid returned and stepped right in where he'd left off. There wasn't much difference, except that he was more careful in his public actions. A high liver who liked fast cars and good times, he was also a businessman and a would-be civic leader in Houston, who donated time and money to various causes. Tucked away in the back of his mind was the idea that one day he might even run for public office. He could not afford to be too crazy. So he sold a Houston nightclub he owned and became more discrete with his social life, though not that discrete. A certain mischievousness still burned within his 33-year-old body, and a Charlotte driver who pulled up beside Reid's black Porsche late in the year might have been startled, especially if the driver were female, to read the contents of a cartoon-style conversation bubble in the rear window of Reid's car: "I'm naked from the waist down." Depending on who was reading it, Reid might accompany the message with a wink or a smile.

Generally, Reid was happy in Charlotte. He missed his wife and children, who, because of the uncertainty of his status due to his unguaranteed contract, had stayed behind in Houston. His two sons were puzzled by this. They had been able to comprehend daddy's forays from home in recent years, because when their mother said "He's off playing basketball," she had been able to prove it by tuning in the Rockets' game on TV. Now, her answer was the same, but where was the proof? Except for a couple of occasions, they couldn't watch daddy on TV. And when the Rockets were on, he was nowhere to be seen. "I'm not sure," Reid said in January, "that they understand what a Hornet is."

This was one reason Reid wanted to straighten out his contract before the next season began. If he knew the money was guaranteed, he'd feel safe in moving his family to Charlotte and settling in. But if it were not guaranteed, he'd continue to live as if he were on an extended road trip. And then there was respect. It always went back to that for Reid. Ten good years, make that 11 now, afforded him a certain status. He would work, but he shouldn't have to sweat out camp like some tin-horn rookie. By season's end, he was ready to issue an ultimatum to the Hornets: Either guarantee my contract or I won't show up next year. He didn't say it quite that strongly, but that was the point. "I've sacrificed for this team and done the job," Reid said. "Now it's time to show some respect, to take care of your people."

The Hornets weren't moved. A contract is a contract and they had Reid's name on the dotted line. "Besides," said Carl Scheer, "we kind of like having him coming in hungry. I don't think that's unhealthy at all."

• • • •

At February's All-Star weekend in Houston, the Hornets were not represented, which was no great surprise. But it was not, surprisingly, because they weren't invited. Tripucka, who had made seven straight three-pointers early in the year and had moved close to the league lead in that department, was invited to participate in the three-point shootout on All-Star Saturday. And Chapman was invited to participate in the slam-dunk contest. Both turned the league down.

Tripucka, a two-time All-Star, didn't want to give up his only vacation until spring for a half-hour exhibition the day before the real show. He would have given it up for a berth in the game itself, but no, not for that. It wasn't beneath him. It just didn't excite him. Chapman came closer to going. He turned down his invitation because of his December back injury, which was still fresh when the invitations first came out. A few weeks later the NBA found itself running out of dunkers as Michael Jordan, Dominique Wilkins and several others backed out. Would Chapman reconsider? He thought about it, but no, not this time. He was still worried about his back, and there would be other chances, other years, to display his talents in that field ... or in the three-point contest. Maybe he could be the first to do both. No one ever had, though Jordan, a modest three-point shooter, had thought about it.

Chapman needed some work on both areas, but showed promise late in the year. His March 19 dunk in Oakland over 7-8 Manute Bol was highlight reel stuff. Chapman, flying downcourt on the break, caught a pass and went in from the right side, cradling the ball behind as he got ready to windmill it over his head and into the basket. Bol, who does not jump to block shots because he doesn't have to, had planted his stick-like frame underneath the basket. As the ball came down toward the cylinder, Bol raised his arm and put a hand on it. For an instant the shot was blocked, but then Chapman's follow-through rammed both the ball and Bol's hand into the basket. "Well that was pretty good," Chapman said, "but I don't think Bol is really all that strong."

The other Hornets, especially the blacks, found Chapman's leaping ability amazing, which seemed to please Chapman. They laughed and exchanged high-fives after his practice dunks and sometimes hung around after the workouts were over to show off for each other. Once, while watching a tape of a past performance in the locker room before a game, a standard NBA ritual, a sensational Chapman dunk flashed across the screen. Earl Cureton, getting dressed in a cubicle near Chapman's, shook his head and clucked his tongue. "My, my Rex. What hops you have." A broad grin spread across Chapman's face. It was fun to be young and have great "hops."

His three-point shooting was, at times, no less remarkable, for the distance didn't seem to have a great effect on the shot. He shot just 31.4 percent for the year from behind the NBA's three-point line, which was placed 23 feet from the basket, more or less, depending on whether you stood in the corner or at the top of the key. It's hard to prove, but considering his total field-goal percentage, it's difficult to imagine that he shot much better on his other jump shots. And at that distance, a lower percentage was considerably more competitive. Chapman finished the year 20th in the NBA in three-point tries, 31st in percentage.

Chapman suffered the same bad start from long range as he did from all others. He missed his first nine three-point attempts and made just two of his first 18. But just after he returned from his back injury, he had a nice run from the line, making 4 of 9 in consecutive games. Then in March, he went on a real tear. He made at least one three-pointer in 14 straight games, and in one 10-game stretch, he was 18 for 36. His bombing became an important weapon for the team.

• • • •

February's trade deadline passed without movement for the Hornets. Harter had indeed called Don Casey about Greg Kite and the teams had talked about a Dell Curry-for-Kite swap. The coaches were both for it. The two general managers were less certain. Scheer thought Curry, who wasn't playing much, was worth more. Elgin Baylor of LA worried about not having a backup center and about the glut of guards Curry would bring. The deal died, as did several others. Atlanta, desperate for rebounding help when Kevin Willis went out for the year, offered a first-round pick for Kurt Rambis. The Utah Jazz, seeking backup help in the backcourt, offered its first-round choice for Michael Holton. Detroit and Milwaukee were both interested in Curry. And, of course, Indiana continued to dangle Stuart Gray.

Harter was still very much interested in Gray, but he had trouble rounding up support for the trade. When the Curry-and- others-for-Gray-and-others deal was publicized in January, callers to Charlotte radio shows came down firmly against it. Why did the Hornets want a stiff like Gray, they wondered. It was just uninformed talk, of course, but a general manager and an owner who were sensitive to public opinion might listen. On the staff, Badger supported Harter, but Littles, who did not think bulk was of major importance anyway, was skeptical.

When Indiana played in Charlotte in February, with Pacer General Manager Donnie Walsh ominously accompanying the team, Gray dropped by the Hornets' locker room after the game. That was a regular occurrence in the NBA. Everyone had friends on opposing teams, and the league did not discourage fraternization. But it carried a little added meaning in this case, and as Gray walked past, Littles said, "I hope he's just visiting."

Littles was miffed that Harter had been able to push the case for Gray and, to lesser extent, John Long, as far as he had, while he, the personnel director, had not been able to get very far with some of his ideas. "Dick wants all these guys he used to coach," Littles said. "I don't know if they can help us or not. But there are some guys out there who are available, who can."

Pressed for a few examples, Littles came up with Gene Banks, the ex-Duke star who was coming back from knee surgery. The Hornets had examined his knee the summer before but had passed on the opportunity to sign him. Now he was just sitting around, waiting for a chance to play. Could he play? Could he help?

"Oh, sure," Littles said. "I had him (coached him) in Chicago." And that, of course, was proof enough.

All of the deals fell through. Scheer thought the price asked for low, first-round picks was too high, especially considering the fan-player loyalty that had already been established in Charlotte. And the small deals that Charlotte wanted to make, deals that would help the Hornets but wouldn't really have much effect on an established team, weren't on most agendas this year. "Everybody's looking for a blockbuster trade," Scheer said. And the Hornets, outside of their future draft choices and their past ones – Chapman – didn't have many blocks to offer. So they resigned themselves to playing out the season with essentially the roster they had.

In February that was not so bad. The schedule offered a handful of possible wins, including a big road game at Miami. Though both sides tried to play down the rivalry between the two expansion teams – it's just a media invention, they said – there was some animosity. Charlotte had been considerably more successful in year one. They had won early and consistently, and, because of their fans, they were the talk of the league. Miami had lost 18 in a row to start the season and was the butt of jokes on late-night TV shows. Entering the second of two games between the teams – Charlotte won in Charlotte in November – the Hornets had 13 victories to just five for the Heat.

The Heat said this was the natural result of the teams' very different building strategies. They had invested heavily in futures, trading for five, second-round picks in the expansion draft and fielding a team that included four rookies. Charlotte had gone for established players. They had just one rookie on the roster. In time, said the Heat theory, their strategy would pay off. The Hornets, of course, thought this was baloney. "This year's rosters don't mean a thing," said Scheer. "We'll both have a lot of new players in three or four years, and that's when you can judge who did the best."

Added Littles, "Sure, Miami has some young players, but do they have any good, young players? I don't think they've got any more than us. If they want to be good in three or four years, they'd better have some different players from the ones they have now."

Whether planned or not, the game quickly turned into an intense and physical battle. Both sides drew technical fouls early. Charlotte's Kempton and Miami's Grant Long squared off at one point, and when Miami shooter Jon Sunvold got a hot hand, the Hornets began knocking him to the floor. "You know, it's funny," Sunvold said afterwards. "It started out as just one of 82, but then it turned into something else, kind of like a playoff game."

Miami, exploiting the defense of Chapman, led most of the first half. The Hornets, behind Tripucka, passed them in the third quarter but couldn't get very far ahead. Rory Sparrow, a journeyman NBA guard, tied the game at 100-100 with a three-pointer with 77 seconds to play. Charlotte muffed a couple of chances to go ahead, and Miami took the lead on Billy Thompson's free throw with 29 seconds left. With eight seconds left, Robert Reid tried his hero act again but missed a contested shot from 15 feet out. The ball hit the back rim and caromed over the heads of several Miami players and right into the hands of Tripucka. He faked several times and lofted a 10-footer over Thompson and into the basket, giving Charlotte a 102-101 lead with five seconds to play. Miami went to Sparrow, who'd had the hot hand, for the last shot. He backed Michael Holton into the lane, then turned and fired at the buzzer. It swished through as a sellout crowd at Miami Arena screamed in unison. The beaten Hornets dashed off the court under of a rain of orange fly swatters, which had been handed out as part of a promotion for the game.

The rivalry may have been just a media concoction, but the Hornets took the defeat as hard as any all year. Holton was defensive about his defense, snapping at a reporter in uncharacteristic fashion, "I think that's a dumb fucking question, that's what I think." Tripucka was critical of his teammates for not helping Holton out on the last play. Reid couldn't believe they let it come down to one play against that team.

Down the hall, Miami celebrated its biggest win of the season. Was it important, coach Ron Rothstein was asked. "Oh yeah," Rothstein said, "this was definitely a big deal."

Charlotte rebounded from that disappointment to beat Indiana at home the next night. Tripucka, on another scoring tear, got 30 for the third night in a row. Back-to-back blowouts against Chicago and New York followed, the first of many as it turned out. But a home game against the struggling San Antonio Spurs hid, for a time, the start of a slump.

The Spurs were a study in disarray. Injuries and dissatisfaction had caused them to churn their roster, running players through in great numbers, and a spat between coach Larry Brown and owner Red McCombs had led to speculation that the nomadic coach might hit the road again. They brought a nine-game losing streak and 10 healthy players to Charlotte that night. Even so, they were for a long time a match for the Hornets, who were not playing well. The game was even for a half, and Charlotte didn't seem to have much spark.

But an incident early in the third quarter seemed to get the Hornets going. After a missed shot and a rebound at San Antonio's offensive end, the teams were streaming back upcourt when the Spurs' Frank Brickowski jerked his right elbow backwards, catching Kurt Rambis on the draw. Rambis dropped to the floor as if shot. Referee Blaine Reichelt had barely glimpsed the play, but he had seen enough to make a call. He ejected Brickowski and gave Rambis two foul shots. With blood dripping from his chin, the dazed Rambis went to the line and made one of two. Then he went to the locker room for stitches. He returned a few minutes later to a thunderous ovation and a few bars from the theme of the Superman movie, and went about dominating the boards for the rest of the night. He finished with 22 rebounds, and the Hornets won going away. It was a typically gritty Rambis performance, the kind that caused Earl Cureton, Rambis' theoretical equal on the court, to remark, "I idolize Kurt and the way he plays. I wish I could be like that." Really Earl? "Really," he said.

Rambis did not take Brickowski's shot personally. The San Antonio player, who was known as a bit of a thug, apologized later, saying he was just swinging his arm to get free from the mass of bodies under the basket. "If he says it, I believe it," Rambis said. "That's the end of it."

Whether Rambis really believed Brickowski is doubtful. Harter certainly did not. He had coached Brickowski at Penn State for awhile, until he had run him off the team. Brickowski was arrogant then and more than a little dirty, something that Harter didn't entirely disapprove of in the right measure, but which he didn't condone either. Asked if he was surprised that Brickowski had laid out Rambis, Harter thought for a moment and said, "Yes ... He usually picks on a little guy. I'd never seen him hit anybody that big before."

Hornets Never Lie

The passing of the trade deadline left Harter with his season-old problem of how to find time for all his perimeter scorers. They were the best players on the team. It seemed silly, on a team that wanted for so much, to leave talented guys sitting on the bench. That, plus some carping from the Chapman family, led to the Rex Chapman point guard experiment, a trial the Hornets had been talking about, in muted tones, since summer.

It came in the final quarter of a February 23 blowout in New York. The game was out of reach, so Harter sent Chapman in for Holton, which surprised Reid, who looked around and said, "Hey, who's running the show?" Chapman was for about four minutes. The results were inconclusive. He had a basket, a turnover and an assist during his one and only stint at the position. Harter suggested afterwards that it was something the Hornets would use more and more in the latter stages of the season. "We've got to see if he can do it," Harter said.

That was okay with Chapman, though he said he really didn't care one way or another. Wayne Chapman had stronger sentiments. "He is a natural point guard," he said of his son, "and that *is* where he will wind up in the NBA."

He would not wind up there this year, however. His brief run in New York was all he would get. The team hit hard times soon afterward, and Harter wasn't about to try to improve them with a crazy experiment. He wondered about Chapman's ability to play the position at this point in his career anyway. He was having a hard enough time just playing without taking on the added duties of worrying about where everybody else was.

So Chapman finished the year as the starter at off guard. Curry, coming on strong at season's end, pushed him to play harder. Harter thought that was good. Very good. Chapman, who had seldom been pushed just to play, didn't always take it well. He chafed during the late-season games when he sat and sat and sat. But perhaps he learned from that, too.

No matter really. By the end of the season, almost everyone had to concede that Chapman, the heralded rookie, had had a good year. There had been the usual first-year ups and downs, but nothing to make anyone believe the Hornets' draft-day hopes were unfounded. By the last two months of the season, he had become a credible NBA player with occasional bursts of greatness. He was good enough to make the all-rookie team, good enough for Harter to say, "He's had a good season, about as good as you could have hoped."

No one thought any of the Hornets' draft-day hopes were unfounded. It was quite clear that Chapman would play in the NBA for years to come. The only question was at what level. Coaches still wondered about that, but Chapman's teammates generally felt they knew the answer. Earl Cureton, who had seen many stars and non-stars in his NBA career, said, "There's something about Rex. He's been compared to Jerry West, Michael Jordan and a whole bunch of guys, but he's not like any of them. He's got his own style. He will be one of those guys that people come to see play, though. I'm glad I got in with him on the ground floor. I've already asked him to get me some tickets so I can be there when he's made it big."

Chapman felt pretty good about his season, too. In that first year, he had gone from confusion to comfort. If he had any doubts about his ability, and he'd never said he had, they were gone. He had felt his way around the NBA without getting too badly burned.

That was not the stuff of legends, of course. But, it was a start.

The Long Road Home

"Well, Kell, at least you've got your tan."
– Dick Harter

March came in like a lion for the Charlotte Hornets. It grabbed them by the throat, shook their mangy carcass, then slowly chewed it up.

Dick Harter's prophecy about post-All-Star game problems proved to be accurate. With their opponents tuning up for the playoffs, Charlotte quit running into teams that had taken the night off. And when the Hornets' own game fell off, the result was a gruesome run in which the team played like ... well, like an expansion team.

Beginning with a February 28 loss at home to the Celtics, who were still a dynasty as far as the Hornets were concerned, Charlotte lost nine straight. That was a tie for the longest losing streak of the season, but it was by far the worst. The Hornets were pummeled regularly in the three-week stretch, losing the nine games by an average of 17.3 points. And that really doesn't tell the story. Some of the blowouts were much worse.

For instance, March 8 in Denver Charlotte trailed 79-46 at the half and was behind by as many as 39 points in the third quarter before a garbage-time rally chopped the final spread to 23. Against Atlanta five days before that, the Hornets were behind 117-83 after three quarters but rallied to lose by only 133-109. And a much-ballyhooed home game with the Lakers was a bust almost before it started. Less than 10 minutes had expired when LA ran its lead to 20 points. Charlotte trailed by 41 early in the fourth quarter and was in danger of being beaten even worse than it had been on opening night, when the benchwarmers rallied to chop LA's lead to just 30 points. Only three times in the nine-game run did Charlotte go to the second half with a realistic chance to win.

It was depressing. After the Boston game that started the streak, during which the Celtics led by 33 points in the third quarter, Kelly Tripucka said, "It's kind of sorrowful to be behind that much that soon. You don't feel like a professional team anymore."

Harter, predictably, blamed the nosedive on the team's lack of size. The Hornets were being ground down by the NBA's grist mill. So was every other team at this point, but in Charlotte's case, there was less grist to begin with.

The streak opener was a good case in point to Harter. Boston, struggling without Larry Bird, simply overwhelmed Charlotte's inside players. When a reporter asked Harter the cause of his team's offensive problems in the 112-87 defeat, he replied with just two words, "McHale and Parrish," meaning Kevin McHale and Robert Parrish, Boston's two giant post players.

A question about Charlotte's defensive troubles brought the same response.

"Size is the difference," Harter said. "They think they can do anything they want in there, and our guys are too tired or too small to stop them. But I said before we were going to have trouble."

Harter took the events of February 28 as a bad sign of things to come. He brooded in his office next to the Hornets' training room after the game. Eventually no one was left but himself, Tripucka, who was undergoing his usual post-game back therapy, trainer Terry Kofler, and manager David Jovanovic. Harter grabbed his coat to leave, turned and looked at Tripucka, a favorite of his, on and off the court. "Well, Kell," Harter finally said, "at least you've got your tan."

Tripucka and Kofler cracked up. Harter smiled. He had not delivered the sentence as the sarcastic one-liner it turned out to be. He and Tripucka both enjoyed the bronzed look, and in the impending gloom that he saw ahead on the Hornets' schedule, it looked to be one of the few redeeming factors left. In the short term, he was right. In fact, if Harter and Tripucka had known what lay ahead, they might have rushed over to the tanning booth right then.

Following the loss to Boston, Charlotte went on a three-game road trip in the East. In the opener, at New Jersey, they played well, particularly in the first half when Rex Chapman scored 18 points. But they faltered down the stretch and lost by a reasonably small margin. The next night in Atlanta, where, as usual, several hundred Hornet fans were in attendance, it was no contest. Atlanta scored 44 points in the first quarter and 40 in the third and was never threatened. The Hawks shot 64 percent from the field in the first three quarters and limited Charlotte to just 11 rebounds in the first half. It was a very soft game, just the kind the Hornets, and most other teams, could not afford to play against Atlanta's army of lithe, quick scorers. Harter fumed at the lack of contact from his big men, jumping to his feet at one point in the second quarter and screaming, "Brian, are you ever going to hit somebody?"

Hornet rebounding and toughness suffered from the absence of Kurt Rambis, who had to sit out when one of his lingering foot injuries worsened. In his place, Harter started Dave Hoppen, who was playing a little better, and shifted Earl Cureton to power forward. But in the end, Harter figured neither that change nor a weird lineup, featuring Robert Reid at the point with Chapman and Tripucka on the flanks, made much difference.

"We didn't have a legitimate excuse tonight," Harter said. "Not Rambis, not anything. They could have given us Wilt Chamberlain and I don't think we'd have won."

Atlanta's Dominique Wilkins, who had five, first-half dunks and scored 35 points in less than three quarters of play, said the Hawks had a point to prove after being upset by the Hornets less than a month before. "After the last time, we had to show these guys they don't belong on the floor with us," Wilkins said.

Charlotte finished its road trip two nights later in Washington, where it had been embarrassed on its last visit. This time they were better. Cureton played a tough game against a front line that, for a change, was no bigger than Charlotte's, and Rambis delivered 21 points and 11 rebounds on a night when it was not easy for him to walk. Just five minutes before the game, Harter was certain Rambis would not play. But just as the public-address announcer was about to introduce the starting lineups, Harter dashed to the scorer's table and said, "Rambis is in, Rambis is in."

Afterwards, Rambis said the decision was hard. "It was a matter of how loose I could get," he said. "For a long time I couldn't get loose, then I finally did. I kept trying to make up my mind. I guess when they started announcing the lineups it was 'eenie-meenie' instead of 'moe.'"

A big third quarter (12 points, five rebounds) from Rambis erased all but two points of a Washington halftime lead and made the game a tossup entering the final quarter. That went well for the Hornets for awhile. Rex Chapman, shooting poorly, suddenly found the range and made two in a row. That tied it at 88-88 with 7:19 left. But the Bullets, with primarily their second team on the floor, exploded, scoring on six straight trips down the floor. Three-point plays by Steve Colter and Ledell Eackles helped the points pile up faster, and a sudden cold streak by the Hornets produced a 102-89 lead for Washington with 4:58 left.

Chapman struck again, hitting a long jumper, a three-pointer and then one of his famous, double-clutch layups off the break to make it 102-96 with 3:24 left. That gave Charlotte some momentum, but it was quickly lost when Bernard King hit a tough jumper from the left wing and Earl Cureton, trapped in backcourt by Washington's press, threw a pass into the seats. Harter, animated as usual in a tight, late-game situation, blew up with uncommon vengeance when Cureton blundered. He leaped, spun around and as he landed, tried to speak. But all he managed to do was sputter and spit his game-long wad of gum onto Hornets radio man Steve Martin, seated beside the Hornets' bench. "It's getting a little sticky here at the Cap Centre," Martin could have said but blessedly didn't.

Harter reigned in his temper after the game. Disintegrating at crunch time was disappointing, but he knew the Bullets had something to do with it. He was a big fan of that underrated team and its peculiar chemistry and was rooting hard for it to catch Boston for the last playoff spot in the Eastern Conference. That was in part a love for how hard and how well Wes Unseld had the Bullets playing and in part a dislike of the Celtics. Harter didn't hate the Celtics for all their winning. He hated them for the sloppy, disorganized brand of basketball they were playing and getting away with, simply because they still had some good players. He longed to bump Boston off in one of the teams' last two meetings.

First, he had to get his own team back on its feet. The Washington game was encouraging in that respect, another reason why Harter wasn't quite so down about the loss. "That was our best game since Seattle," Harter said, referring to his team's upset victory on February 3. "Now, if we can just do that the next two or three nights out, I think we'll be out of this."

Before the game, Harter had looked at the Hornets' schedule, and with unusual optimism, sighted a couple of wins. Well, potential wins. After Washington, Charlotte played three straight at home. One, against the Lakers, was all but a hopeless cause, but the other two, Denver and Sacramento, were possible. The Kings were one of the worst teams in the league and had trailed Charlotte in victories for much of the season. Denver was better, but had been atrocious on the road. "If we could get two of the next four, we'd be in great shape," Harter said.

The Denver game would also offer another test of the Hornets' losing-streak repellent. Despite having lost nearly three out of every four games they played, at this point, the Hornets had not lost more than four in a row. By NBA standards, that was a pittance. The grind of the schedule usually sent all but the very best teams into a longer tailspin at some point during the season. In fact, by the first of the March, fewer than a third of the league's 25 teams could match Charlotte's record in this respect.

Harter had first called attention to this quirk when the Hornets won in Utah in January, ending a four-game streak for the fifth time. "Nobody in this league can beat us five in a row," he joked. It had been amazing. The Hornets had won three times on the road to break a four-game skid and had beaten Chicago at home in December to end another.

On the eve of the Denver game, with the streak once again in jeopardy, Harter said his team should be enshrined in the Basketball Hall of Fame if it kept the streak going all year. "We'll just take them all up there and put them on a wall or something," Harter said.

It might have made an interesting display, right over there next to Bob Lanier's size 22 shoes and one of Red Auerbach's cigars, but alas, it did not happen. Charlotte played a non-descript game against the Nuggets and lost 112-99. The Lakers followed with their mind-boggling blowout, one that Harter compared to the worst mismatches of his career, and suddenly the streak was six. A long road trip was coming up, and for the first time, the Hornets faced some real pressure. If they didn't beat Sacramento at home on Sunday afternoon, two nights after the Laker debacle, they'd head west for five straight with a seven-game losing streak.

The Kings game became as much a "must win" as any game an expansion team could play. The only games that might have rivaled it in the Hornets' first season were the two encounters with Miami.

"We've got to chalk up number 16 against Sacramento," said Robert Reid. "It's big for us. I think everyone understands that. I sure don't want to come back home with some 11-game losing streak or something."

Reid's math was off but not his logic. Sacramento was the only remaining breather left on the schedule. All the patsies left, if indeed the Hornets could be said to have patsies, were played on the road. The remaining home schedule was a depressing mix of playoff teams that would be honing their talents down the stretch. It was hard to see where the next win was coming from. Harter looked at the schedule with his best pained expression and said, "We could lose our last 25 in a row."

He was a pessimist when it came to his team, but his pessimism didn't seem so far-fetched now.

• • • • •

For Sacramento, a befuddled franchise beset by the zany leadership of general manager and sometimes coach Bill Russell, the Charlotte game was a big one, too. The Kings, who had turned over almost their entire roster since the start of the season as a prelude to rebuilding, were struggling home, too. They had lost nine of 11 coming into the game and were a miserable 4-28 on the road. Jerry Reynolds, the team's acerbic coach, said before tipoff, "If we don't get this one, we might not win another road game in the decade."

With two bad teams playing under duress, the game was not pretty. But it was competitive – for a few minutes. Trailing 25-24 with 1:55 left in the first quarter, Charlotte watched in horror as Sacramento ran off eight straight points to take a nine-point lead at quarter's end. Harold Pressley, the Kings' sixth man, did most of the damage. He pumped in two three- pointers, including one with nine seconds left in the period. Charlotte retaliated with three turnovers and a failed Earl Cureton jumper from 19 feet, several feet beyond his range. The second quarter was not much different. Sacramento scored easily and built its lead to 60-45 at the half.

Charlotte rallied and scored 39 points in the third quarter. Chapman, on his way to the biggest scoring day of his career, led the way with help from Tripucka. The Hornets cut the halftime margin in half by the time the fourth period started, and a three-pointer from Chapman and a jumper by Reid made it just 91-89, Sacramento, with more than 10 minutes to play. Momentum was winging the Hornets' way, but the team and its normally useful fans were out of sync this day, and momentum didn't seem to matter. Following Reid's basket, Sacramento got four straight points and a blocked shot from Wayman Tisdale, the power forward obtained the month before from Indiana. A three-point play from point guard Kenny Smith and a jumper from Danny Ainge sent Sacramento up 100-89. That was enough to do the Hornets in. Sacramento held on, and Charlotte packed its bags, expecting the worse.

Reid compared the sensation to driving into the desert low on fuel. "It's like you see that `E' on the gauge and you wish you had stopped at the last filling station 10 miles ago. I think we're where you pull out the map and see that it's from AAA and you think, it's nice to know someone is there. Then, you find out the phone doesn't work."

The next two games brought no relief. Denver blitzed the Hornets on one of their most feeble nights of the season, and the Seattle game, two nights later, was only slightly less depressing. It was amazing. The Hornets weren't quitting. They just looked as if they'd forgotten how to play. At one point during the streak, the long-suffering Harter said, "We're the worst team in the league right now. I can't think of anything to do. I've played everyone. The huddles are terrible. I can't even think of a good play to call. The best I've come up with lately gets us a fallaway 18-footer. It just feels terrible."

Contributing to that feeling, or perhaps causing it entirely, was the team's utter inability to get ahead at the start of a game. In the nine straight losses, Charlotte gave up an average of 34.4 points in the first quarter and found itself behind by an average of 11.2 points. That, despite the fact that they were actually ahead after one quarter once in the streak, at New Jersey. And the first-quarter woes actually went back further than that. In two blowout losses just before they beat San Antonio on February 25, the Hornets fell behind 42-21 and 40-28 in the first quarter to Chicago and New York.

Tyrone Bogues, who usually played looking uphill, found the Hornets' view in March tiresome. "We do the same thing every game," he said. "We get way behind, and then spend the rest of the night trying to catch up."

"It's getting old," Reid agreed, "and I don't know what we're thinking. We're not exactly the kind of team that can spot people 12 points every night and expect to come back to win. We're not like me playing my son to 15, where I give him 14 points and say, 'Okay, I'll shoot left-handed.' We've got to play right from the giddy-up."

This was not exactly a secret, of course, and not long after the problem appeared, the Hornets tried to correct it. That didn't work, and some began to think that maybe the attempt to correct it was itself the problem. "We've talked about getting off to a good start so much that I think we're starting to worry about it," said Tim Kempton. "Sometimes talk doesn't help."

The tightness seemed to affect Charlotte's shooting early in games. Beginning with the Chicago game in late February, the Hornets hit better than 45 percent – their season average – from the field just twice in a 12-game stretch. And the starts within those games were often worse. Against the Hawks, Bullets, Nuggets, Lakers and Kings, Charlotte opened the game one for eight, one for seven, one for seven, two for 12 and three for nine. "We miss our first few shots," said Chapman, one of the few Hornets to shoot well during the streak, "and it really seems to deflate us."

Pressing may have explained the offensive problems, but, as always, the heart of the matter was defense. It does not take a rocket scientist, as NBA coaches are fond of saying, to figure out that a team giving up 40 or more points in a quarter is going to have a hard time winning. Maintain that pace over an entire game and the opposition would average 160. Charlotte was not quite at that level, but to Harter it felt about the same.

The western trip would include several days spent in the San Francisco area, the home of legendary junior-college coach Bud Presley, a man who shared, as few others did, Harter's love of teeth-rattling defense. Presley had come to a Harter basketball camp once, when he was in his late 50s, and to prove a point, had stood at the foul line and taken charges from several dozen campers running at him full speed. Under normal circumstances, a reunion with Presley would have been in order. They would go out to dinner, take a few charges, and Harter would get him a ticket to Charlotte's game with the Warriors. But the way things were going, Harter couldn't bring himself to call his old friend. "I couldn't bear for Bud to see this defense," Harter said.

Just why the defense, which was never very good, had gotten worse, was a matter of conjecture. Part of the problem was the opposition's accelerated pace. But part may have been Harter's decision to make Chapman a starter over Reid, beginning when Tripucka returned to full health in mid-February. Or at least Reid thought so. That lineup, he thought, gave opponents too many easy avenues of attack. Tripucka was not gifted enough physically to deal with many small forwards in the open court, and Chapman was still too inexperienced to consistently handle most off guards. Since those were the two big positions for the scorers in the NBA, Hornet opponents found themselves with a real advantage.

"I ask the guys I know on the other team, 'Yo, what's the scouting report?'" Reid said during the slump. "And they say, 'Easy. Run at Rex and Kelly on defense, then run down the court, because they won't get back.' That seems to be working pretty well. Sometimes Mike (Holton) looks like he's out there by himself.

"Of course, maybe I shouldn't be pointing fingers," Reid went on. "When I've gotten out there, late in the first quarter or in the second, I haven't exactly slowed them down myself."

No, he hadn't. In fact, part of Harter's reasoning for making the switch with Rex was that the one big edge Reid had on the rookie – defense – was slipping fast. Reid had been a tough defender for Charlotte early in the year, almost a stopper against big guards and small forwards. But, in Harter's mind, Reid's age was catching up to him. He couldn't go as hard or as often now. Reid, who prided himself on his condition, disagreed. But his defense wasn't as good, and his court time was passing on to Chapman and, later, to Dell Curry. He averaged almost 29 minutes a game the first half of the season, less than 24 the second. That made it harder for him prove himself right.

• • • • •

With X and O solutions at a minimum, Harter begun pushing his personnel buttons with increased regularity. The team had settled into a rotation very quickly early in the year, largely because things were going well, and there was no reason to change. And, as other, minor bumps had appeared in the road, Harter had steadfastly refused to change lineups or make moves just for the sake of doing so. "What good would that do?" he had asked.

When it was pointed out that many coaches did just that, Harter replied, "Yeah, but how many of them are still working?"

Nonetheless, Harter was finally forced to make a few moves. There was nothing else left to do. The team dumped Rickey Green in late February to make room for Brian Rowsom whose broken foot had mended. That helped balance the frontcourt and backcourt on the guard-heavy team and opened a space for a player who might actually be used. Green had played sparingly since pulling a hamstring muscle four minutes into the season opener. It remained one of the great mysteries of the season whether he'd have played a bigger role if he'd stayed healthy. Harter's attitude toward him suggested otherwise. He was not impressed with Green in training camp – he had trouble learning the plays among other things – and thought it foolish to use a player who was over the hill when he had another who was younger and could do just as well. Green did not take offense at this. He knew his career was close to an end. But he wanted to squeeze a few more years and a few more bucks out of it.

Green was waived just as the trading deadline passed, meaning there was little chance of an addition from outside. So, as the slump started, Harter began juggling his lineup for non-medical reasons for the first time all season. He re-inserted Hoppen in the starting lineup for Cureton against the Lakers, a reward for his improved play, then gave Bogues a start ahead of Holton March 14 at Denver. The former was no problem. The centers were so liable to instant recall during a game that who started hardly seemed to matter. But the point guard switch was a little dicy.

Holton had started since the second game of the season – 60 in a row – and the worldly UCLA grad was sensitive to such maneuvering. Harter pitched it to him at first as a move made to combat Denver point guard Michael Adams, like Bogues, a midget-class scooter who could give Holton problems. Later, when Bogues continued to start against teams with normal-sized point guards, Harter told Holton he liked the spark Bogues provided at the start of games, although earlier in the year he had liked the spark Bogues provided off the bench.

All these sparks ignited suspicions in Holton. He was in the last year of a contract and could become a free agent the next summer. But preliminary talks had already begun between Carl Scheer, the

Hornets' general manager, and Keith Glass, Holton's agent. Both sides wanted Holton to remain in Charlotte. Holton liked the town and its business opportunities. And the Hornets thought Holton a valuable commodity. Just 27 and in good physical condition, he was a decent player who might improve. Certainly the Hornets could do better than Holton, but they could also do worse, especially in the area of character and personality. Holton was a bit of a schemer, a clubhouse lawyer, who looked for all the business angles of pro basketball. But he was still a team guy, very coachable and very stable. His coaches, in fact, thought him a dream come true. That included everyone from Larry Brown to Herb Brown, which, although in the same family, is quite a span. Herb, who had him with two different Continental Basketball Association teams, thought him the most coachable player he'd ever had.

Holton prided himself on that. It was, he thought, his greatest strength. "I really tune in well," he said one afternoon in January. "I think every coach I've played for knows that when I go on the court I'm not going to shoot a flying hook or something. I know the plan. I make it a point to know the plan, whereas some guys don't pay any attention. I'm solid. I think that's had a lot to do with me staying."

Dick Harter agreed with that assessment. But after coaching Holton for half a year, Harter observed that Holton was almost too coachable. Holton was so good in the classroom that when he went out in the field and botched things, as he was wont to do from time to time, it was a huge disappointment. "I don't know," Harter said. "He seems so tied together, so confident and well-schooled off that court ... you expect him to be just the same on it. But he's not always like that. I guess he's probably succeeded more in those off-court situations. He could mature on the court later. Some guys do. If he did that, he might really come on and show everyone something."

Harter kept waiting for that to happen. Holton had shown flashes of brilliance. He recorded the NBA's third-highest number of assists in a quarter (11) on December 1 against Philadelphia. Along with Robert Reid, he put the clamps on Michael Jordan in the big December 23 upset, and in back-to-back games in late January, he had scored 15, 22 and 21 points on 24 of 37 (64.8 percent) shooting. But in general, his performance was average. He was a cautious point guard who did not make many errors, and, conversely, didn't make many big plays either. He could play good defense, but he was not a stopper. "I guess I'm just sort of average across the board," Holton said.

Shooting might have been the area that made the difference. Had Holton been a really good jump shooter, he could have enhanced his point guard skills, hence his value, in a dozen different ways. But instead, his marksmanship was a mixed bag, just like everything else in his game. A left-hander, he was a deadly free throw shooter, third best on the team behind Tripucka and Dell Curry, both noted marksmen. But his jump shot, delivered with a surprisingly awkward motion, was inconsistent. Some nights he could hit, but more often not. Occasionally he produced some really ugly attempts, brick-class balls that thudded against the rim and caromed off at odd angles.

The result was that Holton shot a very poor percentage – less than 42 – until a February surge carried him over that. Combined with Bogues' inability on most nights to punish teams who left him open for the medium or long-range jumper, this created a major deficit at the point for the Hornets. The opposition eventually found that their point guards could cheat off the Hornets' playmakers a little, and perhaps offer some support for teammates trying to handle deadlier threats like Tripucka, Reid or Chapman.

Holton worried about this. As the second half of the season began, the team's biggest number cruncher knew his stats were not what they should be for the minutes he was playing (about 26 a game). "Forty-one percent doesn't cut it," Holton said. "I need to get up to forty-five, forty-six percent. That's respectable. And I think I can. I have before. I'm not that bad a shooter."

Holton figured that if he shot better, his scoring average would also rise. At mid-season, he was averaging about eight points a game. He wanted at least 10. Combined with career highs in assists and steals, plus another good year at the free throw line, that would give his agent something to take to the table. That was important. Holton had struggled for four years and four different teams in the NBA before coming to Charlotte. He had been waived out of the league twice, done his CBA time and had twice come back. But such a pedigree does not earn a player much more than the NBA minimum. In his year with the Hornets, his fifth in the league, he made just $150,000, only $50,000 over the NBA's bottom dollar. In his next contract, Holton was looking for the pay day his hard work told him he deserved.

Consequently, the second half of the year was, as Holton put it, "a real push time." "I'll never be in this position again," he said. "I've got to get it done."

For awhile he did. In January and February, he averaged better than nine points and six assists a game while shooting 46.8 percent from the field. His season averages climbed to 8.5 points and 44 percent from the floor. Then he stumbled. His foot began to hurt. The team started losing, and Harter made a change. Holton's minutes dropped, and he was no longer a starter. That last part was more symbolic than anything in real terms, but at the bargaining table it mattered. As Gene Littles, Charlotte's personnel director, said when negotiations with Holton stalled the next summer, "He wants to be paid like a starter." Of course, as Holton pointed out, for a long time he *was* the starter.

Holton, a big-time recruit out of high school, who, under Larry Brown's orders, had subverted personal achievement to make the team work at UCLA, did not think it unrealistic to think of himself as a starting NBA point guard. He thought he was close to the necessary level and longed to make the next jump. To him, that meant making the big plays with the shot clock running down. That was what differentiated the very good guards in the league from the run of the millers, Holton thought. He had the skills to do that, but, so far, he had had little success at it. At 6-4, he was effective going to the basket. That was one of his more impressive, physical attributes. But he seemed to have trouble finishing the play. He missed a number of opportunities at the end of drives. In the big win at Utah, it was his drive to the basket in the closing seconds that had produced the loose ball that Kurt Rambis scooped up and put in for the game winner. With the clock ticking down, he had stormed into the lane from the left lane only to get knocked down and see the ball go free into the mass of bodies banging under the basket. Was he looking for the foul? "No," Holton said, "I was looking to go up and dunk it."

As usual, it was hard to tell if sharp-witted Holton was serious or not. He could dunk the ball. He could also pull a writer's leg. And he probably was better at the latter.

When the team finally pulled out of its dive, with Bogues at the controls, Holton was asked what he thought had caused the turnaround. He feigned deep thought, then replied, "There's no doubt ... Tyrone Bogues." Then he laughed at his joke. The laughter sounded hollow, though. The flip-flop with Bogues really wasn't funny. And a week later, the humor was gone entirely. Holton's sore right foot turned out to be caused by a stress fracture in his ankle. He was out for the rest of the year.

• • • • •

The added losing brought some simmering discontent on the team to the surface. Those who weren't starting or playing much griped a about those who were. But not much. For a certifiably bad NBA team, the Hornets clashed infrequently. That was a tribute to management's decision to avoid bad people. As Harter noted once, "We knew we weren't going to be very good the first year, so we didn't see any reason to be miserable, too, traveling around the country with a bunch of assholes."

They avoided that and managed to put together a remarkably cohesive team. Rambis thought it the best group he'd been around, an amazing assertion given that the Lakers of the 1980s were known for their chemistry. Earl Cureton recalled similarly compatible squads during his days in Philadelphia. But those were championship teams that won almost nightly. Other losers he had played on, in Chicago and Los Angeles, particularly Los Angeles, were not the same. It was an odd feeling, he thought, to lose so much and still feel so comfortable with your teammates.

Besides the fact that there were no grating personalities to deal with, most felt the Hornets' unity was due to the lifeboat theory. Survivors of a shipwreck who end up in the same lifeboat may develop a strong bond through the mutual experience of being saved by the same lifeboat. For this team of castoffs, the Hornets were the lifeboat that they all shared. And, unlike when they were new players coming onto established teams, there were no cliques in place when they arrived. There were some friendships or acquaintances from previous NBA stops – Curry, Tripucka, and Green were all together in Utah for a year for instance – but nothing that precluded embracing new teammates. They knew no one else in town, at least at the start, so their friends were their teammates. It was either that or have no friends at all.

Some small groups, based loosely on age, race or size, eventually did form. There was the Strawberry Hill gang – Chapman, Bogues, Green and Curry – guards who all lived at the apartment complex of that name; the big white guy group – Hoppen and Kempton, and to an extent Rambis; and the older, married guys Reid, Tripucka, Holton and Cureton, a classification that Green would have seemed to belong to but didn't. The latter was not a group in that they hung together. They didn't, but they really weren't aligned with the rest. Cureton invariably sat with the Strawberry Hill guys in the back of the team bus, as did Rowsom, Ralph Lewis and Tom Tolbert while they were with the team. Holton and Reid were adept at crossing groups and seemed to have more friends away from the team. Tripucka, as mentioned, was something of a loner, though by choice rather than exclusion.

Humor, as is often the case in sports, was a common denominator that helped keep the team from becoming morbid. It ranged in sophistication from none at all to quite a bit. Someone might secretly place a condom – now why would a professional basketball player have a condom? – atop Robert Reid's curly perm in an airport, or Rex Chapman, apparently doing his rookie's duty, might collect room keys when the team checked into a hotel then give Rickey Green the one that opened Dick Harter's room.

Commentary on the passing landscape on bus rides provided outlets for budding comics and social critics. As the team was riding into Manhattan one cold, winter's day, the bus stopped at a stoplight. Out the right side was a furrier, his store windows filled with displays of luxuriant coats. Beneath one of the windows, atop a sidewalk grate venting heat from below, lay a scruffily dressed man.

"Looks like they'd have that guy moved from in front of the store," said a voice from the back of the bus.

"Or," said another, "at least throw one of those coats on him."

"Yeah," said a deeper voice, Cureton's perhaps, "they put one on him and then everybody could see how warm their coats were."

"That's cold, man."

"Very."

Clothing in general was the cause of much intra-team ribbing. Rowsom, whose family owns a chain of funeral homes in eastern North Carolina, took considerable grief for a dour, very plain, blue suit he sometimes wore. "Laying them folks down again?" Tyrone Bogues would ask when Rowsom appeared.

When Cureton showed up for a road trip one day wearing a thigh-length coyote fur coat – a Christmas present from his wife – his teammates started barking and howling. When Bogues stepped onto a bus in a similar coat – maybe it was the same one since it came down to his feet – Kempton looked up and said, "Cousin It!" Bogues did bear, on that day, a remarkable resemblance to the old Addam's Family character.

On a marginally higher plane was Rambis' sardonic lampooning. His favorite target was Hoppen, easy pickings, because there was a lot to lampoon, and because he took it well.

Driving past farmland near Portland one afternoon, Rambis began mooing and oinking in Hoppen's direction. Then he began whistling the theme from *Green Acres* .

"This is you, Dave," Rambis said.

Hoppen just nodded. A truck towing a trailer with a cow in it passed, and Rambis started again. "That's you, Dave. On the way into town for a big night with Bessy."

More Green Acres.

Hoppen said, "You know, I never saw *Green Acres* until it was a rerun."

"What?!" said Rambis incredulously, "Didn't you have TVs out there on the plains?"

"Nope," said Hoppen, getting into the droll spirit of the moment, "we just had the old radio. You know, that could really be some fun. Everybody'd gather round the set on the veranda. Grandpa would whip up some lemonade, and you could sit there and see what came on next. That was exciting. You never, just never knew. It was really some fun."

Rambis shook his head. It was no fun to shoot when the target returned fire. But he wasn't through for the day. A few minutes later, Hoppen resumed a previous conversation about the lack of a movie theater near the team hotel in Portland.

"So there's no theater close, huh?" he said.

"No," said Rambis, "there's one right down town."

Hoppen: "How far?"

Rambis: "Oh, about five or ten minutes."

"Well," Hoppen said, trying to launch his own offensive, "which is it? Five or ten? That's a pretty big difference, you know."

"No it's not," Rambis said.

"Okay," said Hoppen, "well, do you want to go to a movie tonight?"

"Nah," Rambis said, reeling in his line, "it's too far."

Such looseness allowed the team to ride out the many storms of the season without lapsing into the standard NBA bickering that could have made the losing streaks more numerous and much worse. The Hornets did lose a lot, but they were not so miserable as some while doing it. "Probably the best thing we had going during the losing streak," said Michael Holton "was the guys. There aren't any bad guys here, and in a bad streak that makes a world of difference. When things aren't going well we were still getting up and saying good morning to each other."

• • • • •

The losing continued on the first two games of the trip west and looked as if it could go on forever. The Hornets couldn't get started. They really looked as if they might not win again. And then divine providence – perhaps it was all those pre-game prayers at home games – sent them the manna they needed to go on. It was called a game with the LA Clippers. True, it was on the road, but with the Clippers that hardly mattered. The LA Sports Arena where they played was almost like a neutral court. The Clippers were the second basketball show in an entertainment-saturated town. They were terrible, had been for some time, and it was just hard to get anyone to care. Fans rolled into the arena in a trickle, a trickle that once, in the old American Basketball Association days, was counted on a special counter on the scoreboard. Tick.....tick.....tick..... Every five minutes or so, a fan might wander in. Some nights the crowds for the old LA Stars climbed into the thousands.

The Clippers did better than that. They were, after all, in the ultra-popular NBA, and they did have some of the more interesting, if not necessarily the most beautiful cheerleaders in the league. Those who liked to see a lot of female flesh might take in a Clippers' game before heading out to the LA strip joints for the night, just to get them in the mood. Okay, they weren't that bad, but this was definitely a team that depended upon something other than Clipper partisanship to bring the people in. By the time the Hornets arrived, another Clipper season had gone down the tubes. The coach had been fired. The first-round pick, Danny Manning, had blown his knee out, and the Clippers were again killing time, waiting to see where they'd pick in the draft. As a result, the homecourt advantage in the dirty old arena was something less than overwhelming, particularly for a game with the Charlotte Hornets. A little more than 10,000 were alleged by the Clippers to have shown up on this balmy LA night.

Predictably, they saw a peculiar game. The Hornets could not stop Benoit Benjamin, LA's talented but unpredictable center. He made 15 of 18 from the floor for 34 points and hauled down 23 rebounds, but he got only two shots in the last 10 minutes of a very close game. Ken Norman, an LA forward, was given a technical foul for yelling at his own coach. Don Casey screamed at him to take a shot and he replied, "Hey, the guy was holding my fucking arm." Rookie referee Nolan Fine thought the epithet was intended for him and handed Norman a T.

And then, as if on cue, the Clippers just collapsed in the last four minutes. They missed four layups and didn't score in the last three minutes as the Hornets blew by them. But even though they were less confused at this point in the season than the Clippers, the Hornets were still not at the top of their game either. Ahead by one with 90 seconds left, Chapman threw up an air-ball three-pointer on the break. That failed to awaken the Clips, so with six seconds left and Charlotte now ahead by three, Kurt Rambis tried again. After catching a pass on the right wing, he suddenly saw a clear path to the basket and steamed in for the layup when just holding the ball would have won it. "What was Kurt thinking?" Chapman wondered after the game.

"You know, you're always taught to do that," Rambis said. "So I just did."

Some Clippers converged on him, forcing him to alter the shot, which missed. LA rebounded and had a chance to tie, except that Clipper guard Gary Grant launched his shot from a half step *inside* the three-point line. "I just forgot where the line was," Grant said of this extraordinary game's final blow. No matter. His shot missed – too long – and the Hornets' streak was over. Also, the Clippers sewed up a nice 1-5 mark against the expansion teams.

Hornet heroes were Chapman, who had 15 in the fourth period, including a clutch three-pointer with four minutes left, and Tripucka, who returned from a two-game absence with back spasms to score 18 and hit two big free throws with 31 seconds to play. Charlotte also played good defense down the stretch, aided in part by the Clipper coaches who got so excited about getting the ball to 6-10 Charles Smith while he was being guarded by Tripucka that they forgot about Benjamin until the final minute. When they finally went back to the big guy, guard Quintin Dailey was so obvious about the entry pass that Tim Kempton was able to hold Benjamin at just the right moment and keep him from him reaching it. It hopped out of bounds, setting up the Hornet possession that ended in Tripucka's two free throws and the three-point lead.

"That was a terrible game, but the way things have been going for us we'd have taken a win over a CYO (Catholic Youth Organization) team," Tripucka said. "We were getting desperate."

The victory lifted the yoke off Charlotte's shoulders. Two days later, on Sunday afternoon, they played an excellent game against Golden State, a surprise success story in this NBA season, but couldn't quite pull it out. "I'm not happy when we lose," said Harter after the 124-117 defeat, "but we played well. I'd like us to play at that level all the time. If we'd do that we'd be good."

Charlotte did it without Tripucka who, just as he was about to leave his San Francisco hotel room and head to the game, crumpled up in the floor with a severe back spasm. He had to be taken to an Oakland hospital in an ambulance. He received pain medication there and began a series of tests to see if there was a problem beyond the obvious.

The Hornets made up for his absence with contributions from a lot of players. Curry came off the bench to score 10 in the last 4:30 of Charlotte's 37-point first quarter. Reid, who started in Tripucka's place, had 18 points, and Chapman had 22, including a thunderous dunk over 7-8 Manute Bol in the fourth quarter.

Charlotte's point guard tandem was also sharp, combining for 25 assists and just one turnover. Harter left Oakland feeling good. "I think the slump is over," he said.

His team confirmed that diagnosis the next night in Sacramento. Tripucka was still out, but the other shooters poured it on the Kings from the opening gun and never let up. Chapman hit four three-pointers. Curry made nine of 18. Reid hit 10 of 19. Even Bogues hit the jumpers given him.

The Hornets, who made 54 percent from the floor for the night, shot 67 percent in the first 22 minutes and led 66-48 with 2:28 left in the first half. The Kings tried to rally but never got closer than eight.

The Hornets, including owner George Shinn who'd flown in for the last half of the western swing, were like kids at Christmas after the game. That was a neat feature of this team. Unlike some veteran clubs, where most victories meant little other than that they weren't losses, this team doted on every win. They all seemed big. They all were.

In one corner of the locker room, Chapman was talking, expanding no less, to writers about his solid play of late. Not far away, Reid was happy, too. He claimed to have found inspiration for this game in a Sacramento paper that morning which had said, in effect, that the Hornets had no chance because Tripucka wasn't able to play. "That was a personal insult to me," Reid said. And now, flush with victory, he felt vindicated.

Holton was on a trainer's table. His foot and thigh were sore, but he was joking about two drives he'd made during the game in which the ball had, inexplicably, slipped from his grasp. On this night, with the fates with the Hornets, the ball had flown into the hands of teammates who had caught it and scored. "I hope I get an assist," Holton said. A few feet away from him, Hoppen suggested that Curry had an injury that needed treatment, too. "Better get some ice on that arm, Dell," Hoppen said. Curry had launched 18 shots in 26 minutes, about his average of late. No Hornet shot, or scored, more often than Curry. That might be a problem at some times on some teams, but right now, on this one, it was just another reason to laugh.

Harter, who lived and died with the team's fortunes more than any player, was bubbly after the game, almost like he'd been after winning at Utah. "What a sensational road trip," he said. "To come from where we were to win two out of three out here. That's something."

He was now looking forward to the rest of the season. Charlotte had a five-game home stretch. That would give the Hornets a chance to build some momentum for a strong stretch run and a positive ending to what had generally been a very good first year. That seemed very possible.

A little playing time had finally gotten Curry going – he was averaging 18 points a game over the last five – and though playing time might be a problem, another guy playing well could never hurt. Tripucka's injury was not serious. He would, in time, be back. Hoppen was playing a little better. Even Bogues, who had stuck a jumper or two on the trip, looked a little better to Harter. Things just might work out.

"I shouldn't have been so down before," Harter said. "You've just got to be tough because you never know what might happen or where in this league. You might start a nice streak on the road."

He was right. Anything could happen. A team might even start losing at home.

Parting Shots

"Maybe we can still get a bid to the NCAAs."
– Kelly Tripucka, after Charlotte won its 19th game.

The NBA goes to great lengths to keep the hearts of all its teams pumping for an entire season. That is the only reason for holding a draft lottery. If the team with the worst record in the league always got the first pick in the draft, then at some point in the season, several teams would always find themselves in a position where it was no longer in their best interest to win games. If the choice were between drafting Akeem Olajuwon, Patrick Ewing or a large, mobile person of similar skills, and winning 25 games instead of 15, there would be no choice. Olajuwon could make a team a contender for the next 10 years, whereas 10 minutes after the season is over the number of games a non-playoff team won is forgotten.

So, there is the lottery. The names of all the non-playoff teams go into a hat from which the draft order is randomly selected. Keep trying and you still might get the number-one pick. Keep losing and all you may wind up with is a good pick and a bad reputation.

This is sound motivational theory, but it has its limits. For the NBA's have-nots, there comes a time when the lottery is assured and the games just don't matter anymore. Twenty-two victories won't mean any more than 20 when all is said and done, and though the players may hope otherwise, coaches are inclined to forget the guys who shined in April, especially if that's the only time they shined.

It is much like the baseball adage that says, "Don't believe anything you see in September." In baseball, non-contending teams promote minor leaguers for trials in that month, which at least assures those teams of some enthusiasm, if not great professionalism. The NBA has no minors, if you don't count the CBA, so in its Septembers, it is the veterans of an already too-long year who must find a spark. With most of the fires extinguished months ago, it is not an easy task.

Hornets Never Lie

The Charlotte Hornets were somewhat immune to this problem. They had known all along that only the most miraculous string of events could keep their season truly interesting into the final months. Most players had come prepared for this, especially those like Earl Cureton and Kurt Rambis, who had chosen to come to Charlotte. They knew they would not win, would not make the playoffs. But they would play, and when the season headed down toward the wire, they would find a way to make it tolerable, to get up when, in the general scheme of things, it didn't matter.

It was not easy, though. Cureton, the usually calm and thoughtful veteran of so many different NBA wars, found this one hard to fight. In early April he said, "The end of the season coming up makes me kind of sad. It will end, and I'll just go home. That's it. Nothing more.

"That hurts you because what the NBA is all about is the playoffs. That's what you live for. That's the reason you play all these games. To miss it is hard. You go home and turn on the TV, and there they are, all the other guys. I usually watch some, but I always end up turning it off."

Other team members doubtless had the same hollow feelings, but buoyed by their West Coast successes and relieved to be rid of that odious losing streak, the Hornets talked bravely about their stretch upon their return. "Now that we're right again, I'm looking forward to messing up a few seasons," said co-captain Robert Reid. "I won't mind being a spoiler at all. There's no pressure on us. We can have some fun."

Reality turned out to be somewhat harsher. Three days after coming back from the West, the Hornets began an 11-game run against probable playoff teams. Charlotte played reasonably well, but found itself beating its head against an impregnable wall of determination. Teams that might have brushed off a loss to the Hornets early in the year now dug in against the first-year team. Such a defeat could rupture a team's fragile confidence at this crucial stage. It might even cost a playoff berth, or the homecourt advantage. After the Pistons rolled past Charlotte on March 25, Detroit's Bill Laimbeer explained the situation in his own inimitable style. "At this point in the season you just can't afford to fuck up," he said. "And if you're any good, you don't."

The teams the Hornets were playing were all quite good, so they didn't foul up and a pattern emerged. Charlotte would play its opponent roughly even until the fourth quarter, but would lose at the end. They were down six to Washington starting the fourth on March 23, down eight vs. New York on March 27, down one to Philadelphia

April 7, down three to Atlanta on April 10, even down just four to nemesis Cleveland on April 9, but wound up losing every time. After the Cleveland loss, Kelly Tripucka said, "We're like a two-twenty hurdle runner who trips on the last hurdle every race. We just can't make that last ten yards."

The losses were all annoying in their own little ways. Against the Bullets, the first game after coming home from the West, Charlotte's offense died at the start of the fourth quarter, and Washington pulled away. Against the Knicks, the Hornets ran into Pat Ewing on one of the finest shooting days of his career. Despite some decent defense from Earl Cureton and others, Ewing scored 45 points, including a pair of difficult, turnaround jumpers in crunch time when Charlotte was trying to rally. Chicago was within reach in Chicago on April 4, but Michael Jordan took advantage of a defensive gamble by Charlotte guarding him with Tyrone Bogues – and rained in medium-range jumpers in the fourth quarter to break the game open. "It was like target practice," Jordan said.

Bogues was the man on Jordan that night because the taller Michael Holton was on the injured list. His sore foot was diagnosed as a stress fracture on March 26. Charlotte signed Sidney Lowe, the former N.C. State star, as a free agent to replace him a few days later, but Lowe isn't a lot taller than Bogues.

Not surprisingly, Dick Harter saw his team's continued problems in physical terms. "If you guard bigger people with smaller people for a whole year, the smaller people eventually get worn down," he said. "I think that's what's happening to us. We're playing well enough, but our guys are just worn out."

Several of Charlotte's opponents agreed. Old friend Charles Barkley thought "those Hornets just sort of faded on us there at the end. They looked tired."

Knicks' coach Rick Pitino said Charlotte's fourth-quarter fade against his team was anticipated. "We thought their legs might go at the end," Pitino said after Ewing had finished his destruction. "Because of their size they have to run a little harder to keep up."

At Harter's behest, the Hornets moved to rectify the size deficit at the end of March, signing Greg Kite as a free agent. The Clippers, who once could have had Dell Curry in exchange for Kite, unceremoniously dumped him March 23. The move was partly due to financial reasons, but the Clippers said that Kite no longer fit into their plans. The financial part made sense to Kite. He had become the third-string center in mid-March, and teams don't pay $250,000 a year for third-string centers. "Most clubs do think like that, and it makes sense," Kite said. "Whether that's how the Clippers thought ... I don't know. It's been my experience that's it hard to tell what they're thinking or if they're thinking at all."

Kite fit Harter's description of what the team needed most. He was big. A former Celtic, he was 6-11 and at least 255 pounds. But in a five-year NBA career, spent mostly on the Boston bench, he had not shown that he was much more than big. Asked to list his strengths on the basketball court, Kite said, "Well, I show up on time, I'm big and strong and I can play good position defense. I'd say those are the main things."

He did nothing to disprove that assessment during his month with the Hornets. He never missed a plane, a practice, or the chance to lean on an opposing center. How much use this was to the Hornets was hard to say, however. Though Harter lauded him constantly, Kite's contribution to the team was not easy to quantify. In 12 games, all of which he started, he did not go much beyond his meager career statistics of 2.1 points and 2.9 rebounds a game. He was not in great shape, so Harter couldn't use him much. He played 30 minutes one night against his former Boston teammates, but averaged just 18 minutes a game during his stay with the Hornets.

Still, he gave a certain presence to the team. He knocked some people around, and, perhaps, inspired Dave Hoppen to greater deeds. The Hop, who had come to an understanding with Harter in late February over the aggressiveness issue, played his best basketball in April. His confidence restored by the knowledge that Harter did indeed want him to succeed, Hoppen averaged more than eight points and eight rebounds a game for the month. More importantly, he mucked it up inside on occasion. It was enough to make Harter quit shaking his head in disbelief every time Hoppen's name came up. By the end of March, he had come around to the belief that Hoppen might still be a useful player. "He wants to be good," Harter said, "and if you want it, you've always got a chance."

• • • • •

To make room for Kite, the Hornets waived Ralph Lewis, the seldom-used swingman who had dodged the ax twice before. Lewis took it well. Though he thought he could play if given the chance, he realized he was, at best, a marginal NBA player who was fortunate to have squeezed even two seasons out of his talents. He was gifted physically in many ways, but essentially he was a post player in a guard's body. Despite his height, he played around the basket in college and was effective, too. He averaged more than eight rebounds a game for his career at La Salle, more than nine a game each of his last two years. His last season, when he had been told he'd get a chance to move outside some, he had even been his team's center. Another, bigger player, Albert Butts, was denied his last year of eligibility, and Coach Speedy Morris threw Lewis into the breach.

"That," Lewis said, "hurt me. It hurt me drastically." Morris, apologized once for stunting Lewis' development, but Lewis really hadn't minded at the time. He saw the logic in his being a center – he was the best man the Explorers had for the job – and thought himself lucky to have done what he did. Hardly anyone had recruited him out of high school in Philadelphia. He made La Salle's team his freshman year as a walk-on. With so late an entry into the upper echelon's of the sport, it had not dawned on him until late in his senior year that he had a chance to play in the pros.

By then it was too late. Had he been just a little taller, perhaps two inches, with all the commensurate additions to limbs and trunk thrown in, he might have been a fine pro, a Dennis Rodman-type player who could run, jump and defend. As it was, he was forced to perfect his perimeter skills in an arena where most of the performers already approached perfection. Lewis' physical ability was not enough to overcome that. He mastered ballhandling to a degree, but remained a horrible outside shooter due to a odd shooting motion. The jump and ensuing release of the ball were not synchronized, and in his follow-through his shooting hand shot off at an angle towards the intended line of flight. This imparted sidespin to the ball, and along with the spastic release, produced a very hard shot. Lewis didn't benefit from "shooter's bounce" very often, and he knew it. "I think I can score," he said, "but I'm not exactly what you'd call a classic jumper shooter."

But, he was able to roll with the punches. When the news came that he'd been cut, he was already resigned that his basketball days were about over. He might try one more time, but he was thinking more about his next career. He had earned his degree in four years at La Salle. It was in criminal justice. He might take that and go into law enforcement. He might go into business. Whatever, he would not dwell long on what didn't happen for him in basketball. "I've got nothing but good memories of the NBA," Lewis said as he left it.

• • • • •

Kite arrived in Charlotte in time to see the team's Thursday night loss to Golden State. Harter started him two nights later against Portland, a move that did not thrill Tim Kempton, who saw it as his official entry into the doghouse. Kempton's playing time dropped throughout the second half of the season. The last month, he hardly played at all, averaging just 6.4 minutes in the nine games he played. Twice, Harter didn't use him at all. "I just don't understand," Kempton said. "I can't think of anything I really did wrong, but now I'm not playing at all."

The problem was that both he and Hoppen had failed to receive, or failed to act upon, Harter's season-long message of toughness. The acquisition of Kite was one last, extremely loud, transmission of the same idea. But it was nothing new. Kempton's confidence had dropped, and he had stopped being much of a physical presence. In the game against Golden State in Oakland, the spindly Manute Bol, who possessed about a third of Kempton's bulk per square inch, had pushed his way past Kempton to grab a rare offensive rebound and lay it back in. Harter responded with his best sideline stomp and shouted, "C'mon Timmy. You can't let him do that."

Kempton yanked his ever-present mouthpiece out and shouted back, with appropriate hand motions, "He pushed me!"

Harter couldn't believe it. Bol had pushed Kempton out of the way? "You should be pushing him!" Harter screamed, fending off an imaginary Dinka tribesman with his forearm to demonstrate what he meant.

Kempton tried to implement the plan, but his earlier magic was gone. Meanwhile, Hoppen had gone from hitting no one hard to at least hitting a few people. No one had dunked one off his head for several months now. That looked like improvement to Harter, so when Kite arrived, Hoppen became the number-two center. Kempton was third or fourth at that position and at power forward.

Kite's first start was not especially memorable. The game, against Portland, came at the height of Charlotte's wheel-spinning frustration. Charlotte put on a spectacular show against the talented Trailblazers, who had toyed with the Hornets in Portland two months before. Down 10 entering the fourth quarter, still down eight with 2:43 to play, the Hornets rallied to tie the game and send it into overtime. Robert Reid, summoning his sometimes remarkable offensive powers one more time, hit three straight jumpers to keep Charlotte in the game. Then, with 19 seconds left and the Hornets down by three, he caught an inbounds pass from Tripucka and threw in an incredible three-pointer from between two Portland defenders primed to stop that very shot.

Hustling to obtain loose balls at both ends of the court, Charlotte surged ahead 115-114 with 1:32 left in overtime. But the Blazers' superb individual talents took over. Clyde Drexler, Reid's good friend from Houston, spun past Reid and scored on a wild shot from the lane as he was fouled. Tripucka missed a tough shot for the Hornets, and Portland's Terry Porter followed with a 15-footer after scraping Charlotte's Bogues off a pick. Charlotte got two clutch scores – a pair of free throws from Tripucka, who had 38 points on this night, and an offensive rebound basket by Bogues. But Portland just handed the ball to Drexler, who twice held it until the shot clock ran down, then went to the basket against the entire Charlotte team and got the free throws that made the difference.

The outcome pained Harter. It was not so much the close loss, but that his team played well and still lost the only game they really had a chance to win in the waning season. "It's depressing," Harter said. "We've played pretty well for five straight games, but we only get to draw up a play to win it once. I don't know what to do."

And, as usual, he didn't see where the next victory was coming from.

• • • • •

The losing continued, but the faces changed as the Hornets headed down the stretch. True to his word, Harter found minutes for Dell Curry, primarily at Robert Reid's expense, but also at Rex Chapman's. There was no mystery to that. Curry had broken through while Tripucka was out, and he was playing so well that Harter couldn't put him back on the bench. Fans had started bringing signs to the coliseum pushing for more court-time for Curry. When Curry replaced Chapman in the season finale against Milwaukee, many cheered.

Harter wasn't bowing to that pressure. He was just sticking by his dictum that guys who played hard and well got to play. The soft-spoken Curry, a pleasant man from the northern end of Virginia's spectacular Shenandoah Valley, had done what was asked. He was trying harder on defense.

Curry did that even though he wasn't sure just why it was necessary. Not the defense part. He understood that. But the trying harder. It was not as if he hadn't been trying before. It was not that he was a bad defender, so far as he could tell.

"But," Curry had said back when he wasn't playing, "it's like someone came by and stamped on me a long time ago a label that said, 'Cannot play defense.' It doesn't matter what I do. That's what everyone thinks. I guess that happens to a lot of guys who can shoot it a little. And that's the way this league is. You get a reputation, and you could change 180 degrees and no one would pay any attention.

"I think I can play defense well enough. I'm not going to a star at it, and I'm going to look bad at times, because of the position I play. Every team has a two guard who can score. But I think I can hold my own."

Others, obviously, were not as sure. Curry had arrived in the pros with a reputation, built during his days playing for Charlie Moir's loosely structured Virginia Tech teams, as a one-trick pony. He had a marvelous jump shot. His touch was so deft that it sent some scouts into near-orgasmic fits. But that defense ...

Curry was athletic enough to be a good defender. He was not exceptionally fast or quick, but he jumped well, was taller than the average guard (nearly 6-6) and possessed unusually long arms. It came down to fundamentals – and a question of desire. Because of his ability with the ball in his hands, some NBA minds were willing to take a second look when Curry came into the league. No one in Utah much cared. Curry was trade bait almost from the moment he set foot in town. But in Cleveland, it was different. The Cavs wanted him as a player, and Coach Lenny Wilkins, a superior defender during his All-Star caliber playing days, expended a good deal of energy trying to impart some of his defensive wisdom to Curry during Curry's season there.

For whatever reason, it did not seem to take. One lesson in particular stands out to those who were around the Cavs that year. Wilkins was trying to make a point about a fault in Curry's defensive stance. Standing in front of Curry with the ball, the 51-year-old Wilkins would say, "Okay now, I'm going to beat you off the dribble to your left." Curry would nod and Wilkins would dribble past Curry's left side.

"See what I mean?" Wilkins asked. Curry nodded and Wilkins instructed him on knee flex, posture and balance. Then he returned to his position in front. Same drill. "I'm going to beat you off the dribble to your left. Ready?" Wilkins said. Curry nodded, and once again Wilkins drove past Curry's left side.

An exasperated Wilkins eventually gave up. When the playoffs came that year, he went with Craig Ehlo as the backup off guard. Ehlo couldn't shoot like Curry, but he couldn't be beaten off the dribble when he knew it was coming either. Later that summer, the Cavs chose to protect Ehlo instead of Curry against the ravages of the expansion draft. And Curry became a Hornet.

In Charlotte, Dick Harter was never able to beat Curry off the dribble. But he found his defense frustrating all the same. He should be able to do better, Harter thought. Anybody should. He would tell Curry this, hoping it would motivate him, then watch the next time he put him in as Curry's man once again went crazy.

That is what Harter saw. Curry saw something different. He saw himself playing defense roughly on par with his teammates – and being castigated for every slip he made. "It's like I go in there and my man doesn't score for two possessions," Curry said. "Everything is fine. Then he does hit one, and all of sudden I can't play defense again. Every team seems to have a guy who can get away with not playing defense, or not playing it that well. But on this team I can't do that. We have other guys who aren't playing defense, too; at least, they sure aren't doing any better than I am. But they still get to play. I just can't understand it at times."

Curry thought he was getting the shaft, but even so, he didn't sulk or complain. He joined Rickey Green, another player who wasn't getting to play without any real justification, in extra running before games and on off days to stay in shape. And he kept his shooting arm in shape, although his motion and touch were so natural that they hardly seemed to require any maintenance. He also listened to what Harter said and tried, as best he could, to play harder, tougher defense. Nothing much happened for several months, except that he nearly got traded a couple of times. Then, in mid-March, the door finally opened. Tripucka's back went out and Curry was pressed into service as a swingman, filling for Robert Reid, Tripucka's replacement, as well as for Chapman. He even played a little point guard.

Curry took advantage of his break to pour in the points. He scored 21 in 16 minutes in the first game Tripucka missed, and kept on scoring after Tripucka returned. After he lit up Sacramento for 21 in 26 minutes in the Hornets' victory there, Harter publicly promised more playing time for Curry even after Tripucka returned. "He's got to play," Harter said. "He's playing too well, and I mean at both ends. He's really trying. He's playing pretty good defense. Hey, I'm serious."

Curry grinned weakly at this news. He might be from the backwoods of northern Virginia, but he was no dummy. He wasn't getting those minutes because of the way he was shutting everybody down. He was playing because his jumper was falling and he was piling up points. "As long as I continue to hit my shots," he said, "I'll continue to play. ... I think."

Nothing was certain. But Curry did continue to hit his shots, right up to the end of the season. Over the last 19 games of the year, beginning with Tripucka's first back-induced absence at Denver, Curry hit 51.5 percent from the floor, a superior figure for a jump shooter. He was even better in the final month, hitting a sizzling 56.4 percent from the floor while averaging 18.8 points in just more than 21 minutes per game.

He was amazing at times. He scored 13 straight points to keep

Charlotte in the game one night against Philadelphia, scored 31 in 28 minutes against New Jersey to lead the Hornets to their last victory of the year. This did not go unnoticed. He became a fan favorite. The last home game of the year, when fans were hounding Harter to put Curry back in, they chanted his name in unison: "Cur-ree, Cur-ree," over and over. That didn't happen to another Hornet all year.

Harter didn't like that, but it didn't surprise him either. Months before, when Curry had just come off the injured list, Harter had predicted that it would happen.

"There are going to be some nights," he said back then, "when Dell's going to light it up, because he can do that. And the fans are going to be screaming his name, wanting me to put him in."

The only difference between the future Harter saw in January and the one that came to pass, was that in the real future, Harter actually did put Curry back in the game.

• • • • •

There were other changes as the season ground to a halt. Brian Rowsom, the undertaker's kid, undertook a greater role. He had to play. He was a promising player but also a free agent when the season ended. The Hornets thought they wanted to re-sign him, but they had to see more to be sure. Kite took over for Kempton. Lowe took over for Holton. And Tyrone Bogues joined Curry as the Hornets went on a roll.

Bogues' elevation to the starting lineup remained something of a mystery to him. Early in the season, as the point guard who started the second and fourth quarters, he had split time with Holton. But his playing time started to fall after the New Year. In back-to-back games in late January, he played just 16 minutes combined. And from January first until his first game as a starter, he played as much as half the game only six times. The two longest stints came in games when the Hornets got blown out.

Bogues did not understand what had happened, except that he knew the team was losing, and he knew that changes are sometimes made in such a situation. He didn't argue with that. He just rolled up his short little sleeves and went about making the most of it.

In its own way, Bogues' performance at the end of the year was every bit as amazing as Curry's. In his 21 games as a starter, he averaged 12.1 assists and just 1.3 turnovers per game. The former figure, if maintained over an entire season, would be the 12th best in NBA history. As it was, the late burst was enough to raise Bogues to 12th in assists in the 1988-89 season, ahead of, among others, Maurice Cheeks, Doc Rivers and Derek Harper, three veteran points who started all year. And no one in the league handed out assists at a faster rate. Bogues rang up an assist every 2.83 minutes. Utah's John Stockton, the per-game leader, was six thousandths of a minute slower.

Combined with his careful control of the ball – no one stole the ball from Bogues; he only made turnovers on those occasions when he drove too recklessly into traffic and got stuck with no way out – the growing assist pile made for a glittering statistical package. In those last 21 games, Bogues collected nine assists for every turnover, a phenomenal ratio. For the year, Bogues' assist-turnover ratio was 5.5 to one, easily the best in the NBA. This display further endeared him to 5-7 owner George Shinn, who enjoyed seeing another little guy beat the odds, and to General Manager Carl Scheer, who thought Bogues a wonderful marketing tool. Scheer said this view did not cloud his vision of Bogues' other abilities as a player. He would still consider a trade for him if the goods offered in exchange seemed right. But Scheer did gush over several of Bogues' performances down the stretch. When Bogues racked up identical totals of 17 assists and just one turnover on back-to-back nights against Detroit and New York, Scheer shook his head and said, "He's just amazing, isn't he?"

The Hornet coaching staff was less enamored of the "littlest Hornet," although they found it hard to deny that he possessed certain skills. Bogues was a fantastic passer. He had a great sense of timing – that was important, because a shooter in the NBA has to receive the ball just as he pops open, or, more often than not, he would be open no more – and with his quickness, he could create passing angles and opportunities as few others could. He also very much enjoyed the role of "field general," in which he had been cast during his high school days on Bob Wade's most famous teams at Baltimore's Dunbar High. His feeling of confidence with the ball in hand began there and was cemented in college, at Wake Forest, where circumstances transformed Bogues from a novelty recruit into the heart and soul of two modest Deacon teams. Coach Bob Staak, realizing he held few other cards, gave the ball to Bogues and let him do his thing. He monopolized it, running the clock to shorten the game, then darting about, trying to create a scoring opportunity for one of his less-talented teammates. The maneuver was generally successful. Wake won a few more than it should have during those two years, and Bogues became a star.

In the pros, where such tactics were limited in effectiveness,

Bogues displayed a surprisingly astute awareness of the intricacies of the game. He was no scholar. He struggled mightily just to stay eligible during his college days (to his credit, he did). But he understood basketball, understood it the way a coach did. His size sometimes limited him from making a play, but he knew which play to make, when to run off the clock, when to call the number of a player who might be feeling left out of the offense. With Charlotte, he sometimes even anticipated Harter, signaling a play the coach wanted before he had time to call it.

Still, there was his size. Sometimes the other stuff, especially Bogues' obvious courage, blinded scouts to this obvious fact. But most hard-core basketball people were not fooled, including the Hornets' staff. Before training camp even began, assistant Ed Badger identified Bogues as "a luxury we can't afford."

And it was just a few weeks into camp before Dick Harter realized the problems that playing Bogues for extended periods would cause. He could do some nice things, Harter agreed, but for every one of those, he would cause three problems. How could a team with so many problems afford to do that? How could the league's smallest team afford to play a midget, as Harter occasionally called Bogues?

But the case against Bogues was not easy to make. Like bacteria without the aid of a microscope, his flaws were not visible – at least not to the untrained eye. It was hard to realize that a Kelly Tripucka drive was stopped because Bogues' defender could afford to cheat off of Bogues and was able to beat Tripucka to a spot. You had to follow the game with a coach's eye to know that an opposing center scored easily, not because Tim Kempton couldn't handle him, but because, with a 5-3 guy in front of him, the point guard was not pressured while making the entry pass. It took a close observer to see that the teammate who came over to help Bogues prevent the opposing point guard from posting Bogues was the same defender whose man just scored on an uncontested layup. As Harter noted of Bogues at one point late in the season, "He gets you beat in a 100 subtle ways."

Harter was generally subtle in describing this, for despite Bogues' faults, Harter truly liked him. The little guy played harder – he had to, of course – than anyone on the Hornets. He scrapped, he dove for loose balls, he never quit. And Harter's heart went out to him for that. It was never really Bogues whom Harter blamed for the problems the little guy caused. It was more his superiors: Shinn, Scheer and God. The Almighty, meaning God in this case, simply hadn't made Tyrone Bogues to be a basketball player.

One night, Harter's frustration over this immutable point spilled out. The Knicks had just beaten the Hornets on the night when

Patrick Ewing scored 45 points, and Harter was answering questions from sportswriters. Among them was Sam Goldaper of the *New York Times* , the oldest NBA writer still in captivity and a man who liked to focus on minutae of Xs and Os. Why, Goldaper wondered, hadn't Harter ordered his team to double-team Ewing more?

Harter's famous I'm-being-twisted-on-the-rack-for-no-reason look of pain flashed on his face. "Sam," he said, "I've got a 5-3 point guard. Do you know what that looks like to Patrick Ewing?"

Goldaper shook his head, so Harter showed him. He dropped to his knees in front of Goldaper, sat back on his haunches and held his hands in the air in a position of defensive menace at Goldaper's waist. "It looks like that this," Harter said.

"And this," Harter said, standing up and grabbing a nearby chair, "is what it looks like when Patrick Ewing guards Tyrone Bogues." Harter climbed up in the chair and towered over Goldaper. "Go ahead," Harter said. "Hit the open man."

Later, when he was back to his normal size, Harter said, "Don't get me wrong. I love the way Muggsy plays. But he's down here, and the game is up there, and there's not a thing he can do about it. If it were soccer it wouldn't matter. But it's not. It's basketball and the goal is 10 feet off the ground."

For Bogues, all of this was hard to take. He had long ago hardened his shell to the doubts and criticisms of those who said he'd never make it to all of the various levels to which he had already climbed. But every now and then it got to him. Now, late in the season, when he was playing as well as he ever had, was one of those times. "I'm just a little tired of the cheap shots," Bogues said. "I know I'm five-three, and so does everybody else. What else is there to say? To me, the hardest thing about playing in the NBA is keeping your head up when everybody keeps telling you how hard it is."

Bogues knew his liabilities as well or better than anybody, and he thought they were often over-stated. On many nights, the good things he did outweighed the bad. And playing time – the eternal elixir for all players – would cure some of the bad. The more he played, for instance, the better he would shoot, Bogues said.

There was evidence to support that. Just after assuming the starting role, Bogues' shooting picked up. In the final week of the year, it climbed to 43.4 percent, his highest since the first week of the season. His scoring increased. He averaged 7.5 points a game as a starter. But some of that was illusion. His jump shot, except for one stretch at the end of the western trip, was no more dependable than before. And on a per-minute basis, his scoring actually declined after he became a starter.

Harter wished Bogues was right. If just one of Muggsy's failings could be cleaned up, he might be a useful player. If, for example, he could just hit the medium-range jumper with consistency. ... "If he could do that," Harter said, "he might be able to help us for two or three years."

But if not, Harter thought playing Bogues instead of a bigger point guard was a waste of time. "Muggsy's got a place in the league," Harter said. "But I think it's as a spot player – eight or 10 minutes a game – on a championship team. I hope he gets that chance. I hope he gets a ring. He deserves it. But I don't think he'll ever get it here."

Surprisingly, Bogues agreed with most of that. "Not to knock our guys," he said late in the year, "but when you're not on a winning team, when you don't have the personnel, weaknesses show up more. Sometimes, on a championship-type team they can get overlooked."

Of course, Bogues said, that was true for players who were 6-3, too. A weakness was a weakness. What difference did the size make?

• • • • •

Despite everything that Bogues and Curry did, the Hornets continued to lose. And as the streak began to build, the competition did, too. This heightened frustration, not only because it made it harder to win, but because the level of Charlotte's play was increasing to no effect. The feeling built to a crescendo on the weekend of April 9-10, when, in back-to-back games, the Hornets took Cleveland and Atlanta into the final minute before losing. Both those clubs were on their way to winning 50-plus games, the benchmark total for successful NBA teams, and both had slaughtered the Hornets in previous meetings.

But Charlotte was a different team now, tougher and more intense. Somehow, Harter and his staff had managed to draw this out of the team just when it seemed least likely. Practices were no different. They were less demanding at this point, as they had to be to accommodate bodies worn by the long season. But in the games, the team played with a new-found fury and precision. Everything worked a little better. Everything was tied together, as Harter liked to say, as if the pulling, tugging and adjusting of the past four months had suddenly produced a very sound knot.

The Cleveland game, on a blustery Sunday afternoon when snowflakes fell outside the coliseum in Richfield, Ohio, was remarkable. The young Cavs had slowed from their early season pace when they had sprinted to the best record in the NBA and absolutely thrashed the Hornets on three occasions. But they were still a fearsome team with many weapons. One of those, forward Larry Nance, was not available on this day while he rested a sore leg. But the Cavs had beaten Charlotte without Nance before. Easily.

It was not easy on this day, however. The Hornets overcame a poor start and an officiating crew that ruled Mark Price untouchable for the afternoon and suddenly exploded past Cleveland in a second-quarter flurry that silenced the near-sellout crowd. In an amazing run that included Dave Hoppen's turnaround three-pointer to beat the shot clock, Charlotte went from four down at the start of the second quarter to a 70-61 lead at the half.

They could not maintain that furious offensive pace. Cleveland tightened its defense in the third period, and only a barrage of three-pointers kept the Hornets close. With Price making free throw after free throw – he hit 18 straight in the game – Cleveland went ahead 104-95 early in the fourth. But Charlotte hung on. Robert Reid made a three-pointer that hit the back rim, bounced high in the air and dropped in. Sidney Lowe made a driving 15-footer, and Reid made another long jumper. Suddenly it was 114-111.

Cleveland rallied to score twice, and Reid and Dell Curry missed jumpers for Charlotte. But Reid followed a Rex Chapman miss to make it 117-113 with 1:39 left, and at the other end, Hoppen blocked John Williams' shot to force a 24-second violation against the Cavs.

With a minute left, Chapman boldly went for three, but he was rushed by Ron Harper and missed everything. Hoppen snared the air ball just in front of the basket and tried to put it in, all in the same motion. Tantalizingly, it rolled across the back rim and then off the other side. An opportunity missed. Harter stomped his foot. But Hoppen came back to give his team another try. Craig Ehlo missed a shot for Cleveland, and Hoppen, with good position on Brad Daugherty, grabbed the rebound and was fouled by the Cavaliers' center. He had two shots to cut it to two with 36 seconds left. Hoppen missed the first, causing Harter to roll his eyes skyward, but he made the second, meaning there was still a chance, if the Hornets could get a stop.

They couldn't. Price made a nifty cut to set up a nice pick-and-roll to Daugherty, who dunked and was fouled with 19 seconds to go. That finished off the Hornets, but it had not been easy.

The next night at home brought more of the same. Atlanta ran away early, building a 40-29 lead in the second quarter, and a 68-59 margin at intermission. But in the second half, the Hornets punished the Hawks with some of their best defense of the year. Certainly it was their roughest. They limited Atlanta to nine field goals and just 44 second-half points. If a Hawk got the ball close to the basket, he was fouled and fouled hard. The fans whooped it up, cheering the blows as a determined Harter urged them on. Later, Harter said, "If they thought this was something, then get me some real tough guys. I'll really show 'em something then. Nine field goals would be a big half."

The Hornets caught Atlanta early in the fourth quarter and passed them with help from Curry's mini-spree. He scored eight in four minutes, a lot in this game, and Charlotte went ahead 99-95 with 4:49 to play. But the Hornets botched their next two possessions. Tripucka had the ball pulled from his grasp on a drive to the basket, and Curry just dropped it while standing, wide open, on the baseline. Doc Rivers countered with two long jumpers for the Hawks, one a three-pointer, and Atlanta gained the lead. The Hornets never went ahead again. On their next possession they got a poor chance, an Earl Cureton hook shot from 10 feet out. It spun out and the next three Hornet attempts failed, too. Atlanta pounded the ball in to Moses Malone who responded with one goal and five of six free throws to lock up a close one for the Hawks.

"Man," Atlanta's Rivers said afterwards of the Hornets, "what got into those guys?"

Tyrone Bogues, who had 15 assists and no turnovers in the game, said, "We're not backing down. We're playing 'em all tough now. We just can't beat anybody. It's frustrating."

It went beyond that for Carl Scheer. As he stormed from the building after the gut-wrencher, Charlotte's ninth loss in a row, the usually gentlemanly Scheer was driven to a rare outburst of profanity. "Shit," he said. "I thought we had that Goddamn game."

• • • • •

The future looked murky for Charlotte at this point. Seven games were left in the season. Five of those were on the road, including the next three. Games with New Jersey and Indiana, lottery teams like Charlotte, offered the most likely chances for victory. But both were on the road and both were the second game in a back-to-back run. The Hornets' older legs had not moved well in that situation for most of the season, much less now with 75 games worth of wear and tear heaped upon them. Even though the team was playing well, a 16-game losing streak to end the year seemed a good possibility. "Sad to say," said Tripucka as the team headed for the road, "but our goal for the rest of the year has become, 'Win another game.'"

So of course they won two in a row on the road.

In the first game, a mid-weeker against the Knicks in Madison Square Garden, Charlotte finally got a break from the opposition. New York, which had set a club record for consecutive victories on its homecourt earlier in the season and owned one of the five best homecourt records in the league, was coasting toward the playoffs. They could not, at this point, improve or hurt their playoff position. The Atlantic Division crown was theirs, so they were assured of being the second seed in the Eastern Conference, but they were eliminated mathematically from catching Detroit for the best overall record and the first seed. They had no great incentive to play hard and figured they could handle Charlotte in any event. They didn't turn in much of an effort, and the Hornets were sharp, if not exactly brilliant.

With Tripucka playing one of his finest all-around games (25 points, five rebounds, five assists, two steals and a blocked shot) and Chapman and Curry pouring in points from the off guard spot (17 of 31, 36 combined points), Charlotte controlled the game. The Knicks, harassed by Sidney Lowe at the head of a smart Hornet defense, shot poorly (44 percent) and committed 25 turnovers. They stayed in the game because Ewing and Charles Oakley pounded the boards.

It was close down the stretch, but the Hornets hung on. Curry hit a big jumper. Tripucka made some free throws, and Brian Rowsom finished off a Hornet break against a New York press by windmilling in a dunk over Ewing. It was the play of a lifetime for the UNC-Wilmington grad, one that had the Rowsom clan back in Columbia and Tarboro, N.C., talking for days.

At the end, it was up to Dave Hoppen to ice it. He had two free throws with 22 seconds and the Hornets up by two. He missed both, but the second rebound came right back to him. The listless Knicks had failed, even at this crucial juncture, to hustle and box him out. Hoppen was fouled again. This time he converted both, and the Hornets won 104-99.

The result stupefied the Knicks, who never dreamed they'd lose to the Hornets at home. "That's ridiculous," said Mark Jackson, the team's point guard. "That's a team we should handle no matter what, but we just didn't get it done."

The victory was sweet for Harter. It was mostly defensive in nature, the only time in the last 41 games of the year that the Hornets managed to hold their opponents under 100 points. And it was a nifty piece of coaching. Charlotte carved up New York's vaunted presses, forcing the game to a slower speed than the Knicks liked, then baffled New York's halfcourt offense by alternately doubling and not doubling Ewing. As he strode off the court, Coach Harter pounded a press table, startling several statisticians, and slapped an usher's hand – he was giving him five – so hard that the man drew it back and examined it after Harter had passed, looking for some sign of injury.

"This is vindication for all our hard work," Harter said.

More followed. Two nights later in Philadelphia, the Hornets beat up on their favorite whipping boy, the 76ers, for the third time that season, 119-115 at the Spectrum. Philly, like the Knicks, no longer had any chance to change its playoff position. But unlike the Knicks, they had some warning about the Hornets.

Perhaps that helped the Sixers get off to a quick start. With the exception of Charles Barkley, who was lackadaisical at the outset, they pushed hard early, looking for the quick knockout. Philly scored 33 in the first quarter and jumped in front 45-38 early in the second. But then the red-hot Curry went nuts, dropping in seven straight shots, all but one outside 15 feet. Robert Reid and a couple of other Hornets joined in, as the streak of consecutive field goals reached 12. Lowe eventually broke it with a missed layup, but by that time the Hornets had gone from seven down to seven ahead in just five minutes. They finished hitting 69 percent of their shots and scoring 40 points in the torrid quarter.

It was a white-knuckle offensive duel from that point on. Barkley warmed up for the Sixers. Tripucka and Reid took over the scoring load from Curry in the second half. Tripucka, on the way to 34 points, had 18 in the third quarter. Reid, once again taking responsibility in the clutch, scored nine in the fourth.

The Hornets led most of the way, but fell behind with six minutes to play after Barkley hit a fast-break layup and was fouled by Reid. Tripucka, resting while Reid held forth, stepped onto the court fresh from a seven-minute break and promptly threw in a three-pointer to send Charlotte ahead again. The Hornets held Philadelphia twice and went ahead 112-108 with 4:29 left on a jumper by Reid. The Sixers closed again, but Charlotte held them off with another flurry of jump shots, this time from Kurt Rambis, of all people.

Rambis had displayed his perimeter form throughout the season. It was part of his new-found freedom in Charlotte. "I could always shoot the jumper. That's what I did in college," he said earlier in the year. "It's just that in LA, with Byron Scott and Magic and Michael Cooper and everyone else they had, I wasn't exactly the first option for an outside shot. So everybody thinks I can't shoot it."

Philly, struggling to cut off Charlotte's offensive dynamo, twice double-teamed Tripucka, forcing him to pass. Twice, the man uncovered by the double-team was Rambis. Twice, he drilled the shot, running the Hornets' lead to 116-110. Tripucka hit another long one to extend the lead, then the Hornets stopped the Sixers on three straight possessions to wrap things up.

If he had been defiant in victory in New York, Harter was almost silly this time. He had won in his hometown for the second time in the season, and his post-game grin almost split his face. He joked about moving home games to the Spectrum, and about his team's post-season chances.

"We don't have a chance at the NCAAs," Harter said. "But I think this gets us in the NIT. Nineteen wins. That's the NIT isn't it? We've got strength of schedule on our side ... a star, in Kelly Tripucka, who's a draw. I'd say it's a lock."

Tripucka was not so pessimistic. "Maybe we can still get a bid to the NCAAs," he said.

Assistant coach Badger was similarly giddy. "I demand a recount," he said. "This team had to make the playoffs, didn't it?"

Against the Sixers, the Hornets did. Philly, on its way to finishing 10 games over .500, split six with the expansion team and could have lost a couple more. It was embarrassing to lose that many to, "those pesky Hornets," as Barkley called them.

Barkley, for one, was pleased that Charlotte would be moving to another division, another conference. "I'm glad they're going out West next year," he said. "They can't get out of here fast enough for me."

• • • • •

Charlotte closed out its three-game road trip with a loss at Indiana. The underachieving Pacers were finally playing close to their abilities, thanks to a February housecleaning, and the Hornets were whipped from the trip and a long string of strong efforts. Indiana gradually pulled away in the second half and won by a comfortable eight.

That sent the triumphant Hornets home, which at this point wasn't the best news they'd ever had. Having won four of their last eight away and having lost 11 in a row in Charlotte, dating back to the Rambis-chin game against San Antonio on February 25, the Hornets weren't sure the Charlotte Coliseum was where they wanted to be. Be it ever so humbling, there seemed to be no chance at home these days.

The veteran players figured Charlotte's problems at home were just an extension of what happened to the team in late December. Teams finally got used to the idea of really gearing up to play Charlotte at home. That, plus the desperation of the pre-playoff season, had sent the Hornets into combat against teams who were more than ready for battle. A team that might feel comfortable enough to relax against the Hornets at home was on its toes when it came to the Charlotte Coliseum. "I'm sure the coach is coming in and saying, 'Look fellas, these guys play hard here. It's noisy. It's a bitch. We can't let up.'" said Robert Reid. "So they go out, raise it up a little, and we can't make it."

"Yeah," agreed Tripucka, "these other teams may be dumb, but they're not stupid. It's well known now that you've got to play when you come here. We're not catching anybody sitting down."

Harter thought the officials might be similarly affected. Refs at any level don't like people to think they can be swayed or intimidated. So when word got around that the Charlotte crowds were winning a few calls for the home team – Lee Jones' famous charge on Charles Barkley was often mentioned – there was a natural reaction. One official even told Harter his crew wasn't going to let the fans get to them. Harter naturally took this to mean that the officials were going to bend over backwards to help the visitors. And to him, that meant the Hornets would just have to bend over. "We're getting screwed every night," Harter said.

In his agony over a team playing well but not winning, Harter also began to wonder about the true effect of the Hornets' fabled fans. Was it causing a lessening of intensity? Did all the screaming really make that much difference? It was hard to say. Harter loved the coliseum noise but longed for a tangible contribution from the cheering throng. After the bitter loss to Atlanta on April 10, he thought about the crazies who had helped him out – really helped him out – during those wacko years at MacCourt in Oregon.

"I need my old Oregon fans," Harter said. "Steve Prefontaine (a famous Oregon distance runner and a big basketball fan) and those guys ... the other teams were really afraid of them. They were right on top of the other guys and were good for three kicks and a couple of trips a year. Pre (Prefontaine) would get me a couple a year himself. He kicked Bill Walton one time, and he was out for four or five minutes. Now that was a crowd."

Harter stared wistfully into space for a few moments. Then he cracked a smile. Was he joking? Did he really want them back? When the stories about his rough-and-tough, good old days started, it was always hard to tell. Finally, it was pointed out that it was a little hard to expect ticketholders who had paid $50 for a front-row, end-zone seat, to pull leg hairs or kick fallen opponents.

"You're probably right," Harter said. "But I wouldn't mind if they were a little nastier."

Instead, in Charlotte's next home appearance, Harter just got a nasty game. It was against Boston, the season-long nemesis, and like both of the previous Charlotte appearances by the Celtics, it was an ugly, brutal battle. But it was that kind of season for the Celtics. Without the inimitable Bird, out for the year after bone-spur surgery on both feet in November, Boston's best plan of attack was to engage in a general melee and hope its bigger bodies could carry the day. A mid-season trade for Joe Kleine, a 270-pound center, had expanded that concept, which worked especially well against big-body have-nots like the Hornets.

On this night it worked even better. Tim Kempton, who admittedly wasn't playing much but could have added some bulk, was out with a hip injury, and four minutes into the contest, Kurt Rambis stumbled over Tripucka while going for a rebound and sprained his ankle. Harter tried to cover by playing Greg Kite a career-high 30 minutes. That helped, but not much. In a ragged game, Boston out rebounded Charlotte 73-44. Robert Parish, who had 22 rebounds, led the pounding with help from Kevin McHale, Kleine and Kevin Gamble, an ex-CBA player who had become an important player at season's end.

Boston's advantage inside was canceled to some extent by 21 Celtic turnovers and some terrible shooting. The Celtics made just 41 percent from the field. Charlotte took better care of the ball and did a little better from the field, and the game went down to the wire. And beyond.

Tyrone Bogues' three-pointer from midcourt at the halftime buzzer pulled Charlotte within three at the break. And Chapman's more conventional three to open the third period tied the game. The lead swung back and forth after that. Charlotte passed Boston at what appeared to be a decisive moment with 2:05 left. Tripucka bullied his way into the lane, drew a foul and made both shots to make it 99-98. After a Celtic miss, McHale fouled Earl Cureton on a rebound, sending him to the line with a chance to increase the margin.

Cureton, a shaky shooter who could miss free throws by wide margins, received pre-shot counseling from Tripucka, the master. "He just said the same thing he always does," Cureton said. "Slow down." Cureton did on his first shot, and the Hornets led by two, but his second banged off the back rim. Boston tied with two free throws from Lewis and got a chance to go ahead when McHale swatted away a Chapman shot in the lane. But Lewis missed the fast-break try, and Sidney Lowe pried the ball away from Boston's Brian Shaw after the rebound. He fired a pass to Chapman, who went on the break and dunked over Kevin Gamble to make it 102-100 with 53 seconds left.

Hornets Never Lie

Boston went to McHale, suffering through a tough night, for the tying basket, and he got it, dropping in a turnaround from 10 feet out against Cureton with 30 seconds left. Both teams botched late chances to win. Tripucka, double-teamed, threw a desperate pass right to the Celtics' Shaw with about eight seconds left. Shaw raced downcourt but lost track of the time and wasted valuable seconds dribbling around the three-point line. Eventually, his teammate's shouts got his attention, but his 20-footer was too late and no good. The game went to overtime.

The extra period was a microcosm of the whole game. On back-to-back possessions, Parish gobbled up offensive rebounds and scored to push the Celtics to a five-point lead. Charlotte rallied. Lowe cold-cocked Kevin Gamble to stop a fast break. Cureton made a jumper, and Dave Hoppen hit a layup on the run after a nice pass by Chapman. That made it 110-108 with 50 seconds left. And when Boston's Lewis stumbled after catching a pass in the open court – he was called for traveling – the Hornets, unbelievably, had a chance to tie.

Predictably, Harter called Tripucka's number. This time it worked. To an extent. Tripucka drove and drew the foul from Gamble. Then, incredibly, Tripucka missed both shots. It was, by his count, the only time he missed both free throws all year. "I was sure he'd make them," teammate Lowe said after the game. "And if he went out there right now for two more, I'd be even more sure he'd make those."

Shaw made one of two at the line for Boston following that. And Charlotte couldn't score again. Chapman, trying for a conventional three-point play, went to the basket against Parish and drew contact. But he got neither the basket or the foul. The Celtics saved the win and moved within one victory of a playoff berth. Charlotte entered one more could-have-been into its memory bank and headed for New Jersey, a fitting place to go in a state of depression. But on their last trip to the Garden State, the dank surroundings of the Meadowlands and dreary Byrne Arena provided a backdrop for the last celebration of the season.

It was a setup. The Nets, toiling through the final week of another miserable season, their third straight with fewer than 30 wins, were no match for a team playing with great, if not entirely understandable, enthusiasm. Charlotte carved them up. Curry exploded for 31 points, making 13 of 20 from the floor including two three-pointers off the break. Lowe, the Hornets' best point man at this point, in Harter's estimation, had 10 assists. Earl Cureton scored 16 points and Dave Hoppen had a season-high 14 rebounds. Hoppen's work alone was enough to nullify New Jersey's advantage in bigger, better-jumping players. The Hornets stayed even on the boards and won going away.

The team was jubilant. Though there were identifiable heroes every night, Harter's new 11-man rotation spread the credit (and blame) around. Everybody chipped in a little. Those who played well first got to chip in a little more. That produced some motivation where none was thought to exist, and at this point, some was enough.

Said Robert Reid, who had 16 points against the Nets, "You don't always get to play as much as you like, but it seems to work pretty well. We do feel like a team."

Harter, who had stumbled upon the plan almost by accident, agreed. "When everyone does it like that, it's kind of neat. It's just what you'd hope would happen. Of course, it's like that when you win. If we were losing all of them, or not playing very well, they'd be saying, 'I should be playing more.'"

No one was saying that now, not even Chapman, who saw Curry's hot hand and the merit system hack away at his minutes. "I'd like to play more," Chapman said, "but as long we're winning and playing well it's a good system. I'm not going to say any more about it."

• • • • •

Victory at the landfill essentially turned the rest of Charlotte's season into garbage time. They had 20 victories. That was a nice round number and more than anyone had predicted they'd get. So all that was left was the shouting. Harter gave the team extra time off, and at the few remaining practices, everyone yucked it up. At a shootaround the morning before the last home game against Milwaukee, Harter even got into the act, making the players run in a circle around chairs, their foreheads touching the chair backs, before competing in the regular, practice-ending shooting meet. They got very dizzy and launched several strange shots. "That's what we did to get high when we didn't have enough money for beer when I was growing up," Harter said.

Kurt Rambis, stretching his ankle on the sidelines in the odd hope of playing one more game, shook his head. "My generation just took drugs," he said. "It was simpler and you didn't look as dumb doing it."

Charlotte closed its home season on a sour note. The coliseum finale was a Friday night game against Milwaukee. It was "Teal Day" in Charlotte, and there were giveaways and live music before the game. That, along with a liberal sprinkling of coliseum beer, produced an unusual crowd that came looking for a fight. They sat quietly through a first half that saw the Hornets stay within striking distance of the razor-sharp Bucks. But as the game slipped away in the third quarter, the crowd got nasty, at least as nasty as Charlotte fans ever got. They hollered for Harter to put Dell Curry into the game, booed the team in general during a third-quarter timeout called when Charlotte had fallen behind by 17 points, and cheered the contributions of former Hornet Rickey Green, now playing for Milwaukee. As Green shot two free throws, one fan screamed, "Why'd they let him go?"

They cheered when Harter did put Curry in for Chapman, a display that angered the players and coaches, then, when it turned out that Curry couldn't stop Milwaukee either, they built up a modest chant of "We want Rex, we want Rex." The fickleness was all mockery. No one called for Chapman until it was too late. But the whole scene steamed the team, which was not used to such treatment and certainly didn't believe it had done anything to deserve it now.

"That was kind of disappointing," said Tripucka, whose four of 15 shooting deserved a catcall or two. "They've got the right to do that, I suppose, but I'd rather they come and shout and cheer for us like they have all along. They've been so fantastic. I guess maybe they just had a bad night, too."

Said Curry, "It's nice to hear your name, but that really wasn't much fun. I like it better when they just yell."

Harter was disappointed, too, but he figured it was just a sign of things to come. "The next two or three years, that's what it's going to be like," he said. "They're going to want more wins, and we're going to have trouble giving them to them. They'll be on us. I'm just glad we don't have to come back soon. This may be a pretty good night for us to leave on."

• • • • •

Charlotte closed its first season on a windy, Sunday afternoon in Boston, the last play date on the NBA schedule. It was a meaningful contest. Boston stumbled home from the game the Monday before in Charlotte. Needing just one victory to clinch a playoff spot, it had lost a home game to the Bullets, the team that was in hot pursuit, and had been beaten on the road in Indiana and New York. The Celtics came to their final game of the season needing a victory over Charlotte to win their 42nd game and assure themselves a playoff berth. The Celtics could lose and still get in. Washington was playing at Philadelphia simultaneously with the Boston-Charlotte game. If the Bullets lost, it didn't matter what the Celtics did. Emotions were mixed in Beantown over the Celtics' fate. The team had played with so much disinterest, the loss of Bird notwithstanding, that some wondered if it wouldn't be better off to lose the game, miss the playoffs and get into the draft lottery. The Celtics themselves denied any such quandary. To do otherwise would hint at the possibility of a fix. But they were not a fiery bunch that strode onto the parquet floor that afternoon to face the Hornets one last time.

For Charlotte's part, the game represented a juicy spoiler's role, even though the Hornets could beat the Celtics and still not be sure of keeping them out of the playoffs. Harter would have liked nothing better than to win, but he wasn't totally committed to the idea. "If we beat 'em, they'd probably win the lottery, take the player we want in the draft, and be good for the next decade," Harter said. His feelings were further mixed because of the Hornets' own lottery dilemma. If they won, they would be tied in victories with the Spurs and the Clippers – "Those sand-bagging sons of bitches," as assistant coach Badger called them – and could bump Charlotte down the lottery ladder.

One of the plot lines turned to mush early on. At the start of the second quarter, the electronic scoreboard in the Boston Garden flashed a score from Philadelphia: "Sixers 39, Bullets 22 after 1Q." With Washington going into the tank, Boston could do almost anything it wanted. It looked for a long time is if both teams were having trouble deciding just what to do. Boston controlled the desultory game most of the way. The Hornets couldn't keep McHale off the foul line, a situation the Charlotte bench facetiously attributed to a striking resemblance between the Celtic forward and referee Ronnie Garretson. "He's gotta be related to that guy," Badger said at one point in the third quarter, as McHale went to the line for the eighth time in the game.

Garretson turned and said, "Ed, who you looking at?"

Badger replied, "I'm not talking to you." Then he turned to the floor and shouted to McHale, "Hey, Kevin, you related to this guy?" McHale grinned and made two free throws.

Boston slowly crept away. Then a spurt midway through the fourth quarter opened up a 20-point lead with 5:33 left. One more time, Charlotte rallied. The Hornets scored 13 straight, including four quick points when Chapman hit, intercepted an inbounds pass and scored again. That made it 110-103 with 2:43 left. There was a chance. The Celtics, who still didn't know if Philly had won, were choking. McHale and Parish both missed close-in shots. Brian Rowsom cleared a rebound to Bogues, who took it to the basket on a fast-break drive. He was bumped and missed the shot, but no foul was called. Boston's Kevin Gamble was fouled at the other end and made two free throws to end the Celtics' three-minute scoring drought. That stopped Charlotte's momentum and Boston managed a win. It didn't matter. Philadelphia won, too. "So," Harter said, "I guess one more loss isn't any big deal is it?"

• • • • •

The end of the year left most of the team with a certain hollowness. "We're satisfied with 20 wins," said Robert Reid, "because I think that's better than most people, maybe even than most of us, thought we'd do. But we're also dissatisfied that we let six or seven more slip away." Most felt pretty good about the team. Feelings about personal accomplishments varied.

Tripucka was happy with the way he had come back. His scoring average of 22.6 was the second-best of his career, and he had clearly been a force to be reckoned with, a main man. "It's about as good as I could have hoped," he said. Rex Chapman, after a slow start, was pleased with his first year, too. Robert Reid, his contract still unguaranteed, wondered if he'd be back. Tim Kempton, seldom-used the second half of the year, did, too. Dell Curry, on the greatest streak of his career, was sorrier than most to see it end. "Just when I'm finally getting some minutes, finally getting on a roll, we have to quit," he said. It did not seem entirely fair, and of course it was not. It was basketball.

• • • • •

The day after losing to the Celtics, the Hornets were treated to a tickertape parade through downtown Charlotte for the last time. A crowd estimated at 5,000 to 35,000 cheered and showered a team that had lost three times as games many as it had won with roughly 4,500 pounds of shredded paper. The Monday morning schedule of a major business center was suspended for several hours while all this went on.

To paraphrase Winston Churchill, never has so much been done for a group that did so little. Of course, that's not quite right. Although the Hornets had done all that they could on the court, in this silly season, they made up for what they didn't do with the stir they created. Charlotte grew into a big city, almost overnight, because of the team.

Partly because of the Hornets, in the coming summer the city would land three significant future sporting events: the Final Four, the Davis Cup finals and the ACC basketball tournament. And there was talk of much more. Carl Scheer called it the Superman Theory. "It's a feeling you get when you finally come to realize that you can do anything you want," he said. "A lot of people who had been in Charlotte for a long time didn't see that. They were the ones who were most surprised the way the NBA succeeded here. I think it's a case of being too close to the forest to see the trees. Something had to open their eyes, and the NBA, George Shinn's big dream, was what did it."

The dreaming continued after the parade was over. The Hornets went up to a stage erected in front of the newspaper building and spoke a few words to their fans. Robert Reid, wearing a strange-looking black hat that might have been stolen from Zorro, told the faithful, in his standard braggadocio style, that the team had knocked on the door this year and next year, they would kick it in. Radio man Steve Martin, the emcee for the day, waxed eloquently about the history of Hornet parades in Charlotte. There was one for getting the team, one, today's, for a successful first season, and there would be one in the very near future, when the Hornets won the NBA Championship.

On the back row of the stage, Ed Badger and Dick Harter heard this, rolled their eyes, and tried to keep from snickering aloud. Didn't these people know what they were getting into? Didn't they know how hard it was to win in the NBA?

And the answer, of course, was that they didn't. At least not yet.

Epilogue

Early in April of 1989, each of George Shinn's three Hornet partners received a message from the chief. He was buying them out.

It was stunning news. Although all three had signed contracts which included buyout clauses, none had expected Shinn to exercise them. At least not anytime soon. But he had, and just a little more than a year after the partnership had been officially formed.

Reactions from the partners varied. Rick Hendricks, Shinn's closest friend in the triumvirate, took it well. He was disappointed to have to give up his part of the Hornets, but if it was what George wanted, well, he was all for it. Felix Sabates, who, like Hendricks owned a seven percent share, was less enthusiastic, particularly when he heard Shinn's offer: his original investment of $1.2 million plus 10 percent, paid out, as stipulated, over the course of the next five years. It seemed niggardly. The franchise had at least doubled in value, and Sabates and the rest had stuck their financial necks out to help Shinn get it. "I just went crazy," Sabates told the *Charlotte Observer*. "I said, 'What the hell is this?'"

Sabates kicked and screamed enough that Shinn came up with a better offer. A much better one, though neither side will say just what it was. That mollified Sabates, though like Hendricks, he was unahappy to have to let go. An avid golfer and a sports fan, Sabates immensely enjoyed the role he now had to give up, that of being part owner of an NBA team.

Cy Bahakel, who had a much larger stake – $6 million – was more than unhappy. And when Shinn's attorneys called to see when he could sign the papers sealing the deal, he had a surprising response: never.

Mediation by the NBA and others followed, but to no avail. Shinn's legal rights were irrefutably documented, but Bahakel wouldn't budge. He felt he had been wronged. With the situation at an impasse, Shinn sued Bahakel. Bahakel followed by suing Shinn, and an ugly, public fight ensued. The two millionaires called each other names in print and over the city's airwaves. Bahakel claimed Shinn had coerced him into the signing the buyout agreement, which was included in a second agreement between the two men, signed in November of 1987, long after the original partnership had been formed. Bahakel said Shinn never would have gotten the team without his money. In return for it, Bahakel said, Shinn had promised him a share of management and profits.

Relying on his already favorable image, Shinn used the media to pound Bahakel. He called Bahakel's charges "hogwash" and said that his former partner made up conversation between them that was central to Bahakel's case for coercement. He claimed that if Bahakel hadn't come along, he'd have found another partner with the necessary money. He said that it was Bahakel, not himself, who instigated the second partnership agreement, threatening to withhold his part of a scheduled payment to the NBA unless Shinn sweetened the Hornet broadcast deal for Bahakel's Charlotte TV station. Shinn had extended the station's rights by 10 years. But in return, he added the buyout clause, a one-time lump payment he could make to gain Bahakel's 35 percent if executed before 1990.

Bahakel, who went to several Charlotte PR firms seeking help, countered that it was Shinn who was making up stories. Bahakel claimed that he hadn't threatened to withold a payment, but Shinn had threatened to say he did if Bahakel wouldn't sign the new agreement.

And on and on it went, the two millionaires slugging it out for all to see. And given the intricacies of the legal process, no end seened in sight.

Ego complicated this dispute. Bahakel, a one-time politician, was thought by some to envy Shinn for the power and prestige he enjoyed as the Hornets' majority owner and progenitor. But Bahakel had one edge on Shinn. He had more money, four or five times as much in some estimates.

And, as Bahakel told it, Shinn had had to beg him to get the capital needed to make his dream fly. Shinn might always have control of the team, but Bahakel would have that.

For his part, Shinn thought that one reason Bahakel signed the second partnership agreement was that he didn't think Shinn, with his lesser millions, could pull off the buyout within the given time. And probably never. Doing it gave Shinn a certain satisfaction, even though he had to sell off his chain of business colleges, the cornerstone of his empire, to make it possible.

"I'm sure Cy was surprised," Shinn said happily amidst the turmoil.

Shinn said his November stroke had precipitated the move. His advisors had warned him that he could not continue burning so many candles at so many ends. Something had to go, and it would certainly not be his newest and shiniest possession. There was nothing else like the Hornets in George Shinn's life. And there wasn't going to be anybody in control of the team except George Shinn. As both sides prepared evidence and assembled their legal armies, the case headed for a preliminary hearing in early 1990.

• • • • •

The Hornets looked to their second college draft with optimism and trepidation. Early evaluations indicated that no matter where it drafted, Charlotte could not expect to fill its most pressing need at center. There simply was no first-line big man available. Indeed, the class of 1989 was an odd lot, creating a level draft. The 10th pick might turn out as well as the first. The Hornets hoped to have a shot at Danny Ferry, the multi-talented All-America from Duke. He was their preference. Beyond that it was a muddle.

The next best player in the draft, in most estimations, was Sean Elliott, a sleek forward from Arizona. But he was not an inside player. If he came to Charlotte, he would further jam the situation at small forward and off guard. Gene Littles, the team's personnel director, didn't think that would be all that bad. "There could be worse things for us than having a little competition," he said. But other members of the braintrust were more skeptical. The Hornets didn't quite have to draft for need yet, but they couldn't ignore their most serious shortcomings either.

So their attention turned to the biggest good players available. That included Pervis Ellison, a 6-9 center from Louisville; 6-10 Stacey King of Oklahoma; 6-8 Randy White, a beefy rebounder from Louisiana Tech; and North Carolina's J.R. Reid, the logical choice.

A 6-9, 260-pounder, Reid was a basketball legend almost before he reached college, and he held an unusually strong lure for the Hornets. George Shinn had talked of acquiring Reid almost as long as he had talked about getting an NBA team. Reid's appeal was undeniable even if all the seats were already sold, for he was not only a local guy, he was a local guy who was born to be in the spotlight.

Unusually quick and co-ordinated for his size and sporting a slanted, flat-top haircut that added to his menacing countenance, Reid attracted attention. A native of Virginia's athletically rich Tidewater area, he was one of the nation's most highly sought players in high school, and his arrival at North Carolina was heralded.

Reid did not disappoint at first. Making the most of the miserly minutes doled out to him by Dean Smith, UNC's careful coach, he had a superb freshman year. As a sophomore, he made most All-America teams. Julius Erving even suggested that an NBA team just starting out would be smart to make Reid its cornerstone.

But just before the start of his junior year, Reid broke his foot. That slowed him and kept him out of the first nine games. When he returned, the team was unbeaten and playing well. Reid did not immediately recapture his starting role, and he never regained his position as the Tar Heels' top dog. Tough opponents sometimes embarrassed him. He was occasionally booed at home by fans who normally are the world's most polite and loyal. He did not have a bad year, but neither did he dominate. His rebounding average fell to a relatively meager 6.3 a game. Reid finished the season with a flourish, though, scoring 26 points in the season-ending loss to Michigan in the NCAA Tournament.

That helped repair his sagging reputation in the pros to the point that he and Smith could be sure he'd make a lot of money by joining the NBA a year early. And he did. But many questions lingered. To many scouts, Reid seemed one-dimensional. He was burly and a highly efficient scorer when he got the ball near the basket. But he wasn't effective outside the lane. He didn't rebound or block shots that well for a man his size either. He was compared to Wayman Tisdale, a former number-two pick out of Oklahoma, who becane a decent NBA player but not a star. Reid's personality was called into question, too. He had been disciplined at least twice by Smith during his UNC career, once for spitting on an N.C. State student in a Raleigh bar and once for missing curfew by two minutes the night before an NCAA Tournament game his last year. He had gotten into a fight with a teammate on another occasion.

Reid pooh-poohed his troubles. "I'm not denying them," he said, "but if spitting in some jerk's face and missing curfew by a few minutes are the worst things I ever do, then I won't be too bad off."

Nonetheless, some NBA teams were queasy about Reid. His problems and sometimes arrogant public persona made them wonder if his potential was worth the trouble.

Charlotte wondered, too, but after failing to improve their position at the May lottery – Sacramento won the drawing, while Charlotte retained fifth pick – Reid more and more looked to be their lot. Conventional wisdom said that Ferry, Elliott and Ellison would all be gone when Charlotte got to pick. The Hornets correctly figured that they would have a choice between Reid, White and King. In that scenario, Reid had no more warts than anybody else.

Dick Harter, who would have to coach Reid his first season, worried about how he would fit in. So did assistant coach Ed Badger.

Personnel director Gene Littles waffled on Reid's abilities almost daily. He liked other players better, but Reid, he said, had great possibilities. Most enthusiastic about Reid were Carl Scheer and George Shinn. And, in the uncertain atmosphere of this draft, that was enough to turn the Hornets to Reid.

A week before the draft, Shinn told the *Charlotte Observer* that he thought the team should draft Reid if the decision was close between Reid and another player. His reasoning was that North Carolina's team could not afford to be haunted by a Tar Heel star it could have picked but didn't. And he was the boss.

Shinn was criticized for airing what he had already told his staff in private. As usual, he didn't take it well.

"I read where someone, talking about me, said an owner should just sign the checks and be happy," he said after the Hornets drafted Reid. "Well, if all you do is sign the checks, you won't be very happy. This is my team. I said I was going to be involved from the start and I am. I had a gut feeling about J.R., and I've always run my business on gut feelings. I couldn't just ignore this feeling."

Although Scheer had protested, Shinn's announcement essentially had settled the issue by the time the draft rolled around. The Hornet braintrust was left to ponder what to do with the second-round pick and to listen to the deals being pitched their way.

Some were intriguing. The Golden State Warriors wanted to dump 7-4 Ralph Sampson, the talented but enigmatic ex-Virginia star. He was hurt and had a huge contract. The Hornets were interested until they heard Golden State's asking price: Charlotte's first-round pick. Other would-be deals would have sent centers Alton Lister, Dave Corzine and even, yes, Stuart Gray, to Charlotte.

Charlotte listened but didn't budge until the day of the draft, when, almost a year after it started talking about him, it finally landed Gray. The price was not steep. The Hornets sent Indiana its second-round pick which the Pacers used to draft Dyron Nix. A provision of the trade would have allowed Charlotte to exercise its own pick and take Gray in exchange for a future second-round pick, if either Dana Barros, a high-scoring point guard, or Shawn Kemp, a raw, 19-year-old forward with amazing potential, were available when the Hornets picked. Neither was. Both were taken by Seattle with back-to-back picks in the middle of the first round.

So, on draft day 1989, the Hornets moved in the beef. The first four picks went about as expected, and with the fifth pick, the Hornets took J.R. Reid, who had been flown to town several hours earlier. He arrived at a draft-night party at the Charlotte Coliseum less than an hour after his selection and was cheered by a crowd of

15,000. A small group hung around to hear the Hornets' second pick and were puzzled when it was announced that the team had selected Dyron Nix. The puzzlement wore off a short time later when it was explained that Nix had been traded for ... Stuart Gray. That touched off a few moans. Gray had been on Charlotte tongues for months, and many fans didn't like the taste. Even the Hornets were tired of it. "It does seem like he's been part of the team for awhile," said Scheer.

One man who had never tired of the idea, of course, was Dick Harter. He did not get a contract extension in the spring, but on draft day he did get his man. One of them at least.

Harter tried to downplay the acquisition. "Aw, I never said he would be a savior," Harter said. "I just said he would help us."

Harter's gigantic smile, similar to the one that often spread his face after a victory, betrayed him, however. He had had a good night. His wimpy team had picked up more than 500 pounds of beef.

Staring out at the vacant coliseum floor, Harter said, "I see an empty lane out there. At times the lane was empty last year when we were playing, but I think you'll see someone in there next year. We've at least got a chance to be a strong team now."

The two new Hornets were happy to be wearing teal, particularly Gray, who had languished four years in Indiana and waited most of a season for his former coach to spring him.

"I've had my bags packed for awhile," Gray said on draft night. "But I'd about started to unpack them. I thought we were done. But then I heard on TV what had happened. I'm ecstatic."

Gray was as eager to get to Charlotte as any player in the Hornets' short history. When Harter called to give him the good news, Gray offered to pass up his impending honeymoon in Europe and report early for some extra work. "I told him that wouldn't be necessary," Harter said. "But he might come anyway."

Reid promised to turn over a new leaf in the pros. "You will see a different J.R. Reid," he said. Parroting a famous line about Smith's UNC program, Reid complained that he had been restricted by the Tar Heel's team-oriented system. His offensive repertoire, his rebounding, his game, had all been limited by the way Smith teaches his players to play unselfishly.

Smith, an unyielding promoter of his offspring, concurred. Reid would be a great pro rebounder, he said. And, in a speech to a Charlotte civic club, he said that Reid already shot better from 15 feet than any player over 6-5 on the Hornets' roster. Harter laughed at that. He and Smith had seldom crossed paths in college, so there was little professional jealousy between them. But he had to tweak Smith's nose on that one.

"The first day of practice," Harter said, "we'll have a little contest. We'll get J.R. out there to shoot with Dell Curry. I won't even use Kelly. Who knows? Maybe Dean is right."

• • • • •

Charlotte had five free agents on its roster at season's end: Michael Holton, Dave Hoppen, Greg Kite, Sidney Lowe and Brian Rowsom. In May, Scheer said the team "would do everything in its power to sign them all."

That was an unbelievable and impractical statement. Signing all five would hamstring the team's roster with guaranteed contracts even worse than the year before. And it could run the Hornets into salary cap problems. Scheer's true meaning: the team would consider re-signing all five.

In the end, the Hornets signed three. Hoppen and Rowsom, both of whom were restricted free agents, came to terms rather easily. Hoppen's deal, signed in early August, sent him house hunting. He received a three-year contract, and his play at the end of the season left him believing he'd have a long and fruitful career in Charlotte.

Holton, who could have gone to another team, took longer. He and his agent negotiated with several teams. Eventually, they settled for less than they wanted, but stayed in Charlotte. Holton and his family liked the place, and it was rich with business opportunities for a few men who wore teal tank tops with matching, pleated shorts.

Sidney Lowe had also hoped to stay. He and his wife already lived in Charlotte when the Hornets called him late in the season. He played well in his brief trial, and for a time the team seemed close to re-signing him. But they never got around to it. Then, in early July, his old CBA coach, Bill Musselman, offered him a better deal. He wanted him to play for the new team in Minnesota. The Timberwolves would pay him a modest sum, about $160,000, for two years. But they would guarantee three fourths of that each season. The Hornets guarantee was much lower and was only for one year.

Lowe hoped the Hornets would match the Minnesota offer. "That would be the best thing that could happen," he said. But it didn't happen. Scheer decided a $100,000 guarantee was too stiff for Sidney Lowe. So Lowe was off to the land of frozen engine blocks.

Charlotte never made a serious attempt to sign Greg Kite, and Kite and his agent didn't press the issue. When Gray was acquired on draft night, Kite became superfluous. A team, even a Dick Harter team, only needs so much pure meat on the hoof.

Charlotte's second NBA draft was not kind to Tim Kempton. Both

Reid and Gray played his position and no doubt were better at it. With his contract for the coming season only partially guaranteed, the fabulous Dr. K looked to be a good candidate to get cut. He had, after all, barely been used at the end of the previous season.

Kempton knew this, knew the odds were against him, but he wasn't going down without a fight. He spent the spring and summer honing his body and working on his game. He lopped 15 pounds, lifted weights, ran. He played basketball wherever he could find a game. He impressed the coaches. By the time of the draft, Dick Harter said, "I'd love to see Timmy make the team. The way he's worked he deserves it."

Perhaps Kempton was deserving, but nothing more. When he approached Scheer in August to get a reading on his future, he was told there was none. His chances for making the team were, in Scheer's word, "marginal." So he and his agent found a team in Spain looking for a big, hard-working power forward.

It was not what Kempton wanted, but it wasn't bad. The money was better. "They're not cheap like the Hornets," Kempton said. And he would go from a complementary player to the starring role. Three days before he was to leave for Spain, he was in good spirits, joking about his new position in basketball.

"Instead of me passing to Kelly and Rex, there will be a bunch of guys passing to me," he said. "Instead of shaking my head over those crazy shots Rex takes, I'll be shaking my head over the crazy shots I take. Dr. K will live on in Spain. I will not pass the ball on the break."

Dr. K never made it to Spain, however. The day he was to leave, the NBA invoked a year-old agreement with the Spanish Basketball Association that prevented players under contract in either organization from jumping to the other. Kempton couldn't go to Spain unless the Hornets released him, which they wouldn't do unless they could retain his rights. The good doctor was stuck. "Unless something changes, he'll report to Charlotte's camp in October," said his agent, Eric Fleisher, "although I'm not sure how much enthusiasm he'll have."

"Tim is still an asset to us," said Carl Scheer. "How big an asset, we'll see. We could get something for him in a trade. He could help us in practice. Who knows? He might even make the team."

• • • • •

The Hornets' second summer camp for free agents turned up the same number of prospects as the first. One. His name was Clifford Lett, and he was a point guard. Charlotte hoped to bring him to camp to challenge Michael Holton and Tyrone Bogues in the fall.

Gene Banks, the ex-Duke star, also came to camp. He was trying to revive his NBA career after an ankle injury and a one-year exile in Italy. He now lived in North Carolina, and like Lowe, thought playing for the Hornets a perfect setup. He was not impressive in his summer trial, but there remained an outside chance he could make the team.

• • • • •

No one enjoyed being a Charlotte Hornet that first year more than Robert Reid. He reveled in the attention he regained and made the most of it. Suave and self-assured, he dropped into the city like a relative and made himself right at home.

But it wasn't home. The uncertainty of Reid's non-guaranteed contract made him a boarder instead of a resident. His family had to stay behind because he could be cut at any time without pay.

In that first season, the euphoria surrounding the team and Reid's generally rosy outlook allowed him to breeze past this ugly fact. But as the Hornets' second season drew near, he grew first impatient, then angry at the team that had given him new life. Why wouldn't they renegotiate? Why wouldn't they prevent the humiliation caused by being the only veteran in the league without a guarantee?

"The Hornets preach family this, family that all the time," Reid said in August. "But doesn't that include me? I guess not. Where's my family? That's right, they're back in Houston. They won't let me be family up here."

As the Hornets pondered Reid's future with fall less than a month away, Carl Scheer was leaning toward Reid's point of view. He wanted to be a nice guy. But the coaching staff held steady to its view that the make-good contract, however unfair, provided superb motivation for a 33-year-old swing man. They liked him "hungry."

"I want to throw up when I hear that," Reid said. "Have I not proven that I will work hard? Don't they know what I can do by now? And what about the other *old* guys on the team? Kelly? Kurt? What are they hungry for? What's the difference?

Reid was known to overreact on occasion, to overstate his case. But this anger was real. It had been building over a season and a summer. And it was one of several darkening clouds on the Hornets' horizon.

As Dick Harter said, the climate in the season season would be different. Fans would expect more. Players would want more. And just as with any real NBA team, there might be a few storms.

NOV. 4, 1988 — AT CHARLOTTE

CLEVELAND CAVALIERS (133)

Player	MP	FG	FT	R	A	PF	S	TP
Sanders	24	4-5	0-0	3	3	1	3	8
Nance	25	6-11	4-6	7	1	2	0	16
Daugherty	29	7-13	6-8	8	4	3	2	20
Harper	31	10-17	2-4	4	5	2	5	22
Price	30	6-11	1-1	2	10	2	0	13
Williams	12	2-3	0-0	4	0	4	0	4
Dudley	16	2-3	1-4	9	1	2	0	5
Valentine	23	5-7	3-3	3	5	1	3	13
Ehlo	25	5-7	1-2	6	3	3	2	12
Rollins	8	3-6	1-1	5	1	1	1	7
Keys	12	4-6	3-3	0	0	3	0	11
Hubbard	5	0-3	2-2	3	0	0	0	2
TOTALS	240	54-92	24-34	54	33	24	16	133

CHARLOTTE HORNETS (93)

Player	MP	FG	FT	R	A	PF	S	TP
Tripucka	35	7-13	2-2	3	4	2	1	16
Rambis	32	7-9	2-2	6	0	2	1	16
Hoppen	28	4-6	0-0	4	0	4	0	8
Green	8	0-3	0-0	0	4	1	1	0
Reid	25	5-12	0-4	2	2	3	0	10
Chapman	24	5-15	4-6	4	2	1	3	14
Bogues	20	2-4	2-2	1	6	2	1	6
Kempton	13	4-6	0-0	3	2	3	0	8
Rowsom	19	3-8	2-2	4	1	1	0	8
Holton	25	2-8	1-2	3	4	3	1	5
Tolbert	4	1-1	0-0	0	1	2	0	2
Cureton	7	0-1	0-0	1	1	1	0	0
TOTALS	240	40-86	13-20	31	27	25	8	93

Cleveland	26	40	34	33	133
Charlotte	26	16	27	24	93

Turnovers: Cle. 20 (Daughtery 6); Char. 24 (Tripucka 8).
3-Pointers–Cle. 1-2 (Ehlo 1-1, Harper 0-1); Char. 0-0.
Technical Fouls: None.
Officials: O'Donnell, Thompson, Vaden.
Attendance: 23,338.

NOV. 5, 1988 — AT AUBURN HILLS, MI.

CHARLOTTE HORNETS (85)

Player	MP	FG	FT	R	A	PF	S	TP
Tripucka	38	2-12	5-5	5	1	5	4	9
Rambis	24	3-9	0-0	8	1	3	0	6
Hoppen	16	2-5	0-0	3	0	2	1	4
Reid	23	5-13	0-0	5	3	3	0	10
Holton	30	4-13	4-4	0	3	0	0	12
Chapman	35	6-19	0-0	6	1	0	1	12
Kempton	23	4-5	0-0	3	3	4	0	8
Bogues	18	2-6	2-2	1	4	0	2	6
Rowsom	24	4-10	8-8	7	0	3	0	16
Cureton	9	1-3	0-0	2	2	1	0	2
TOTALS	240	33-95	19-19	40	18	21	8	85

DETROIT PISTONS (94)

Player	MP	FG	FT	R	A	PF	S	TP
Dantley	24	7-8	4-4	3	5	3	0	18
Mahorn	27	6-8	1-1	11	1	2	1	13
Laimbeer	34	6-10	2-2	12	4	4	0	14
Dumars	35	2-10	1-2	3	7	2	2	5
Thomas	39	4-11	7-7	3	7	4	0	15
Salley	21	4-5	1-2	3	1	2	1	9
Rodman	24	4-5	0-0	10	0	3	0	8
Johnson	16	1-7	0-0	1	2	0	0	2
Edwards	12	3-8	2-4	2	0	3	0	8
Williams	6	1-1	0-0	0	1	0	1	2
Dawkins	2	0-0	0-0	0	0	0	0	0
TOTALS	240	38-73	18-22	48	28	23	5	94

Charlotte	20	20	16	29	85
Detroit	27	21	26	20	94

Turnovers: Char. 11 (Rambis 3); Det. 22 (Mahorn 5).
3-Pointers: Char. 0-1 (Tripucka 0-1); Det. 0-0.
Technical Fouls: Detroit 1 (Coach Daly).
Officials: Strom, Capers, Mayfield.
Attendance: 21,454.

NOV. 8, 1988 — AT CHARLOTTE

LOS ANGELES CLIPPERS (105)

Player	MP	FG	FT	R	A	PF	S	TP
Norman	34	6-15	3-7	15	2	5	0	15
Smith	32	6-10	1-4	5	2	4	2	13
Benjamin	33	7-12	3-5	8	2	5	0	17
Nixon	40	4-9	4-6	2	4	1	2	12
Williams	25	6-15	2-2	4	1	5	1	15
Grant	8	1-2	0-0	1	2	4	0	2
Dailey	23	8-13	2-5	0	4	0	2	18
Gondrezick	19	2-7	4-6	4	3	5	0	8
Wolf	10	1-1	1-2	2	0	4	0	3
Kite	16	0-1	2-2	7	1	1	1	2
TOTALS	240	41-85	22-39	48	21	34	8	105

CHARLOTTE HORNETS (117)

Player	MP	FG	FT	R	A	PF	S	TP
Tripucka	39	7-16	10-11	6	5	3	3	24
Rambis	30	7-9	3-7	14	1	3	1	17
Hoppen	17	2-3	2-2	6	1	4	0	6
Holton	26	2-8	2-2	1	6	3	4	6
Reid	27	6-17	4-5	9	3	3	0	16
Chapman	27	9-20	0-0	1	1	4	0	18
Bogues	25	5-8	4-6	4	3	3	1	14
Rowsom	18	1-3	3-4	5	1	3	0	5
Kempton	15	3-3	3-5	6	4	4	0	9
Cureton	16	1-3	0-0	3	3	1	0	2
TOTALS	240	43-90	31-42	55	28	31	9	117

L.A. Clippers	26	29	24	26	105
Charlotte	27	30	33	27	117

Turnovers: L.A. 20 (Benjamin, Nixon 4); Char. 17 (Rambis 4).
3-Pointers: L.A. 1-8 (Norman 0-2, Nixon 0-1, Williams 1-3, Gondrezick 0-2); Char. 0-2 (Chapman 0-2).
Technical Fouls: None.
Officials: Bavetta, Reichelt, Wood.
Attendance: 18,865.

NOV. 11, 1988 — AT LANDOVER, MD.

CHARLOTTE HORNETS (87)

Player	MP	FG	FT	R	A	PF	S	TP
Rambis	36	2-4	4-6	9	2	4	2	8
Tripucka	38	6-10	4-4	4	4	4	1	16
Hoppen	12	0-3	0-0	7	1	1	0	0
Holton	23	3-6	0-2	1	6	2	1	6
Reid	37	9-18	5-5	3	1	6	2	23
Bogues	25	6-12	2-2	3	6	0	2	14
Chapman	21	3-15	0-0	2	1	5	0	6
Kempton	19	2-2	2-2	4	0	2	0	6
Rowsom	12	1-4	2-3	5	0	1	0	4
Cureton	17	2-3	0-1	5	1	1	1	4
TOTALS	240	34-77	19-25	43	22	26	9	87

WASHINGTON BULLETS (96)

Player	MP	FG	FT	R	A	PF	S	TP
Catledge	23	3-9	2-4	3	1	2	0	8
King	29	8-13	2-3	6	3	2	0	18
Jones	24	0-0	0-0	5	0	4	1	0
Malone	31	7-17	7-10	2	2	2	1	21
Walker	33	2-12	0-0	4	8	2	5	4
Williams	24	8-11	3-3	5	4	2	0	19
Feitl	19	1-8	0-0	4	1	2	2	2
Pressley	15	2-4	0-0	1	1	0	0	4
Grant	25	3-4	0-2	7	1	4	3	6
Eackles	17	5-8	4-4	3	0	5	1	14
TOTALS	240	39-86	18-26	40	21	25	13	96

Charlotte	30	13	25	19	87
Washington	23	21	23	28	96

Turnovers: Char. 23 (Tripucka 8); Wash. 17 (Walker 5).
3-Pointers: Char. 0-4 (Tripucka 0-1, Reid 0-1, Bogues 0-2); Wash. 0-0.
Technical Fouls: None.
Officials: Mihalak, Nies, Toliver.
Attendance: 12,731.

NOV. 12, 1988 AT ATLANTA

CHARLOTTE HORNETS (111)

Player	MP	FG	FT	R	A	PF	S	TP
Rambis	21	2-4	3-4	5	2	2	1	7
Tripucka	30	7-14	3-4	7	2	5	0	18
Hoppen	25	6-9	2-3	5	3	4	1	14
Holton	32	7-10	3-3	2	5	3	4	17
Reid	30	6-16	1-1	1	3	3	2	13
Chapman	28	5-15	2-2	2	4	2	2	12
Bogues	22	2-9	0-0	1	7	1	1	4
Kempton	16	2-2	6-8	4	1	2	0	10
Rowsom	24	4-8	6-7	7	3	3	0	14
Cureton	10	1-1	0-0	1	0	1	1	2
Tolbert	2	0-0	0-0	0	0	0	0	0
TOTALS	240	42-88	26-32	35	30	26	12	111

ATLANTA HAWKS (132)

Player	MP	FG	FT	R	A	PF	S	TP
Carr	11	3-4	2-2	0	0	5	0	8
Wilkins	35	7-18	5-5	7	5	4	1	19
Malone	35	8-12	5-6	10	3	3	0	21
Rivers	28	5-8	4-4	4	7	1	2	14
Theus	32	9-15	8-8	2	7	4	2	27
Levingston	37	9-13	2-3	7	1	4	3	20
Webb	20	0-3	1-2	3	8	1	1	1
Koncak	14	2-4	1-2	7	1	2	0	5
Battle	14	1-2	2-4	2	3	1	0	4
Tolbert	8	4-4	1-2	3	0	0	0	9
Bradley	2	1-2	0-0	0	0	0	0	2
Ferrell	4	0-0	2-2	0	0	0	0	2
TOTALS	240	49-85	33-40	45	35	25	9	132

Charlotte	25	29	32	25	111
Atlanta	39	30	23	40	132

Turnovers: Char. 19 (Bogues 5); Atl. 16. (Wilkins 5)
3-Pointers: Char. 1-3 (Tripucka 1-1, Chapman 0-2); Atl. 1-1 (Theus 1-1).
Technical Fouls: Atl. 1 (Koncak).
Officials: Rooney, Salvatore, Bernhardt.
Attendance: 16,155.

NOV. 15, 1988 AT CHARLOTTE

NEW JERSEY NETS (106)

Player	MP	FG	FT	R	A	PF	S	TP
Berry	22	2-7	1-1	6	1	2	0	5
Williams,B	34	5-11	1-5	9	0	4	1	11
Carroll	36	10-15	5-5	10	4	4	1	25
Bagley	36	4-8	1-2	1	5	2	2	10
McGee	38	12-22	1-2	5	3	3	1	26
Hinson	22	4-8	2-5	4	1	4	0	10
Conner	21	2-7	2-3	3	4	1	4	6
Shackleford	6	2-4	0-2	5	0	1	0	4
Hopson	5	0-0	0-0	2	3	0	0	0
Morris	7	2-2	1-2	0	1	2	0	5
Williams, K	13	2-3	0-0	1	0	1	0	4
TOTALS	240	45-87	14-27	46	22	24	9	106

CHARLOTTE HORNETS (99)

Player	MP	FG	FT	R	A	PF	S	TP
Tripucka	37	8-16	7-8	2	1	5	1	25
Rambis	34	4-7	2-2	3	0	4	0	10
Holton	37	5-11	2-3	1	10	2	2	12
Hoppen	20	4-8	0-1	8	0	1	0	8
Reid	22	4-11	1-2	3	0	2	1	9
Chapman	19	1-10	2-2	5	4	2	0	4
Rowsom	3	0-0	1-2	0	1	0	0	1
Bogues	24	1-6	0-0	6	6	4	2	2
Kempton	16	6-13	4-5	8	1	2	1	16
Cureton	23	5-8	2-5	9	2	3	0	12
Green	5	0-2	0-0	0	0	0	0	0
TOTALS	240	38-92	21-30	45	25	25	7	99

New Jersey	21	24	31	30	106
Charlotte	21	30	24	24	99

Turnovers: N.J. 19 (Berry 5); Char. 19 (Rambis 4).
3-Pointers: N.J. 2-6 (Bagley 1-2, McGee 1-4); Char. 2-4 (Tripucka 2-3, Chapman 0-1).
Technical Fouls: None.
Officials: Mathis, Capers, Mayfield.
Attendance: 21,748.

NOV. 17, 1988 AT DALLAS

CHARLOTTE HORNETS (93)

Player	MP	FG	FT	R	A	PF	S	TP
Tripucka	35	3-11	9-9	4	5	2	0	15
Rampis	28	4-8	0-0	10	2	2	0	8
Hoppen	26	2-6	2-2	9	0	2	0	6
Holton	24	5-16	3-3	1	6	4	0	14
Reid	22	3-12	2-2	6	0	1	0	8
Chapman	22	2-9	0-0	3	1	3	0	4
Bogues	17	2-6	0-0	1	4	3	0	4
Cureton	9	1-3	2-2	1	2	1	0	4
Kempton	22	5-5	2-3	2	0	1	0	12
Lewis	12	5-8	0-0	3	0	0	1	10
Green	12	0-3	0-0	1	8	0	1	0
Tolbert	11	4-4	0-2	2	0	3	0	8
TOTALS	240	36-91	20-23	43	28	22	2	93

DALLAS MAVERICKS (105)

Player	MP	FG	FT	R	A	PF	S	TP
Aguirre	35	10-20	6-9	3	2	1	1	26
Perkins	34	5-14	3-5	13	1	5	0	13
Donaldson	32	4-5	0-0	11	1	4	0	8
Harper	34	8-11	4-4	4	10	2	1	21
Blackman	35	8-16	5-8	2	6	2	1	21
Wennington	20	0-1	2-2	2	0	5	0	2
Davis	22	3-7	0-0	2	3	1	0	6
Tyler	21	1-3	0-0	7	0	2	0	2
Alford	3	1-2	0-0	0	1	0	0	2
Wiley	2	1-2	0-0	0	0	0	0	2
Blab	2	1-1	0-0	1	0	0	0	2
TOTALS	240	42-82	20-28	45	24	22	3	105

Charlotte	26	23	12	32	93
Dallas	29	19	34	23	105

Turnovers: Char. 14 (Tripucka 4); Dallas 15 (Aguirre, Harper 3).
3-Pointers: Char. 1-3 (Tripucka 0-1, Holton 1-2); Dallas 1-2 (Harper 1-1, Wiley 0-1).
Technical Fouls: Dallas 2 (Illegal defense, Donaldson).
Officials: Oakes, Crawford, Herring.
Attendance: 16,512.

NOV. 19, 1988 AT SAN ANTONIO

CHARLOTTE HORNETS (107)

Player	MP	FG	FT	R	A	PF	S	TP
Tripucka	38	9-21	11-12	4	5	1	2	31
Cureton	23	4-5	2-2	6	1	5	1	10
Hoppen	29	5-5	1-4	9	0	3	2	11
Holton	20	4-8	0-0	2	4	2	0	8
Reid	32	5-12	2-4	5	3	4	2	12
Tolbert	22	3-5	0-0	4	1	2	0	6
Chapman	26	5-20	6-6	5	3	2	0	16
Kempton	22	3-5	3-4	3	0	3	2	9
Bogues	28	2-6	0-0	3	11	3	2	4
TOTALS	240	40-87	25-32	41	28	25	11	107

SAN ANTONIO SPURS (105)

Player	MP	FG	FT	R	A	PF	S	TP
Greenwood	25	1-2	3-3	8	0	6	0	5
Anderson, W.	41	12-21	0-0	9	5	2	1	24
Anderson, G.	40	8-14	3-4	13	0	3	4	19
Robertson	39	9-16	6-8	2	5	6	1	24
Dawkins	44	8-19	7-7	4	7	3	2	23
Comegys	28	2-7	3-4	6	0	4	1	7
Cook	18	1-3	1-2	1	0	2	1	3
Jones	3	0-1	0-0	1	0	0	0	0
Maxwell	2	0-0	0-0	0	0	0	0	0
TOTALS	240	41-83	23-28	44	17	26	10	105

Charlotte	21	29	27	30	107
San Antonio	22	19	32	32	105

Turnovers: Char. 19 (Tripucka 5); S.A. 25 (W. Anderson 6).
3-Pointers: Char. 2-3 (Tripucka 2-2, Chapman 0-1); S.A. 0-0.
Technical Fouls: Char. 1 (Tripucka); S.A. 1 (Cook).
Officials: Bavetta, Thompson, Clark.
Attendance: 10,863.

NOV. 22, 1988 AT CHARLOTTE

DETROIT PISTONS (99)

Player	MP	FG	FT	R	A	PF	S	TP
Mahorn	31	4-8	2-2	10	1	2	0	10
Dantley	21	1-8	4-4	3	0	3	1	6
Laimbeer	26	7-12	5-5	9	0	2	0	19
Dumars	33	10-16	6-6	4	5	1	0	26
Thomas	35	2-10	2-3	3	8	2	1	6
Rodman	29	6-9	0-0	9	3	1	1	12
Johnson	28	6-17	1-1	5	1	1	1	13
Salley	27	2-3	2-2	2	0	1	0	6
Edwards	10	0-3	1-2	4	0	2	0	1
TOTALS	240	38-86	23-25	49	18	15	4	99

CHARLOTTE HORNETS (93)

Player	MP	FG	FT	R	A	PF	S	TP
Tripucka	29	5-17	1-1	4	4	3	2	11
Rambis	33	7-11	2-3	14	1	1	4	16
Hoppen	22	3-5	0-0	6	0	4	0	6
Holton	24	1-6	2-2	0	8	0	0	4
Reid	32	9-21	1-1	5	1	5	0	19
Chapman	23	4-11	3-4	1	1	1	0	11
Kempton	26	4-6	2-3	9	1	3	1	10
Bogues	9	0-6	0-0	1	1	0	1	0
Cureton	15	1-2	0-0	3	1	2	0	2
Green	15	7-8	0-0	0	2	0	1	14
Lewis	12	0-1	0-0	1	0	2	0	0
TOTALS	240	41-94	11-14	44	20	21	9	93

Detroit	28	26	25	20	99
Charlotte	29	17	21	26	93

Turnovers: Det. 17 (Dumars 5); Char. 13 (Hoppen 3).
3-Pointers: Det. 0-0; Char. 0-3 (Tripucka 0-1, Reid 0-1, Chapman 0-1).
Technical Fouls: None.
Officials: Strom, Alexander, Fine.
Attendance: 23,388.

NOV. 23, 1988 AT BOSTON

CHARLOTTE HORNETS (109)

Player	MP	FG	FT	R	A	PF	S	TP
Tripucka	32	7-16	8-8	2	2	2	2	23
Rambis	34	5-5	5-6	6	1	2	3	15
Hoppen	26	2-4	3-3	3	4	3	0	7
Holton	17	0-3	2-2	1	6	1	1	2
Reid	34	9-18	2-2	6	5	4	0	20
Chapman	30	10-16	0-0	0	5	4	0	21
Bogues	24	3-8	2-2	1	8	2	3	8
Cureton	17	1-3	0-0	3	0	4	0	2
Kempton	19	4-6	1-2	6	1	1	0	9
Green	7	1-2	0-0	0	1	0	0	2
TOTALS	240	42-81	23-25	28	33	23	9	109

BOSTON CELTICS (114)

Player	MP	FG	FT	R	A	PF	S	TP
Paxson	25	6-13	0-0	2	2	3	4	12
McHale	33	10-16	6-6	12	4	3	0	26
Parish	33	7-10	0-0	7	2	2	3	14
Johnson	22	2-6	0-0	1	2	1	0	4
Ainge	32	4-11	8-9	4	9	2	1	16
Shaw	26	2-7	4-4	5	4	1	1	8
Lohaus	20	4-7	0-0	2	2	4	1	8
Lewis	26	8-15	4-5	4	1	2	4	20
Grandison	8	0-1	0-0	0	2	2	0	0
Acres	15	3-4	0-0	3	0	1	0	6
TOTALS	240	46-90	22-24	40	28	21	14	114

Charlotte	28	28	27	26	109
Boston	26	26	33	29	114

Turnovers: Char. 18 (Tripucka 5); Boston 14 (McHale, Parish 3).
3-Pointers: Char. 2-5 (Tripucka 1-1, Hoppen 0-1, Chapman 1-2, Bogues 0-1); Boston 0-2 (Ainge 0-1; Lewis 0-1).
Technical Fouls: None.
Officials: Mathis, Durham, Borgia.
Attendance: 14,890.

NOV. 25, 1988 AT PHILADELPHIA

CHARLOTTE HORNETS (116)

Player	MP	FG	FT	R	A	PF	S	TP
Tripucka	37	14-22	4-4	5	6	4	0	33
Cureton	25	2-7	0-0	3	2	6	0	4
Hoppen	25	4-5	2-2	9	1	4	0	10
Holton	18	3-5	0-0	0	6	3	0	6
Reid	32	11-18	4-4	8	3	5	0	27
Chapman	22	4-7	2-2	1	4	0	0	11
Green	3	1-1	0-0	0	2	1	0	2
Tolbert	23	3-7	0-0	4	2	4	1	6
Lewis	5	0-3	0-0	1	0	1	0	0
Kempton	23	2-2	2-2	4	3	4	0	6
Bogues	27	4-9	3-4	2	8	2	4	11
TOTALS	240	48-86	17-18	37	37	34	5	116

PHILADELPHIA 76ERS (123)

Player	MP	FG	FT	R	A	PF	S	TP
Robinson	37	9-17	5-9	5	4	0	1	23
Barkley	41	12-18	13-16	15	3	3	1	37
Gminski	35	5-11	7-8	8	3	3	0	17
Cheeks	35	5-15	3-4	3	8	1	2	13
Hawkins	32	2-8	4-4	1	2	5	0	8
Anderson	30	7-12	3-4	3	3	1	3	17
Welp	8	3-4	0-0	3	1	1	0	6
Brooks	13	0-2	0-0	2	3	0	0	0
Wingate	9	1-3	0-0	1	1	1	0	2
TOTALS	240	44-90	35-45	41	28	15	7	123

Charlotte	24	32	35	25	116
Philadelphia	33	28	24	38	123

Turnovers: Char. 17 (Bogues 4); Phil. 11 (Barkley 3).
3-Pointers: Char. 3-5 (Tripucka 1-1, Reid 1-1, Chapman 1-1, Tolbert 0-2); Phil. 0-2 (Hawkins 0-1, Brooks 0-1).
Technical Fouls: None.
Officials: Crawford, Javie, Herring.
Attendance: 10,588.

NOV. 26, 1988 AT CHARLOTTE

WASHINGTON BULLETS (120)

Player	MP	FG	FT	R	A	PF	S	TP
King	38	10-17	2-3	4	6	5	2	22
Catledge	38	6-11	5-7	13	1	4	0	17
Feitl	16	0-2	0-0	2	2	4	0	0
Walker	36	6-11	0-0	8	2	4	0	12
Malone	37	10-20	9-11	2	5	3	2	29
Williams	31	7-15	6-8	9	3	2	2	20
Alarie	9	2-2	0-0	2	1	0	1	4
Grant	9	1-2	2-2	1	0	1	0	4
Colter	13	0-0	0-0	1	2	1	0	0
Eackles	13	5-7	2-2	0	3	1	0	12
TOTALS	240	47-87	26-33	42	25	25	7	120

CHARLOTTE HORNETS (113)

Player	MP	FG	FT	R	A	PF	S	TP
Tripucka	26	7-11	6-6	2	0	0	1	21
Cureton	20	3-3	0-1	4	2	2	1	6
Hoppen	21	1-2	2-2	2	3	4	0	4
Holton	30	4-8	6-6	3	6	3	0	14
Reid	34	10-21	4-4	7	3	3	1	25
Chapman	28	8-19	0-0	2	2	5	1	16
Bogues	26	1-2	2-4	1	6	2	1	4
Kempton	30	7-11	1-2	9	1	6	4	15
Lewis	5	0-1	0-0	0	0	2	0	0
Tolbert	20	3-5	2-4	4	2	2	0	8
TOTALS	240	44-83	23-29	34	25	29	9	113

Washington	30	26	42	22	120
Charlotte	30	24	23	36	113

Turnovers: Wash. 17 (Malone 7); Char. 18 (Cureton 5).
3-Pointers: Wash. 0-0; Char. 2-5 (Tripucka 1-1, Reid 1-2, Chapman 0-1, Tolbert 0-1).
Technical Fouls: None.
Officials: Evans, Salvatore, Mauer.
Attendance: 23,388.

NOV. 29, 1988 AT CHARLOTTE

MIAMI HEAT (84)								
Player	MP	FG	FT	R	A	PF	S	TP
Gray	17	2-6	2-2	2	1	0	0	6
Long	35	6-11	2-4	10	2	4	1	14
Seikaly	23	1-10	2-8	9	0	5	0	4
Sparrow	29	5-13	0-0	4	2	0	2	10
Taylor	20	4-10	0-0	3	1	4	1	8
Edwards	16	1-5	1-2	2	5	1	1	3
Hastings	25	0-3	0-0	3	1	3	0	0
Thompson	22	4-6	0-0	10	1	3	2	8
Washington	31	8-14	2-2	3	2	0	2	18
Cummings	21	6-10	1-2	7	0	6	0	13
Sundvold	1	0-0	0-0	0	0	0	0	0
TOTALS	240	37-88	10-20	53	15	26	9	84
CHARLOTTE HORNETS (99)								
Rambis	24	5-11	3-4	8	1	2	2	13
Hoppen	25	3-4	2-2	7	2	2	1	8
Holton	26	2-6	6-6	1	3	2	0	10
Reid	35	7-18	3-5	5	1	1	0	17
Green	21	2-5	2-2	1	0	1	0	6
Chapman	32	8-20	6-7	5	4	0	2	22
Bogues	17	2-3	0-0	2	7	2	2	4
Cureton	23	1-1	1-2	4	3	3	1	3
Kempton	23	1-2	6-8	8	1	3	1	8
Lewis	13	4-6	0-0	0	1	0	0	8
Tolbert	1	0-1	0-0	0	0	0	0	0
TOTALS	240	35-77	29-36	41	23	16	9	99

Miami	22	15	26	21	84
Charlotte	22	27	19	31	99

Turnovers: Miami 19 (Sparrow 5); Char. 14 (Bogues 5).
3-Pointers: Miami 0-3 (Sparrow 0-2, Taylor 0-1): Char. 0-3 (Chapman 0-3).
Technical Fouls: None.
Officials: Kersey, Delaney, Armstrong.
Attendance: 23,388.

DEC. 1, 1988 AT CHARLOTTE

PHILADELPHIA 76ERS (107)								
Player	MP	FG	FT	R	A	PF	S	TP
Anderson	35	14-20	2-3	5	2	6	0	30
Barkley	47	9-17	13-18	12	4	4	2	31
Gminski	40	7-13	9-9	15	4	4	1	23
Hawkins	40	5-16	1-1	1	0	1	1	12
Wingate	18	0-3	2-4	1	4	2	1	2
Thornton	4	0-0	0-0	0	0	1	0	0
Welp	8	0-1	0-0	0	0	1	0	0
Brooks	18	2-4	0-0	2	3	1	0	4
Henderson	20	2-4	0-0	2	3	4	1	5
Myers	10	0-2	0-0	1	1	1	0	0
TOTALS	240	39-80	27-35	39	21	25	6	107
CHARLOTTE HORNETS (109)								
Tripucka	33	11-22	3-4	7	1	3	0	25
Rambis	32	4-9	0-0	9	2	6	1	8
Hoppen	23	5-5	2-2	7	1	4	0	12
Holton	31	5-12	0-1	3	15	4	4	10
Reid	29	8-15	0-1	7	2	4	0	16
Chapman	32	8-15	3-4	2	3	0	2	19
Kempton	18	3-5	2-5	2	0	4	1	8
Cureton	21	0-1	1-4	4	3	1	0	1
Bogues	19	5-6	0-1	3	2	0	1	10
Tolbert	2	0-0	0-0	0	0	0	0	0
TOTALS	240	49-90	11-22	44	29	26	9	109

Philadelphia	23	23	33	28	107
Charlotte	35	24	22	28	109

Turnovers: Phil. 19 (Barkley 4); Char. 18 (Tripucka 5).
3-Pointers: Phil. 2-4 (Hawkins 1-3, Henderson 1-1); Char. 0-2 (Chapman 0-2).
Technical Fouls: Char. 1 (Hoppen).
Officials: Jones, Fryer, Mayfield.
Attendance: 21,716.

DEC. 3, 1988 AT HOUSTON

CHARLOTTE HORNETS (104)								
Player	MP	FG	FT	R	A	PF	S	TP
Rambis	32	1-4	0-0	8	8	3	2	2
Tripucka	39	11-20	6-7	5	3	3	2	30
Hoppen	21	6-9	1-2	8	1	4	0	13
Holton	18	2-5	0-1	1	5	4	1	4
Reid	30	12-18	0-0	7	1	6	2	24
Green	6	0-1	0-0	0	1	0	0	0
Chapman	27	3-15	2-5	3	3	3	0	8
Kempton	27	4-7	3-4	9	4	3	0	11
Bogues	24	3-7	0-0	0	7	6	2	6
Cureton	16	3-4	0-0	6	0	5	1	6
TOTALS	240	45-90	12-19	47	33	37	10	104
HOUSTON ROCKETS (108)								
Johnson	31	4-10	2-2	2	1	4	2	10
Thorpe	44	4-10	8-10	9	3	2	3	16
Olajuwon	45	11-18	6-7	14	0	5	3	28
Floyd	45	4-11	9-13	7	13	1	4	17
Woodson	43	9-16	11-11	0	3	2	0	29
McCormick	7	1-2	2-2	1	1	3	0	4
Short	13	1-4	2-2	1	0	3	0	4
Chievous	7	0-3	0-0	1	0	0	0	0
Leavell	3	0-1	0-0	0	0	0	0	0
Brown	2	0-0	0-0	0	1	1	0	0
TOTALS	240	34-75	40-47	35	22	21	12	108

Charlotte	24	31	25	24	104
Houston	24	23	30	31	108

Turnovers: Char. 27 (Tripucka 6); Houston 23 (Olajuwon 6).
3-Pointers: Char. 2-5 (Tripucka 2-2, Holton 0-2, Chapman 0-1); Houston 0-3 (Floyd 0-3).
Technical Fouls: Char. 1 (Illegal defense); Houston 1 (Delay of game).
Officials: Middleton, Lauerman, Wood.
Attendance: 16,611.

DEC. 9, 1988 AT CHARLOTTE

NEW JERSEY NETS (95)								
Player	MP	FG	FT	R	A	PF	S	TP
Hinson	30	7-15	1-2	8	0	5	0	15
Williams, B	30	2-6	5-6	6	1	2	1	9
Carroll	38	7-15	7-8	19	1	3	0	21
McGee	31	3-9	0-0	1	0	2	1	6
Conner	27	2-7	2-4	3	2	1	5	6
Hopson	17	2-8	0-0	2	3	4	1	4
Shackleford	9	2-3	2-2	3	1	2	0	6
Bagley	25	5-8	1-1	2	5	3	1	12
Morris	24	5-8	4-5	6	1	1	1	16
Williams, K	9	0-4	0-0	1	0	1	0	0
TOTALS	240	35-83	22-28	51	14	24	10	95
CHARLOTTE HORNETS (96)								
Tripucka	37	12-22	5-5	3	3	0	1	30
Rambis	35	3-5	5-6	8	3	4	0	11
Hoppen	22	4-9	2-2	6	1	5	0	10
Holton	16	1-3	0-0	2	3	3	0	2
Reid	23	1-12	1-2	8	0	2	2	3
Green	8	1-3	0-0	0	2	0	0	2
Chapman	36	12-20	0-0	4	6	0	3	24
Bogues	24	0-5	3-4	4	8	3	2	3
Cureton	24	2-3	0-0	5	0	4	0	4
Kempton	15	3-6	1-3	3	1	2	1	7
TOTALS	240	39-88	17-22	43	27	23	9	96

New Jersey	24	14	22	35	95
Charlotte	19	32	20	25	96

Turnovers: N.J. 20 (Hinson, Carroll, K. Williams 3); Char. 15 (Kempton 4).
3-Pointers: N.J. 3-4 (Bagley 1-1, Morris 2-3); Char. 1-2 (Tripucka 1-1, Chapman 0-1).
Technical Fouls: None.
Officials: Maden, Alexander, Fine.
Attendance: 23,388.

DEC. 10, 1988 AT E. RUTHERFORD, N.J.

CHARLOTTE HORNETS (112)

Player	MP	FG	FT	R	A	PF	S	TP
Tripucka	37	10-23	10-11	3	3	4	0	31
Rambis	36	3-5	0-0	7	1	4	2	6
Hoppen	24	3-10	2-4	3	2	4	0	8
Holton	27	0-6	3-4	3	5	0	1	3
Reid	26	11-22	1-2	7	2	3	1	23
Cureton	23	1-1	2-2	8	0	3	0	4
Chapman	33	4-11	8-8	3	1	1	2	19
Bogues	18	2-4	3-4	0	5	2	2	7
Kempton	23	2-6	3-4	1	1	6	0	7
Green	8	2-3	0-0	0	2	0	2	4
TOTALS	265	38-91	32-39	35	22	27	10	112

NEW JERSEY NETS (121)

Player	MP	FG	FT	R	A	PF	S	TP
Hinson	35	9-16	5-5	7	0	5	0	23
Williams, B.	42	4-7	2-2	18	0	4	0	10
Carroll	37	7-17	8-9	9	0	2	3	22
Conner	28	5-7	3-3	2	3	4	4	13
McGee	19	4-14	1-2	3	2	1	0	9
Morris	29	6-13	2-2	5	0	5	0	14
Bagley	39	3-6	6-6	8	11	1	2	12
Hopson	25	5-9	3-4	6	1	2	1	13
Shackleford	2	1-2	1-1	1	0	1	0	3
Williams, K.	9	1-6	0-0	1	0	2	0	2
TOTALS	265	45-97	31-34	60	17	27	10	121

Charlotte	21	20	24	34	4	112
New Jersey	28	18	27	35	13	121

Turnovers: Char. 14 (Rambis 3); N.J. 17 (Bagley 5).
3-Pointers: Char. 4-11 (Tripucka 1-4, Holton 0-1, Chapman 3-5, Kempton 0-1). N.J. 0-5 (McGee 0-3, Morris 0-2).
Technical Fouls: None.
Officials: O'Donnell, Reichett, Olesiak.
Attendance: 9,460.

DEC. 13, 1988 AT INDIANAPOLIS

CHARLOTTE HORNETS (104)

Player	MP	FG	FT	R	A	PF	S	TP
Rambis	32	4-7	0-0	9	1	4	3	8
Tripucka	33	9-17	7-9	7	2	3	3	26
Hoppen	30	5-14	4-4	4	1	3	1	14
Holton	31	4-10	6-7	0	6	3	1	14
Reid	23	5-13	2-3	4	2	3	0	13
Chapman	22	3-14	0-0	4	4	2	2	6
Bogues	2	0-1	0-0	0	1	1	1	0
Cureton	16	0-2	0-0	0	0	3	2	0
Kempton	14	1-3	0-4	5	1	4	0	2
Green	22	4-10	0-0	1	7	1	2	8
Tolbert	4	2-3	3-4	1	0	1	0	7
Lewis	11	2-3	2-7	2	0	1	1	6
TOTALS	240	39-97	24-38	37	25	29	16	104

INDIANA PACERS (115)

Player	MP	FG	FT	R	A	PF	S	TP
Tisdale	29	4-10	2-2	7	1	5	1	10
Williams	36	6-13	4-4	13	1	4	0	16
Smits	21	6-10	0-1	6	0	5	0	12
Fleming	37	4-8	2-4	13	12	2	2	10
Miller	37	6-13	10-10	7	6	2	2	22
Gray	10	0-2	0-0	1	0	1	0	0
Frederick	12	3-5	3-3	2	1	5	0	9
Skiles	15	1-2	2-2	3	2	2	1	4
Dreiling	15	0-1	7-10	7	0	3	0	7
Long	27	9-15	6-6	2	2	1	2	25
Stephens	1	0-0	0-0	0	0	0	0	0
TOTALS	240	39-79	36-42	61	25	30	8	115

Charlotte	30	21	23	30	104
Indianapolis	27	27	25	36	115

Turnovers: Char. 15 (Kempton 4); Ind. 27 (Tisdale 7).
3-Pointers: Char. 2-5 (Tripucka 1-3, Holton 0-1, Reid 1-1); Ind. 1-6 (Williams 0-1, Miller 0-3, Skiles 0-1; Long 1-1).
Technical Fouls: Ind. 2 (Bench).
Officials: Saar, Javie, Stafford.
Attendance: 8, 670.

DEC. 14, 1988 AT CHARLOTTE

INDIANA PACERS (106)

Player	MP	FG	FT	R	A	PF	S	TP
Miller	35	5-13	5-6	6	3	2	1	16
Williams	33	7-14	2-2	7	0	2	0	16
Smits	26	7-11	5-5	3	1	4	0	19
Fleming	29	3-6	1-2	3	5	1	1	7
Long	36	4-17	1-1	6	3	6	0	9
Tisdale	31	7-17	5-5	7	0	2	0	19
Frederick	22	4-5	2-2	6	1	3	0	10
Gray	7	0-0	1-2	1	0	1	0	1
Skiles	17	3-5	1-1	1	6	4	1	7
Dreiling	4	1-1	0-0	1	0	0	0	2
TOTALS	240	41-89	23-26	41	19	25	3	106

CHARLOTTE HORNETS (115)

Player	MP	FG	FT	R	A	PF	S	TP
Tripucka	41	13-22	13-14	5	1	1	0	40
Rambis	33	6-14	0-4	13	4	1	0	12
Hoppen	11	1-3	0-0	3	0	5	1	2
Holton	24	2-4	0-0	1	11	2	2	4
Reid	29	9-19	0-0	4	1	4	0	18
Chapman	5	2-3	0-0	1	0	0	0	4
Kempton	31	6-9	9-10	9	3	2	3	21
Green	24	4-10	2-2	2	4	0	1	10
Cureton	19	0-2	0-0	1	0	3	1	0
Lewis	21	2-8	0-0	6	3	1	0	4
Tolbert	2	0-1	0-0	1	0	0	0	0
TOTALS	240	45-95	24-30	46	27	19	8	115

Indiana	27	21	36	22	106
Charlotte	30	26	32	27	115

Turnovers: Ind. 17 (Williams, Frederick 4); Char. 11 (Tripucka, Holton, Reid 2).
3-Pointers: Ind. 1-4 (Miller 1-3, Skiles 0-1); Char. 1-4 (Tripucka 1-2, Reid 0-1, Green 0-1).
Technical Fouls: Ind. 1 (Tisdale); Char. 1 (Illegal defense).
Officials: Garretson, Crawford, Herring.
Attendance: 22,601.

DEC. 16, 1988 AT CHARLOTTE

DALLAS MAVERICKS (107)

Player	MP	FG	FT	R	A	PF	S	TP
Aguirre	35	7-18	10-11	1	3	2	2	24
Perkins	36	7-15	7-8	14	0	1	0	21
Donaldson	33	2-7	1-2	10	0	3	1	5
Harper	38	4-10	6-6	2	7	1	1	14
Blackman	35	6-13	3-3	3	1	2	3	15
Tarpley	21	5-10	3-7	10	0	5	1	13
Davis	25	3-6	0-0	4	6	2	1	7
Schrempf	14	4-7	0-1	3	0	0	0	8
Tyler	3	0-0	0-0	1	0	0	0	0
TOTALS	240	38-86	30-38	48	17	16	9	107

CHARLOTTE HORNETS (98)

Player	MP	FG	FT	R	A	PF	S	TP
Tripucka	36	10-17	1-4	3	5	3	2	21
Rambis	36	4-12	1-2	21	3	3	0	9
Hoppen	25	4-7	1-2	4	0	4	1	9
Holton	36	7-15	2-2	3	9	2	0	16
Reid	33	9-23	2-2	6	1	3	1	20
Curry	14	2-5	0-0	0	0	2	1	4
Green	21	4-10	1-1	2	3	3	1	10
Cureton	12	1-3	0-0	4	1	3	0	2
Kempton	23	3-7	1-2	6	4	5	1	7
Lewis	4	0-1	0-0	2	0	0	0	0
TOTALS	240	44-100	9-15	51	26	28	7	98

Dallas	25	29	29	24	107
Charlotte	26	18	30	24	98

Turnovers: Dallas 13 (Harper 4); Char. 12 (Kempton 5).
3-Pointers: Dallas 1-4 (Aguirre 0-1, Harper 0-1, Davis 1-1, Schrempf 0-1); Char. 1-3 (Tripucka 0-1, Reid 0-1, Green 1-1).
Technical Fouls: Dallas 1 (Donaldson); Char. 2 (Holton, Rambis).
Officials: Oakes, Nunn, Willard.
Attendance: 23,388.

DEC. 17, 1988 AT AUBURN HILLS, MI.

CHARLOTTE HORNETS (91)

Player	MP	FG	FT	R	A	PF	S	TP
Tripucka	36	8-13	2-3	3	6	3	4	18
Rambis	23	3-10	0-0	5	2	2	2	6
Hoppen	19	1-9	0-0	6	1	3	0	2
Reid	30	3-15	0-0	6	1	4	1	6
Holton	30	2-3	1-3	2	6	3	1	5
Curry	17	7-10	2-2	3	2	1	1	17
Kempton	25	5-7	4-6	7	5	4	0	14
Cureton	16	0-4	0-0	0	0	2	0	0
Green	23	5-9	4-4	0	3	2	3	14
Tolbert	13	1-5	1-2	2	1	3	1	3
Lewis	8	3-4	0-0	0	0	2	1	6
TOTALS	240	38-89	14-20	34	27	29	14	91

DETROIT PISTONS (100)

Player	MP	FG	FT	R	A	PF	S	TP
Dantley	38	5-14	11-15	9	2	3	0	21
Mahorn	27	0-2	3-4	12	1	0	1	3
Laimbeer	28	4-9	0-0	3	1	5	0	8
Dumars	25	6-7	2-2	0	4	1	1	14
Thomas	41	10-15	5-5	7	7	4	0	25
Johnson	26	7-15	1-1	8	3	1	1	15
Salley	20	2-6	1-1	1	2	0	0	5
Rodman	25	1-6	2-2	8	0	4	0	4
Williams	2	1-2	0-0	0	0	1	0	2
Edwards	8	0-0	3-4	4	1	1	0	3
TOTALS	240	36-76	28-34	52	21	20	3	100

Charlotte	23	18	23	27	91
Detroit	30	22	23	25	100

Turnovers: Char. 16 (Tripucka 6); Det. 27 (Mahorn, Thomas 5).
3-Pointers: Char. 1-5 (Tripucka 0-1, Curry 1-2, Green 0-1, Lewis 0-1); Det. 0-1 (Rodman 0-1).
Technical Fouls: Detroit 1 (Coach Daly).
Officials: Hollins, Reichelt, Clark.
Attendance: 21,454.

DEC. 20, 1988 AT MILWAUKEE

CHARLOTTE HORNETS (115)

Player	MP	FG	FT	R	A	PF	S	TP
Rambis	23	5-6	4-6	5	3	2	0	14
Tripucka	30	8-18	5-6	2	4	1	2	21
Hoppen	28	2-3	3-4	4	1	3	0	7
Holton	27	4-6	2-2	2	7	4	3	10
Reid	32	5-13	1-2	8	3	4	1	11
Green	22	6-10	1-2	4	8	2	0	13
Curry	17	3-8	0-0	1	3	3	4	6
Kempton	20	1-2	5-6	3	3	3	0	7
Cureton	25	7-11	1-2	2	3	1	1	15
Bogues	11	2-3	2-2	1	4	0	0	6
Lewis	5	2-2	1-1	0	0	0	0	5
TOTALS	240	45-82	25-33	32	39	23	11	115

MILWAUKEE BUCKS (125)

Player	MP	FG	FT	R	A	PF	S	TP
Cummings	35	14-22	9-9	8	5	3	4	37
Krystkowiak	27	6-10	1-2	2	2	2	0	13
Sikma	31	4-9	2-2	8	8	4	0	10
Grayer	24	4-7	0-0	3	1	2	1	8
Pressey	34	6-11	0-0	2	6	4	3	12
Humphries	28	6-12	0-0	2	4	4	5	12
Pierce	31	11-17	6-9	4	7	3	0	28
Horford	4	0-0	1-2	1	0	0	0	1
Breuer	6	2-4	0-0	3	1	0	0	4
Roberts	13	0-1	0-0	1	1	2	0	0
Mokeski	7	0-0	0-0	3	0	2	0	0
TOTALS	240	53-93	19-24	37	35	26	13	125

Charlotte	32	27	30	28	115
Milwaukee	40	17	31	37	125

Turnovers: Char. 21 (Tripucka, Reid 5); Mil. 18 (Pressey 5).
3-Pointers: Char. 0-3 (Tripucka 0-1, Holton 0-1, Curry 0-1); Mil. 0-4 (Sikma 0-2, Pressey 0-1, Pierce 0-1).
Technical Fouls: None.
Officials: Evans, Delaney, Bernhardt.
Attendance: 15,075.

DEC. 21, 1988 AT CHARLOTTE

MILWAUKEE BUCKS (112)

Player	MP	FG	FT	R	A	PF	S	TP
Cummings	40	13-21	6-7	6	2	3	2	32
Krystkowiak	22	1-4	4-5	6	2	2	1	6
Sikma	35	11-18	2-2	16	0	4	1	25
Grayer	18	2-6	1-2	2	3	1	1	5
Pressey	36	4-9	0-0	4	7	3	4	8
Breuer	13	0-0	7-8	4	0	1	0	7
Pierce	28	6-13	3-4	2	1	2	0	15
Humphries	29	3-5	2-2	4	5	4	3	8
Roberts	19	3-4	0-0	4	1	1	1	6
TOTALS	240	43-80	25-30	48	21	21	13	112

CHARLOTTE HORNETS (100)

Player	MP	FG	FT	R	A	PF	S	TP
Tripucka	36	10-24	10-11	5	8	3	2	30
Rambis	22	2-3	2-6	8	0	2	0	6
Hoppen	15	3-5	0-0	2	0	2	0	6
Holton	28	5-6	1-3	2	4	4	0	11
Reid	17	1-11	2-2	1	2	1	0	4
Kempton	30	4-11	0-0	6	4	2	1	8
Curry	21	6-13	1-1	6	1	2	2	13
Cureton	28	6-7	0-0	5	0	6	1	12
Green	21	2-4	0-0	2	3	0	1	4
Tolbert	1	0-2	0-0	0	0	0	0	0
Lewis	6	0-1	2-2	1	1	0	0	2
Bogues	15	1-2	2-2	1	2	0	1	4
TOTALS	240	40-89	20-27	39	25	22	8	100

Milwaukee	28	27	26	31	112
Charlotte	30	18	34	18	100

Turnovers: Mil. 22 (Pressey, Humphries 4); Char. 19 (Tripucka 6).
3-Pointers: Mil. 1-4 (Sikma 1-2, Pressey 0-1, Humphries 0-1); Char. 0-3 (Tripucka 0-2, Curry 0-1).
Technical Fouls: Mil. 1 (Pierce).
Officials: Mihalak, Nies, Huetter.
Attendance: 23,010.

DEC. 23, 1988 AT CHARLOTTE

CHICAGO BULLS (101)

Player	MP	FG	FT	R	A	PF	S	TP
Sellers	34	2-7	1-2	3	1	4	2	5
Grant	36	6-8	3-4	6	2	5	2	15
Cartwright	35	6-8	4-6	12	2	3	0	16
Vincent	26	6-9	1-1	5	10	0	0	13
Jordan	41	14-26	5-6	5	4	5	6	33
Pippen	17	2-4	3-4	4	1	3	1	7
Paxson	21	4-7	0-0	2	1	0	1	9
Corzine	8	0-2	1-2	2	0	1	0	1
Hodges	22	1-4	0-0	3	1	2	0	2
TOTALS	240	41-75	18-25	42	22	23	12	101

CHARLOTTE HORNETS (103)

Player	MP	FG	FT	R	A	PF	S	TP
Tripucka	36	10-22	9-12	1	4	5	2	30
Rambis	31	3-8	2-2	7	3	1	6	8
Hoppen	18	2-4	0-2	7	1	3	1	4
Holton	39	4-12	1-1	4	10	3	2	9
Reid	37	6-22	2-2	6	2	5	0	14
Curry	15	5-7	0-0	3	0	0	1	11
Cureton	21	2-7	3-4	9	0	0	1	7
Kempton	26	7-10	2-4	5	2	4	0	16
Green	3	0-1	0-0	1	0	0	0	0
Bogues	13	2-5	0-2	2	2	1	0	4
Lewis	1	0-0	0-0	0	0	0	0	0
TOTALS	240	41-98	19-29	45	24	22	13	103

Chicago	24	22	26	29	101
Charlotte	20	24	29	30	103

Turnovers: Chi. 23 (Jordan 7); Char. 14 (Rambis 6).
3-Pointers: Chi. 1-3 (Paxson 1-2, Hodges 0-1); Char. 2-5 (Tripucka 1-2, Reid 0-1, Curry 1-1, Bogues 0-1).
Technical Fouls: None.
Officials: Rooney, Salvatore, Mauer.
Attendance: 23,388.

DEC. 26, 1988 — AT CHARLOTTE

HOUSTON ROCKETS (97)

Player	MP	FG	FT	R	A	PF	S	TP
Johnson, B.	43	4-9	2-2	4	5	3	1	10
Thorpe	32	6-12	4-5	8	1	4	0	16
Olajuwon	38	10-17	3-4	15	2	4	4	23
Floyd	34	2-6	7-8	3	4	2	3	11
Woodson	26	8-15	5-7	3	0	1	2	22
McCormick	21	0-2	2-2	2	0	1	0	2
Short	5	1-3	2-2	1	0	2	0	4
Johnson, F.	13	0-1	3-3	3	2	0	0	3
Chievous	6	0-3	0-0	1	0	1	0	0
Nevitt	5	0-0	0-0	1	0	2	0	0
Thompson	17	2-4	2-2	3	0	3	2	6
TOTALS	240	33-72	30-35	44	14	23	12	97

CHARLOTTE HORNETS (95)

Player	MP	FG	FT	R	A	PF	S	TP
Tripucka	30	9-21	0-1	6	2	4	0	19
Rambis	29	2-7	0-0	7	3	5	2	4
Cureton	35	6-8	0-0	10	2	3	2	12
Holton	25	4-9	0-0	3	9	2	2	8
Reid	32	11-22	3-4	2	4	2	1	25
Curry	22	5-11	2-3	2	0	3	1	12
Kempton	25	3-5	5-6	4	1	3	4	11
Green	11	2-4	0-0	0	3	0	0	4
Tolbert	7	0-1	0-0	1	0	3	0	0
Bogues	16	0-2	0-0	2	4	0	0	0
Lewis	8	0-1	0-0	2	0	1	1	0
TOTALS	240	42-91	10-14	39	28	26	13	95

Houston	29	27	24	17	97
Charlotte	29	28	21	17	95

Turnovers: Hou. 29 (Olajuwon 7); Char. 20 (Tripucka, Kempton 5).
3-Pointers: Hou. 1-3 (Floyd 0-1, Woodson 1-2); Char. 1-4 (Tripucka 1-2; Reid 0-2).
Technical Fouls: Hou. 1; Char. 1.
Officials: Bavetta, Laverman, Olesiak.
Attendance: 23,388.

DEC. 28, 1988 — AT RICHFIELD, OHIO

CHARLOTTE HORNETS (98)

Player	MP	FG	FT	R	A	PF	S	TP
Tripucka	33	6-16	5-6	0	0	1	2	17
Rambis	25	5-6	2-4	5	2	3	1	12
Cureton	31	5-7	2-2	6	4	3	2	12
Holton	25	2-5	2-2	0	7	2	0	6
Reid	26	8-17	3-4	4	4	2	0	19
Kempton	26	4-9	0-0	4	3	4	1	8
Curry	25	9-17	0-0	5	2	2	0	18
Green	22	1-3	0-0	2	8	0	1	2
Hoppen	9	1-2	2-2	3	0	2	0	4
Lewis	8	0-2	0-0	2	1	0	0	0
Bogues	5	0-0	0-0	0	1	1	0	0
Tolbert	5	0-2	0-0	2	0	0	0	0
TOTALS	240	41-86	16-20	33	32	20	7	98

CLEVELAND CAVALIERS (122)

Player	MP	FG	FT	R	A	PF	S	TP
Nance	26	6-8	3-4	8	2	1	0	15
Sanders	10	3-5	0-0	2	0	5	0	6
Daugherty	30	3-10	7-10	8	3	2	1	13
Harper	37	8-17	2-2	4	6	3	4	19
Price	33	6-12	3-3	2	12	0	4	16
Ehlo	34	6-11	0-2	9	4	3	1	13
Valentine	21	3-5	2-2	2	3	0	2	8
Dudley	18	6-7	2-2	3	0	1	0	14
Williams	21	6-10	0-0	7	0	1	0	12
Keys	5	2-4	0-0	1	0	0	0	4
Rollins	5	1-1	0-0	0	0	0	0	2
TOTALS	240	50-90	19-25	46	30	16	12	122

Charlotte	22	26	29	21	98
Cleveland	26	28	37	31	122

Turnovers: Char. 19 (Holton, Kempton 4); Cle. 20 (Price 4).
3-Pointers: Char. 0-2 (Reid 0-1, Curry 0-1); Cle. 3-6 (Harper 1-2, Price 1-3, Ehlo 1-1).
Technical Fouls: Char. 1 (Kempton).
Officials: Mathis, Durham, Forte.
Attendance: 17,353.

DEC. 30, 1988 — AT CHARLOTTE

NEW YORK KNICKS (111)

Player	MP	FG	FT	R	A	PF	S	TP
Newman	34	8-17	2-3	1	0	4	1	19
Oakley	33	5-8	2-2	11	2	4	2	12
Ewing	41	11-14	3-10	11	2	4	1	25
Jackson	33	6-7	0-2	2	6	1	2	13
Wilkins, G.	34	1-6	1-2	2	2	0	0	3
Tucker	20	2-9	2-2	0	1	1	3	8
Walker	17	4-5	0-0	5	0	4	0	8
Green	8	1-7	0-0	4	0	0	0	2
Strickland	9	5-8	2-2	0	5	5	1	12
Wilkins, E.	3	2-4	3-4	0	0	1	1	7
Myers	4	0-1	2-2	0	0	1	0	2
Butler	4	0-1	0-0	1	0	0	0	0
TOTALS	240	45-87	17-29	37	18	25	11	111

CHARLOTTE HORNETS (122)

Player	MP	FG	FT	R	A	PF	S	TP
Tripucka	27	8-19	4-5	2	3	3	2	21
Rambis	33	7-9	7-8	16	3	1	1	21
Cureton	33	7-12	1-5	10	2	5	1	15
Holton	19	0-2	4-4	2	6	2	2	4
Reid	37	10-20	3-3	1	0	3	0	23
Hoppen	14	0-0	1-2	1	1	4	0	1
Chapman	31	6-12	0-0	2	7	2	2	13
Green	9	3-4	1-1	1	1	0	0	7
Bogues	20	4-6	3-4	4	7	3	3	11
Kempton	15	3-9	0-0	3	1	2	1	6
Lewis	2	0-0	0-0	0	0	0	0	0
TOTALS	240	48-93	24-32	42	31	25	12	122

New York	26	30	26	29	111
Charlotte	33	26	32	31	122

Turnovers: N.Y. 18 (Ewing 5); Char. 16 (Tripucka, Holton 4).
3-Pointers: N.Y. 4-17 (Newman 1-4, Jackson 1-1, G. Wilkins 0-3. Tucker 2-6, Green 0-1, Strickland 0-1, Butler 0-1); Char. 2-7 (Tripucka 1-3, Reid 0-1, Chapman 1-3.
Technical Fouls: Char. 1; N.Y. 1.
Officials: Crawford, Javie, Stafford.
Attendance: 23,388.

JAN. 3, 1989 — AT CHARLOTTE

NEW JERSEY NETS (109)

Player	MP	FG	FT	R	A	PF	S	TP
Hinson	36	11-15	0-0	3	0	2	0	22
Williams, B	26	3-9	6-6	11	0	5	0	12
Carroll	36	7-12	8-9	8	2	4	1	22
Conner	38	3-8	5-8	5	3	2	3	12
McGee	31	3-9	4-5	0	0	3	0	10
Morris	16	4-7	1-1	4	1	1	0	9
Shackleford	12	2-3	0-0	3	0	1	0	4
Hopson	20	4-8	4-5	3	1	4	0	12
Bagley	25	2-6	2-2	4	10	0	1	6
TOTALS	240	39-77	30-36	41	17	22	5	109

CHARLOTTE HORNETS (106)

Player	MP	FG	FT	R	A	PF	S	TP
Tripucka	28	6-13	4-4	5	4	4	0	17
Rambis	34	3-8	4-4	16	3	5	1	10
Cureton	38	5-7	1-3	8	2	4	0	11
Holton	22	3-4	0-0	2	6	4	2	6
Reid	24	6-17	4-4	1	0	3	2	16
Chapman	28	9-22	0-0	2	3	2	1	21
Hoppen	7	1-1	0-2	3	1	1	0	2
Lewis	10	3-6	2-4	1	0	0	1	8
Green	10	2-4	0-0	0	2	0	0	4
Bogues	16	1-1	0-0	1	5	0	0	2
Kempton	17	4-7	1-1	4	0	2	1	9
Curry	6	0-5	0-0	1	0	1	1	0
TOTALS	240	43-95	16-22	44	26	26	9	106

New Jersey	30	25	25	29	109
Charlotte	25	23	32	26	106

Turnovers: N.J. 17 (B. Williams 4); Char. 14 (Tripucka 4).
3-Pointers: N.J. 1-3 (Conner 1-2, McGee 0-1); Char. 4-10 (Tripucka 1-3, Reid 0-1, Chapman 3-6).
Technical Fouls: Char. 1 (Coach Harter).
Officials: Middleton, Clark, Grillo.
Attendance: 23,388.

JAN. 4, 1989 AT LANDOVER, MD.

CHARLOTTE HORNETS (86)

Player	MP	FG	FT	R	A	PF	S	TP
Rambis	30	5-10	6-8	14	1	1	1	16
Tripucka	30	3-17	4-4	3	4	1	0	10
Cureton	28	2-5	4-4	8	0	2	1	8
Holton	24	2-6	2-2	0	9	2	0	6
Reid	23	6-12	0-0	3	2	3	2	12
Hoppen	18	0-7	0-0	5	1	3	1	0
Chapman	23	6-15	0-0	1	2	2	1	12
Bogues	19	2-4	1-1	1	0	0	1	5
Kempton	20	2-6	3-6	7	0	3	0	7
Lewis	10	0-1	0-0	3	2	2	0	0
Green	5	1-2	0-0	0	0	0	0	2
Curry	10	4-8	0-0	3	0	3	0	8
TOTALS	240	33-93	20-25	48	21	22	7	86

WASHINGTON BULLETS (109)

Player	MP	FG	FT	R	A	PF	S	TP
Catledge	31	9-16	3-5	11	1	2	0	21
King	26	6-12	1-1	2	1	3	0	13
Feitl	24	5-9	0-0	5	1	2	2	10
Malone	30	7-16	5-6	2	5	2	1	19
Walker	28	2-3	0-0	11	3	3	1	4
Williams	19	2-6	0-2	5	2	1	0	4
Alarie	17	2-7	0-0	2	0	0	0	4
Colter	20	2-6	0-2	8	0	1	5	4
Grant	22	5-11	2-3	0	2	3	1	12
Eackles	18	3-8	8-8	5	3	0	0	14
Jones, C.A.	5	1-1	2-3	1	2	1	0	4
TOTALS	240	44-95	21-30	52	20	18	10	109

Charlotte	20	10	30	26	86
Washington	32	27	24	26	109

Turnovers: Char. 19 (Bogues, Tripucka 4); Wash. 13 (Malone 4).
3-Pointers: Char. 0-4 (Tripucka 0-1, Chapman 0-2, Curry 0-1); Wash. 0-2 (Malone 0-1, Eackles 0-1).
Technical Fouls: None.
Officials: Garretson, Forte, Fine.
Attendance: 4,832.

JAN. 6, 1989 AT BOSTON

CHARLOTTE HORNETS (92)

Player	MP	FG	FT	R	A	PF	S	TP
Tripucka	28	7-14	10-12	2	3	2	2	25
Rambis	28	5-9	0-0	7	2	2	2	10
Cureton	38	5-9	1-2	10	3	1	2	11
Holton	21	2-5	1-2	1	3	4	1	5
Reid	31	6-13	1-2	2	1	3	2	13
Green	7	0-2	0-0	0	1	0	0	0
Chapman	20	5-7	2-3	0	1	4	0	13
Hoppen	9	1-2	0-0	2	1	4	0	2
Bogues	24	1-2	0-0	0	11	2	0	2
Kempton	21	1-6	2-2	4	0	6	2	4
Curry	10	3-6	1-2	1	0	0	2	7
Lewis	3	0-0	0-0	0	1	0	0	0
TOTALS	240	36-75	18-25	29	27	28	13	92

BOSTON CELTICS (115)

Player	MP	FG	FT	R	A	PF	S	TP
McHale	36	7-13	4-4	11	4	3	0	18
Lewis	36	8-13	2-3	5	2	3	4	18
Parish	37	3-7	6-9	8	4	2	2	12
Johnson	31	4-7	0-0	5	11	2	2	8
Ainge	29	9-17	6-6	2	4	2	3	25
Shaw	17	5-6	0-0	4	1	3	1	10
Grandison	12	0-0	2-2	4	1	3	1	2
Lohaus	15	3-7	2-3	1	1	2	1	8
Acres	7	1-1	0-0	1	0	0	0	2
Paxson	18	4-8	2-2	0	2	4	2	10
Rivas	1	1-1	0-1	0	0	0	0	2
Gamble	1	0-1	0-0	0	0	0	0	0
TOTALS	240	45-81	24-30	41	30	24	16	115

Charlotte	16	36	23	17	92
Boston	33	25	24	33	115

Turnovers: Char. 21 (Cureton 5); Boston 18 (McHale, Parish, Johnson 3).
3-Pointers: Char. 2-4 (Tripucka 1-1, Chapman 1-3); Boston 1-2 (Ainge 1-2).
Technical Fouls: None.
Officials: Kersey, Salvatore, Toliver.
Attendance: 14,890.

JAN. 7, 1989 AT CHARLOTTE

WASHINGTON BULLETS (104)

Player	MP	FG	FT	R	A	PF	S	TP
King	37	9-24	2-3	4	9	4	0	20
Catledge	32	7-10	3-5	10	0	6	0	17
Feitl	15	2-4	0-0	4	2	3	0	4
Walker	21	3-7	0-0	3	5	2	1	6
Malone	28	8-17	1-2	3	3	4	1	17
Williams	23	0-7	3-4	4	5	3	2	3
Eackles	21	5-14	3-4	1	1	3	1	14
Grant	14	2-7	1-2	2	0	0	0	5
Colter	26	4-7	2-2	6	3	1	1	10
Alarie	6	2-3	0-0	3	0	0	0	4
Jones, C.A.	17	2-2	0-0	3	0	1	0	4
TOTALS	240	44-102	15-22	43	28	27	6	104

CHARLOTTE HORNETS (107)

Player	MP	FG	FT	R	A	PF	S	TP
Tripucka	39	15-27	2-2	9	2	3	0	32
Rambis	26	2-5	5-5	14	4	3	4	9
Cureton	28	3-6	0-1	5	1	3	1	6
Holton	32	4-10	4-4	3	9	5	0	12
Reid	27	7-17	0-0	4	3	1	0	14
Hoppen	23	3-3	2-2	11	0	3	0	8
Chapman	30	9-20	2-6	2	1	3	0	21
Bogues	16	0-2	2-2	1	9	1	1	2
Kempton	19	1-1	1-2	2	2	1	0	3
TOTALS	240	44-91	18-24	51	31	23	6	107

Washington	22	27	24	31	104
Charlotte	29	26	28	24	107

Turnovers: Wash. 13 (King 4); Char. 17 (Holton 4).
3-Pointers: Wash. 1-2 (Eackles 1-1, Colter 0-1); Char. 1-5 (Tripucka 0-2, Chapman 1-2, Reid 0-1).
Technical Fouls: None.
Officials: Mathis, Durham, Borgia.
Attendance: 23,388.

JAN. 9, 1989 AT CHARLOTTE

UTAH JAZZ (114)

Player	MP	FG	FT	R	A	PF	S	TP
Malone	36	15-25	8-10	19	3	3	2	38
Iavoroni	26	4-6	1-2	2	0	2	0	9
Eaton	23	1-3	0-0	5	0	4	1	2
Stockton	35	5-9	2-2	3	10	2	2	12
Griffith	27	5-11	0-2	3	1	0	3	10
Bailey	28	5-10	4-5	3	5	1	0	14
Farmer	21	5-8	2-3	3	3	1	1	13
Brown	8	0-1	1-2	0	0	3	0	1
Les	13	1-3	0-0	0	7	0	0	2
Leckner	20	4-5	1-1	6	0	4	0	9
Ortiz	3	2-2	0-0	1	0	0	0	4
TOTALS	240	47-83	19-27	45	29	20	9	114

CHARLOTTE HORNETS (92)

Player	MP	FG	FT	R	A	PF	S	TP
Tripucka	34	7-16	5-7	4	3	4	0	19
Rambis	27	1-5	4-4	6	0	4	2	6
Cureton	32	6-10	1-2	7	0	2	0	13
Holton	18	3-6	0-0	0	5	0	0	6
Reid	27	4-13	0-0	1	2	1	0	8
Hoppen	19	2-4	3-6	4	1	2	0	7
Chapman	21	5-15	0-0	3	3	1	2	10
Bogues	17	3-5	0-0	3	2	2	1	6
Kempton	18	2-3	2-3	3	2	4	1	6
Curry	10	1-3	1-1	2	0	0	0	3
Green	13	2-4	0-0	2	3	0	1	4
Lewis	4	2-3	0-0	1	0	0	0	4
TOTALS	240	38-87	16-23	36	21	20	7	92

Utah	28	32	26	28	114
Charlotte	20	13	23	36	92

Turnovers: Utah 18 (Bailey 5); Char. 16 (Tripucka 6).
3-Pointers: Utah 1-5 (Stockton 0-1, Griffith 0-3, Farmer 1-1); Char. 0-1 (Chapman 0-1).
Technical Fouls: Char. 1 (Kempton).
Officials: Saar, Garretson, Benson.
Attendance: 23,388.

JAN. 11, 1989 — AT CHARLOTTE

CHICAGO BULLS (106)

Player	MP	FG	FT	R	A	PF	S	TP
Pippen	40	8-12	8-11	9	3	3	3	24
Grant	38	8-11	0-0	7	2	4	0	16
Cartwright	23	1-3	7-8	5	1	2	0	9
Paxson	29	4-7	0-0	1	4	1	0	9
Jordan	40	7-15	10-11	4	10	4	3	24
Hodges	33	6-14	2-2	3	3	4	2	14
Corzine	16	0-1	0-0	2	0	0	0	0
Sellers	20	3-5	4-4	5	0	1	0	10
Haley	1	0-0	0-0	0	0	0	0	0
TOTALS	240	37-68	31-36	36	23	19	8	106

CHARLOTTE HORNETS (101)

Player	MP	FG	FT	R	A	PF	S	TP
Tripucka	33	8-23	8-10	5	1	4	1	24
Rambis	34	6-9	0-0	14	3	2	3	12
Cureton	39	3-7	0-0	5	4	3	1	6
Holton	35	1-6	0-0	0	4	2	3	2
Reid	35	10-19	4-4	3	2	4	0	24
Chapman	24	9-18	5-5	2	1	5	0	25
Hoppen	15	0-1	0-0	1	1	4	0	0
Bogues	17	2-2	2-2	0	10	1	3	6
Kempton	8	1-1	0-0	1	0	3	0	2
TOTALS	240	40-86	19-21	31	26	28	10	101

Chicago	23	26	31	26	106
Charlotte	20	28	24	29	101

Turnovers: Chi. 19 (Jordan 6); Char. 11 (Tripucka, Reid 3).
3-Pointers: Chi. 1-6 (Paxson 1-2, Hodges 0-3, Corzine 0-1); Char. 2-7 (Tripucka 0-3, Rambis 0-1, Chapman 2-3).
Technical Fouls: Chi. 1 (Illegal defense).
Officials: Hollins, Nunez, Vaden.
Attendance: 23,388.

JAN. 12, 1989 — AT NEW YORK

CHARLOTTE HORNETS (89)

Player	MP	FG	FT	R	A	PF	S	TP
Rambis	25	1-6	1-2	8	2	1	2	3
Tripucka	31	5-13	6-6	5	1	1	2	16
Cureton	35	6-20	2-2	14	2	4	2	14
Holton	20	2-4	0-1	0	4	0	2	4
Reid	30	3-13	0-0	3	4	1	1	6
Chapman	29	7-17	4-5	4	1	3	3	19
Hoppen	25	6-8	1-2	5	0	5	2	13
Bogues	18	1-4	2-2	1	6	2	0	4
Kempton	11	0-0	1-2	2	0	1	0	1
Green	8	0-2	0-0	1	1	0	0	0
Lewis	5	2-5	0-0	1	1	1	1	4
Curry	3	2-5	0-0	2	0	0	0	5
TOTALS	240	35-97	17-22	46	22	19	15	89

NEW YORK KNICKS (106)

Player	MP	FG	FT	R	A	PF	S	TP
Newman	26	1-8	2-2	3	2	1	0	4
Oakley	25	6-9	0-0	12	2	2	3	12
Ewing	29	5-8	3-3	13	3	2	2	13
Jackson	29	6-13	5-6	8	5	1	4	18
Wilkins, G.	17	2-6	3-3	2	2	4	0	7
Strickland	27	6-9	2-2	4	6	3	0	14
Tucker	26	3-11	0-0	2	2	1	1	6
Walker	22	5-11	0-1	9	0	3	3	10
Green	18	4-9	3-5	7	2	3	1	11
Wilkins, E.	8	1-4	1-1	2	0	0	0	3
Butler	8	0-3	2-2	1	0	1	0	2
Myers	5	2-2	2-2	1	0	0	0	6
TOTALS	240	41-93	23-27	64	24	21	14	106

Charlotte	31	17	13	28	89
New York	29	19	32	26	106

Turnovers: Char. 23 (Tripucka 6); N.Y. 26 (Jackson 5).
3-Pointers: Char. 2-4 (Chapman 1-3, Curry 1-1); N.Y. 1-12 (Newman 0-2, Jackson 1-3, G. Wilkins 0-2, Tucker 0-5).
Technical Fouls: None.
Officials. Rush, Javie, Kinsey.
Attendance: 16,943.

JAN. 15, 1989 — AT CHARLOTTE

PHILADELPHIA 76ERS (116)

Player	MP	FG	FT	R	A	PF	S	TP
Jones	16	2-3	2-4	2	2	3	0	6
Barkley	40	8-13	7-12	15	6	3	1	24
Gminski	35	7-13	8-10	13	3	2	0	22
Cheeks	33	6-10	3-4	4	4	2	2	15
Hawkins	29	4-13	3-4	2	0	1	0	12
Henderson	19	4-6	5-6	1	4	4	0	13
Anderson	32	9-13	0-1	4	0	1	0	18
Brooks	15	0-3	0-0	1	2	0	1	0
Welp	7	0-0	0-0	0	1	5	1	0
Coleman	8	2-4	0-0	0	0	1	0	4
Thornton	6	1-2	0-0	3	0	0	0	2
TOTALS	240	43-80	28-41	45	22	22	5	116

CHARLOTTE HORNETS (109)

Player	MP	FG	FT	R	A	PF	S	TP
Tripucka	39	8-18	9-9	6	2	2	3	25
Rambis	27	6-10	3-4	14	0	6	1	15
Cureton	30	5-10	0-0	6	1	6	1	10
Holton	24	4-7	2-3	1	8	2	2	10
Reid	20	2-7	2-2	3	2	1	1	6
Chapman	37	9-23	3-4	3	3	2	0	22
Kempton	30	4-5	3-6	5	1	2	0	11
Bogues	24	5-12	0-0	3	9	2	2	10
Hoppen	9	0-0	0-0	0	1	0	0	0
TOTALS	240	43-92	22-28	41	27	23	10	109

Philadelphia	37	21	26	32	116
Charlotte	26	31	26	26	109

Turnovers: Phil. 14 (Barkley, Anderson 3); Char. 10 (Rambis, Chapman 3).
3-Pointers: Phil. 2-9 (Barkley 1-5, Hawkins 1-3, Brooks 0-1); Char. 1-4 (Tripucka 0-1, Chapman 1-2, Holton 0-1).
Technical Fouls: Char. 2 (Bench, Cureton); Phil. 1 (Illegal defense).
Officials: Rooney, Rush, Toliver.
Attendance: 23,388.

JAN. 16, 1989 — AT PHILADELPHIA

CHARLOTTE HORNETS (127)

Player	MP	FG	FT	R	A	PF	S	TP
Tripucka	40	16-25	7-9	4	2	3	0	40
Rambis	38	5-7	0-0	6	2	4	1	10
Cureton	32	3-9	1-3	17	3	2	2	7
Holton	24	3-6	0-0	0	10	1	0	6
Reid	27	5-14	8-8	3	2	2	1	18
Chapman	39	11-26	2-2	6	2	2	1	25
Hoppen	24	3-3	3-3	6	2	4	0	9
Kempton	12	1-2	2-2	6	1	0	0	4
Bogues	29	4-7	0-0	3	14	0	2	8
TOTALS	265	51-99	23-27	51	38	18	7	127

PHILADELPHIA 76ERS (122)

Player	MP	FG	FT	R	A	PF	S	TP
Jones	13	1-2	0-0	0	2	1	0	2
Barkley	34	6-14	4-6	11	6	4	0	16
Gminski	42	11-20	3-3	17	4	2	2	25
Cheeks	42	6-12	2-3	4	8	2	1	14
Hawkins	42	6-14	6-6	3	5	3	1	19
Anderson	40	8-19	0-0	3	2	3	1	16
Coleman	17	5-8	2-2	3	0	2	0	12
Welp	11	2-3	0-0	3	0	3	0	4
Henderson	11	2-4	2-2	0	1	1	0	7
Brooks	11	2-3	0-0	0	2	0	0	6
Thornton	2	0-0	1-2	1	0	1	0	1
TOTALS	265	49-99	20-24	45	30	22	5	122

Charlotte	33	32	18	27	17	127
Philadelphia	27	33	31	19	12	127

Turnovers: Char. 12 (Tripucka 4); Phil. 13 (Gminski, Cheeks 3).
3-Pointers: Char. 2-3 (Tripucka 1-1, Chapman 1-2); Phil. 4-12 (Barkley 0-2, Gminski 0-1, Hawkins 1-3, Welp 0-1, Henderson 1-2, Brooks 2-3).
Technical Fouls: Phil. 1 (Barkley).
Officials: Strom, Durham, Thompson.
Attendance: 10,116.

JAN. 18, 1989 — AT MILWAUKEE

CHARLOTTE HORNETS (106)

Player	MP	FG	FT	R	A	PF	S	TP
Cureton	32	4-9	0-0	7	3	3	0	8
Tripucka	30	9-14	1-1	3	4	2	1	20
Rambis	24	4-7	0-0	6	2	1	0	8
Holton	23	2-3	0-0	0	7	3	0	4
Reid	27	9-14	0-0	3	4	2	0	20
Chapman	26	6-11	2-2	3	2	2	0	15
Hoppen	24	3-5	4-5	2	2	3	1	10
Bogues	11	2-3	1-2	1	6	2	3	5
Kempton	16	2-3	2-2	4	1	4	0	6
Green	14	2-4	0-0	1	3	3	0	4
Lewis	7	0-1	2-2	1	0	0	0	2
Curry	6	2-6	0-0	0	0	0	2	4
TOTALS	240	45-80	12-14	31	34	25	7	106

MILWAUKEE BUCKS (118)

Player	MP	FG	FT	R	A	PF	S	TP
Cummings	35	11-22	4-4	8	0	3	0	26
Roberts	29	5-10	2-2	3	3	2	0	12
Sikma	33	7-12	0-1	10	8	4	1	14
Humphries	34	1-4	5-6	1	9	1	4	7
Pressey	34	5-10	5-8	5	6	3	4	15
Pierce	25	8-9	2-4	2	1	1	1	18
Mokeski	13	2-2	4-4	2	0	3	1	8
Davis	27	7-13	3-4	3	2	4	1	17
Horford	6	0-1	1-2	0	1	0	0	1
Turner	4	0-1	0-0	1	0	1	1	0
TOTALS	240	46-84	26-35	35	30	22	13	118

Charlotte	31	26	26	23	106
Milwaukee	24	35	36	23	118

Turnovers: Char. 27 (Tripucka 8); Mil. 18 (Roberts, Humphries, Pressey, Turner 3).
3-Pointers: Char. 4-7 (Tripucka 1-2, Reid 2-2, Chapman 1-2, Curry 0-1); Mil. 0-4 (Roberts 0-1, Sikma 0-1, Humphries 0-1, Davis 0-1).
Technical Fouls: Char. 1 (Kempton); Mil. 1 (Sikma).
Officials: O'Donnell, Nunez, Grillo.
Attendance: 16,145.

JAN. 19, 1989 — AT CHARLOTTE

PHOENIX SUNS (126)

Player	MP	FG	FT	R	A	PF	S	TP
Chambers	36	10-22	11-12	13	3	2	1	31
Gilliam	23	2-7	0-0	3	0	1	0	4
Perry	24	5-9	1-2	8	0	2	0	11
Johnson, K.	40	4-10	2-2	8	12	2	1	10
Hornacek	42	11-15	6-6	5	6	2	0	28
Johnson, E.	31	10-22	4-5	4	3	4	0	24
Corbin	12	0-2	0-0	1	0	0	0	0
West	19	5-6	3-4	7	0	5	0	13
Nealy	7	0-0	2-2	1	0	2	0	2
Dunn	6	1-1	1-1	0	0	2	0	3
TOTALS	240	48-94	30-34	50	24	22	2	126

CHARLOTTE HORNETS (112)

Player	MP	FG	FT	R	A	PF	S	TP
Tripucka	35	12-26	2-2	5	3	3	1	27
Rambis	40	7-13	5-6	16	4	4	3	19
Cureton	33	5-11	2-4	9	3	4	1	12
Holton	33	6-15	3-4	2	2	3	1	15
Reid	24	5-10	3-3	7	1	4	1	14
Chapman	37	5-19	6-6	3	4	4	2	16
Kempton	13	1-3	3-6	2	1	3	0	5
Bogues	15	1-4	0-0	0	5	0	0	2
Hoppen	8	1-3	0-0	3	1	1	0	2
Green	2	0-1	0-0	0	0	0	0	0
TOTALS	240	43-105	24-31	47	24	26	9	112

Phoenix	32	31	33	30	126
Charlotte	26	30	31	25	112

Turnovers: Pho. 13 (Gilliam 3); Char. 8 (Rambis 3).
3-Pointers: Pho. 0-1 (E. Johnson 0-1); Char. 2-10 (Tripucka 1-3; Holton 0-2; Reid 1-1; Chapman 0-4).
Technical Fouls: None.
Officials: Evans, Salvatore, Mauer.
Attendance: 23,388.

JAN. 21, 1989 — AT ATLANTA

CHARLOTTE HORNETS (113)

Player	MP	FG	FT	R	A	PF	S	TP
Rambis	27	6-9	2-2	3	4	3	0	14
Reid	35	11-19	4-4	3	1	4	2	26
Cureton	31	6-7	3-4	5	2	2	1	15
Chapman	37	10-19	2-2	6	5	3	4	22
Holton	24	2-5	3-4	1	10	4	0	7
Lewis	9	1-2	0-0	2	0	1	0	2
Hoppen	24	3-5	1-2	4	1	6	0	7
Bogues	20	3-4	0-0	0	7	2	2	6
Curry	15	4-10	0-0	0	2	3	1	8
Kempton	14	2-3	2-2	1	1	2	0	6
Green	4	0-2	0-0	0	2	1	0	0
TOTALS	240	48-85	17-20	25	35	31	10	113

ATLANTA HAWKS (137)

Player	MP	FG	FT	R	A	PF	S	TP
Levingston	30	7-9	4-8	9	0	2	0	18
Wilkins	36	10-19	1-2	4	3	2	3	21
Malone	31	7-10	7-8	12	2	1	0	21
Rivers	31	2-4	6-7	3	13	3	2	11
Theus	22	6-10	8-8	3	4	4	0	20
Battle	26	7-12	0-0	2	7	0	0	14
Webb	17	3-3	4-4	1	2	1	1	10
Carr	22	5-9	2-4	6	2	1	0	12
Koncak	14	1-1	0-0	4	0	0	0	2
Ferrell	8	1-3	2-3	1	0	2	0	4
Tolbert	3	1-2	2-2	1	0	1	0	4
TOTALS	240	50-82	36-46	46	33	17	6	137

Charlotte	34	22	29	28	113
Atlanta	33	34	34	36	137

Turnovers: Char. 15 (Reid, Cureton 3); Atl. 17 (Malone, Theus 5).
3-Pointers: Char. 0-6 (Reid 0-2, Chapman 0-2, Curry 0-1, Green 0-1); Atl. 1-4 (Rivers 1-1, Battle 0-3).
Technical Fouls: None.
Officials: Bavetta, Reichelt, Wood.
Attendance: 16,371.

JAN. 24, 1989 — AT PHOENIX

CHARLOTTE HORNETS (103)

Player	MP	FG	FT	R	A	PF	S	TP
Rambis	37	4-13	3-4	14	3	1	5	11
Reid	23	10-18	0-0	3	0	4	1	21
Cureton	28	1-3	2-4	10	1	5	0	4
Chapman	33	10-22	2-2	4	3	3	1	23
Holton	24	3-8	4-4	1	2	1	0	10
Kempton	30	1-5	5-6	7	3	3	0	7
Lewis	23	2-8	2-2	6	2	1	1	6
Bogues	24	2-8	1-2	5	7	2	0	5
Curry	18	6-9	3-3	0	1	2	0	16
TOTALS	240	39-94	22-27	50	22	22	8	103

PHOENIX SUNS (106)

Player	MP	FG	FT	R	A	PF	S	TP
Gilliam	29	4-11	0-0	5	2	1	0	8
Perry	9	2-4	1-2	3	0	0	0	5
Chambers	44	8-20	9-10	8	7	2	0	25
Hornacek	38	6-8	2-4	2	3	1	4	14
Johnson, K.	44	5-9	1-2	4	10	3	2	11
West	17	2-3	0-0	3	1	5	0	4
Johnson, E.	37	10-18	9-10	10	3	3	2	31
Corbin	17	4-8	0-0	6	0	4	0	8
Dunn	5	0-0	0-0	2	0	0	0	0
TOTALS	240	41-81	22-28	43	26	19	8	106

Charlotte	23	28	24	28	103
Phoenix	26	24	31	25	106

Turnovers: Char. 15 (Chapman 4); Pho. 14 (K. Johnson 5).
3-Pointers: Char. 3-8 (Reid 1-3, Chapman 1-4, Curry 1-1); Pho. 2-3 (Chambers 0-1, E. Johnson 2-2).
Technical Fouls: Pho. 1 (Coach Fitzsimmons).
Officials: Madden, Borgia, Forte.
Attendance: 11,089

JAN. 26, 1989 AT SALT LAKE CITY

CHARLOTTE HORNETS (89)

Player	MP	FG	FT	R	A	PF	S	TP
Rambis	26	4-9	0-0	15	3	3	1	8
Reid	24	8-19	2-3	3	1	4	1	18
Cureton	38	3-8	1-2	11	2	2	0	7
Chapman	27	8-19	1-1	6	2	1	1	18
Holton	36	3-7	2-2	5	6	3	1	8
Bogues	7	0-1	0-0	1	1	0	0	0
Kempton	25	1-6	4-4	3	4	3	0	6
Lewis	1	0-0	0-0	1	0	0	0	0
Curry	21	3-10	0-0	4	0	0	0	6
Tripucka	24	4-11	8-8	5	1	1	1	16
Green	5	0-1	0-0	0	1	1	0	0
Hoppen	6	1-3	0-1	4	2	2	0	2
TOTALS	240	35-94	18-21	58	23	20	5	89

UTAH JAZZ (88)

Player	MP	FG	FT	R	A	PF	S	TP
Malone	39	9-28	7-11	12	0	4	0	25
Iavaroni	14	2-3	0-0	3	0	0	1	4
Eaton	30	7-10	1-1	11	0	2	0	15
Stockton	39	2-12	0-0	6	16	2	4	4
Griffith	36	7-15	1-1	5	0	2	3	18
Bailey	37	5-16	6-8	7	2	2	0	16
Farmer	12	0-2	0-0	2	3	1	0	0
Les	9	0-2	0-0	1	2	1	0	0
Brown	13	1-4	0-0	3	0	2	0	2
Leckner	11	1-1	2-2	3	0	4	0	4
TOTALS	240	34-93	17-23	53	23	20	8	88

Charlotte	19	23	26	21	89
Utah	20	35	13	20	88

Turnovers: Char. 18 (Holton 5); Utah 14 (Malone 4).
3-Pointers: Char. 1-5 (Reid 0-1, Chapman 1-3, Curry 0-1); Utah 3-6 (Griffith 3-6).
Technical Fouls: Utah 1 (Malone).
Officials: Alexander, Mathis, Fine.
Attendance: 12,444.

JAN. 27, 1989 AT LOS ANGELES

CHARLOTTE HORNETS (97)

Player	MP	FG	FT	R	A	PF	S	TP
Rambis	32	8-14	3-4	9	2	2	1	19
Reid	21	4-14	0-0	3	4	2	1	8
Cureton	26	3-11	0-0	13	4	3	0	6
Chapman	28	6-15	0-0	2	4	1	0	12
Holton	23	7-10	1-1	1	5	2	2	15
Tripucka	25	4-10	4-6	1	3	2	0	12
Kempton	25	5-8	0-0	6	5	5	2	10
Curry	23	4-9	1-2	3	0	1	0	9
Green	13	1-4	0-0	1	3	0	1	2
Hoppen	6	1-3	0-0	2	0	2	0	2
Bogues	9	0-1	0-0	0	2	2	0	0
Lewis	9	1-2	0-0	1	1	1	1	2
TOTALS	240	44-101	9-13	42	33	23	8	97

LOS ANGELES LAKERS (114)

Player	MP	FG	FT	R	A	PF	S	TP
Green	31	11-15	2-3	11	1	3	1	24
Worthy	39	6-13	1-1	4	5	1	0	13
Abdul-Jabbar	23	9-13	1-1	6	1	3	0	19
Cooper	29	5-10	0-0	4	10	0	1	11
Johnson	31	4-14	4-5	10	10	0	2	12
Thompson	19	2-5	2-4	2	1	1	0	6
Woolridge	22	3-8	3-4	5	2	2	0	9
Campbell	17	7-10	1-1	3	0	2	3	15
Rivers	22	1-6	0-0	2	4	1	1	2
McNamara	4	0-1	1-2	2	1	0	0	1
Lamp	3	1-1	0-0	1	0	1	0	2
TOTALS	240	49-96	15-21	50	35	14	8	114

Charlotte	23	19	37	18	97
Los Angeles	32	24	39	19	114

Turnovers: Char. 15 (Tripucka 4); L.A. 14 (Johnson 3).
3-Pointers: Char. 0-4 (Reid 0-1, Curry 0-2, Green 0-1); L.A. 1-3 (Cooper 1-2, Johnson (0-1).
Technical Fouls: None.
Officials: Mihalak, Salvatore, Mauer.
Attendance: 17,505.

JAN. 30, 1989 AT PORTLAND

CHARLOTTE HORNETS (118)

Player	MP	FG	FT	R	A	PF	S	TP
Rambis	33	3-11	2-2	10	5	5	2	8
Reid	20	6-12	2-2	2	0	2	0	14
Cureton	24	2-4	4-4	2	4	5	0	8
Chapman	34	7-15	0-0	3	2	3	4	16
Holton	30	9-16	3-4	4	4	4	1	22
Tripucka	33	10-22	6-8	3	2	2	0	26
Kempton	24	3-6	6-9	8	1	5	0	12
Bogues	18	1-2	0-2	0	6	2	2	2
Curry	10	2-10	0-0	5	2	0	1	4
Hoppen	14	2-3	2-2	4	0	1	0	6
TOTALS	240	45-101	25-33	41	26	29	10	118

PORTLAND TRAIL BLAZERS (130)

Player	MP	FG	FT	R	A	PF	S	TP
Kersey	29	5-8	4-6	4	4	2	1	14
Jones	15	2-3	1-1	7	1	2	1	5
Duckworth	34	6-17	7-9	9	0	2	1	19
Drexler	35	13-19	6-7	6	4	3	2	32
Porter	34	5-8	7-7	8	10	3	1	17
Johnson	21	5-12	4-5	6	0	5	1	14
Sichting	21	4-6	0-0	3	4	1	0	8
Bryant	20	4-8	0-0	7	1	5	0	8
Branch	6	1-4	1-2	1	0	2	3	3
Vandeweghe	19	4-11	0-0	3	4	1	0	8
Anderson	6	1-2	0-0	0	0	1	0	2
TOTALS	240	50-98	30-37	54	28	27	10	130

Charlotte	31	35	22	30	118
Portland	40	28	36	26	130

Turnovers: Char. 14 (Reid, Tripucka, Bogues 3); Port. 18 (Kersey, Porter 4).
3-Pointers: Char. 3-6 (Chapman 2-3, Holton 1-1 Tripucka 0-1, Bogues 0-1); Port. 0-2 (Kersey 0-1, Vandeweghe 0-1).
Technical Fouls: Port. 1 (Illegal defense).
Officials: Oakes, Crawford, Benson.
Attendance: 12,848.

FEB. 1, 1989 AT CHARLOTTE

BOSTON CELTICS (107)

Player	MP	FG	FT	R	A	PF	S	TP
McHale	30	6-12	9-10	8	1	5	0	21
Lewis	33	6-17	2-2	7	4	4	2	14
Parish	39	11-18	2-3	24	2	4	2	24
Johnson	15	0-1	0-0	2	2	1	0	0
Shaw	34	6-14	1-4	11	6	3	1	13
Ainge	28	5-13	1-2	2	5	2	0	12
Paxson	28	5-11	7-8	2	2	0	0	17
Lohaus	9	0-3	0-0	2	0	1	1	0
Acres	17	1-2	0-0	3	0	3	0	2
Rivas	1	1-1	0-0	0	0	1	0	2
Gamble	3	1-2	0-0	0-0	0	0	0	2
Grandison	3	0-1	0-0	0	0	0	0	0
TOTALS	240	42-95	22-29	61	22	24	6	107

CHARLOTTE HORNETS (94)

Player	MP	FG	FT	R	A	PF	S	TP
Tripucka	29	3-13	10-10	3	0	4	1	16
Rambis	31	0-4	3-4	8	1	2	3	3
Cureton	31	1-4	2-4	15	0	4	0	4
Chapman	31	5-18	3-4	2	1	0	0	13
Holton	30	8-11	5-7	4	5	2	0	21
Kempton	13	1-2	1-3	1	0	2	0	3
Reid	20	4-15	3-4	6	2	2	1	11
Hoppen	21	4-5	1-2	5	0	3	0	9
Bogues	18	2-5	0-0	1	5	2	4	4
Curry	13	5-10	0-0	2	0	0	0	10
Lewis	3	0-1	0-0	0-0	0	0	1	0
TOTALS	240	33-88	28-38	47	14	21	10	94

Boston	31	27	24	25	107
Charlotte	24	25	21	24	94

Turnovers: Boston 18 (Shaw 4); Char. 13 (Cureton 3).
3-Pointers: Boston 1-6 (Ainge 1-5, Lohaus 0-1); Char. 0-2 (Chapman 0-1, Curry 0-1).
Technical Fouls: Boston 2 (Bench, McHale).
Officials: Bavetta, Clark, Wood.
Attendance: 23,388.

FEB. 3, 1989 AT CHARLOTTE

SEATTLE SUPERSONICS (106)

Player	MP	FG	FT	R	A	PF	S	TP
McKey	42	6-12	1-1	6	3	3	1	13
Cage	27	6-13	2-2	10	1	1	1	14
Lister	17	2-5	4-4	5	1	5	0	8
Ellis	42	9-24	9-10	5	1	0	1	27
McMillan	30	1-5	5-5	8	8	4	4	7
McDaniel	24	8-14	2-2	4	2	3	2	18
Lucas	8	0-1	0-0	1	1	0	3	0
Polynice	3	0-0	0-0	0	0	0	0	0
Reynolds	24	5-9	4-4	4	2	1	2	14
Johnson	13	1-2	0-0	1	3	0	0	2
Schoene	10	1-3	0-0	1	1	1	0	3
TOTALS	240	39-88	27-28	45	23	18	14	106

CHARLOTTE HORNETS (108)

Player	MP	FG	FT	R	A	PF	S	TP
Rambis	34	6-9	3-5	13	2	6	0	15
Reid	36	12-22	4-4	4	3	5	3	28
Cureton	42	4-8	3-3	11	3	4	0	11
Chapman	40	7-21	6-6	2	2	1	2	23
Holton	20	2-9	0-0	3	4	3	0	4
Green	5	0-2	0-0	0	2	0	0	0
Kempton	12	3-6	0-0	3	3	1	1	6
Bogues	23	1-2	0-0	2	10	3	1	2
Lewis	17	5-6	0-1	1	0	2	0	10
Curry	8	3-5	0-0	2	0	0	0	6
Hoppen	3	1-1	1-1	1	0	1	1	3
TOTALS	240	44-91	17-20	42	29	26	8	108

Seattle	25	34	27	20	106
Charlotte	29	26	25	28	108

Turnovers: Sea. 21 (McDaniel 7); Char. 18 (Rambis 5).
3-Pointers: Sea. 1-7 (McKey 0-1, Cage 0-1, Ellis 0-3, Lucas 0-1, Schoene 1-1); Char. 3-9 (Reid 0-1, Chapman 3-8).
Technical Fouls: None.
Officials: Garretson, Reichelt, Vaden.
Attendance: 23,388.

FEB. 5, 1989 AT CHARLOTTE

CLEVELAND CAVALIERS (110)

Player	MP	FG	FT	R	A	PF	S	TP
Sanders	29	4-10	2-2	4	0	2	2	10
Williams	39	5-12	2-2	10	4	2	0	12
Daugherty	33	9-14	5-7	9	6	1	0	23
Harper	35	10-13	4-5	6	8	2	1	25
Price	32	9-15	0-0	3	5	1	0	20
Ehlo	23	2-6	3-5	5	4	3	0	7
Valentine	16	1-7	3-4	0	0	1	1	5
Dudley	13	1-2	0-2	4	0	2	0	2
Hubbard	6	0-1	0-0	1	0	1	0	0
Keys	9	2-6	0-0	3	0	0	0	4
Rollins	5	1-3	0-0	1	0	0	1	2
TOTALS	240	44-89	19-27	46	27	15	5	110

CHARLOTTE HORNETS (91)

Player	MP	FG	FT	R	A	PF	S	TP
Rambis	28	8-12	0-0	8	2	2	0	16
Reid	22	6-14	0-0	0	2	2	1	13
Cureton	33	2-3	0-0	7	1	4	1	4
Chapman	27	4-12	1-2	2	2	0	1	9
Holton	18	1-3	0-0	0	4	1	0	2
Tripucka	22	5-13	4-6	4	5	3	0	14
Kempton	12	1-2	0-0	2	0	1	0	2
Bogues	30	2-5	1-2	7	9	4	2	5
Curry	20	5-12	2-2	2	3	2	0	12
Hoppen	18	4-4	0-0	7	0	3	0	8
Lewis	5	0-1	0-0	1	0	0	0	0
Green	5	3-6	0-0	0	0	0	1	6
TOTALS	240	41-87	8-12	40	28	22	6	91

Cleveland	33	21	35	21	110
Charlotte	22	21	20	28	91

Turnovers: Cle. 13 (Daugherty 3); Char. 16 (Hoppen 5).
3-Pointers: Cle. 3-6 (Harper 1-2, Price 2-3, Ehlo 0-1); Char. 1-5 (Reid 1-2, Tripucka 0-1 Chapman 0-1, Curry 0-1).
Technical Fouls: None.
Officials: Mathis, Alexander, Hunter.
Attendance: 23,388.

FEB. 7, 1989 AT CHICAGO

CHARLOTTE HORNETS (93)

Player	MP	FG	FT	R	A	PF	S	TP
Reid	17	2-9	0-0	1	2	1	0	4
Rambis	27	4-6	2-2	10	1	1	0	10
Cureton	31	3-4	0-0	2	1	3	2	6
Chapman	27	3-11	2-2	2	0	1	0	8
Holton	26	2-5	7-8	1	7	1	0	11
Tripucka	30	8-15	11-14	1	3	0	1	27
Kempton	23	1-5	3-4	5	0	5	0	5
Bogues	16	2-2	0-0	1	6	0	2	4
Curry	16	2-9	0-0	2	1	2	1	4
Hoppen	15	3-7	2-2	8	1	4	1	8
Green	8	1-2	2-2	1	2	0	1	4
Lewis	4	1-2	0-0	1	0	0	1	2
TOTALS	240	32-77	29-34	35	24	18	9	93

CHICAGO BULLS (118)

Player	MP	FG	FT	R	A	PF	S	TP
Pippen	32	8-9	1-3	7	3	4	7	17
Grant	37	6-10	0-0	12	5	2	2	12
Cartwright	21	4-8	3-4	9	1	3	0	11
Vincent	18	0-4	2-2	1	3	1	0	2
Jordan	32	11-20	9-10	7	5	3	2	32
Hodges	26	5-14	0-0	1	2	2	3	10
Paxson	26	2-4	0-0	2	9	0	0	5
Corzine	20	5-6	2-2	6	0	1	0	12
Sellers	10	2-5	2-2	1	0	1	1	6
Davis	4	3-5	0-0	3	0	1	1	6
Haley	7	1-3	3-4	1	0	4	0	5
Perdue	7	0-3	0-0	1	2	1	1	0
TOTALS	240	47-91	22-27	51	30	23	17	118

Charlotte	21	29	19	24	93
Chicago	29	31	29	29	118

Turnovers: Char. 20 (Tripucka 5); Chi. 19 (Jordan 3).
3-Pointers: Char. 0-3 (Chapman 0-2, Reid 0-1); Chi. 2-9 (Jordan 1-2, Hodges 0-3, Paxson 1-2, Davis 0-2).
Technical Fouls: None.
Officials: Nies, Rush, Benson.
Attendance: 17,385.

FEB. 9, 1989 AT CHARLOTTE

ATLANTA HAWKS (108)

Player	MP	FG	FT	R	A	PF	S	TP
Malone	38	6-14	6-7	13	1	3	0	18
Wilkins	38	11-28	1-1	9	2	4	0	23
Koncak	28	2-6	0-0	8	0	5	2	4
Theus	36	5-14	10-10	3	7	4	2	20
Rivers	24	5-11	3-5	4	2	6	4	13
Carr	13	2-4	0-0	3	3	1	1	4
Webb	19	1-1	1-1	2	4	2	0	3
Ferrell	9	1-2	1-2	2	0	1	0	3
Battle	21	5-9	4-6	0	1	4	0	14
Tolbert	14	3-4	0-0	4	0	2	0	6
TOTALS	240	41-93	26-32	48	20	32	9	108

CHARLOTTE HORNETS (110)

Player	MP	FG	FT	R	A	PF	S	TP
Tripucka	31	7-15	7-9	5	4	2	0	21
Rambis	29	6-11	4-5	4	1	3	1	16
Cureton	42	6-8	0-0	15	4	4	1	12
Chapman	35	5-17	5-6	1	3	2	2	15
Holton	29	4-8	0-0	0	5	3	1	8
Kempton	25	2-5	2-3	6	0	3	0	6
Reid	30	14-23	0-2	9	3	4	1	28
Bogues	19	2-4	0-0	2	10	4	2	4
TOTALS	240	46-91	18-25	42	30	25	8	110

Atlanta	23	26	34	25	108
Charlotte	22	23	33	32	110

Turnovers: Atl. 20 (Malone 5); Char. 17 (Tripucka 5).
3-Pointers: Atl. 0-1 (Wilkins 0-1); Char. 0-4 (Chapman 0-2, Holton 0-1, Reid 0-1).
Technical Fouls: Char. 3 (Illegal defense, Coach Harter, Kempton).
Officials: Mihalak, Rooney, Bernhardt.
Attendance: 23,388.

FEB. 14, 1989 AT CHARLOTTE

NEW YORK KNICKS (129)

Player	MP	FG	FT	R	A	PF	S	TP
Newman	31	8-14	5-5	3	3	3	3	22
Oakley	29	8-17	2-4	6	2	2	0	18
Ewing	34	6-10	2-4	13	7	5	2	14
Tucker	29	5-6	0-0	2	4	3	0	13
Jackson	31	3-8	1-2	2	11	3	3	7
Green	18	3-4	2-2	1	0	2	0	8
Wilkins, G.	25	9-15	2-2	5	4	1	0	20
Strickland	16	5-7	4-4	1	3	1	0	14
Walker	10	1-2	0-0	0	0	0	0	2
Wilkins, E.	17	5-7	1-1	6	0	1	0	11
TOTALS	240	53-90	19-24	39	34	21	8	129

CHARLOTTE HORNETS (117)

Player	MP	FG	FT	R	A	PF	S	TP
Tripucka	35	9-16	12-12	3	2	1	0	31
Rambis	38	7-13	3-3	10	3	4	0	17
Cureton	34	4-9	2-6	6	5	5	1	10
Chapman	40	10-20	2-2	3	0	1	0	23
Holton	28	1-6	2-2	0	9	1	2	4
Kempton	18	2-6	1-2	4	2	5	2	5
Reid	21	5-11	6-8	0	0	3	0	17
Bogues	20	3-5	0-0	3	8	1	1	6
Hoppen	6	2-2	0-0	4	0	1	0	4
TOTALS	240	43-88	28-35	33	29	22	6	117

New York	28	30	39	32	129
Charlotte	26	29	31	31	117

Turnovers: N.Y. 13 (Newman, Ewing 3); Char. 12 (Tripucka 5).

3-Pointers: N.Y. 4-10 (Newman 1-3, Tucker 3-3, Jackson 0-2, G. Wilkins 0-1, Strickland 0-1); Char. 3-7 (Tripucka 1-3, Chapman 1-3, Reid 1-1).

Technical Fouls: N.Y. 3 (Coach Pitino, Oakley, Ewing); Char. 1 (Tripucka).

Officials: Kersey, Salvatore, Rush.

Attendance: 23,388.

FEB. 17, 1989 AT MIAMI

CHARLOTTE HORNETS (102)

Player	MP	FG	FT	R	A	PF	S	TP
Rambis	31	2-6	0-0	2	0	4	0	4
Tripucka	36	12-25	7-9	5	1	2	1	31
Cureton	37	3-6	3-5	16	3	5	0	9
Chapman	34	7-15	2-3	2	4	3	1	16
Holton	28	3-10	2-2	3	9	3	1	9
Kempton	19	3-4	0-0	2	2	3	1	6
Reid	26	7-14	3-3	4	0	1	2	17
Bogues	20	1-5	0-0	2	7	0	1	2
Hoppen	9	3-5	2-2	6	0	3	0	8
TOTALS	240	41-90	19-24	42	26	24	7	102

MIAMI HEAT (103)

Player	MP	FG	FT	R	A	PF	S	TP
Long	45	4-10	4-5	11	0	2	1	12
Thompson	26	8-11	1-2	5	2	4	1	17
Cummings	12	2-4	0-0	8	1	4	0	4
Edwards	38	9-21	1-3	6	9	4	1	19
Sparrow	35	6-14	0-0	3	6	2	2	13
Sundvold	28	9-18	2-3	2	1	0	0	20
Washington	19	3-3	1-1	3	7	0	0	7
Hastings	27	1-4	4-4	2	1	4	0	6
Seikaly	10	2-4	1-1	3	0	2	0	5
TOTALS	240	44-89	14-19	43	27	22	5	103

Charlotte	28	24	25	25	102
Miami	32	23	24	24	103

Turnovers: Char. 13 (Tripucka, Holton 3); Miami 15 (Washington 5).

3-Pointers: Char. 1-3 (Tripucka 0-1, Holton 1-1, Chapman 0-1); Miami 1-2 (Sparrow 1-1, Sundvold 0-1).

Technical Fouls: Char. 1 (Reid); Miami 1 (Cummings).

Officials: Madden, Fryer, Huetter.

Attendance: 15,008.

FEB. 18, 1989 AT CHARLOTTE

INDIANA PACERS (114)

Player	MP	FG	FT	R	A	PF	S	TP
Tisdale	41	8-14	5-6	12	2	4	2	21
Person	42	9-15	2-5	6	3	6	3	20
Smits	40	4-11	2-2	6	1	4	0	10
Fleming	28	3-4	5-10	6	12	3	1	11
Miller	38	11-15	8-8	3	0	4	0	32
Gray	8	0-2	0-0	3	1	1	0	0
Skiles	25	6-10	0-0	2	8	1	0	12
Long	12	3-7	2-2	0	1	1	2	8
Dreiling	5	0-0	0-0	0	1	2	0	0
Stephens	1	0-0	0-0	0	0	0	0	0
TOTALS	240	44-78	24-33	38	29	26	8	114

CHARLOTTE HORNETS (119)

Player	MP	FG	FT	R	A	PF	S	TP
Tripucka	35	11-20	8-8	1	2	2	2	30
Rambis	33	4-12	5-6	20	5	1	2	13
Cureton	28	1-7	0-0	4	1	3	0	2
Chapman	39	12-25	2-2	3	5	3	3	27
Holton	24	3-9	2-2	2	10	2	1	8
Reid	22	5-11	4-4	0	2	3	0	14
Kempton	17	3-5	1-1	4	2	2	0	7
Hoppen	18	1-2	4-4	7	1	3	0	6
Bogues	24	4-5	4-4	0	8	4	3	12
TOTALS	240	44-96	30-31	41	36	23	11	119

Indiana	29	21	29	35	114
Charlotte	23	33	31	32	119

Turnovers: Ind. 18 (Person 4); Char. 11 (Tripucka 4).

3-Pointers: Ind. 2-5 (Person 0-1, Smits 0-1, Miller 2-3); Char. 1-8 (Tripucka 0-1, Chapman 1-7).

Technical Fouls: Ind. 1 (Skiles).

Officials: Rush, Garretson, Kinsey.

Attendance: 23,388.

FEB. 22, 1989 AT CHARLOTTE

CHICAGO BULLS (130)

Player	MP	FG	FT	R	A	PF	S	TP
Pippen	31	7-12	3-5	4	6	3	2	17
Grant	30	9-13	2-3	10	1	0	1	20
Corzine	33	6-6	7-7	7	4	4	1	19
Vincent	25	6-9	0-0	4	8	2	1	12
Jordan	37	10-14	4-5	4	5	4	1	24
Hodges	22	6-7	4-4	3	6	2	0	17
Perdue	11	0-3	0-0	2	0	3	0	0
Sellers	22	2-4	3-3	1	1	2	0	7
Paxson	23	4-5	1-1	1	5	3	0	10
Haley	3	0-1	0-0	1	0	1	0	0
Davis	3	2-2	0-0	1	0	0	0	4
TOTALS	240	52-76	24-28	38	36	24	6	130

CHARLOTTE HORNETS (102)

Player	MP	FG	FT	R	A	PF	S	TP
Tripucka	26	5-14	8-11	4	3	3	1	18
Rambis	22	5-6	1-1	3	1	3	0	11
Cureton	28	3-8	0-0	2	1	3	1	6
Chapman	36	10-22	1-1	2	5	0	2	22
Holton	17	2-2	0-0	1	7	3	0	4
Kempton	17	1-4	2-4	6	0	2	0	4
Bogues	31	0-3	2-4	6	7	1	1	2
Reid	22	6-12	3-4	2	1	4	0	17
Hoppen	18	4-5	0-0	2	0	2	0	8
Rowsom	11	3-3	2-4	1	1	0	1	8
Lewis	5	0-1	0-0	0	0	1	0	0
Curry	7	0-2	2-2	0	1	0	0	2
TOTALS	240	39-82	21-31	29	27	22	6	102

Chicago	42	29	37	22	130
Charlotte	21	28	33	30	102

Turnovers: Chi. 17 (Jordan 6); Char. 13 (Tripucka, Kempton 3).

3-Pointers: Chi. 2-4 (Jordan 0-1, Hodges 2-4, Paxson 1-1; Char. 3-4 (Chapman 1-1, Reid 2-2, Curry 0-1).

Technical Fouls: None.

Officials: Capers, Clark, Hollins.

Attendance: 23,388.

FEB. 23, 1989 AT NEW YORK

CHARLOTTE HORNETS (114)

Player	MP	FG	FT	R	A	PF	S	TP
Rambis	27	4-9	5-7	7	3	3	1	13
Tripucka	23	6-9	3-5	2	1	2	1	15
Cureton	12	1-2	0-0	2	0	1	0	2
Chapman	19	2-9	0-0	4	2	0	0	4
Holton	26	3-8	3-3	1	6	2	1	9
Kempton	19	6-11	0-1	4	2	4	0	12
Reid	25	4-13	5-5	2	2	2	0	13
Bogues	22	1-1	2-2	1	11	1	0	4
Hoppen	17	2-6	1-1	7	1	4	1	5
Rowsom	21	7-14	2-4	6	1	3	0	17
Curry	22	8-13	2-2	2	3	0	3	19
Lewis	7	0-1	1-4	1	0	1	0	1
TOTALS	240	44-96	24-34	39	32	23	7	114

NEW YORK KNICKS (139)

Player	MP	FG	FT	R	A	PF	S	TP
Newman	21	4-7	3-3	1	2	3	0	11
Oakley	25	5-8	5-8	10	5	2	0	15
Ewing	28	12-20	4-5	9	1	3	3	28
Jackson	32	7-10	4-4	3	15	2	7	20
Tuckner	27	5-11	0-0	4	4	1	2	12
Green	20	5-7	4-4	10	1	3	1	14
Wilkins, G.	23	6-11	0-0	3	2	3	1	12
Strickland	23	3-8	5-6	6	5	2	3	11
Walker	21	4-5	1-2	3	0	5	0	10
Wilkins, E.	11	1-5	0-0	2	0	1	1	2
Butler	9	2-7	0-0	0	0	4	0	4
TOTALS	240	54-99	26-32	51	35	29	18	139

Charlotte	28	30	26	30	114
New York	40	37	37	25	139

Turnovers: Char. 24; N.Y. 20.
3-Pointers: Char. 2-6 (Chapman 0-1, Reid 0-2, Rowsom 1-1, Curry 1-2); N.Y. 5-12 (Newman 0-1, Jackson 2-3, Tucker 2-6. G. Wilkins 0-1, Walker 1-1).
Technical Fouls: Char. 2; N.Y. 1.
Officials: O'Donnell, Nunez, Wood.
Attendance: 16,130.

FEB. 25, 1989 AT CHARLOTTE

SAN ANTONIO SPURS (113)

Player	MP	FG	FT	R	A	PF	S	TP
Comegys	32	7-13	7-10	9	0	5	0	21
Anderson, G.	34	5-11	2-2	7	1	4	0	12
Brickowski	21	7-12	0-0	10	1	2	0	14
Maxwell	41	5-19	5-5	2	5	1	1	15
Anderson, W.	43	12-25	4-7	8	5	4	1	28
King	13	1-6	1-2	2	1	2	0	3
Smrek	13	1-2	0-2	4	0	3	0	2
Anderson, M.	31	2-8	7-10	5	5	5	0	11
Roth	12	2-5	3-6	1	1	2	0	7
TOTALS	240	42-101	29-44	48	19	28	2	113

CHARLOTTE HORNETS (124)

Player	MP	FG	FT	R	A	PF	S	TP
Tripucka	38	15-22	10-11	5	9	4	4	40
Rambis	36	5-9	6-8	22	3	3	1	16
Cureton	32	7-11	3-8	12	3	4	1	17
Chapman	37	9-24	2-4	3	3	4	0	21
Holton	28	9-14	0-0	1	9	4	0	18
Reid	21	2-8	0-0	0	1	3	0	4
Kempton	19	1-3	3-4	7	1	4	2	5
Lewis	1	0-0	0-0	0	0	0	0	0
Bogues	19	0-1	0-0	0	11	3	0	0
Rowsom	9	1-2	1-4	5	0	1	0	3
TOTALS	240	49-94	25-39	55	40	30	8	124

San Antonio	29	31	28	25	113
Charlotte	35	18	36	35	124

Turnovers: S.A. 13 (G. Anderson, W. Anderson 3); Char. 15 (Tripucka, Holton 3).
3-Pointers: S.A. 0-3 (Maxwell 0-3); Char. 1-4 (Chapman 1-3, Rambis 0-1).
Technical Fouls: S.A. 1 (Brickowski); Char. 1 (Kempton).
Officials: Middleton, Reichelt, Herring.
Attendance: 23,388.

FEB. 28, 1989 AT CHARLOTTE

BOSTON CELTICS (112)

Player	MP	FG	FT	R	A	PF	S	TP
McHale	25	8-13	5-5	5	1	0	0	21
Lewis	33	11-21	6-7	5	3	1	1	28
Parish	25	7-9	2-3	13	3	2	0	16
Johnson	28	3-7	0-2	0	2	2	2	6
Shaw	32	2-6	0-0	6	10	4	1	4
Paxson	20	0-5	0-0	2	2	1	0	0
Kleine	19	2-5	4-4	6	1	1	0	8
Pinckney	16	3-4	3-4	3	0	1	0	9
Gamble	9	1-3	0-0	1	0	1	1	2
Grandison	22	3-5	9-10	8	1	5	1	15
Acres	7	0-1	0-0	0	1	0	1	0
Rivas	4	1-2	1-2	2	0	1	0	3
TOTALS	240	41-81	30-37	51	24	19	7	112

CHARLOTTE HORNETS (87)

Player	MP	FG	FT	R	A	PF	S	TP
Tripucka	37	8-22	4-4	6	3	3	0	21
Rambis	31	4-10	0-0	12	2	3	5	8
Cureton	19	0-4	0-0	4	1	1	0	0
Chapman	28	4-12	3-4	1	0	3	0	11
Holton	32	8-13	0-0	2	9	2	2	16
Reid	22	4-12	0-0	1	1	2	0	8
Kempton	17	2-5	0-0	3	0	4	0	4
Bogues	16	1-3	0-0	1	6	0	1	2
Rowsom	19	5-5	0-0	5	2	3	2	10
Hoppen	10	1-2	0-0	0	0	2	0	2
Lewis	4	2-2	1-1	0	0	0	0	5
Curry	5	0-4	0-0	1	1	1	0	0
TOTALS	240	39-94	8-9	36	25	24	10	87

Boston	28	31	21	32	112
Charlotte	19	14	24	30	87

Turnovers: Bos. 16; Char. 11.
3-Pointers: Bos. 0-1 (Johnson 0-1); Char. 1-3 (Tripucka 1-2, Chapman 0-1).
Technical Fouls: None.
Officials: Javie, Crawford, Thompson.
Attendance: 23,388.

MAR. 2, 1989 AT E. RUTHERFORD, N.J.

CHARLOTTE HORNETS (103)

Player	MP	FG	FT	R	A	PF	S	TP
Tripucka	41	7-18	12-14	6	7	1	3	26
Rambis	27	3-4	2-2	8	1	2	0	8
Cureton	20	1-4	0-0	7	1	2	0	2
Chapman	33	12-28	1-1	6	1	2	1	27
Holton	21	1-3	0-0	0	5	5	0	2
Bogues	27	4-5	0-0	2	6	3	2	8
Kempton	15	1-3	0-0	3	1	3	0	2
Rowsom	19	4-8	0-0	5	0	3	0	8
Reid	22	3-13	4-6	1	0	3	0	10
Hoppen	15	5-5	0-0	5	0	5	0	10
TOTALS	240	41-91	19-23	43	22	29	6	103

NEW JERSEY NETS (114)

Player	MP	FG	FT	R	A	PF	S	TP
Hinson	39	8-18	5-5	10	1	5	0	21
Morris	41	11-17	8-8	7	2	2	0	31
Carroll	32	10-12	6-8	8	0	4	0	26
Hopson	34	5-21	2-2	2	3	3	1	12
Conner	44	4-10	5-7	13	11	2	6	13
Lee	18	1-3	0-0	6	1	4	1	2
McGee	21	4-9	0-1	0	1	1	0	9
Gaines	4	0-0	0-0	0	0	1	0	0
Jones	2	0-0	0-0	1	0	1	0	0
TOTALS	240	43-90	26-31	47	19	23	8	114

Charlotte	33	32	21	17	103
New Jersey	30	27	27	30	114

Turnovers: Char. 14 (Tripucka 5); N.J. 12 (Conner 5).
3-Pointers: Char. 2-5 (Tripucka 0-2, Chapman 2-2, Reid 0-1); N.J. 2-7 (Morris 1-3, Hopson 0-1, McGee 1-3).
Technical Fouls: None.
Officials: Evans, Delaney, Tolliver.
Attendance: 8,011.

MAR. 3, 1989 AT ATLANTA

CHARLOTTE HORNETS (109)

Player	MP	FG	FT	R	A	PF	S	TP
Cureton	29	8-15	0-0	7	2	0	1	16
Tripucka	24	7-11	4-4	1	3	5	0	18
Hoppen	27	5-8	4-5	6	4	5	1	14
Chapman	27	5-12	0-0	1	1	2	0	11
Holton	17	1-7	4-4	5	1	3	3	6
Kempton	15	1-6	3-4	4	2	5	2	5
Bogues	22	2-5	0-0	2	5	1	2	4
Reid	20	3-4	2-2	2	3	3	0	8
Curry	20	3-7	2-2	3	1	4	1	8
Rowsom	23	2-6	4-5	8	2	3	0	8
Lewis	16	4-8	3-6	5	0	2	0	11
TOTALS	240	41-89	26-32	44	24	33	10	109

ATLANTA HAWKS (133)

Player	MP	FG	FT	R	A	PF	S	TP
Levingston	22	2-5	4-5	2	0	2	0	8
Wilkins	28	16-24	3-4	3	0	0	6	35
Malone	26	6-10	12-14	13	1	3	3	24
Rivers	27	5-5	7-8	4	11	1	5	17
Theus	28	6-11	5-6	1	4	3	2	17
Koncak	17	1-7	0-0	4	1	4	1	2
Battle	11	5-6	1-4	2	2	1	0	11
Webb	21	1-3	0-1	2	5	0	0	2
Carr	23	2-5	3-3	6	2	2	0	7
Ferrell	14	3-6	0-1	3	0	1	1	6
Tolbert	14	1-5	0-0	5	1	4	0	2
Mannion	9	1-3	0-0	1	1	1	1	2
TOTALS	240	49-90	35-46	46	28	22	19	133

Charlotte	29	32	22	26	109
Atlanta	44	33	40	16	133

Turnovers: Char. 26 (Cureton, Bogues 4); Atl. 18 (Levingston, Wilkins, Malone, Tolbert 3).
3-Pointers: Char. 1-4 (Chapman 1-3, Lewis 0-1); Atl. 0-3 (Koncak 0-1, Webb 0-1, Mannion 0-1).
Technical Fouls: Char. 1; Atl. 1.
Officials: O'Donnell, Clark, Olesiak.
Attendance: 16,371.

MAR. 5, 1989 AT LANDOVER, MD.

CHARLOTTE HORNETS (101)

Player	MP	FG	FT	R	A	PF	S	TP
Rambis	31	8-15	5-5	11	0	1	0	21
Tripucka	36	4-13	9-12	1	3	4	4	17
Cureton	36	4-7	0-0	13	4	3	0	8
Chapman	37	9-21	3-4	1	2	2	2	22
Holton	26	4-9	3-4	2	6	2	1	11
Reid	23	2-10	2-2	5	1	3	0	6
Bogues	22	2-6	2-2	0	7	1	0	6
Rowsom	18	2-5	4-4	2	0	2	1	8
Hoppen	7	1-1	0-0	1	0	1	0	2
Kempton	4	0-0	0-0	0	0	2	0	0
TOTALS	240	36-87	28-33	36	23	21	8	101

WASHINGTON BULLETS (114)

Player	MP	FG	FT	R	A	PF	S	TP
Catledge	28	6-12	0-1	8	1	4	1	12
King	30	12-18	3-3	5	3	1	1	27
Jones, C.	19	0-0	0-0	1	1	3	0	0
Malone	33	11-22	12-12	2	5	0	2	34
Walker	25	1-4	0-0	8	4	4	0	2
Eackles	15	4-8	3-3	2	0	2	0	11
Williams	29	1-4	1-2	7	4	2	4	3
Colter	23	3-4	3-3	3	0	4	1	8
Grant	18	2-8	2-4	3	3	3	0	6
Alarie	20	5-9	0-0	7	1	2	0	10
TOTALS	240	45-89	24-28	46	22	25	9	113

Charlotte	27	21	32	21	101
Washington	31	23	28	32	114

Turnovers: Char. 12 (Cureton 4); Wash. 16 (Catledge, King, Walker, Colter 3).
3-Pointers: Char. 1-7 (Rambis 0-1, Tripucka 0-1, Chapman 1-4, Reid 0-1); Wash. 0-0.
Technical Fouls: None.
Officials: Strom, Jones, Borgia.
Attendance: 6,661.

MAR. 8, 1989 AT CHARLOTTE

DENVER NUGGETS (112)

Player	MP	FG	FT	R	A	PF	S	TP
English	35	12-20	7-7	3	8	0	0	31
Schayes	30	4-7	1-1	7	0	5	0	9
Rasmussen	31	9-16	0-0	8	0	1	2	18
Cook	29	2-8	0-0	2	5	5	0	4
Adams	42	7-18	4-6	6	12	0	2	20
Turner	31	4-7	0-0	6	2	2	1	8
Cooper	24	3-7	2-3	12	1	5	1	8
Davis	18	5-12	4-5	3	4	4	2	14
TOTALS	240	46-95	18-22	47	32	22	8	112

CHARLOTTE HORNETS (99)

Player	MP	FG	FT	R	A	PF	S	TP
Tripucka	35	9-20	3-4	4	2	3	0	21
Rambis	37	5-13	6-9	18	5	3	1	16
Cureton	17	0-0	0-0	4	2	2	0	0
Chapman	28	5-16	6-6	0	2	3	0	17
Holton	25	2-7	2-2	4	5	0	0	6
Reid	25	6-14	1-2	5	1	4	0	13
Kempton	11	2-2	0-0	1	0	1	1	4
Bogues	23	2-5	0-0	6	11	1	0	4
Rowsom	6	0-1	0-0	1	0	1	0	0
Hoppen	25	5-9	4-6	8	1	2	0	14
Curry	8	1-2	2-2	0	1	0	1	4
TOTALS	240	37-89	24-31	51	30	20	3	99

Denver	31	24	34	23	112
Charlotte	24	23	29	23	99

Turnovers: Den. 11 (Adams 4); Char. 16 (Rambis, Kempton, Bogues 3).
3-Pointers: Den. 2-6 (Adams 2-6); Char. 1-4 (Chapman 1-2, Reid 0-2).
Technical Fouls: None.
Officials: Vaden, Oakes, Forte.
Attendance: 23,388.

MAR. 10, 1989 AT CHARLOTTE

LOS ANGELES LAKERS (123)

Player	MP	FG	FT	R	A	PF	S	TP
Worthy	32	10-15	0-0	1	1	1	4	20
Green	27	4-7	5-6	15	32	2	2	13
Abdul-Jabbar	25	5-9	0-0	9	1	3	1	10
Scott	29	10-16	2-2	2	2	1	0	25
Johnson	28	7-8	2-3	7	14	1	0	16
Cooper	15	3-6	2-2	0	4	0	1	10
Thompson	16	0-3	2-2	5	1	2	1	2
Campbell	18	5-7	1-2	1	1	2	1	11
Woolridge	21	3-5	1-2	6	2	1	2	7
Lamp	8	1-3	0-0	0	0	0	1	2
Rivers	12	1-3	0-0	1	5	1	1	2
McNamara	9	1-4	3-4	5	0	0	0	5
TOTALS	240	50-86	18-23	52	34	14	14	123

CHARLOTTE HORNETS (90)

Player	MP	FG	FT	R	A	PF	S	TP
Tripucka	28	7-14	3-4	0	1	1	1	17
Rambis	27	1-5	2-2	8	3	1	4	4
Hoppen	22	3-6	0-0	5	0	3	0	6
Chapman	34	7-18	1-2	1	3	2	1	16
Holton	31	6-13	3-3	1	4	3	0	15
Cureton	21	3-5	1-2	4	2	1	3	7
Reid	26	4-14	2-2	5	1	1	0	10
Bogues	17	0-6	0-0	2	10	0	5	0
Rowsom	18	3-9	0-0	5	2	4	0	6
Lewis	4	0-0	0-0	0	0	0	0	0
Curry	4	3-3	0-0	1	0	0	0	6
Kempton	8	1-2	1-2	2	0	1	0	3
TOTALS	240	38-95	13-17	34	26	17	14	90

Los Angeles	37	30	30	26	123
Charlotte	21	21	22	26	90

Turnovers: L.A. 23 (Johnson, Rivers 5); Char. 19 (Holton 3).
3-Pointers: L.A. 5-7 (Scott 3-4, Johnson 0-1, Cooper 2-2); Char. 1-3 (Chapman 1-2, Tripucka 0-1).
Technical Fouls: Char. 1 (Holton).
Officials: Rush, Kinsey, Garretson.
Attendance: 23,388.

MAR. 12, 1989 AT CHARLOTTE

SACRAMENTO KINGS (114)

Player	MP	FG	FT	R	A	PF	S	TP
McCray	40	6-7	0-0	7	8	3	2	12
Tisdale	35	9-16	10-10	10	2	5	1	28
Petersen	31	6-14	2-2	9	1	4	3	14
Ainge	37	6-13	2-4	2	10	4	1	15
Smith	42	7-12	7-8	4	4	0	0	22
Del Negro	13	1-4	1-2	2	1	2	2	3
Pressley	30	7-12	2-2	3	2	3	1	18
Lohaus	12	1-6	0-0	2	0	2	0	2
TOTALS	240	43-84	24-28	39	28	23	10	114

CHARLOTTE HORNETS (105)

Player	MP	FG	FT	R	A	PF	S	TP
Tripucka	39	11-21	5-7	6	5	3	2	28
Rambis	31	6-8	5-8	8	0	2	0	17
Hoppen	17	0-2	0-0	4	0	2	0	0
Chapman	39	16-28	3-3	4	3	4	0	37
Holton	22	2-3	2-2	0	2	3	1	6
Cureton	15	1-4	0-0	2	2	1	0	2
Reid	19	2-7	1-2	4	1	3	1	5
Rowsom	13	0-4	4-4	3	0	1	0	4
Bogues	26	0-1	0-0	4	8	3	1	0
Kempton	19	3-8	0-0	7	3	3	1	6
TOTALS	240	41-86	20-26	42	24	25	6	105

Sacramento	33	27	31	23	114
Charlotte	24	21	39	21	105

Turnovers: Sac. 15 (Petersen 4); Char. 21 (Tripucka 6).

3-Pointers: Sac. 4-10 (McCray 0-1, Ainge 1-2, Smith 1-1, Del Negro 0-1, Pressley 2-5); Char. 3-9 (Tripucka 1-3, Chapman 2-6).

Technical Fouls: None.

Officials: Kersey, Delaney, Bernhardt.

Attendance: 23,388.

MAR. 14, 1989 AT DENVER

CHARLOTTE HORNETS (102)

Player	MP	FG	FT	R	A	PF	S	TP
Rambis	24	4-6	3-3	10	0	4	0	11
Reid	30	8-19	2-2	1	1	4	0	18
Hoppen	16	1-2	0-2	4	1	3	0	2
Bogues	29	2-7	0-0	1	10	3	1	4
Chapman	32	4-12	1-1	2	3	2	1	9
Cureton	24	4-7	1-2	8	1	2	0	9
Lewis	18	7-11	2-4	3	2	3	0	17
Kempton	8	0-1	3-4	0	0	1	0	3
Rowsom	24	2-7	2-2	12	1	5	2	6
Curry	16	9-15	2-2	0	1	1	3	21
Holton	19	0-5	2-2	1	6	2	1	2
TOTALS	240	41-92	18-24	42	26	30	8	102

DENVER NUGGETS (125)

Player	MP	FG	FT	R	A	PF	S	TP
English	21	7-13	2-2	3	5	2	0	16
Rasmussen	25	6-11	2-2	7	3	6	2	14
Schayes	20	7-9	5-6	5	4	1	1	19
Adams	21	5-8	0-0	1	7	1	2	13
Turner	25	1-1	1-2	5	3	0	2	3
Davis	19	5-13	0-0	3	0	0	3	10
Greenwood	28	3-8	4-4	6	1	2	0	10
Cook	22	6-11	2-2	2	4	2	1	14
Lane	21	6-11	3-9	11	1	5	1	15
Cooper	20	2-5	1-1	4	0	2	0	5
Hanzlik	18	2-3	2-2	4	3	2	0	6
TOTALS	240	50-93	22-30	51	31	23	12	125

Charlotte	27	19	19	37	102
Denver	44	35	22	24	125

Turnovers: Char. 22 (Chapman 5); Den. 21 (Hanzlik 5).

3-Pointers: Char. 2-4 (Reid 0-1, Lewis 1-1, Curry 1-1, Holton 0-1); Den. 3-5 (Adams 3-4, Lane 0-1).

Technical Fouls: Char. 1 (Cureton).

Officials: Crawford, Javie, Stafford.

Attendance: 10,522.

MAR. 16, 1989 AT SEATTLE

CHARLOTTE HORNETS (88)

Player	MP	FG	FT	R	A	PF	S	TP
Rambis	22	2-3	2-2	5	1	5	0	6
Reid	27	6-14	0-0	4	2	4	0	12
Hoppen	22	2-4	2-4	6	0	4	1	6
Bogues	39	4-10	2-2	0	14	1	4	10
Chapman	30	8-16	0-1	2	1	2	0	18
Cureton	25	3-5	1-2	5	1	2	0	7
Rowsom	21	1-5	0-0	5	1	4	0	2
Lewis	18	2-8	0-3	4	0	0	0	4
Curry	30	9-22	0-0	5	2	4	2	19
Kempton	6	1-2	2-2	4	0	0	0	4
TOTALS	240	38-89	9-16	40	22	26	7	88

SEATTLE SUPERSONICS (108)

Player	MP	FG	FT	R	A	PF	S	TP
Cage	21	1-2	2-2	6	1	1	1	4
McKey	28	2-8	5-8	4	2	1	1	9
Lister	17	5-10	1-2	10	0	4	0	11
Ellis	35	12-20	7-9	3	0	1	2	32
McMillan	31	1-2	0-0	10	6	1	4	2
McDaniel	27	6-10	3-3	2	2	2	0	15
Threatt	17	2-4	0-0	0	5	2	0	4
Polynice	15	1-3	1-2	4	0	2	0	3
Reynolds	23	7-13	2-4	5	0	2	2	16
Schoene	16	2-8	2-4	5	0	1	1	6
Lucas	6	3-4	0-0	1	0	0	0	6
Johnson	4	0-2	0-0	1	1	1	1	0
TOTALS	240	42-86	23-34	51	17	18	12	108

Charlotte	26	16	26	20	88
Seattle	33	32	18	25	108

Turnovers: Char. 22 (Bogues 7); Sea. 18 (McKey 4).

3-Pointers: Char. 3-10 (Chapman 2-3, Curry 1-7); Sea. 1-4 (Ellis 1-2, Schoene 0-2).

Technical Fouls: Sea. 1 (Lister).

Officials: Jones, Thompson, Forte.

Attendance: 9,665.

MAR. 17, 1989 AT LOS ANGELES

CHARLOTTE HORNETS (108)

Player	MP	FG	FT	R	A	PF	S	TP
Rambis	37	8-13	1-2	9	2	3	3	17
Tripucka	27	8-19	2-2	2	3	2	0	18
Hoppen	10	2-6	0-0	5	1	4	0	4
Chapman	32	10-21	2-2	2	3	2	3	24
Bogues	25	3-7	0-0	2	9	1	4	6
Cureton	25	3-7	0-0	8	1	5	2	6
Curry	16	5-11	0-0	1	1	2	1	12
Reid	21	7-11	2-2	5	1	2	1	16
Holton	23	2-6	1-1	2	12	2	1	5
Kempton	24	0-2	0-0	9	3	5	1	0
TOTALS	240	48-103	8-9	45	36	28	16	108

LOS ANGELES CLIPPERS (105)

Player	MP	FG	FT	R	A	PF	S	TP
Smith	40	7-12	4-5	11	1	1	0	18
Norman	35	7-16	1-4	10	4	1	1	15
Benjamin	42	15-18	4-8	23	1	3	0	34
Dailey	36	9-18	2-3	0	8	1	1	20
Grant	35	5-10	2-3	2	16	1	1	12
Wolf	27	1-8	2-5	7	0	4	0	4
Garrick	20	0-3	2-2	0	1	2	1	2
White	5	0-2	0-0	2	0	0	0	0
TOTALS	240	44-87	17-30	55	31	13	4	105

Charlotte	26	30	21	31	108
Los Angeles	33	20	28	24	105

Turnovers: Char. 13 (Chapman 4); L.A. 24 (Grant 7).

3-Pointers: Char. 4-7 (Tripucka 0-1, Chapman 2-4, Curry 2-2); L.A. 0-0.

Technical Fouls: L.A. 1 (Norman).

Officials: Alexander, Fine, Mayfield.

Attendance: 10,758.

MAR. 19, 1989 — AT OAKLAND

CHARLOTTE HORNETS (117)

Player	MP	FG	FT	R	A	PF	S	TP
Rambis	29	6-12	7-7	13	0	2	2	19
Reid	26	9-19	0-2	5	0	2	0	18
Hoppen	27	3-5	6-6	8	0	5	0	12
Bogues	29	5-10	2-2	2	14	3	4	12
Chapman	35	9-20	2-2	3	1	3	0	22
Curry	22	7-15	1-1	4	2	3	1	16
Lewis	10	1-3	1-2	4	0	0	1	3
Cureton	24	1-4	2-4	1	4	3	0	4
Kempton	14	1-2	1-2	2	0	4	1	3
Holton	24	3-11	2-2	3	11	4	1	8
TOTALS	240	45-101	24-30	45	32	29	10	117

GOLDEN STATE WARRIORS (124)

Player	MP	FG	FT	R	A	PF	S	TP
Mullin	36	10-21	7-9	3	1	0	3	27
Teagle	32	8-15	4-4	4	0	4	4	20
Sampson	10	1-1	1-2	1	1	1	1	3
Garland	35	4-8	7-7	3	7	4	0	15
Richmond	37	9-19	5-9	12	4	3	1	23
Smith, L.	14	2-6	0-0	10	2	3	0	4
Smith, O.	19	1-6	6-6	5	3	2	0	8
Higgins	26	5-10	0-0	8	2	3	3	14
Bol	18	2-4	1-1	3	0	1	0	5
Alford	13	2-2	1-2	1	0	2	0	5
TOTALS	240	44-92	32-40	50	20	23	12	124

Charlotte	37	28	27	25	117
Golden State	31	38	27	28	124

Turnovers: Char. 16 (Rambis, Reid, Hoppen 3); G.S. (Mullin, Garland, Richmond 4).
3-Pointers: Char. 3-7 (Chapman 2-5, Curry 1-2); G.S. 4-8 (Mullin 0-1, Higgins 4-6, Bol 0-1).
Technical Fouls: G.S. 2 (Teagle, Coach Nelson).
Officials: Mihalak, Salvatore, Armstrong.
Attendance: 15,025.

MAR. 20, 1989 — AT SACRAMENTO

CHARLOTTE HORNETS 117)

Player	MP	FG	FT	R	A	PF	S	TP
Reid	30	10-19	4-6	5	1	1	0	24
Rambis	31	4-8	2-2	6	3	2	1	10
Hoppen	17	3-4	0-0	5	0	1	1	6
Bogues	27	3-5	5-6	5	11	4	1	11
Chapman	34	10-18	1-2	1	1	2	0	25
Cureton	21	0-1	0-0	6	0	3	1	0
Curry	26	9-18	2-2	3	1	1	1	21
Kempton	24	1-2	4-4	8	3	4	1	6
Holton	21	3-7	2-3	2	10	4	1	8
Lewis	6	1-1	0-0	0	0	1	0	2
Rowsom	3	2-3	0-0	1	0	0	0	4
TOTALS	240	46-86	20-25	42	30	23	7	117

SACRAMENTO KINGS (110)

Player	MP	FG	FT	R	A	PF	S	TP
McCray	38	3-9	0-0	9	3	2	0	6
Tisdale	44	14-24	6-8	9	2	1	2	34
Petersen	20	2-6	0-2	5	2	3	1	4
Smith	44	8-13	6-7	4	11	2	2	25
Ainge	40	8-18	2-3	1	6	4	0	20
Pressley	30	6-14	4-4	5	1	5	0	18
Berry	15	1-5	0-0	5	2	2	0	2
Lohaus	5	0-1	1-4	1	0	1	0	1
Del Negro	4	0-2	0-0	1	0	0	0	0
TOTALS	240	42-92	19-28	40	27	20	5	110

Charlotte	34	32	25	26	117
Sacramento	36	18	25	31	110

Turnovers: Char. 10 (Reid, Bogues, Cureton, Curry, Kempton 2); Sac. 11 (Smith 3).
3-Pointers: Char. 5-11 (Reid 0-1, Bogues 0-1, Chapman 4-7, Curry 1-2); Sac. 7-14 (Smith 3-5, Ainge 2-6, Pressley 2-3).
Technical Fouls: Sac. 1 (Illegal defense).
Officials: Middleton, Nunn, Bernhardt.
Attendance: 16,517.

MAR. 23, 1989 — AT CHARLOTTE

WASHINGTON BULLETS (102)

Player	MP	FG	FT	R	A	PF	S	TP
King	36	12-25	5-8	4	3	3	1	29
Alarie	27	6-10	2-2	7	3	3	1	14
Jones, C.	28	1-2	0-0	5	1	5	0	2
Walker	40	3-11	3-5	10	3	3	0	9
Colter	43	5-11	5-6	6	4	1	2	15
Williams	32	10-17	2-3	8	3	2	1	22
Eackles	13	3-5	1-1	0	0	0	1	7
Grant	14	0-2	2-2	0	0	1	0	2
Jones, C.A.	7	1-2	0-0	2	0	0	0	2
TOTALS	240	41-85	20-27	42	17	18	6	102

CHARLOTTE HORNETS (97)

Player	MP	FG	FT	R	A	PF	S	TP
Rambis	36	7-12	3-5	15	3	2	2	17
Reid	27	10-17	4-6	1	3	5	1	25
Hoppen	25	2-5	2-2	9	1	2	1	6
Bogues	28	1-5	2-2	4	11	1	1	4
Chapman	38	6-19	1-2	3	2	6	0	14
Curry	25	8-21	0-0	3	0	0	0	17
Cureton	24	2-4	0-0	2	1	3	0	4
Holton	20	1-3	0-0	1	5	2	1	2
Kempton	8	1-1	0-0	1	0	1	0	2
Lewis	6	2-2	0-0	2	0	0	0	4
Rowsom	3	1-1	0-0	1	1	0	0	2
TOTALS	240	41-90	12-17	42	27	22	6	97

Washington	23	32	26	21	102
Charlotte	26	24	26	21	97

Turnovers: Wash. 13 (Walker, Williams 3); Char. 12 (Holton 3).
3-Pointers: Wash. 0-1 (Colter 0-1); Char. 3-10 (Reid 1-1, Chapman 1-6, Curry 1-3).
Technical Fouls: None.
Officials: Hollins, Clark, Olesiak.
Attendance: 23,388.

MAR. 25, 1989 — AT CHARLOTTE

DETROIT PISTONS (113)

Player	MP	FG	FT	R	A	PF	S	TP
Aguirre	31	7-12	3-3	4	2	2	0	17
Mahorn	27	4-6	2-2	5	0	2	1	10
Laimbeer	29	8-9	0-0	11	1	3	0	16
Dumars	30	7-11	4-4	2	5	1	0	18
Thomas	34	6-11	0-0	1	6	3	3	12
Rodman	27	7-12	2-2	10	5	4	0	16
Johnson	28	4-14	2-4	4	4	1	0	11
Edwards	17	5-6	1-1	3	1	0	0	11
Long	1	0-0	0-0	0	0	0	0	0
Williams	3	0-1	0-0	0	0	0	0	0
Salley	13	0-1	2-4	3	2	1	0	2
TOTALS	240	48-83	16-20	43	26	17	4	113

CHARLOTTE HORNETS (101)

Player	MP	FG	FT	R	A	PF	S	TP
Rambis	30	3-9	3-4	10	2	3	2	9
Reid	31	6-18	1-1	5	2	3	1	14
Hoppen	23	1-4	5-6	5	2	3	0	7
Bogues	35	2-7	0-0	5	17	1	1	4
Chapman	33	9-19	2-2	2	1	3	0	21
Holton	20	4-8	0-0	1	3	2	1	8
Curry	22	9-14	0-0	1	1	2	0	18
Cureton	24	5-8	0-1	6	1	2	1	10
Kempton	9	0-3	1-2	3	0	3	0	1
Rowsom	10	2-3	1-2	2	0	0	0	5
Lewis	3	2-2	0-0	0	0	0	0	4
TOTALS	240	43-95	13-18	40	29	22	6	101

Detroit	28	29	28	28	113
Charlotte	19	28	24	30	101

Turnovers: Det. 15 (Dumars 5); Char. 8 (Hoppen 2).
3-Pointers: Det. 1-5 (Thomas 0-1, Johnson 1-4); Char. 2-7 (Reid 1-1, Chapman 1-4, Curry 0-2).
Technical Fouls: None.
Officials: Madden, Forte, Thompson.
Attendance: 23,388.

MAR. 27, 1989 — AT CHARLOTTE

NEW YORK KNICKS (121)

Player	MP	FG	FT	R	A	PF	S	TP
Newman	24	4-6	0-0	2	3	5	0	8
Oakley	39	4-7	2-2	8	7	3	0	10
Ewing	37	18-25	9-10	14	0	3	3	45
Jackson	33	8-13	5-8	4	9	2	1	21
Wilkins, G.	32	5-11	3-4	1	6	2	1	14
Tucker	15	1-3	0-0	0	0	3	0	2
Walker	13	1-2	1-2	4	0	3	0	3
Vandeweghe	19	1-6	4-4	4	2	1	0	6
Strickland	15	1-1	4-6	0	1	1	0	6
Green	10	2-4	0-0	3	0	1	1	4
Myers	1	0-0	0-0	0	0	0	0	0
Wilkins, E.	2	1-2	0-0	0	0	0	0	2
TOTALS	240	46-80	28-36	40	28	24	6	121

CHARLOTTE HORNETS (105)

Player	MP	FG	FT	R	A	PF	S	TP
Rambis	37	3-8	6-7	14	3	4	0	12
Reid	31	6-17	5-6	1	2	2	2	18
Hoppen	9	2-2	0-0	4	0	4	0	4
Bogues	40	6-10	0-0	1	17	3	1	12
Chapman	36	9-22	5-9	1	0	3	1	24
Cureton	28	5-9	0-0	7	0	3	0	10
Curry	22	5-10	0-1	2	1	5	1	10
Lewis	7	2-3	0-0	2	0	2	0	4
Rowsom	11	1-2	0-0	2	0	3	1	2
Lowe	8	1-1	0-0	1	3	1	0	2
Kempton	11	2-3	3-4	2	0	1	0	7
TOTALS	240	42-87	19-27	37	26	31	6	105

New York	29	36	29	27	121
Charlotte	31	31	24	19	105

Turnovers: N.Y. 19 (Ewing 6); Char. 20 (Rambis 6).
3-Pointers: N.Y. 1-11 (Newman 0-1, Oakley 0-3, Jackson 0-2, G. Wilkins 1-2, Tucker 0-2, Vandeweghe 0-1); Char. 2-5 (Reid 1-1, Chapman 1-4).
Technical Fouls: N.Y. 1 (Ewing).
Officials: Middleton, Grillo, O'Donnell.
Attendance: 23,388.

MAR. 30, 1989 — AT CHARLOTTE

GOLDEON STATE WARRIORS (113)

Player	MP	FG	FT	R	A	PF	S	TP
Mullin	40	13-23	9-11	7	2	1	1	36
Teagle	37	9-21	6-6	6	1	2	2	24
Smith, L.	16	0-2	0-0	3	0	2	1	0
Garland	39	5-11	4-4	12	4	1	1	14
Richmond	39	9-17	10-12	12	3	3	1	28
Sampson	11	1-2	0-0	4	0	3	0	2
Higgins	25	3-9	0-1	5	5	5	1	7
Smith, O.	13	0-3	0-0	1	2	0	0	0
Bol	20	1-4	0-1	2	1	2	0	2
TOTALS	240	41-92	29-35	52	18	19	7	113

CHARLOTTE HORNETS (104)

Player	MP	FG	FT	R	A	PF	S	TP
Rambis	33	11-16	1-3	12	4	3	0	23
Reid	32	3-14	0-0	5	5	2	0	6
Hoppen	15	1-1	0-0	2	0	2	0	2
Bogues	36	4-10	0-0	3	12	3	2	8
Chapman	32	10-20	1-3	1	2	3	0	22
Cureton	33	4-6	0-0	12	1	2	0	8
Tripucka	18	7-17	7-7	3	3	4	2	21
Curry	14	2-8	0-0	3	0	2	0	4
Lowe	12	0-1	1-2	2	3	1	1	1
Kempton	8	1-3	3-4	5	0	1	0	5
Rowsom	7	2-5	0-0	3	1	1	0	4
TOTALS	240	45-101	13-19	51	31	24	5	104

Golden State	27	31	36	19	113
Charlotte	30	25	24	25	104

Turnovers: G.S. 15 (Richmond 6); Char. 14 (Kempton 4).
3-Pointers: G.S. 2-8 (Mullin 1-1, Richmond 0-1, Higgins 1-3, Bol 0-3); Char. 1-5 (Reid 0-1, Chapman 1-3, Curry 0-1).
Technical Fouls: G.S. 1 (Coach Nelson).
Officials: J. Crawford, D. Crawford, Stafford.
Attendance: 23,388.

APR. 1, 1989 — AT CHARLOTTE

PORTLAND TRAIL BLAZERS (125)

Player	MP	FG	FT	R	A	PF	S	TP
Kersey	40	9-15	3-3	13	5	5	1	21
Jones	15	2-2	0-0	2	0	1	1	4
Duckworth	42	11-18	8-10	13	0	4	1	30
Drezler	47	12-23	11-11	5	3	3	2	36
Porter	43	6-16	2-4	4	13	1	0	15
Johnson	32	3-10	2-8	4	0	6	0	8
Wheeler	15	1-2	2-2	2	2	0	1	4
Bryant	13	2-4	1-2	3	1	4	1	5
Steppe	10	1-2	0-0	0	0	1	0	2
Branch	5	0-1	0-0	0	1	1	0	0
Anderson	3	0-0	0-0	2	0	1	0	0
TOTALS	265	47-93	29-40	48	25	27	7	125

CHARLOTTE HORNETS (121)

Player	MP	FG	FT	R	A	PF	S	TP
Tripucka	43	11-21	16-18	3	4	5	2	38
Rambis	39	4-9	7-11	8	3	3	0	15
Kite	15	1-3	0-0	6	0	4	2	2
Bogues	33	5-12	0-0	3	8	2	0	10
Chapman	30	6-17	1-3	4	3	3	0	13
Cureton	38	4-6	2-4	6	4	2	0	10
Rowsom	14	3-5	2-3	2	0	0	0	8
Reid	33	10-20	2-2	6	5	5	1	23
Lowe	20	1-2	0-0	3	6	3	3	2
TOTALS	265	45-95	30-41	41	33	27	8	121

Portland	29	28	31	20	17	125
Charlotte	22	25	31	30	13	121

Turnovers: Por. 15 (Drexler 4); Char. 13 (Reid 4).
3-Pointers: Por. 2-5 (Drexler 1-3, Porter 1-2); Char. 1-3 (Bogues 0-1, Chapman 0-1, Reid 1-1).
Technical Fouls: Por. 1 (Drexler).
Officials: Strong, Borgia, Alexander.
Attendance: 23,388.

APR. 4, 1989 — AT CHICAGO

CHARLOTTE HORNETS (101)

Player	MP	FG	FT	R	A	PF	S	TP
Tripucka	26	5-11	7-7	2	4	3	1	17
Rambis	24	5-8	1-3	6	3	1	0	11
Kite	28	2-3	1-1	4	0	4	0	5
Bogues	26	1-3	0-0	3	12	1	0	2
Chapman	34	9-23	1-1	1	4	4	1	21
Cureton	17	0-2	2-2	3	0	1	2	2
Lowe	16	0-1	0-0	0	6	3	1	0
Rowsom	18	4-6	4-4	4	1	3	0	12
Reid	23	7-14	2-2	4	3	3	1	16
Curry	17	6-10	0-0	2	2	2	0	13
Hoppen	6	0-2	0-0	1	0	0	0	0
Kempton	5	1-1	0-0	1	0	1	0	2
TOTALS	240	40-84	18-20	31	35	26	6	101

CHICAGO BULLS (121)

Player	MP	FG	FT	R	A	PF	S	TP
Pippen	35	4-14	3-3	3	8	2	1	11
Grant	26	6-9	4-4	9	2	4	1	16
Cartwright	26	5-9	3-4	5	1	1	1	13
Paxson	1	0-0	0-0	0	2	0	0	0
Jordan	40	10-15	13-15	10	12	1	6	33
Vincent	34	5-15	4-4	6	1	3	3	14
Davis	26	5-9	2-2	8	0	3	0	12
Sellers	24	4-9	3-4	5	3	2	1	11
Corzine	17	3-7	2-3	1	1	2	0	8
Perdue	7	1-4	1-2	3	0	0	2	3
Haley	4	0-1	0-0	1	0	0	0	0
TOTALS	240	43-92	35-41	51	30	18	15	121

Charlotte	22	26	31	22	101
Chicago	32	37	26	26	121

Turnovers: Char. 19 (Chapman 5); Chi. 10 (Jordan 3).
3-Pointers: Char. 3-7 (Bogues 0-1, Chapman 2-4, Reid 0-1, Curry 1-1); Chi. 0-4 (Pippen 0-1, Jordan 0-2, Vincent 0-1).
Technical Fouls: None.
Officials: Rush, Saar, Garretson.
Attendance: 17,578.

APR. 7, 1989 AT CHARLOTTE

PHILADELPHIA 76ERS (118)

Player	MP	FG	FT	R	A	PF	S	TP
Barkley	44	9-16	13-15	20	9	2	1	31
Smith	17	2-4	0-0	2	2	4	0	4
Gminski	35	10-15	9-9	5	1	1	0	29
Cheeks	37	2-14	4-4	4	5	2	2	8
Hawkins	31	8-12	6-6	8	1	4	0	23
Henderson	17	3-5	3-4	4	1	2	0	9
Anderson	31	4-12	1-1	6	3	2	0	9
Coleman	13	2-7	1-2	4	0	1	0	5
Brooks	11	0-3	0-0	1	1	0	0	0
Welp	4	0-1	0-0	1	0	1	0	0
TOTALS	240	40-89	37-41	55	23	19	3	118

CHARLOTTE HORNETS (108)

Player	MP	FG	FT	R	A	PF	S	TP
Tripucka	33	8-18	4-4	3	2	3	1	21
Rambis	28	4-10	2-2	3	2	6	2	10
Kite	13	1-2	0-0	1	1	5	0	2
Bogues	24	4-6	0-0	0	11	3	0	8
Chapman	26	8-17	8-8	1	1	1	2	24
Cureton	26	3-3	0-0	8	1	3	0	6
Reid	15	1-6	0-0	4	0	3	0	2
Curry	22	12-19	1-1	3	1	1	0	25
Lowe	24	0-2	1-2	3	11	0	1	1
Kempton	16	0-1	2-2	0	3	3	0	2
Hoppen	13	3-3	1-1	6	0	2	0	7
TOTALS	240	44-87	19-20	32	33	30	6	108

Philadelphia	34	21	28	35	118
Charlotte	28	22	32	26	108

Turnovers: Phi. 13 (Hawkins 4); Char. 10 (Reid, Kempton 2).
3-Pointers: Phi. 1-8 (Barkley 0-1, Hawkins 1-4, Henderson 0-1, Brooks 0-2); Char. 1-5 (Tripucka 1-2, Chapman 0-2, Curry 0-1).
Technical Fouls: Phi. 1 (Barkley); Char. 1 (Kite).
Officials: Nies, Oakes, Benson.
Attendance: 23,388.

APR. 9, 1989 AT RICHFIELD, OHIO

CHARLOTTE HORNETS (116)

Player	MP	FG	FT	R	A	PF	S	TP
Rambis	22	3-5	0-2	7	1	4	2	6
Tripucka	26	8-14	8-10	4	8	5	0	26
Kite	18	2-2	0-0	6	2	4	0	4
Chapman	25	9-16	1-2	0	2	5	1	21
Bogues	28	3-6	0-0	1	9	5	0	6
Lowe	18	1-1	0-2	1	6	1	0	2
Rowsom	21	3-5	6-6	5	0	2	0	12
Cureton	10	0-1	0-0	2	1	3	0	0
Reid	29	8-21	2-2	6	3	2	0	20
Curry	19	4-12	1-1	3	3	1	2	9
Hoppen	19	3-5	1-2	6	1	6	0	8
Kempton	5	1-2	0-0	0	1	1	0	2
TOTALS	240	45-90	19-27	41	37	39	5	116

CLEVELAND CAVALIERS (122)

Player	MP	FG	FT	R	A	PF	S	TP
Sanders	25	4-8	5-7	3	1	5	1	13
Williams	41	8-15	3-6	6	1	3	1	19
Daugherty	40	9-16	4-8	15	4	3	2	22
Price	39	8-13	18-18	0	6	0	0	35
Harper	40	6-9	9-11	9	7	2	2	21
Hubbard	7	1-1	1-2	2	0	1	0	3
Ehlo	28	3-9	0-2	5	6	2	1	7
Keys	3	0-0	0-0	0	0	2	0	0
Rollins	8	0-1	0-0	1	1	2	0	0
Valentine	9	0-4	2-2	0	1	1	0	2
TOTALS	240	39-76	42-56	41	27	21	7	122

Charlotte	33	37	21	25	116
Cleveland	37	24	34	27	122

Turnovers: Char. 12 (Chapman, Bogues 3); Cle. 10 (Harper 4).
3-Pointers: Char. 7-11 (Tripucka 2-2, Chapman 2-5, Reid 2-2, Curry 0-1, Hoppen 1-1); Cle. 2-4 (Price 1-2, Ehlo 1-2).
Technical Fouls: None.
Officials: Nunez, Bavetta, Olesiak.
Attendance: 19,276.

APR. 10, 1989 AT CHARLOTTE

ATLANTA HAWKS (112)

Player	MP	FG	FT	R	A	PF	S	TP
Wilkins	40	8-26	6-8	6	4	1	4	22
Koncak	35	3-3	2-3	11	1	3	1	8
Malone	37	4-15	16-22	14	2	2	0	24
Theus	25	6-13	2-2	3	5	2	0	14
Rivers	35	6-10	8-9	7	6	3	0	21
Levingston	17	3-4	0-0	2	0	5	0	6
Battle	14	1-6	1-1	0	4	0	0	3
Webb	22	0-1	2-2	6	3	1	0	2
Carr	15	3-7	6-7	4	1	1	0	12
TOTALS	240	34-85	43-54	53	26	18	5	112

CHARLOTTE HORNETS (105)

Player	MP	FG	FT	R	A	PF	S	TP
Tripucka	29	4-11	9-9	7	6	4	2	17
Rambis	30	5-9	4-5	11	2	3	2	14
Kite	15	1-3	1-2	5	1	6	0	3
Bogues	33	6-14	1-2	4	15	3	0	13
Chapman	29	4-16	1-1	1	1	2	1	10
Curry	19	9-13	0-0	0	1	1	0	18
Cureton	20	1-3	0-0	5	2	3	1	2
Rowsom	5	0-1	0-0	1	0	1	0	0
Reid	20	5-13	2-2	1	4	4	0	12
Lowe	15	0-0	0-0	2	2	1	1	0
Hoppen	23	7-8	2-2	6	0	6	1	16
Kempton	2	0-1	0-0	0	0	1	0	0
TOTALS	240	42-92	20-23	43	34	35	8	105

Atlanta	35	33	18	26	112
Charlotte	29	30	24	22	105

Turnovers: Atl. 12 (Malone 5); Char. 11 (Tripucka 3).
3-Pointers: Atl. 1-3 (Wilkins 0-2, Rivers 1-1); Char. 1-7 (Tripucka 0-1, Bogues 0-1, Chapman 1-3, Curry 0-2).
Technical Fouls: Char. 1 (Coach Badger).
Officials: Huetter, Strom, Durham.
Attendance: 23,388.

APR. 12, 1989 AT NEW YORK

CHARLOTTE HORNETS (104)

Player	MP	FG	FT	R	A	PF	S	TP
Tripucka	28	8-20	9-10	5	5	4	2	25
Rambis	25	4-5	0-0	3	1	2	1	8
Kite	18	2-3	0-0	4	1	2	0	4
Bogues	22	1-2	0-0	3	14	3	0	2
Chapman	25	8-17	2-2	2	1	2	1	18
Lowe	26	0-2	2-2	4	7	3	2	2
Cureton	10	0-0	1-2	0	0	0	0	1
Hoppen	20	4-9	3-5	5	1	2	0	11
Reid	20	5-11	1-2	2	1	1	2	11
Curry	23	9-14	0-0	2	3	0	2	18
Rowsom	18	2-3	0-0	6	0	2	1	4
Kempton	5	0-1	0-0	0	0	1	0	0
TOTALS	240	43-88	18-23	36	34	22	11	104

NEW YORK KNICKS (99)

Player	MP	FG	FT	R	A	PF	S	TP
Newman	17	1-5	2-3	1	0	1	1	4
Oakley	31	6-13	2-2	14	6	4	2	14
Ewing	42	13-19	4-8	12	2	5	0	30
Jackson	35	4-14	2-5	3	8	2	3	10
Wilkins, G.	30	3-12	0-0	5	1	3	1	6
Strickland	15	3-7	0-0	4	3	1	0	6
Walker	20	3-6	2-2	7	0	3	1	9
Tucker	21	2-8	0-0	2	4	1	1	5
Vandeweghe	21	4-6	3-3	0	2	2	0	11
Green	8	2-3	0-0	5	0	1	1	4
TOTALS	240	41-93	15-23	53	26	23	10	99

Charlotte	29	26	26	23	104
New York	40	18	19	22	99

Turnovers: Char. 15 (Tripucka 4); N.Y. 25 (Jackson 7).
3-Pointers: Char. 0-6 (Chapman 0-5, Curry 0-1); N.Y. 2-13 (Newman 0-2, Oakley 0-1, Jackson 0-2, G. Wilkins 0-3, Walker 1-1, Tucker 1-4).
Technical Fouls: Char. 2 (Coach Badger, Coach Harter).
Officials: Mathis, Thompson, Lauerman.
Attendance: 18,385.

APR. 14, 1989 AT PHILADELPHIA

CHARLOTTE HORNETS (119)

Player	MP	FG	FT	R	A	PF	S	TP
Tripucka	29	13-18	7-8	6	2	3	3	34
Rambis	33	4-7	1-2	7	4	2	1	9
Kite	15	3-5	0-0	6	1	3	0	6
Bogues	24	4-10	0-0	3	9	2	3	8
Chapman	19	3-10	0-0	2	1	0	0	6
Cureton	17	0-2	0-0	3	2	3	0	0
Curry	24	11-16	0-0	3	1	3	1	23
Reid	24	9-14	2-3	4	1	2	0	20
Lowe	24	1-3	0-0	3	14	4	0	2
Rowsom	11	2-2	2-2	1	0	0	0	6
Hoppen	20	2-3	1-2	2	1	4	0	5
TOTALS	240	52-90	13-17	40	36	26	8	119

PHILADELPHIA 76ERS (115)

Player	MP	FG	FT	R	A	PF	S	TP
Smith	25	3-8	4-4	1	2	2	2	10
Barkley	44	7-17	11-16	13	5	2	1	25
Gminski	35	8-13	5-6	10	2	0	0	21
Cheeks	35	6-8	2-3	1	7	2	0	14
Hawkins	32	8-14	0-2	3	2	3	0	17
Anderson	28	6-12	3-3	2	3	1	0	15
Brooks	13	0-2	0-0	0	4	0	0	0
Welp	7	0-1	2-2	2	0	1	1	2
Coleman	10	4-5	1-2	4	0	2	1	9
Henderson	11	1-2	0-0	1	1	1	0	2
TOTALS	240	43-82	28-38	37	26	14	5	115

Charlotte	27	40	27	25	119
Philadelphia	33	30	28	24	115

Turnovers: Char. 13 (Tripucka 4); Phi. 12 (Barkley, Coleman 3).
3-Pointers: Char. 2-6 (Tripucka 1-1, Bogues 0-1, Chapman 0-1, Reid 0-2, Curry 1-1); Phi. 1-14 (Smith 0-1, Barkley 0-6, Gminski 0-1, Cheeks 0-1, Hawkins 1-3, Brooks 0-1, Henderson 0-1).
Technical Fouls: Phi. 1 (Coach Carter).
Officials: Jones, Fryer, Stafford.
Attendance: 14,321.

APR. 15, 1989 AT INDIANAPOLIS

CHARLOTTE HORNETS (105)

Player	MP	FG	FT	R	A	PF	S	TP
Rambis	23	2-7	2-4	6	3	2	1	6
Tripucka	29	7-15	0-0	2	5	2	0	14
Kite	17	1-2	1-2	7	0	3	1	3
Bogues	34	5-10	2-2	5	12	1	2	12
Chapman	29	9-19	2-2	2	1	0	0	21
Cureton	25	5-10	0-0	4	2	1	0	10
Lowe	14	1-1	0-0	2	3	2	1	2
Curry	20	6-18	2-2	3	1	0	1	15
Hoppen	19	0-1	4-4	8	0	6	0	4
Reid	19	4-10	0-0	2	1	1	1	8
Rowsom	9	4-4	1-1	4	1	1	0	9
Kempton	2	0-0	1-2	1	1	0	0	1
TOTALS	240	44-97	15-19	46	30	19	7	105

INDIANA PACERS (115)

Player	MP	FG	FT	R	A	PF	S	TP
Person	36	16-27	1-2	5	2	0	0	37
Schrempf	28	1-7	0-0	4	6	1	1	2
Thompson	34	6-12	1-2	11	2	3	2	13
Fleming	29	1-4	2-2	5	10	0	2	4
Miller	36	8-15	0-0	5	2	0	2	17
Stephens	16	2-4	2-3	2	6	0	0	6
Smits	34	9-18	9-11	12	0	3	1	27
Gray	1	0-0	0-0	1	0	1	0	0
Wittman	7	0-3	0-0	0	1	1	0	0
Skiles	8	1-1	0-0	1	4	0	0	2
Dreiling	11	3-5	1-2	3	0	3	0	7
TOTALS	240	47-96	16-22	49	33	12	8	115

Charlotte	33	25	20	27	105
Indiana	33	31	22	29	115

Turnovers: Char. 8 (Tripucka 3); Ind. 8 (Miller 2).
3-Pointers: Char. 2-9 (Tripucka 0-2, Chapman 1-4, Curry 1-2, Reid 0-1); Ind. 5-7 (Person 4-6, Miller 1-1).
Technical Fouls: None.
Officials: Garretson, Javie, Willard.
Attendance: 11,860

APR. 17, 1989 AT CHARLOTTE

BOSTON CELTICS (113)

Player	MP	FG	FT	R	A	PF	S	TP
McHale	40	7-22	4-4	11	0	2	0	18
Lewis	45	8-20	10-12	10	6	4	0	26
Parish	43	10-19	1-4	22	4	4	1	21
Shaw	42	0-5	5-6	12	6	3	4	5
Gamble	47	9-15	7-8	6	7	5	1	25
Kleine	10	1-3	1-1	6	1	3	0	3
Pinckney	13	3-6	5-7	3	1	1	0	11
Upshaw	15	2-5	0-0	2	3	1	0	4
Birdsong	5	0-3	0-0	0	0	0	0	0
Grandison	5	0-0	0-0	1	0	2	0	0
TOTALS	265	40-98	33-42	73	28	25	6	113

CHARLOTTE HORNETS (108)

Player	MP	FG	FT	R	A	PF	S	TP
Tripucka	36	6-22	7-10	2	2	5	3	19
Rambis	4	0-0	0-0	3	0	0	0	0
Kite	30	1-3	1-2	6	1	3	0	3
Bogues	31	4-6	0-0	2	15	2	1	9
Chapman	37	12-25	3-4	2	2	1	1	29
Cureton	28	5-10	2-4	7	0	5	1	12
Reid	17	5-12	1-6	1	0	1	1	11
Hoppen	23	2-3	1-2	7	1	2	2	5
Rowsom	21	2-5	0-0	6	3	6	1	4
Curry	16	6-14	2-2	4	1	3	1	14
Lowe	22	1-3	0-0	4	6	3	2	2
TOTALS	265	44-103	17-30	44	31	31	13	108

Boston	23	30	27	22	11	113
Charlotte	21	29	24	28	6	108

Turnovers: Bos, 21 (Shaw 6); Char. 10 (Tripucka 3).
3-Pointers: Boston 0-1 (Kleine 0-1); Char. 3-9 (Tripucka 0-1, Bogues 1-1, Chapman 2-5, Cureton 0-1, Lowe 0-1).
Technical Fouls: None.
Officials: Rush, Nunn, Toliver.
Attendance: 23,388.

APR. 18, 1989 AT E. RUTHERFORD, N.J.

CHARLOTTE HORNETS (121)

Player	MP	FG	FT	R	A	PF	S	TP
Tripucka	26	5-13	8-8	5	1	0	1	18
Cureton	28	7-10	2-5	5	1	4	2	16
Kite	14	0-0	1-2	3	0	3	0	1
Bogues	24	4-6	2-2	2	8	2	3	10
Chapman	24	3-9	4-6	1	4	3	1	10
Hoppen	29	5-6	0-0	14	1	5	1	10
Lowe	24	1-6	3-3	5	10	1	1	5
Reid	22	8-17	0-0	3	2	3	1	16
Curry	28	13-20	2-3	1	2	2	2	31
Rowsom	23	0-4	4-4	4	1	1	0	4
Kempton	2	0-0	0-0	1	0	0	0	0
TOTALS	240	46-91	26-33	44	30	24	12	121

NEW JERSEY NETS (105)

Player	MP	FG	FT	R	A	PF	S	TP
Morris	34	5-18	2-4	5	2	4	3	15
Williams	26	3-7	5-10	14	0	4	0	11
Carrolll	28	2-8	2-2	10	0	2	0	6
Conner	30	6-9	3-4	2	8	4	2	15
McGee	35	13-23	3-4	4	2	3	1	30
Bagley	25	1-4	0-1	1	5	1	0	2
Hinson	26	7-9	4-6	3	1	5	0	18
Lee	16	1-5	2-2	4	0	1	0	4
Jones	15	2-3	0-0	2	1	3	0	4
Gaines	5	0-1	0-0	0	2	0	0	0
TOTALS	240	40-87	21-33	45	21	27	6	105

Charlotte	30	24	33	34	121
New Jersey	28	23	27	27	105

Turnovers: Char. 11 (Bogues 3); N.J. 21 (Carroll, Bagley 4).
3-Pointers: Char. 3-8 (Tripucka 0-2, Bogues 0-2, Lowe 0-1, Curry 3-3); N.J. 4-11 (Morris 3-7, McGee 1-2, Bagley 0-2).
Technical Fouls: Char. 3 (Illegal defense, Coach Harter, Tripucka).
Officials: Jones, Durham, Mayfield.
Attendance: 8,991.

APR. 21, 1989 AT CHARLOTTE

MILWAUKEE BUCKS (117)

Player	MP	FG	FT	R	A	PF	S	TP
Cummings	30	5-15	4-4	4	0	4	0	14
Krystkowiak	36	7-11	9-9	8	0	1	1	23
Sikma	29	6-8	3-3	5	5	1	0	16
Moncrief	32	2-2	5-6	4	4	2	0	9
Humphries	31	4-6	5-5	4	4	2	3	13
Pierce	23	9-14	3-4	4	5	5	3	21
Roberts	25	4-5	2-2	4	3	1	0	10
Green	19	2-3	2-2	0	5	0	0	6
Breuer	7	2-2	0-2	1	0	0	0	4
Mokeski	8	0-0	1-2	0	2	1	0	1
TOTALS	240	41-66	34-39	34	28	17	7	117

CHARLOTTE HORNETS (110)

Player	MP	FG	FT	R	A	PF	S	TP
Tripucka	23	4-15	0-0	3	4	3	0	9
Cureton	24	2-3	0-2	1	0	3	0	4
Kite	13	2-2	1-1	2	0	3	0	5
Bogues	27	1-5	0-0	4	8	3	4	2
Chapman	23	9-18	3-4	3	2	4	0	22
Hoppen	28	4-6	2-2	7	0	4	1	10
Rowsom	23	6-8	3-3	5	0	4	0	15
Reid	25	7-15	2-2	1	5	4	0	16
Curry	27	9-17	5-5	2	2	2	0	23
Lowe	21	1-2	0-0	2	12	1	0	2
Kempton	6	1-1	0-0	2	0	1	0	2
TOTALS	240	46-92	16-19	32	33	32	5	110

Milwaukee	30	26	28	33	117
Charlotte	22	22	25	41	110

Turnovers: Mil. 14 (Cummings 5); Char. 11 (Tripucka 3).
3-Pointers: Mil. 1-2 (Sikma 1-1, Pierce 0-1); Char. 2-7 (Tripucka 1-1, Chapman 1-4, Curry 0-2).
Technical Fouls: Mil. 3 (Illegal defense, Pierce, Trainer Snedeker).
Officials: Bavetta, Clark, Capers.
Attendance: 23,388.

APR. 23, 1989 AT BOSTON

CHARLOTTE HORNETS (110)

Player	MP	FG	FT	R	A	PF	S	TP
Tripucka	37	9-16	10-11	3	2	3	0	28
Cureton	23	2-4	0-0	4	1	3	0	4
Kite	17	0-2	0-0	3	0	3	1	0
Bogues	33	2-10	0-2	6	19	1	0	4
Chapman	33	9-19	2-2	5	5	5	2	21
Hoppen	25	6-8	2-4	6	0	5	0	14
Kempton	15	1-1	1-2	0	0	3	0	3
Curry	19	9-15	1-2	3	0	1	1	20
Lowe	6	0-0	0-0	2	4	4	1	0
Reid	14	4-7	1-2	2	3	2	0	9
Rowsom	18	3-3	1-3	4	0	4	1	7
TOTALS	240	45-85	18-28	38	34	34	6	110

BOSTON CELTICS (120)

Player	MP	FG	FT	R	A	PF	S	TP
McHale	34	9-17	10-12	7	2	2	0	28
Lewis	33	6-15	5-5	5	2	4	0	17
Parish	28	3-9	2-3	7	1	4	0	8
Shaw	32	4-7	3-3	2	10	3	1	11
Gamble	43	11-14	9-12	5	6	2	4	31
Kleine	19	2-2	4-4	3	2	3	3	8
Birdsong	11	3-5	0-0	1	1	0	0	6
Upshaw	16	2-3	0-0	1	7	1	0	4
Pinckney	15	3-7	1-2	2	0	0	0	7
Grandison	9	0-1	0-0	1	0	3	1	0
TOTALS	240	43-80	34-41	34	31	22	9	120

Charlotte	23	31	30	26	110
Boston	32	31	32	25	120

Turnovers: Char. 16 (Tripucka 4); Bos. 14 (Shaw 3).
3-Pointers: Char. 2-6 (Tripucka 0-1, Chapman 1-3, Curry 1-2); Bos. 0-2 (Lewis 0-1, Gamble 0-1).
Technical Fouls: Char. 1 (Coach Harter); Bos. 1 (Illegal defense).
Officials: Saar, Garretson, Stafford.
Attendance: 14,000.

1988-89 Hornets Final Statistics

Player	GP	GS	FG	Pct.	3FG	Pct.	FT	Pct.	Reb./PG	A/PG	PF	S/PG	TO/PG	TP/PG
Tripucka	71	65	568-1215	.467	30-84	.357	440-508	.866	2673.8	224/3.2	196	88/1.24	236/3.3	1606/22.6
Chapman	75	44	526-1271	.414	60-191	.314	155-195	.795	187/2.5	176/2.3	167	70/0.93	113/1.5	1267/16.9
Reid	82	54	519-1214	.428	17-52	.327	152/196	.776	302/3.7	153/1.9	235	53/0.65	106/1.3	1207/14.7
Curry	48	0	256-521	.491	19-55	.345	40-46	.870	104/2.2	50/1.0	68	42/0.88	44/0.9	571/11.9
Rambis	75	75	325-627	.518	0-3	.000	182-248	.734	703/9.4	159/2.1	208	100/1.33	148/2.0	832/11.1
Holton	67	60	215-504	.427	3-14	.214	120-143	.839	105/1.6	424/6.3	165	66/0.99	119/1.8	553/8.3
Rowsom	34	0	80-162	.494	1-1	1.00	65-81	.802	137/4.0	24/0.7	69	10/0.29	18/0.5	226/6.6
Hoppen	77	36	199-353	.564	1-2	.500	101-139	.727	384/5.0	57/0.7	239	25/0.32	77/1.0	500/6.5
Cureton	82	41	233-465	.501	0-1	.000	66-123	.537	488/6.0	130/1.6	230	50/0.61	114/1.4	532/6.5
Kempton	79	0	171-335	.510	0.1	.000	142-207	.686	304/3.8	102/1.3	215	41/0.52	121/1.5	484/6.1
Bogues	79	21	178-418	.426	1-13	.077	66-88	.750	165/2.1	620/7.8	141	111/1.41	124/1.6	423/5.4
Green	33	2	57-132	.432	1-5	.200	13-14	.929	23/0.7	82/2.5	16	18/0.55	28/0.8	128/3.9
Lewis	42	0	58-121	.479	1-3	.333	19-39	.487	61/1.5	15/0.4	28	11/0.26	24/.06	136/3.2
Tolbert	14	0	17-37	.459	0-3	.000	6-12	.500	21/1.5	7/0.5	20	2/0.14	2/0.1	40/2.9
Kite	12	12	16-30	.533	0-0	.000	6-10	.600	53/4.4	7/0.6	43	4/0.33	12/1.0	38/3.2
Lowe	14	0	8-25	.320	0-2	.00	7-11	.636	34/2.4	93/6.6	28	14/1.00	9/0.6	23/1.6
TOTALS	82	–	3426-7430	.461	134-430	.312	1580-2060	.767	3338/40.7	2323/28.3	2068	705/8.60	1318/16.1	8566/104.5
OPP.	82	–	3555-7113	.500	115-399	.288	2040-2629	.776	3812/46.5	2061/25.1	1791	710/8.66	1425/17.4	9265/113.0

Autographs

Autographs

Autographs

Autographs